'AUTISTIC' CHILDREN
new hope for a cure

'AUTISTIC' CHILDREN

new hope for a cure

Niko Tinbergen FRS and Elisabeth A. Tinbergen

with contributions from **Martha Welch MD (New York)**
and Michele Zappella MD (Siena, Italy)

London
GEORGE ALLEN & UNWIN
Boston   Sydney

**George Allen & Unwin (Publishers) Ltd,
40 Museum Street, London WC1A 1LU, UK**

George Allen & Unwin (Publishers) Ltd,
Park Lane, Hemel Hempstead, Herts HP2 4TE, UK

Allen & Unwin Inc.
9 Winchester Terrace, Winchester, Mass 01890, USA

George Allen & Unwin Australia Pty Ltd,
8 Napier Street, North Sydney, NSW 2060, Australia

First published in 1983
Second impression 1985

First published in paperback 1985

British Library Cataloguing in Publication Data

Tinbergen, N.
   Autistic children.
1. Autism
I. Title
618.92′8′982   RJ506.A9
ISBN 0-04-157010-3 Cased
ISBN 0-04-157011-1 Paper

Library of Congress Cataloging in Publication Data

Tinbergen, Niko, 1907–
   Autistic children: new hope for cure.
Bibliography: p.
Includes index.
1. Autism—Treatment.   I. Tinbergen, Elisabeth A.
II. Title.
RJ506.A9T56   1983   618.92′8982   82-18490
ISBN 0-04-157010-3 Cased
ISBN 0-04-157011-1 Paper

Set in 11 on 12 Imprint by Wyvern Typesetting Ltd, Bristol
and printed in Great Britain
by Mackays of Chatham

Dedicated to the memory of
Corinne Hutt
who pioneered the ethological study of autism
and to
the 'do-it-yourself' mothers,
who have done so much to raise our hopes

Contents

1

Preface

'Autistic children are ineducable.'[1]* 'You can't make them relate but you can teach them simple skills.'[2] 'Most autistic children will remain dependent all their lives.'[3] 'The prognosis for autistic children is poor.'[4]

These and similar depressing pronouncements are made so often that it would be easy to believe that they are the last words on the subject. Their phrasing suggests that they are statements about the present state of knowledge about autism. In reality they are negative statements, expressing our *lack* of understanding, and our helplessness with regard to the curing or the prevention of autism. The words written by O'Gorman in 1970 – 'In the absence of clear ideas on causation, our efforts in the past have been largely empirical, and largely ineffectual' – are still as valid today as they were ten years ago.[5]

The couching of an admission of ignorance and helplessness in the misleading form of positive statements is unfortunate, for it leads to complacency and, worse, to defeatism – in doctors, in therapists, in teachers and in parents. This is not only morally indefensible; it is also scientifically wrong. Detached consideration makes it highly unlikely that a final conclusion can already have been reached, for autism has been studied for no more than a few decades, and by a handful of people at that. And, until recently, attempts at treatment have been no more than tentative, not to say haphazard. Both issues (only partly interconnected) – that of understanding and of treatment – are still wide open, and further study alone can decide if and when we can arrive at more positive statements.

In this book we report the results of some ten years of such further study. In it we describe a two-pronged attack: one on the problem of a better understanding of autism, and one on a search for more effective treatment, and perhaps prevention. On both issues we believe we have helpful contributions to offer.

Scientifically, the position is that in spite of a large and fast-growing number of papers and books on the subject, autism is no better understood than when O'Gorman wrote the lines quoted above.[6] A growing number of facts is being published but, because of certain methodological shortcomings in this field of psychiatry (which we will discuss in some detail in Ch. 7), it is no exaggeration to say that what is being built up is *a*

*Numbers refer to 'Notes and references' at the end of each chapter.

mass of disconnected information in search of a theory. Those attempts that are being presented as theories do not qualify for that name.[7]

This scientific part of our attack is to be found in Chapters 3 to 7. They contain, first, a description of a method of approach which we consider fruitful but which has so far hardly been applied in this field, even though earlier work (in particular that of J. S. & C. Hutt) had already shown its potential before 1970. In our studies, started in 1970, we pooled our experiences as a lifelong student of animal behaviour (N.T.) and as a lifelong childwatcher and childminder (E.A.T.) and found that this dual expertise helped us to understand a great deal about autism that the experts in the field have so far been unable to explain. In fact, the application of our 'ethological' methods led us to interpretations, and even to the framework of an overall theory of autism, that were very different from what is often presented (as we shall see, wrongly) as being 'generally accepted'.

With regard to the problem of treatment: those who, ignoring expert opinions, refuse to write off their children, can take heart by realising that these forecasts about the future are in reality *no more than statements about the failures of past attempts* at treatment. In the absence of anything like an understanding of the nature of autism, such attempts at treatment have inevitably been of a haphazard, hit-or-miss nature; and even if they had been based on some degree of understanding, we must not forget that even experts cannot look into the future. (Anyway, let us not overrate the value of expert opinion. Such opinions have a habit of changing.) Until the main causes of cholera, smallpox and many other illnesses were discovered, they too were (naturally) considered incurable – or nearly so.

But the main thing about the question of treatment of autists is that in recent years it has become no longer true that treatments cannot be successful. Partly unknown to and partly ignored by the rather closed circle of experts, several new ways of treating autistic children and their parents have been developed and are being tried out, which are already achieving very considerable successes. We shall discuss some aspects of these new, more successful, procedures in Chapters 6 and 9. It is because we address ourselves to caregivers as well as to research psychiatrists that we have, throughout the book, avoided the use of technical terms as far as possible. We do not apologise for this, for we know from experience that the use of simple language can clear the mind wonderfully – only too often verbosity suggests understanding where there is in fact confusion.

Our first communications on autism, in which the essence of our present views was already given, appeared in 1972, 1973 and 1974.[8] They received a curiously, but interestingly, mixed reception. The majority of professional students of autism (and, in their wake, the National Societies for Autistic Children) rejected our methods as irrelevant, and our views as ill founded. By contrast, numerous personal communications, which we received from many parts of the world, expressed a surprising degree of understanding and support.

Very few of these concurring responses came from psychiatrists; the bulk came either from fellow ethologists, or from persons involved in the day-to-day care and education of autistic children. Because very few of these 'grassroot' responses appeared in print, the extent of this support is greatly underrated.[9]

We realise now that the sharp dichotomy in the reaction to our publications could have been predicted. Those in daily contact with autistic children understood us because, much like we field ethologists, they had always studied the children in their home environment. Psychiatrists and psychologists rarely do 'fieldwork'; instead they rely largely on office interviews (often with the parents rather than with the child), on questionnaires, and on a variety of 'tests'; and their criticisms of our work reflected this methodological bias. So far, they seem not to have understood our procedure at all. Therefore, far from discouraging us, even the negative reactions to our first publications rather strengthened us in our resolve to continue on our chosen road, and prompted us at the same time to make a new attempt at explaining to non-ethologists our methods and the conclusions to which they had led us. This meant spelling them out in a much more elaborate treatise, which soon assumed the volume of a book.

While struggling to make ourselves clear to our different kinds of readers (and to ourselves), we have often interrupted our writing by continuing to observe a fair number of autistic children (and their parents) in their own environments; we have visited clinics and schools in several countries both in the Old and the New World; we have had numerous discussions with colleagues, likewise of a number of countries; and we have followed developments in the literature. Although we keep receiving new and illuminating information, we feel that the time has come to publish this new, elaborated and updated version of our earlier papers.

We want to make clear at the outset what our book does *not* purport to be. It does not claim to give an 'exhaustive' review of the literature on autism. Nor, of course, do we claim it to be 'the last word' on autism, the final solution to an extremely intricate set of problems. What we do describe is a method of study which we have applied in a renewed reconnaissance of the field, and what we do claim is that this new approach has led to a set of plausible hypotheses and even to the design of promising therapies. Although more evidence is certainly desirable, we feel that we should not postpone publication of our work until it could be 'fully substantiated'. Too many children are at the moment denied access to treatments that are beginning to be available and that could well cure them.

We received invaluable help from many people – far too many for them all to be mentioned by name. Our special thanks are due to Professor J. S.

and the late Dr Corinne Hutt of Oxford, later of Keele University, who first called our attention to autism and with whom we had stimulating discussions; to Dr J. Richer of Reading, later Oxford; to Dr Tsuneo Taguchi of Tokyo, Japan; to Dr M. Zappella of Siena, Italy and other colleagues with whom we discussed various aspects of their and our own work; to Geraldine Flanagan of Oxford for many helpful discussions and for her invaluable help in selecting relevant literature references; to Professor K. Pyck of Louvain, Belgium; to Dr Th. Compernolle of Philadelphia and Louvain; to Professor N. L. J. Kamp of Utrecht, the Netherlands; Dr B. A. A. Ruttenberg of Philadelphia and Dr Martha Welch of New York whose clinics we were allowed to visit; to Dr M. Heatley of Oxford who allowed us to follow an educational experiment with some autistic children; and to a number of devoted and talented tutors of autistic children, notably Mrs J. Bayley of Teddington, Mrs P. Elmhirst of Stillingfleet and Mrs M. Ormerod of Oxford, who gave us the benefit of their extensive experience. Mrs Elmhirst kindly read the entire manuscript and gave us valuable criticism; and Drs R. and M. Dawkins of the Animal Behaviour Research Group of the Oxford University's Department of Zoology gave us valuable comments on Chapter 7. Our thanks are also due to the very large number of people, among them parents, who have given us personal information, some of which has to be considered confidential. Finally, we received much valuable criticism and advice during the discussions following the many lectures in which N. T. has been trying to present our methods and views to non-ethologists. That we owe a great debt to the important category of 'do-it-yourself' parents is acknowledged by the fact that we have dedicated the book to them.

Acknowledgements

All illustrations are by N. T., with the exception of the following, for which we are indebted to the persons and publishers listed below:

Collins, London (Figs 3.9 &10, from Tinbergen, N. *The herring gull's world* 1953); Mrs P. Elmhirst (Plates 3–11); Mr Nathan Cabot Hale (Plates 1 & 2, from *Birth of a family*, Garden City, NY: Anchor Books/Doubleday 1979); Professor S. J. Hutt and Charles C. Thomas, Publisher, Springfield, Illinois (Fig. 2.1, from Hutt, S. J. & C. Hutt, *Direct observation and measurement of behaviour* 1970); Professor S. J. Hutt and Dr C. Ounsted (Figs 3.1 & 2); Methuen, London (Figs 3.11 & 12, from Tinbergen, N. *Social behaviour in animals* 1953); Dr M. Norton-Griffiths (Figs 3.3–6, from *The feeding behaviour of the oystercatcher*, Hematopus ostralegus. D. Phil. thesis, Oxford 1968); Oxford University Press (Figs 3.7, 3.13 & 14, from Tinbergen, N. *The study of instinct* 1951); Paul Parey Verlag (Figs 3.1 & 2, from Tinbergen, E. A. & N. Tinbergen *Early childhood autism – an ethological approach* 1972).

Notes and references

Without in any way pretending to deal exhaustively with 'the literature', we have added at the end of each chapter a limited number of references, and also notes which, if they had been incorporated in the main text, would have interrupted its flow. Most of the relevant titles of the (rapidly growing) literature can be found in the bibliographies of the books mentioned in note 4 below, where the reader can also find the names of the scientific journals in which the majority of research workers publish their results.

1 Repeatedly stated on BBC Television in a programme giving the views of representatives of the British Society for Autistic Children, in the early 1970s; these views have not been greatly changed since.
2 Said verbatim by Sybil Elgar, at the time Headmistress of Somerset Court, in a lecture given in Oxford in the autumn of 1978.
3 Wing, L. (ed.) 1976. *Early childhood autism*, 48. Oxford: Pergamon.
4 Stated in most of the best known works on early childhood autism, to which we refer for further reading of the more conventional literature.
 DesLauriers, A. M. and C. F. Carlson 1969. *Your child is asleep – early infantile autism.* Homewood, Ill.: Dorsey Press.
 Furneaux, B. and B. Roberts (eds) 1977. *Autistic children – teaching, community and research approaches.* London: Routledge and Kegan Paul.
 O'Gorman, G. 1970. *The nature of childhood autism.* London: Butterworth.
 Ornitz, E. M. 1973. Childhood autism – a review of the clinical and experimental literature. Medical progress. *Calif. Med.* **118**, 21–47.
 Rimland, B. 1965. *Infantile autism.* London: Methuen.
 Ritvo, E. R., B. J. Freeman, E. M. Ornitz and P. E. Tanguay (eds) 1976. *Autism, current research and management.* New York: Spectrum.
 Wing, L. 1976 (see Note 3 above).
 The most recent comprehensive work published so far (June 1981) is the extended version of the 1976 International Symposium on Autism, held in St Gallen:
 Rutter, M. and E. Schopler 1978. *Autism – a reappraisal of concepts and treatment.* London and New York: Plenum Press.
 There is a special journal devoted almost exclusively to autism: the *Journal of Autism and Childhood Schizophrenia* (now, *Journal of Autism and Developmental Disorders);* many contributions have appeared in the *Journal of Child Psychology and Psychiatry* and other journals.
5 Empirical attempts (which could have led to effectual cures without necessarily being based on an understanding of autism) have not been consistently successful.
6 That this is not just our opinion, but begins to be heard in medical and psychiatric circles as well, is shown by the following quotations taken from reviews, in a medical and in a psychiatric journal respectively, of the St Gallen volume mentioned in note 4 above.
 Stephen Wolkind (1979) writes in *Br. J. Psychiat.* **134**, 120: 'The aim of the editors is to present a picture of the "current state of the art". In this they have undoubtedly succeeded and any frustration the reader feels is probably a true reflection of that state . . . there are few attempts to bring these (authoritative accounts on particular topics) together into an integrated whole. The basic problem of the nature of autism remains as difficult to reach as the sufferers themselves.'
 From the (unsigned) review of the same volume in the *Lancet* of September 1978, p. 714: 'An "obsessive insistence on the maintenance of sameness" is said to be the hallmark of autistic children; this characteristic also applies to most of those who write about them . . . Serious workers in this field will learn little that is new . . .'.
 A recent editorial in the *Br. Med. J.* still reflects the familiar resigned, and in our

view now outdated, view that 'there is no medical treatment' for autism. Childhood autism and related conditions. 1980. *Br. Med. J.* **281**, 761–2.

7   The almost endless repetition of statements to the effect that 'it is generally agreed that a cognitive-cum-language handicap is the central feature of autism' cannot convince because they are nowhere supported by relevant arguments.

8   Tinbergen, E. A. and N. Tinbergen 1972. Early childhood autism; an ethological approach. *Advances in ethology* (supplement series to *Z. Tierpsychol.*) Vol. 10. Berlin: Paul Parey.

Tinbergen, N. 1974. Ethology and stress diseases. Nobel Prize (Medicine) Acceptance Address in *Les Prix Nobel en 1973*. Stockholm: Nobel Foundation (reprinted in *Science* **185**, 20–27 in 1974).

Our views were severely criticised by several authors, e.g:

Schopler, E. 1974. The stress of autism in ethology (sic). *J. Aut. Childhd. Schizophrenia* **4**, 193–5.

Wing, L. and D. M. Ricks 1976. The aetiology of childhood autism; a criticism of the Tinbergens' ethological theory. *Psychol. Med.* **6**, 533–44.

We replied to this paper by briefly restating our methods and our views and ended with: 'It is for the sake of the children and their families that we urge those working in this field to consider our approach and our interpretations without prejudice.' (ibid., p. 549).

9   However, a number of case histories have been published in a variety of books, largely written by parents and other 'laymen'. With few exceptions, these 'non-scientific' accounts have been ignored by the experts. We consider this wrong, and discuss samples of the valuable evidence to be gleaned from these books in Chapters 6 and 9.

2

Introduction

Because the label 'autistic' is not always applied consistently, we have to settle first of all what kind of children we shall be talking about. It is in principle not possible to delineate this sharply, if only because (a) different children show different grades of severity of the syndrome; (b) autism may take different forms in different children, and (c) the symptoms (i.e. the observable behaviours) change as a child grows up. There is also the practical difficulty (d) that even now many doctors, specialists included, notice different parts of any particular child's abnormal behaviour, and as a consequence do not always arrive at the same diagnosis. This has been strikingly demonstrated by Rimland, who has, for several hundred children who had been seen and diagnosed independently by more than one doctor, examined the degree of correlation between first and second opinions.[1] Table 2.1 shows the eight most commonly given diagnoses, and the extent to which first and second opinions corresponded. If there were general agreement on what characterises an autistic child (as there is almost without exception on, say, typhoid, mumps and smallpox), the diagonal that runs from the top left to bottom right should of course have very high scores, and few scores should be found in other places. In fact, the scatter appears to be random.

When trying to make a diagnosis, many experts adhere more or less to the well-known 'nine points', originally agreed on by the working party convened in 1961 by M. Creak.[2] These were a more detailed and elaborate version of the description given originally by Kanner.[3]

In 1970, O'Gorman[4] proposed the use of a slightly altered list of 'criteria of diagnosis', as follows.

(1) Withdrawal from, or failure to become involved with, reality; in particular, failure to form a normal relationship with people.
(2) Serious intellectual retardation with islets of higher, or nearly normal or exceptional intellectual functions or skills.
(3) Failure to acquire speech, or to maintain or improve on speech already learned, or to use what speech has been acquired for communication.
(4) Abnormal response to one or more types of sensory stimulus (usually sound).
(5) Gross and sustained exhibition of mannerisms or peculiarities of movement, including immobility and hyperkinesis, and excluding tics.

Table 2.1 Comparison of first and second opinions about 445 children showing severe behaviour disorders. From Rimland (1971).

2nd opinion → 1st opinion ↓	Autistic	Infantile autism or early infantile autism	Childhood schizophrenia	Emotionally disturbed or mentally ill	Brain damaged or neurologically damaged	Retarded	Psychotic (symbiotic psychosis) etc.	Deaf or partly deaf	Total
Autistic	**33**	5	53	18	23	51	10	7	200
Infantile autism or early infantile autism	1	**10**	6	0	4	6	0	2	29
Childhood schizophrenia	17	3	**1**	2	8	1	0	0	32
Emotionally disturbed or mentally ill	12	2	4	**2**	9	13	3	0	45
Brain damaged or neurologically damaged	14	3	2	5	**4**	15	0	1	44
Retarded	21	2	6	18	16	**5**	2	2	72
Psychotic (symbiotic psychosis) etc.	4	0	1	1	2	2	**0**	0	10
Deaf or partly deaf	4	1	0	2	0	5	1	**0**	13
Total	106	26	73	48	66	98	16	12	445

(6) Pathological resistance to change. This may be shown by:
   (a) Insistence on observance of rituals in the patient's own behaviour or in those around him.
   (b) Pathological attachment to the same surroundings, equipment, toys and people (even though the relationship with the person involved may be purely mechanical and emotionally empty).
   (c) Excessive preoccupation with particular objects or certain characteristics of them without regard for their accepted functions.
   (d) Severe anger or terror or excitement, or increased withdrawal, when the sameness of the environment is threatened (e.g. by strangers).

A fuller description of the syndrome, a number of its details and of its many variations can be found, e.g., in Wing (1976).[5]

Rutter (1978)[6] lists as 'essential criteria' (of the behaviour of a child before the age of five): '(1) an onset before the age of 30 months; (2) impaired social development which has a number of special characteristics and which is out of keeping with the child's intellectual level; (3) delayed and deviant language development which also has certain defined features and which is out of keeping with the child's intellectual level; and (4) "insistence on sameness" as shown by stereotyped play patterns, abnormal preoccupations, or resistance to change'.

'However . . . cases must also be described in terms of I Q level and neurological or medical status' (p. 19).

We feel that on the whole the characterisations we have read do not differ all that much. They put the emphasis perhaps on different aspects of the syndrome, and some ignore symptoms mentioned by others (thus Rutter does not mention the 'islets of good performance' which to many are a very intriguing characteristic of many autists, while, for example, I Q and onset before the age of 30 months are not considered diagnostically relevant by several other authors), but this does not seem to us to be too important. At least the criteria used are on the whole descriptive, or very nearly so.[7] What has to be avoided is, of course, the inclusion of mere inferences in a characterisation. Rutter seems to be in danger of doing so when he insists on the use of 'I Q level and neurological and medical status'; also, although this is not usually mentioned in print, there is, at least at the moment in America and Britain, a tendency to consider 'ineducability' a part of the definition. Time and again we have, when describing cases of partial or complete recovery which we had witnessed, received the answer: 'Oh, but if they recovered they cannot have been true autists'. We suggest that such incorporation of what are really inferences (for 'ineducability' is related to the notion that autism must be due to 'organic' or even genetic damage alone) has to be avoided if we are not to become hopelessly confused right at the start.

For practical purposes we have found it sufficient to state that when we are speaking of autistic children we refer to children who show all or the majority of the following behaviour peculiarities: (a) failure or near-failure to form normal social relationships (Fig. 2.1); (b) reluctance to venture out into an unfamiliar world; (c) non-development or regression of speech; (d) the frequent performance of a limited repertoire of 'mannerisms' or 'stereotypies'; (e) avoidance of and resistance to changes in their (physical and social) world, including changes in routine; (f) overall retardation, but often with 'islets of good or excellent performance'; and often (g) sleeping difficulties.

The question is often asked, is autism an 'entity'; is it a distinct and consistent enough syndrome to be set off from other disorders and to receive a name of its own? The same question applies undoubtedly to all mental disorders; diagnosis and classification in psychiatry are notoriously difficult. It is of course quite possible that classifications as neat as that of, for instance, illnesses due to infection by a recognisable parasite, will never be possible. Even so, if we take into account the differences of severity and the qualitatively different sets of symptoms that may be shown and the changes that occur as a child grows up, it looks as if the use of 'early childhood autism' as the name for a fairly well delineated

Figure 2.1 'A characteristic posture and position adopted by an autistic child (right foreground) relative to other children playing in the same room (drawn from an 8 mm motion picture film)' From Hutt and Hutt (1970).

syndrome is justified and useful. Yet it must never be forgotten that in mental disorders, borderline cases and mixtures of a variety of syndromes (to mention only two phenomena) make it impossible to distinguish really sharply between 'autistic' and 'non-autistic', and if the latter, whether normal or otherwise afflicted. We repeat: we are going to speak of children who show most or all of the symptoms that we have just listed, and 'autistic' seems to be as good a label as, if not a better one than most others used in psychiatry.

When in our Preface we said that we consider none of the interpretations of the nature of autism to deserve the name of a theory, this is not necessarily a reflection on the value of the work done by all investigators (even though much in the research effort made so far *is* open to severe criticism). It must be expected that we will live for a long time with many uncertainties about autism, if only because it belongs to what are without doubt *the most complex natural phenomena in our universe*. The organisation and functions of the adult human brain are more complex than those of other organs; certainly much more complex than chemical or physical processes in the inanimate world. Even the most complicated of man-built machines such as, say, spacecraft, are crude contraptions compared with our brain. The *growth* of that human brain – the 'programming' not only for adult functioning but also for functioning correctly at every stage of development, for changing its function *while* it develops – is a process of a very much higher level of complexity again than the proper functioning of the brain at any given moment. Thus *deviations* from this normal growth process must be expected to be even more difficult to understand than the normal course of events. It would be naïve, and not a little arrogant to think that, after such a comparatively short time of research by little more than a handful of people, understanding could have been reached. Psychiatric science is at the moment doing no more than grappling with the problems, probing now here then there, gropingly searching to find its way in this exceedingly difficult field. It has to make the human brain understand not only its own functioning, but its own development and the 'derailments' of that development that produce autistic children. It is this state of affairs that makes it important that 'no stone shall be left unturned', that no way of studying the problem must be left unexplored, that no hypothesis, however 'strange', must be rejected out of hand.[9]

The various aspects in which our approach differs from those hitherto attempted will be discussed in the course of our text, but we want to emphasise here that we believe it to be important, indeed essential, to distinguish conceptually, more clearly than is generally done, between four different questions. One of these – that of how to recognise and characterise autism – we have dealt with. The others are given below.

(a) How can we understand the autistic *condition*, that of *being autistic*, and what is its essence – how are the different symptoms interconnected? This will be discussed in Chapters 3 and 4.

(b) What can *make* a child autistic, what can cause the 'derailment' of his development? This question of aetiology, of ontogenesis, will be investigated separately in Chapter 5.

(c) Finally, how can we influence the course of events; how can we ameliorate the condition, perhaps cure it and, if at all possible, prevent it? This issue will be dealt with in Chapter 6.

On all these three issues (a, b & c) we find ourselves in disagreement with the prevailing expert opinion. With regard to the autistic condition, we shall argue that it is in essence an emotional or motivational[10] disturbance; more specifically, a state of anxiety-dominated imbalance, which seriously impairs the child's ability to interact with the environment that offers so many opportunities for behavioural development that are utilised by normal children as a matter of course. The various peculiarities in the perceptual, the cognitive and the motor skills (including speech) are in our view peripheral; they are symptoms in comparison with this central emotional impairment.

Regarding the question of how a child becomes autistic in the first place, and how, together with his parents, he can then get caught in a fatal downward spiral, we will argue that (a) the genetic contribution is not decisive but is at best involved in making some children more vulnerable, more likely to develop autism than others; (b) that there is at best doubtful evidence that 'organic', i.e. gross structural damage or chemical abnormality, is at the root of autism; and (c) that there are many indications that early traumatic experiences are of much greater importance than is usually assumed.[11] Unfortunately, ever since Kanner suggested that a special type of parent (called by some 'refrigerator parents') might have a higher chance of having an autistic child than other parents, and in particular, since Bettelheim even more explicitly put the main *blame* for autism (and for other emotional disturbances) on the parents and the home environment, parents have felt themselves unjustly accused, and have quite understandably felt such views not only to be *unfair* and cruel but have rejected them as *wrong*. But we want to emphasise at the start that when we ascribe autism largely to traumatic influences of the early environment we are referring to more than 20 different circumstances, of which the majority cannot be said to be the 'fault' of the parents: for instance, a difficult delivery (or an overall anaesthetic during delivery); a week's separation when either mother or child is in hospital; moving house when the child is less than 30 months of age and while the parents are under stress; a new baby being born when the previous child is still very young. While none of these alone is likely to harm a child, a combination of even a few of them may in our experience be enough to put child and mother on the wrong track from the start, and once the wrong turning has been taken, the chances are that child and parent damage each other progressively. Many of the 'autismogenic' environmental factors victimise the parents as much as the child. Even if the parents have perhaps unwittingly traumatised their child, it is of course better to help them overcome possible feelings of guilt than to add to them by blaming them. The reasons for these views, and the reason why the mother is so often more involved than the father, are discussed in Chapters 5, 6 and 8.

As for treatment, we have over the years become more rather than less convinced that the pessimistic prognosis so widely publicised, and the resultant limited attempts at education, are not justified. We see one of the causes of this pessimism in the fact that the experts who hold these views know only a part of the total population of autists. We will submit, on the basis of first-hand experience, that in very young children there is a smooth continuum from very mildly autistic children all the way to severely afflicted autists; that many parents, notably mothers, manage to coax their autistic child back to normality, whereas in other cases either child or mother, or both, have been so damaged from the start that the chasm that separates them cannot be bridged. Thus a dichotomous division between autists and non-autists is a secondary development which appears in later years,[12] and it is the non-recovered category that comes much more often to the notice of doctors than those who are cured by 'do-it-yourself' parents. We will argue in particular that if autistic children are spotted early, and both mother and child are helped in establishing a close, warm bond with each other, the recovery rate can be much higher than is now generally believed. We will substantiate this claim by showing that the most successful treatments of children of various ages we have seen or read about are indeed those in which top priority is given to the reduction of the child's abnormal feelings of insecurity and of the mother's inability to cope emotionally with her child; that this is best done by re-establishing a strong bond between the child and his mother; that if this is done successfully, the child will prove both to have learned more while he was sick than was realised, and that, as he recovers emotionally, he will be prepared, indeed keen, to develop socially and intellectually. Our points about traumatising events in the early environment and about new, more successful treatments will both be illustrated in Chapters 6 and 9 and a number of case histories will be described briefly in Chapter 10.

Finally, we emphasise once more that, in view of what we said about the extreme complexity of this and other distortions of behaviour development in the human species, we feel unable to claim to have found the final solution. What we advocate is that a renewed, unprejudiced attempt must be made at understanding autism; that methods are available that can lead to such understanding but that these have so far hardly been applied; and that a more constructive educational policy has to be followed.

Notes and references

1 Rimland, B. 1971. The differentiation of childhood psychoses. *J. Aut. Childhd. Schizophrenia* **1**, 161–75.
2 Creak, M. (Chairman) 1961. The schizophrenic syndrome in childhood. Progress of a working party. *Brit. Med. J.* **2**, 889–90.
3 Kanner, L. 1943. Autistic disturbances of affective contact. *Nerv. Child* **2**, 217–50.
4 O'Gorman, G. 1970 (see Ch. 1, note 4).
5 Wing, L. 1976 (see Ch. 1, note 3).
6 Rutter, M. 1978. Diagnosis and definition. In Rutter, M. and E. Schopler (see Ch. 1, note 4).
7 The books that try to give an overview of the 'state of the art' and/or give opinions on the prognosis, and that are most often quoted, are: (a) the more pessimistic or at least resigned ones:
DesLauriers, A. M. and C. F. Carlson 1969 (see Ch. 1, note 4);
Furneaux, B. and B. Roberts 1977 (see Ch. 1, note 4);
Ornitz, E. M. 1973 (see Ch. 1, note 4);
Ritvo, E. R. *et al.* (eds) 1976 (see Ch. 1, note 4).
The most persistent advocate of the view of autism as a perceptual/cognitive/language handicap is:
Rutter, M. 1966. Behavioural and cognitive characteristics of a series of psychotic children. In *Early childhood autism*, J. Wing (ed.), 51–81. Oxford: Pergamon. See also:
Rutter, M. 1978. Developmental issues and prognosis. In Rutter, M. and E. Schopler (see Ch. 1, note 4), 497–507.
(b) A modest, no longer quite up-to-date, but in our opinion still excellent, and above all open-minded account is given by O'Gorman, G. 1970 (see Ch. 1, note 4).
(c) The following authors strike, each for his own reasons, a more optimistic note:
Bettelheim, B. 1967. *The empty fortress: infantile autism and the birth of self.* London: Collier-Macmillan.
As the title reveals, this is a book by a psychoanalyst. We find it long winded, but full of interesting thoughts and facts, including bits of many case histories. As we shall argue in Chapter 5, Bettelheim over-emphasises the role played by parents in the aetiology of autism, and this has unfortunately antagonised many people to such an extent that his work is at present either ignored or dismissed as simply wrong (see e.g. Wing, L. 1976, 72–92).
Delacato, C. H. 1974. *The ultimate stranger – the autistic child.* Garden City, New York: Doubleday.
An interesting if rather sketchy book, written in '*Reader's Digest* style' and considered by its author, with a degree of justification, to be 'revolutionary'. Together with G. Doman, Dr Delacato worked out the therapies now applied in the Doman Institutes in Philadelphia (see Ch. 6). On the whole, Delacato seemed to think at the time that 'autism is sensoryism', i.e. that its root cause is sensory or perceptual malfunctioning. Like Doman, however, he does not seem to distinguish very clearly between autistic children, in the sense as used by us, and a wide range of other children with a variety of differently malfunctioning brains, or at least not to find such distinctions material to the therapist.
Doman, G. 1974. *What to do about your brain-injured child.* Garden City, New York: Doubleday.
Like Delacato's book, this work is written in '*Reader's Digest* style' and deals with a huge variety of 'hurt' children. We describe our visit to his Institutes in Chapter 6 and mention here merely that, whatever the theoretical basis for his work, his

therapeutical results are impressive and must not be dismissed, even though it is not clear to us how effective his methods are with autistic children in our sense. (Our repeated inquiries on this latter point were never answered.)

Ruttenberg, B. A. A. 1971. A psychoanalytic understanding of infantile autism and its treatment. In *Infantile autism*, D. W. Churchill, G. D. Alpern and M. K. DeMyer (eds), 145–84. Springfield, Ill.: Charles C. Thomas.

We refer to our visit to Dr Ruttenberg's Clinic in Philadelphia in Chapter 6.

8 Foudraine, J. 1974. *Not made of wood*. London: Quartet Midway.

The case of Sylvia, described in stages in Foudraine's book, is of particular interest, since she had as a child been diagnosed as autistic (a diagnosis in which L. Kanner himself was involved), and is throughout the book referred to as 'the adult autist'. Through application of the 'graded task' therapy (see Ch. 6), Foudraine managed to cure Sylvia fully when she was 46 (!) years old and had been as totally institutionalised as could be imagined. Foudraine (who argues that many institutionalised 'schizophrenics' can likewise be cured) makes at the end of this case history the astonishing remark that, *since she has recovered, she cannot have been an autist* (our emphasis) – a telling example of the extraordinary influence of authority on the thinking of one of the psychiatric profession's most independently thinking rebels.

Wing, L. (1971) in her *Austistic children – a guide for parents* (London: Constable), advises, consistent with her view of autism, that the best parents can do is to be resigned, though she urges them to treat their children well on their limited intellectual levels. On pp. 126 and 127 she writes: 'One or two cases have been reported (without much documentary evidence) of people with autistic behaviour as children who grew up and married, but they seem to have grown out of the symptoms completely by the time of adolescence. In these circumstances *it is difficult to know if they really did have early childhood autism.*' (emphasis is ours). We summarise our comments on current methodology in this field in Chapter 7.

9 One of our criticisms (which we have also heard expressed by various psychiatrists, including some working on autism) is that there is among the workers on autism an abnormal attitude of possessiveness linked with, it seems, fear of intrusion by unfamiliar ideas or interpretations (hence the reproach of 'adherence to sameness' in the review in the *Lancet* mentioned in note 6 to Ch. 1). We ourselves have been at the receiving end of this type of response (which is exemplified by, for example, the review of our writings by Schopler, and the criticism of our views on aetiology by Wing and Ricks – see note 8 to Ch. 1). The former simply dismisses our work without really entering into our arguments; and Wing and Ricks attack (distorted) descriptions of our views on aetiology and, rather than urge their readers to be *critical*, advise them 'to *discard*' our work.

10 When we use in this book both the terms 'motivation(al)' and 'emotion(al)', we refrain deliberately from making a sharp distinction. We consider that, for our present purpose, it is sufficient and helpful if we apply the words 'motivation(al)' when we speak in objectivistic terms and 'emotion(al)' when we refer to what we believe to be a child's subjective feelings.

11 As will be clear in the course of our argument, we believe (with other authors such as J. and L. Wing, M. Rutter and others) that the cause of autism must be considered to be multifactorial, i.e. that genetic, 'organic' and 'psychogenic' are not mutually exclusive or incompatible aspects of its aetiology. Our thinking, not just in psychiatric but in other medical issues as well, conforms rather to the ideas discussed explicitly in a recent issue of *Encounter* by the former Chief Editor of *New Scientist*, Bernard Dixon (Beyond the magic bullet – reconciling health and disease. *Encounter* June 1980, 64–8).

12 When we suggested, in 1972, that there is a gliding scale from severely autistic on the one hand, through more or less mildly autistic, to 'shy', 'timid' or 'socially withdrawn' children on the other, this idea was fairly generally rejected, and a sharp distinction

between 'truly' autistic children and 'children with autistic (or autistiform) behaviour' was maintained. Everyone who has followed the literature will have noticed that the 'gliding scale' idea (amended as we suggest in Ch. 5) begins to be more generally accepted.

3

Analysis of the autistic condition – methods and concepts

Introduction

THE ABSENCE OF AN OVERALL THEORY

We begin this chapter by submitting that, so far, no acceptable *comprehensive* theory about the nature of the autistic condition has been presented. A variety of pronouncements and suggestions has been made, but we feel that none of them carries conviction. Some statements are so vague as to be almost meaningless; thus Ritvo's claim[1] that 'I feel we can say with certainty that autism is a *physical disease of the brain*' (Ritvo's italics) cannot be said to represent a theory, and is perhaps not really intended as such. There are, however, more specific hypotheses, and of these the notion that the central characteristic of the autistic condition is a 'cognitive-language handicap' (Rutter 1978)[2] is at the moment, at least in Britain, persistently advocated by leading workers. Clearly, Ricks and Wing (1976)[3] think along similar lines and write that 'The central problem, which is present even in the most mildly handicapped autistic people, appears to be a specific kind of difficulty in handling symbols, which affects language, non-verbal communication and many other aspects of cognitive and social activity' (p. 120). This view is widely accepted by parents' associations and by others who follow the lead of these authorities. For more than one reason, however, we do not find this notion helpful, and even feel it to be unacceptable.

First of all, the statement itself, that autism is primarily 'a cognitive-language handicap', is not altogether in accordance with the facts. It is true that autistic children perform very poorly in many interviews and standard tests but, as we shall argue, this is largely the consequence of inappropriate methodology: in such situations autistic children are simply too daunted (or sometimes too bored) to show what they are capable of. When they are observed properly – we shall describe the required procedures presently – many autistic children, quite possibly even the majority, reveal on occasion quite considerable cognitive and language abilities. This is well known to many parents and to those teachers who have, and use, the time for unobtrusively studying the children. In fact, the professional students do know a little of this, at any rate enough to point out that many autists show 'islets of good performance'. We intend to show that under suitable circumstances the abilities of most autists are not at all confined to those, admittedly very striking 'islets'.

Secondly, the notion of the centrality of the cognitive-language handicap has so far not been satisfactorily tested for its overall explanatory power. As we shall argue in more detail below, it is rarely possible in a science such as psychiatry to 'prove' or 'refute' hypotheses; at the very early stage in which this science finds itself – that of tentative reconnaissance – hypotheses have to be judged mainly by the criterion of how many of the known facts they can make understandable; by *their overall plausibility*. Admittedly, the claim of comprehensiveness is sometimes made. Thus, L. Wing (1976)[4] writes: 'The new formulations link the children's behaviour to underlying organic impairments, the most important of which are cognitive problems affecting the comprehension and use of linguistic symbols and the interpretation of all kinds of sensory experience. Looked at in this way, the elements making up the complete syndrome *form a logical pattern* . . .' (our italics) (p. 22). We fail to see, however, that this claim is substantiated in her contribution.

What would be required is a demonstration that, and how, a cognitive-language handicap could explain, for instance, the islets of good performance, social withdrawal, the performance of stereotypies, resistance against change in the environment or in routine, and the (often astonishingly good) *understanding* of speech. That such a demonstration is not attempted seems to mean that the pressing need for such attempts is not recognised; that the importance of the criterion of overall plausibility is underrated.

Thirdly, the possibility that cognitive-language handicaps could be a consequence rather than a central cause of other 'elements of the syndrome' is not convincingly eliminated. And yet the task of distinguishing between (a) *correlations* between elements of a complex system, and (b) the nature of the *cause–effect relationships* between them that are responsible for these correlations is (as everywhere in the natural sciences) of paramount importance.

Other hypotheses, put forward tentatively (or merely implied), such as that which considers a state of general arousal[5] to be the core of the autistic condition, or that autism is primarily due to defective perception,[6] or (an idea often expressed by neurologists) to structural defects somewhere in the periphery of the nervous system (even in, for instance, the motor periphery, in separate parts of the body such as the hand) have in our opinion even less general explanatory power, and it must be said in fairness that some of the advocates of these ideas do not claim such a wide applicability of their interpretations. We repeat, however, that progress will be possible only if comprehensive theories are formulated and their plausibility argued.

Rather than elaborating this criticism we shall try to explain how we have proceeded in our search for a constructive interpretation of the nature of the autistic state.

Some points of method

Since the conclusion that a child is autistic is always based primarily on his behaviour peculiarities – as these are in fact almost the *only* observables – we submit that it is this behaviour which has to be studied before inferences are made about the child's internal condition, of which his aberrant behaviour is the outcome. One has to remind oneself all the time that all such inferences are nothing but guesses unless and until they are based on, have been checked with, and can account for what is observed directly.

This study of the visible 'output' of the wrong, 'derailed' development of the behaviour machinery has to proceed step by step. Intense, long, repeated 'plain' or 'simple' observation, guided by a truly inquiring, not prematurely prejudiced state of mind, has to come first. This phase of the work must not be hurried, in fact it is just at the moment more needed than anything else. If done properly, it will lead to the emergence, first tentatively, then in more and more conscious and explicit form, of 'hunches' about what makes the child behave so strangely, about his internal condition (in fact such hunches usually guide the observational work from the start as well as being formed as a result of it). During further study, such initially vague ideas are gradually tested and sorted out into, on the one hand, the more plausible, and on the other the less plausible or clearly wrong hypotheses. Once a set of possible hypotheses has been formulated, more specific observations and, when possible, experiments can help to consolidate or, conversely, to refute some of them until, with luck, something emerges that deserves the name of a theory. In other words, we advocate a 'descending' analytic procedure; one which begins by scrutinising the behaviour as a whole and which leads gradually to digging deeper and deeper into the details of its causation. In this step-by-step process, too large and too hasty 'jumping to conclusions' (i.e. to premature hunches) has to be avoided or has at least to be distinguished from the formulation of well founded hypotheses. There is of course nothing wrong with the jumping as such – in fact, it is an essential part of the exercise – but what is wrong is the premature elevation of mere hunches to the status of conclusions, for this closes the mind to further exploration.[7]

The way in which we ourselves have tried to apply this general method in our studies of autistic children requires some elucidation.

(a) We made our observations as *unobtrusively* as possible. This was necessary because, to a far greater extent than normal children, autists respond to the slightest intrusion or (to them) unfamiliar circumstances and events by withdrawing into their shells. In fact, their behaviour is one of the most striking examples of natural processes that are vulnerable to 'observer interference'. The result of such interference on the part of the observer of autistic children is of course not that he sees nothing at all, but that he is shown only a minor part of their overall behaviour repertoire, viz. either persistent attempts at escape or, if this is impossible, a complete shutting off from their environment, a retreat into their private world, or a sudden determined defence – in extreme cases even a surprisingly violent physical attack.

One of the valuable skills that ethologists have developed – have *had* to develop in their studies of often extremely wary wild animals – is just the one we need when studying autistic children: that of observing without the animal or the child (the 'subject') being aware of the observer's presence. Much of the ethologists' work on animal behaviour that is relevant to our study of autism has been done from 'hides' or 'blinds' which, provided they are used with expert 'field craft', give the subjects no visual, auditory or any other signs of the observer's presence (with wild mammals, even the giving of scent clues has to be avoided; this, fortunately, is rarely necessary with the children, normal or abnormal, of our own species, for human beings have a very poor sense of smell). However, when we are 'childwatching' we are hampered by two difficulties that we do not encounter in work with animals. Firstly, children not only react momentarily to even subtle signs, for instance to the slightest sound coming from behind a one-way screen (the laboratory equivalent of the ethologists' hides), but deduce at once that these sounds mean that 'there is someone behind that black mirror' and, unlike most animals, they *do not forget* this inference and may even elaborate on it.[8] Secondly, secretive prying into a person's, even a child's, behaviour without permission (permission which, because it would require that person's knowledge of the exercise, would defeat its very purpose) borders upon the unethical and is often resented, particularly when adults and their more intimate kinds of behaviour are concerned. Therefore both manwatching and childwatching are often best done with a substitute method, not ideal but next best, viz. by making one's subject(s) so completely used to one's presence that one is accepted as 'part of the furniture'. Surprisingly few people have this required double gift of 'making themselves scarce' and at the same time observing with concentrated attention; yet this skill can, and should, be learned if one is to succeed. Even so, however, moral considerations do demand discretion, and much valuable information simply cannot be published because the parents involved might recognise their case even when expertly camouflaged, and might feel hurt, raise objections and withdraw their collaboration.

As we shall argue later in specific cases, failure to meet fully the need for unobtrusiveness while observing makes many of the psychological tests that are so widely, even routinely, used in this field of medicine, relatively uninformative, and sometimes positively misleading. Like most normal children who perform less well at their exams than when 'the pressure is off', so autistic children are so to speak 'exam shy', only very much more so than normal children; they can be said to be virtually allergic to being tested. This is why all that is revealed by most tests is simply that the anxiety caused by the situation suppresses most of the achievements of which the child is capable and so presents a distorted, often unrealistically poor picture of his real abilities. As we shall see later, a number of other tests, such as neurological examinations and the taking of blood samples, may even have definite deleterious effects; many of them are not only cruel but worsen the child's condition. We shall later describe a striking example of this.

(b) More and more workers recognise now that it is not just the autistic child himself who is malfunctioning; what is actually ill is something larger: the child *in the web of his relationships* with the social and physical outside world. As is invariably mentioned in the 'nine points' for purposes of diagnosis (though not put in the centre of things, as we consider necessary), an autistic child (a) fails to establish social bonds; and (b) insists on 'sameness', i.e. withdraws from, rather than ventures out into (i.e. interacts with and explores) the non-social outside world. It is because of this that it is not enough to study an autistic child on his own, nor even merely in the presence of, say, his mother. The problem of autism can be understood only if the children are studied in their interactions with their total environment; with their mothers to begin with (with whom they have their first contacts); next with their fathers, their sibs and other children; and, as 'affiliation' with them develops into 'socialisation', with even more persons, with a steadily growing circle of acquaintances. It is just as important to study their interactions (and often their failure to interact) with their non-social environment: with toys, with their own rooms and their own corners; with their own 'comforter'; and with things in the garden, in the street, in shops and in other people's homes, with pets etc.

For all these reasons we have observed children as much as possible in their natural environments, i.e. in their social settings and in the non-social, explorable but not explored world, of which they are the, so sadly malfunctioning, centres. Very few psychiatrists do even a minimal amount of such 'fieldwork'.

(c) As we have already indicated, it was helpful, indeed essential, to compare autistic children and their parents, associates and overall environments all the time with the behaviour of *normal* children in the same contexts,[9] and (for reasons that will become clear later) to extend this comparison to the behaviour both of children of the same age as one's subject and of younger, on occasion very much younger, children. As we shall see, this comparison can throw light on the nature of the peculiar type of retardation found in autistic children, and also on the causes of many details of their 'bizarre' behaviour.

It may be thought that the normal behaviour development of the human child is sufficiently well known and does not require more special study. Admittedly, it is 'known' in the sense of 'being familiar', but the *scientific* study of child behaviour and its development is in reality still in its early stages.[10] Even so, there is now a veritable explosion of such research, and much that is relevant to our theme is now being published in readable summarising books. Yet, as we shall see, we keep discovering behaviour patterns of children of certain age groups that have so far not been described. Experienced observers will agree at once when we say that we are sure that we are still very far from a complete inventory of child behaviour, let alone from an understanding of causes and functions.

(d) Further, we found it important to keep a close watch on the possible influence of short-term changes in the *environment* on an autist's behaviour; it is often revealing to notice in particular what changes in the environment immediately precede (and so *may* have *produced*) observed changes in the child's behaviour. Of course, this too had to be done with both normal and autistic children.

(e) Since severely autistic children do not speak, we had to concentrate on their *non-verbal behaviour* – as well as, of course, on that of all those who interacted with them. (Under 'non-verbal' we do not rank, as some have thought, anything equivalent to the official 'deaf and dumb' sign language, for this is largely recoded speech. Admittedly, some autists develop their own sign language, and this is, of course, worth studying in its own right.) Our main clues come from those behaviours that are called, since Darwin,[11] 'expressions of the emotions': gesturing, facial and body expressions, details of where the children go, of their starting or stopping, of the orientation of their bodies or body parts etc. After Darwin had pioneered the scientific study of these behaviours (as distinct from the intuitive understanding that every one of us develops) very little was done in this fascinating field until, in the early 20th century, birdwatchers, and later the comparative ethologists – both of whom were likewise faced with non-speaking subjects – began to study 'expressions' with new methods, especially aimed at finding out what exactly it is that they express, what determines their form, and what functions they serve. As a result, our understanding of the expressive behaviour of animals is now much farther advanced than that of human expressions;[12] it is no exaggeration to say that this area of animal ethology is decades ahead of our corresponding knowledge of human and in particular of child behaviour, although, as we said, the general ethology of normal child behaviour is rapidly catching up.

We believe that there are three main reasons why we, laymen and scientists alike, have so long neglected the conscious and objectivistic study of human non-verbal behaviour, of which 'expressions of the emotions' form part.

(a) Scientific curiosity and the wish to understand is aroused by the unexpected. Hence, whatever is familiar to us, i.e. all events to which we are used, is unlikely to spur us to investigate, and to many people normal child behaviour is too familiar for study, just as the facts that we walk on two legs, eat when hungry, fall asleep when tired, feed our children, hardly cause curiosity but are simply accepted.

(b) Like animals of every other species, human beings acquire an understanding of the non-verbal signs of their own species, intuitively and unconsciously, through refining (by learning) a relatively crude 'innate', 'pre-programmed' or non-learnt understanding. But since we have no such intuitive understanding of the sign language of other species, we *have* to apply our scientific methods of analysis to animal 'language'. Almost paradoxically, this (and also the fact that we often respond intuitively while we observe, and so *interfere* in what we intend merely to *register*) makes the scientific study of our own expressive behaviour more difficult than that of animal language.

(c) Modern education, which is based largely (and in our opinion excessively) on verbal instruction, and also the fact that, as children begin to acquire speech, their reliance on non-verbal expressions begins to take second place, are additional factors that have led to the neglect of using non-verbal expressions for the purpose of understanding human motivation.

Whatever the explanation, poor analytic understanding by adults of human non-verbal behaviour is a fact, and it does hamper scientific analysis. Fortunately, most of us improve with practice once our interest is aroused.

While these circumstances may at least in part explain our ignorance, they no longer excuse it, and we believe that child psychiatry (and psychiatry in general) could profit greatly from taking notice of this 'growing point' of the behavioural sciences.

Finally, before we apply our approach to autism in concrete detail, we have to make a few more specific remarks about aims and methods. We are often asked: what is it exactly that ethologically oriented childwatchers are trying to do, and how do they go about it?

While this question, like those about other scientific methods, can best be answered by inviting those who ask it to join us for a year or so in the actual business of 'watching and wondering' and to learn by joint practice, we are not in a position to offer such assistance. Instead, some general directives will have to do; and they *can* be helpful.

With regard to the overall *aim* of 'straightforward observation': at first glance, 'behaviour' seems to be an endlessly variable, almost chaotic flow of events (movements, postures and gestures, involving the whole individual or merely such tiny parts as, say, the eyelids, and including absence of movement), a random jumble in which no order can be detected at all, let alone a connection with the equally irregular events in the environment. The aim of the observer is to refuse to believe that all these events are in fact random; he 'feels in his bones' (because he has noticed it unconsciously and intuitively) that it is possible to discern some kind of order, of patterns, and of patterns-within-patterns, both in the behaviour itself and in its connection with outside events, and he cannot help wanting to discern this order more clearly.

As to how the observer tries to reach his aim: in order to recognise this suspected orderliness in the apparent chaos, he has to try to give equal attention to 'all' he sees – to notice (and record) ideally, 'everything that is happening'. In practice, this is of course impossible. Fortunately, it is not desirable either. Modern philosophers of science recognise that no observer takes in outside happenings randomly and without bias. If observing is to lead to scientific understanding, it has (like that of the artist) to be selective and therefore restricted. The selection is done on the basis of, initially unconscious, (a) *questions*, of (b) *expectations* about the likely answers to those questions, and of (c) *amazement* at finding those answers 'wrong', of finding the *un*expected. (This importance of expectancy in the approach of the observer made us speak above of observation being both guided by and leading to 'hunches'.)

Even though the return to observation by ethologists has not led to attempts to see and record 'everything', it has in two ways let 'a breath of fresh air' (Huxley) into the behavioural sciences.[13] Ethology has revived interest in a host of behaviours that had so far hardly been studied; and in its selection of what was most worth studying it was guided by many questions that had not hitherto been asked.

THE PROBLEM OF RECORDING BEHAVIOUR

In order to cope with the many details of observed behaviour that become worth studying, the behaviour student uses a variety of new, or especially designed apparatuses to help him register more, and also to analyse better and more quickly, all those aspects of the bewildering mass of phenomena that his event recorders did capture for him. A variety of such new recording apparatuses, from simple keyboard machines to videotape cameras and audiotape recorders, has superseded the clumsy shorthand writing we used in the past, and increasingly sophisticated computers have made analyses possible beyond the wildest dreams of even 20 years ago.

This mechanising of observational, analytical and interpretative work has on the whole been extremely helpful. But it has not been an unmixed blessing; it carries serious dangers with it. One of these is that it tempts the observer to let the machines decide for him *beforehand* what he has to record, and it forces him, in his sometimes frantic attempts to master the recording techniques, to concentrate on its technicalities so that he forgets to 'wonder' (i.e. think) *while* he observes and, unlike the unmechanised observer, fails to adjust a faulty course of inquiry while his own thinking machine is at work; the 'data', he argues when tackled about this, will make sense when the time comes for 'processing' them. In itself, this intense concentration on the technical side even of merely videotaping is good and indispensable: the cameraman has to set his stop, to aim, to focus, to prepare for zooming and panning etc. before he can profitably shoot, and the computer has to be fed 'digestible' material; but just because of this even the best cameraman cannot possibly record more than a tiny fraction of what a good observer sees. Moreover, he works with a built-in delay, which makes him miss a great deal, e.g. the often highly revealing initiation of a series of events, many things that go on in the environment, and much detail that appears blurred on the record. But perhaps most important of all is that over-reliance on recording machines, with all their demands on one's technical skills, tends to make one forget that they are *servants* of our brains and cannot *replace* our thinking machine.

We further believe that it is important that the maxim 'man must measure' (the idea that science is mature only when it can express itself in numbers, graphs and equations, that science deserves its name *only* when it is 'quantitative') be seen in perspective. *Premature* quantifying, counting and measuring for the sake of our recorders and computers is a misapplication of this respectable notion and, particularly in a subject such as ours, where health and illness, happiness and misery and other things that figures cannot touch are at stake, the arch-quantifier cannot really penetrate to the core of the problems. We admit that we ourselves are not fond of counting and measuring as such, but we are not merely expressing this dislike when we emphasise as strongly as we can that in the present state of the study of autism it is not primarily figures that we need, but ideas, observation, discipline of thought and, last but not least, compassion. Without these attributes, research will remain barren in spite of the most beautiful graphs. We even submit that in fact a great deal of published 'research' on our present subject *is* barren, largely because of an uncritical belief in the intrinsic value of quantification. For instance, the often quoted number of 'approximately 6000 autistic children in England'[14] is based on the extrapolation of a very few regional censuses, of which, incidentally, the figures themselves were not exactly reliable because of the confusion surrounding diagnosis. (In addition, as we shall argue later, large numbers of autistic children never come to the attention of either doctors or health visitors.) Another example of practically meaningless counting is the comparison of the effects of different kinds of schooling on the recovery or otherwise of autistic children; we shall argue our rejection of this kind of research in Chapter 5.

Finally, even the most sensible and, as we said, extremely useful application of modern techniques carries with it another, perhaps still more serious, danger than those mentioned already. The non-initiated 'laymen' (i.e. the observant and intelligent mother, father, social worker, family doctor and all those teachers and caregivers who see so much more of the children than the consultant in his office or during his brief visits, however well armed he may be with the most modern array of testing apparatus; and further all those 'who know children') may be cowed into believing (as we know many of them are) that science has left them behind, that they can no longer contribute anything of value. They think that the expert is the only one who knows – an attitude incidentally not discouraged by the latter. We would urge all those 'laymen' emphatically not to adopt this over-humble attitude towards the (often far from humble) expert. At the present juncture, with psychiatry as a science still in its infancy, our hope must not lie exclusively with the many books and papers by professionals, but just as much in the continued work of the many devoted, observant, patient and often intuitively very perceptive observers and therapists considered to be, scientifically speaking, 'laymen'.

With all this in mind, we will now turn to our actual investigation and consider *in concreto* what regularities we believe to be most illuminating in the seemingly chaotic, 'bizarre' behaviour of autistic children, and how we arrived at a definite hypothesis about what exactly is 'being autistic'. We shall precede our arguments by a brief discussion of the methods that have been developed by ethologists who have been interested especially in the motivation behind what Darwin called the 'expressions of the emotions'.[15] We shall start by referring to (normal) child behaviour, but since the methods have been derived from animal studies we will often have to illustrate those methods by giving animal examples.

Meeting a person or a situation

APPROACH AND AVOIDANCE

The most straightforward and simple, yet very fruitful, procedure starts with observing the seemingly commonplace movements we can see when a child encounters a person or a situation (to be called the 'stranger' or the 'new situation' irrespective of whether the child or the other 'party' is the initiator). These movements are first of all those of going towards a person or situation and its opposite, withdrawing from them, including all their variations, such as changes in speed, signs of perhaps slight hesitation, switching from 'go' to 'stop' and *vice versa*, changes in the direction of the course taken, the type of locomotion (e.g. walking, running, or crawling etc.), the often very slight, incipient form of these movements, and many other details. In normal children, such behaviours are often more easily understood than in autists, who are either less mobile or make more 'bizarre' movements, but once one knows the basic patterns of normal behaviour, one develops an 'eye' for the same, but often modified, sometimes even hardly recognisable forms of these movements that are performed by autists. In a normal child the two extremes are either crawling, walking or even running *towards* the newcomer (person or object), or its opposite, backing away and/or turning round, then walking or even running *away* from her/it.* Just because these movements are so commonplace, observers tend to overlook them; or they take them for granted and as not worth recording in detail. Yet it is these movements that often provide us with our primary clues. In addition, one can see a number of expressions or gestures that accompany the overall movements. Combined with approach are, for instance, facial expressions that reveal interest, or show friendly or other moods; the child may extend his arms towards the newcomer; he may make 'friendly' sounds; certainly he usually turns his face towards her and looks at her etc. At the other extreme, a withdrawn or withdrawing child will look tense, anxious or angry; he may hide and/or curl up, or he will cry and even scream; or he may assume a 'blank' eye expression and 'look through' or just past her, and/or assume an overall posture that expresses indifference. These two extremes of approach and avoidance occur in a normal child only in equally extreme conditions. Most often, a normal child will show a kind of intermediate behaviour. For instance he may approach slowly, with a hardly noticeable smile but at the same time a slightly suspicious or investigatory look; or he may stop before he has reached the newcomer. The moment he stops he may partly or totally turn away; he will usually avoid looking straight at the newcomer; he may suck his thumb, may turn his entire face away or face the newcomer, or he may adopt the 'blank' eye expression already mentioned. These are only a few examples: the total spectrum of behaviour patterns is extremely rich. As a rule, it also changes, usually within minutes and often even from second to second; either the hesitant approach will develop into an increasingly confident, faster approach, or the child may withdraw after all; most often he will oscillate for quite a time between the two. The changes may be abrupt but in stationary or near-stationary situations they are usually smooth and continuous; they can be arranged on a gliding scale.

When we observe the behaviour of autistic children in similar situations, we soon discover that when they meet other persons, in particular adults, they show the same rich spectrum of approach and avoidance behaviour as normal children, but that close approach is much, often very much, rarer (yet occasionally observable) and that avoidance is the almost invariable rule (Fig. 3.1). When they are in a strange room, for

---

* Rather than saying consistently 'he/she', 'his/her' etc. we have, in what follows, used (where at all possible) the feminine when speaking of an adult, and 'he/his' when speaking of a child.

Figure 3.1 'Typical response of an autistic child to outstretched arms of an adult (drawn from an 8 mm motion picture).' From Hutt and Hutt (1970), after Hutt and Ounsted (1960).

instance at school, and sometimes even at home – in rooms where they spend hours every day and with which we would expect them to be familiar, as a normal child would be – autistic children will not only withdraw from almost every person but also avoid the centre of the room; they will hide in corners or under tables, and when they move they will prefer to walk round and round, hugging the wall, at the same time keeping as large a distance from others as they can. If an observer sits quietly somewhere in such a room, with her back against the wall (as we have often done), neither making movements nor addressing the child, if possible not even looking too obviously straight at him, an autist will, upon approaching the observer, slow down at a distance of a few feet or so, then walk or crawl round her, keeping his distance (sometimes with surprising constancy) and resume his wall-hugging progress after having passed the 'danger'.

OTHER BEHAVIOURS

During such encounters, autists also show behaviour that cannot be easily classified as parts of either approach or withdrawal; they almost invariably show one or more 'nervous', usually more or less stereotyped, seemingly meaningless little movements, such as blinking their eyes, making a variety of finger, hand or even foot movements, facial grimaces, rocking, pivoting or twirling, spinning of objects etc. These movements are usually typical of each child, but differ between one child and another and they are usually most frequent and most pronounced when the child is near the unfamiliar person or object. When, as they do on occasion, the child approaches the newcomer and even touches her, he selects a part of her, often (though not always) far from her face, e.g. he will touch a foot or a hand, and most children will not even look at the observer's face (Fig. 3.2) (this accounts for the statement, often found in the literature, that autists do not interact with you 'as a person'). The child may even use the observer's hand or foot as a tool, by grasping it and so 'by proxy' pushing away or raking towards him the toy or other object that has attracted his

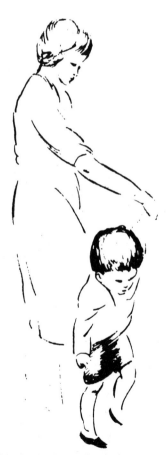

Figure 3.2 'Autistic child attempting to lead an adult, keeping face averted (drawn from an 8 mm motion picture film).' From Hutt and Hutt (1970), after Hutt and Ounsted (1966).

attention. This 'keeping their distance' from objects or persons and avoidance of direct contact, with all their correlated behaviour details, have their equivalent in the auditory sphere: most autistic children will, for instance, ignore or seem to avoid listening to many sounds, in particular what people say *to* them, and they can then behave exactly as if they were deaf – in fact many of them *are even now* often diagnosed as deaf, very often by their teachers, but also, as we have seen in Table 2.1, by the examining physicians.

When autistic children are left alone, even in surroundings to which they are not yet fully accustomed such as the schoolroom or playroom, the various avoidance and 'nervous' behaviours, as mentioned above, will gradually become less pronounced. Given time, a child will approach a new object and investigate it; he will even approach a quietly behaving stranger. But if the stranger does not stay completely motionless (and sometimes even then), or if she interrupts her own behaviour, even in subtle ways (e.g. by slight intention movements of approach, or by looking at the child, in however friendly a way – even a friendly look can be disturbing), the child will stop his approach, may withdraw and hide and on occasion begin to scream and even throw a 'temper tantrum' (which we shall discuss in more detail later). Paradoxically, he may, particularly when restrained during a tantrum, turn limp. Another response in such a situation, at first glance seemingly far less intense than screaming and kicking and similar to, yet different from, turning limp, and in reality expression of a very strong emotional upset, is 'freezing', i.e. motionless but often very tense crouching, either in a corner or under a table, in general as well hidden as possible. A (quite considerable) number of autists will, when pressed in such a meeting, have a 'seizure' or even a genuine epileptic fit (about which we shall also have to say more later). Without for the present going into more details, we shall anticipate at this point and stress that overt approach and avoidance behaviour, together with innumerable correlated 'expressions', are frequent in autistic as well as in normal children, with the difference that the autistic pattern is almost perpetually shifted very considerably towards avoidance and related behaviours. We shall not attempt to compile a complete catalogue of such 'nervous' movements, because every parent of an autistic child and every teacher knows these behaviours only too well, and the literature is full of the most diverse examples. How they fit into the general pattern of avoidance and approach behaviour we shall discuss in due course.

SEEING ORDER IN APPARENT CHAOS

Apart from knowing these behaviours so well, many parents and certainly the more perceptive teachers and playgroup leaders understand intuitively what at least some of them reveal about the child. The contribution that the ethologist can make is to study them more consciously, more objectively, more systematically, and in more detail, and also to observe such behaviour-cum-expressions simultaneously with what happens in the environment. This, as we shall show, allows us to discover a number of (with hindsight, surprisingly simple and clear-cut) regularities, which follow relatively few rules.

What the ethologist does systematically has in fact already been done in the (very sketchy and fragmentary) 'mere descriptions' given above. In fact, what we did was much more than merely describing. We have (a) *classified* (and in the process *interpreted* to a certain extent) the single movements that we saw, and (b) done so according to two, different and independent, criteria.

As to (a), we have relegated a number of the component, single movements to *either* 'approach' (of various forms such as, for instance, a half-hearted approach, or even the merest intention movement of an approach) *or* 'avoidance' and its correlates, from an all-out retreat to merely stopping an approach, turning away, or even no more than averting the eyes. In other words, we have arranged the multitude of single movements and gestures into two systems – approach and avoidance – which differ clearly in their *function* (i.e. in the *effects* they achieve), but obviously also in their *causation* (in what makes them happen). In almost every encounter these *two functional systems* appear in one form or another and time after time, now signs of approach, then a form of withdrawal, and often mixtures of the two. In addition, we mentioned a number of movements which could not at first glance be so classified, e.g. 'nervous' movements, facial expressions, often co-occurring with mild, tentative forms of both approach and avoidance, or with staying at a 'safe distance'. We shall discuss these less straightforward behaviours later.

As to (b), we have, *within* each of these two major functional systems (approach and avoidance), distinguished between on the one hand 'complete', 'unhesitating', 'intensive' forms of the behaviour shown; and 'incomplete', 'hesitating', 'mild' or 'low-intensity' forms on the other extreme. In other words, we have arranged the observed behaviour within each of the two categories, according to *completeness* or, as is often said, on an *'intensity'* scale.

The interpretation of these two aspects of the 'hidden orderliness' of everyday and seemingly chaotic behaviour is based on procedures that require some elucidation. When one follows the activities of one of the higher animals, such as a mammal or bird, or those of normal human beings for a considerable time, one cannot help noticing that they perform different activities at different times. There are times when an animal ('a subject') will feed; at other times it will rest and sleep; at others it may flee from a predator or from an aggressive member of its own species; or it may build a nest, preen its plumage or groom its fur; it may show sexual behaviour etc. Some of these activity patterns have a daily, some a seasonal rhythm; others occur less regularly. Each of them is not just a single movement, but a *system of movements*. We group them together and distinguish them from each other as we have done here because each of them, however variable its component movements may seem to be, serves a particular major *function*, achieves (if the animal or person is successful) a certain, definite end. In other words, the total repertoire of movements which an animal of a given species performs has to be analysed, as a first step, into 'major *functional* systems'. From the fact that in each of these systems the behaviour is not chaotic but ordered in such a way that its function is indeed served, we must conclude that the causal organisation of the machinery underlying the behaviour is such that 'what belongs together functionally' is also performed together, and performed in the most useful way. The rapidly growing science of behaviour physiology, or the study of the moment-to-moment control of behaviour (which aims at understanding how the underlying machinery works) is revealing the exceedingly complicated nervous (more precisely 'sensory-neural-motor') mechanisms that are responsible for ensuring that the behaviour does achieve, at any time and anywhere, what is necessary for success. Most details of these mechanisms need not concern us here – we are as yet merely reconnoitering – but a few fairly general empirical rules are relevant and have to be discussed briefly.

First of all, the behaviour of each of these major functional systems is as a rule controlled by two categories of causes: (a) internal conditions (such as certain hormones in the case of sexual behaviour, the 'hunger' state in the case of feeding behaviour, and numerous other internal conditions, different for each system), and (b) external events, which provide the outside stimuli that are effective as sensory input, for which each of the major systems is receptive (such as stimuli from the mate in the case of sexual behaviour, from food in that of feeding behaviour etc.). Put in the simplest terms, the internal conditions together determine the *degree of readiness* with which a subject will respond to outside stimuli. We will use the term 'motivation' to indicate both the *type* of this specific readiness (whether an individual is 'hungry' or 'afraid' or 'broody' or 'sleepy' etc.) and its *strength* (e.g. *how* hungry etc. an individual is). (Although it is useful to keep in mind that this strength need not reflect, as was claimed in the times of early 'Lorenzian' ethology,[16] that of any endogenous, 'spontaneous' nervous rhythm but can itself be due to the accumulating effect of other internal or even external 'priming' stimuli, this issue need not really concern us here.) What we have to keep in mind is that, in general, the stronger the motivation is, the weaker need the external stimulation be in order to trigger off the behaviour in question (i.e. the lower the 'threshold' is for this stimulus, the greater is its effect). In extreme cases, very poor substitutes for the normal stimuli can elicit the response, as anyone will know who has been really hungry, or who has been extremely apprehensive or 'jittery'; and when one is long deprived of breathable air, the 'urge' to inhale becomes so strong that, for instance, a drowning person cannot stop himself from inhaling water. Conversely, a satiated animal or person will not eat even the most tempting delicacies; likewise, the readiness to perform sexual behaviour wanes as the effect of having mated; a series of frequent deep breathing movements makes one 'forget' to inhale.

Since an animal (and humans) has a number of different functional systems, and since the readiness of each system fluctuates to a large extent independently of the others, and further some external stimuli are 'used' by more than one of these systems, a complication can arise: dependent on its motivational state, an animal may respond to a given object now with this, then with that behaviour. For instance, a predatory bird such as a gull will eat even its own eggs if it is not 'broody'; it is only when it is in a state of readiness to incubate (and when the eggs are in its own nest) that it will perform the (complex set of) activities called together 'incubation'. Or, to mention one other example, a mother cat will furiously attack the very same dog, however large, from which she will run in panic when she has no kittens to defend.

This reciprocal, supplementary relation between motivation and relevant stimuli, and also the variable response an animal or a person shows to one and the same object, are both issues of the greatest importance for our understanding of, our interaction with, and even our treatment of autistic children. Perhaps the most striking example is found in the different ways children can respond to the approach, or even merely the direct gaze, of an adult.

A smiling face directed at a normal child will usually elicit a socially positive response of some kind; an angry stare will cause the opposite behaviour; and a neutral face will have an intermediate effect. A very insecure or socially apprehensive child is much more easily cowed by all these types of faces: neutral and even relatively friendly faces make him withdraw, and the response to a really angry face is one of cringing or running away. One could express this by saying that in this latter case the avoidance system 'poaches' on the socialising system: it 'uses' sensory input (the smile) that would normally be channelled to socially positive behaviour, so that now the output 'flows out through' the avoidance system.

We shall encounter many occasions on which a child does not respond to stimuli to which we are used to see children react. This can be due to any of a variety of conditions. (a) A child who does not respond to a sound may be really deaf; that is, his ear, and/or the nerve that sends acoustical messages to the brain, may be 'out of order', either temporarily or permanently damaged or underdeveloped. (b) A child may not react to certain sounds because he has decided they do not concern or interest him. In neurophysiological terms: the brain inhibits the passing-on of the input to the motor control or even to the brain centres. Thus a child may be totally impervious to talk from adult to adult but respond at once when his name is cheerfully called. (c) A child may not respond to, for example, the promise of 'more pudding' because he is satiated; the motivation has gone down as a consequence of having eaten. (d) A child may not respond to, for instance, his name or any talk clearly addressed to him because he is 'shy' or frightened by the speech, or unwilling to respond for other reasons; he *refuses* to, or perhaps *dares* not, respond; his readiness is not itself weak, but is *suppressed*, by fear or perhaps another system that inhibits a positive response. We call special attention to these second, third and fourth conditions. The technical term for this 'refusing to respond' is 'cut-off', and it can happen with sounds, with visual stimuli, with touch stimuli, and also with pain – in fact with stimuli of any sensory modality. The issue is important because neurologists and, following them, many doctors (including even some psychiatrists) tend to assume that absence of response invariably means that the sensory–neuro-motor apparatus is unable to function because it, or a part of it, is structurally damaged or as yet underdeveloped. Neurologists in particular are regrettably prone to take dysfunction as a certain sign of structural damage.

MOTIVATIONAL CONFLICTS[17]

When, with all this in mind, we study the behaviour of a child, autistic or for that matter normal, during an *encounter* with a person or with an object or an environment, we can see evidence of the simultaneous activity of two of these major systems: during such an encounter an autistic child (and in milder form every normal child, indeed every person) acts largely under the influence of two different, in fact opposite and incompatible, types of motivation. He responds to the encountered person or situation *at the same time* by approaching (either as part of making social contact or as the start of exploration) and by withdrawal (avoidance, or fleeing – for our present purposes the terms can be used interchangeably). As we shall argue presently, this is true even though many of the behaviours shown are not obviously overt approach or overt avoidance but are, say, 'nervous' movements, or even total immobility. We describe such a motivational state by saying that the child is in a state of an internal, a *motivational* or *emotional* (to use the two most often applied, objective and subjective, terms for roughly the same thing) *conflict*.

Now, such 'conflict behaviour' (by which we mean *not* behaviour shown in a hostile clash, but behaviour shown under the influence of a dual or multiple motivation inside a person) has been studied both intensely and extensively (i.e. comparatively) in animals. In fact, this particular field of study has been and still is one of several exceptionally fruitful growing points of animal ethology. It approaches the problem of motivation in a different way, but in part with the same aim, as some forms of psychoanalysis. We shall, however, refer very little to this latter field, partly because of its many semi- and unscientific aspects and its elaborate sets of concepts and technical terms which we do not need for our present, provisional study; partly because much psychoanalytic writing, certainly that on autism, is beyond our comprehension. And more

Because of the importance of animal studies for our subject, we have now to interrupt our analysis of problems of autism in order to discuss in some depth how these animal studies proceed, and what they have so far revealed. We shall try to do this with the use of as few technical terms as possible. We stress once more that we shall avoid the *extrapolation of results* of animal studies to problems of human behaviour – a criticism sometimes levelled at work on human ethology – and use animal examples merely to elucidate *points of method*. Whenever we discuss issues of human behaviour, we shall use data obtained from work on human beings themselves.

Conflict behaviour in animals and Man

The study of motivational conflicts in animals can be said to have started in earnest when ethologists began to interpret the so-called 'displays' or 'expressions of the emotions' and related types of behaviour. Most of these movements happen to act as signals, largely between animals of the same species, though occasionally also between animals of different species. It is the signalling movements acting within the species that are relevant to our topic. The term 'display' (originally referring to the fact that in many of these signalling movements or postures, brightly coloured parts of the body are made visible, or 'shown off') is now generally applied to many behaviours that seem at first glance to have no clear function, and which the uninitiated observer is liable to call merely 'bizarre', or 'strange antics', or 'expressions of great excitement', or similar terms that say no more than that the observer does not understand them. It is by analysis of their use in social contexts that they have become understood. To put it at its simplest: they *function* as signals, and they are *motivated* by internal conflicts. We shall mention examples as our discussion proceeds.

The line of argument that has led to our present understanding of motivational conflicts can be discussed in the following six steps.

(1) THE ADAPTEDNESS OF COMPLEX BEHAVIOUR SYSTEMS

The meaning of the term 'functional' in our expression 'major functional systems' (as applied to social avoidance, exploratory approach etc.) requires some elaboration. Briefly, it refers to the fact that behaviour and its underlying mechanisms of any animal, and Man, are part of the 'equipment for survival' just as much as are, for example, lungs, kidneys, legs and all the other innumerable 'organs' which we know have to function healthily to ensure the organism's success, just as the component parts of a motor car have to function 'healthily' to prevent a breakdown, or death, i.e. a write-off.

This seemingly commonplace statement indicates what is in reality *the* fundamental aspect not only of behaviour but of living in general, the property of living systems that biological science has to explain in terms that are not contradictory to the physical sciences even though they may describe processes of the highest integrative levels. *No scientific understanding of (and therefore no control over) autism or any other form of human conduct will be possible if this fact of adaptedness is not seen as central.*

To give an impression, however superficial, of what we mean we will describe very briefly a few (out of thousands of other more or less analysed) examples of the adaptedness of behaviour. We select seemingly commonplace, unspectacular types of behaviour because, unlike more extraordinary activities, their adaptedness is so easily overlooked.

The oystercatcher, a seabird common along the coasts of Britain, feeds among other things, on edible mussels.[18] These molluscs live on large banks or 'beds' well below the high tide mark. The birds spend the high tide resting on high stretches of the shore or on estuarine meadows. They respond to the onset of low tide (even – guided by unknown stimuli – when the shore itself is out of sight) by flying towards the mussel beds where they start feeding. They walk round, and soon take up a suitable mussel. In order to get at the mussel's flesh, the bird opens its shells either by quickly inserting its long, sharp bill between the two slightly gaping shell halves, or by turning the whole mussel upside down and hammering a hole in its shell (Fig. 3.3). While it is entering the mussel, the bill 'scissors' through the strong adductor muscle that had so far kept the two shells together (Fig. 3.4), so that the mussel can no longer 'keep the doors

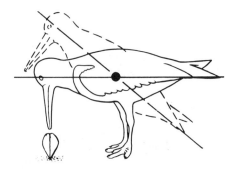

Figure 3.3 Oystercatcher (compare with Plate 5) hammering open an edible mussel. From Norton-Griffiths (1968).

closed'. Next, the bird performs very quickly a series of extremely skilful chiseling movements, by which it cuts the mussel proper out of its shells (Figs 3.5 & 6). Then, after shaking it completely loose, it swallows it. This is a (condensed) description of only one of several feeding systems of the oystercatcher; for other prey animals (worms, limpets, occasionally fish, eggs, crabs) it uses different but always suitable techniques.

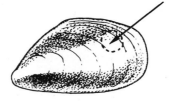

Figure 3.4   Side view of a mussel. The arrow indicates the adductor muscle that holds the two shells together and has to be severed. From Norton-Griffiths (1968).

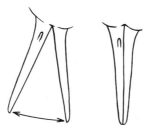

Figure 3.5   The 'prizing' movement by which the oystercatcher forces the shell halves further apart once the adductor has been cut. From Norton-Griffiths (1968).

Figure 3.6   How the mussel shells are prized apart. From Norton-Griffiths (1968).

A squirrel manages to get at the contents of a hazel nut[19] by first searching for and selecting the nut, then turning it round in its 'hands', by next weakening the existing groove in the shell by rapid, precisely aimed gnawing movements, after which it cracks open the shell and chews and swallows the contents – a likewise very complex and sophisticated technique of dealing with one of its foods. This species too can deal with a variety of foods and does so in equally well adapted ways.

A male three-spined stickleback[20] builds a 'nest' in spring, after having selected a suitable site, by digging a shallow pit in the substrate, selecting suitable strands of weed and carrying them into the pit, stamping them down with his snout and glueing them to the substrate with the aid of a secretion of his kidneys; after which he bores a tunnel in the 'nest' by wriggling his entire body through its axis. All this too is done so smoothly, so without fuss or acrobatics that it is easily taken for granted instead of for the exceedingly 'clever', beautifully adapted behaviour it is.

In this nest, one or more females lay their eggs, which are then taken care of by the male. In due course, he bores several holes in the roof and, while the eggs develop, he spends a steadily increasing time fanning fresh water into the nest entrance, thus keeping up with the increasing need of the eggs for fresh oxygen and removing excess carbon dioxide. The fanning movement is the consequence of backward-swimming movements of the pectoral fins and simultaneous forward-swimming movements of the tail, exactly modulated so that the fish stands still facing the nest entrance (Fig. 3.7).

It is through analyses such as these that one discovers, in ever-

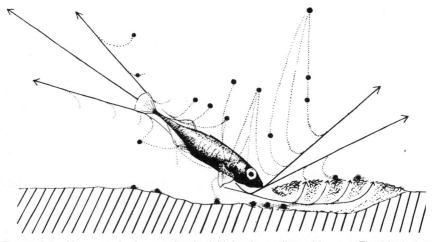

Figure 3.7 How a male three-spined stickleback ventilates his nest. The black dots indicate potassium manganate crystals; the dotted lines indicate the coloured solution emanating from them; and the arrowed lines indicate the resulting water currents. From Kristensen, in Tinbergen, N. 1951. *The study of instinct.* Oxford: Clarendon Press.

increasing detail, how intricately adapted literally *all* behaviour is, i.e. in how many respects it has to be done just so or the effect would misfire (i.e. fail to achieve the end necessary for success – for survival and, ultimately, reproduction). The more clearly one realises the extreme improbability of this adaptedness, the more urgently one wants to understand how these behaviour systems work, how their effects are caused, what mechanisms are responsible for them. As we said before, this next step in the research – in the broadest sense of the word, the physiology, or the study of the mechanics, of behaviour – has its formidable task continuously made more taxing as the complexity of what the animal *has* to do is better understood.

When the function and causation are studied side by side, it becomes increasingly clear that there is (i.e. that natural selection has produced) an extremely intricate correlation, a 'fit' between the functions served by each system and its causal organisation. The description alone of this in detail would require a massive volume. For our present purpose it is sufficient to state that, in the behaviour of each animal, as in its other physiological functions, there exists a close correlation, more precisely a *sufficient fit* between what is *required* for survival and reproductive success and what is actually *done*. As one of us has elsewhere expressed this often forgotten fundamental truth about living: '. . . living is like a tightrope act . . . there are infinitely more ways in which (an organism) can fail than the one narrow road that leads to success . . . (the life of animals) is so to speak a multidimensional tightrope act . . . their success depends on coping with a bewildering variety of obstacles in the environment, of environmental pressures' (N. Tinbergen 1972, p. 385).[21]

These basic facts, viz. that behaviour, just as for instance the functioning of an animal's digestive and circulatory systems, or of kidneys, is adapted, i.e. (a) the opposite of random, and more precisely (b) non-random in only one, very narrow, sense, apply to human behaviour just as much as to that of any animal. But again, because we are so familiar with our own behaviour we rarely stop to wonder about this aspect. Yet, as we will see later on, the various types of normal social behaviour, of exploratory behaviour and of avoidance behaviour of the human infant and child are intricately adapted systems that have evolved in our long evolutionary history under the pressure of natural selection, and were and still are of vital importance for every child's survival. True, we will see that child behaviour does not fit *everything* in our modern, modified world (thus modern children have to be taught, for instance, curb drill and fear of cars, and 'unnatural' caution when faced with electrical gadgets) – in fact we shall argue that autism is in part a response to new conditions that overstretch a child's ability to adjust – but this must not make us forget that the very fact of survival of any organism means that all its life processes are functioning 'properly', i.e. in a manner adapted to the requirements imposed by the outside world. We have to keep *this basic 'fact of life'* continuously in mind.

Apart from having produced this adaptedness, natural selection also keeps it in good trim by ruthlessly eliminating individuals who malfunction in one way or another. When an antelope does not flee fast enough from the pursuing pack of wild dogs, it is killed and eaten. A camouflaged insect that does not sit absolutely motionless by day and on the matching substrate, is in grave danger of being detected and eaten by a keen-eyed bird. A redwing thrush migrating from Iceland in the autumn perishes at sea or on Greenland's east coast if its delicate navigating machinery is not functioning properly. In short, every species, including Man, has not only been produced by *creative* evolution (genetic and, in the case of Man, cultural evolution as well) but is also prevented from losing adaptedness, is kept continuously 'on its toes' by *stabilising* selection.[22]

Contrary to a widespread, but wrong, belief, Man has not *freed* himself from natural selection. Ever since he started to control and change his environment he has merely *changed* the pattern of pressures, not altogether eliminated them. With respect to clothing, housing, communication, mobility, disease of many kinds, food production, protection against predators and parasites, the original pressures have been greatly reduced, if only for the time being. Other pressures have remained roughly the same; no amount of genetic adaptation and individual adjustability can free us from the consequences of real starvation, of drowning, or of lack of water, of freezing or over-heating. But, as unexpected consequences of the many man-made improvements in our environment begin to be recognised, we discover that we have ourselves created new pressures against which natural selection has not armed us: car accidents, wars, drug-resistant strains of parasites, psychological stress, unhealthy food, and many other dangers to our health, indeed our very survival. In fact, far from being the Lord of Creation, Man is at present facing what is perhaps the most challenging crisis of his evolutionary career, and we ignore this new turn in our fortunes at our peril. As we intend to show, this issue of weaknesses and even dangers inherent in our modern civilisation is relevant to the problems surrounding autism.

(2) DOING ONE THING AT A TIME

When one registers the behaviour of an animal over a certain time – seconds, minutes, hours, days or years – one discovers soon that on the whole an animal engages in no more than one of these major behaviour systems at a time. An animal, even when hungry, will stop feeding when threatened by a predator and evade it, fight it or perform other forms of anti-predation defence. But long starvation or intense thirst will make it feed or drink even in the face of perceived danger instead of taking defensive action. In other words, the mechanisms that control these major functional patterns compete with each other (so to speak), and their activities are mutually exclusive. The causal connections that ensure this obviously vital 'single-mindedness' are the subject of intensive study, but the various theories about their nature need not concern us here; it is for the moment enough to state as a fact that these mutually exclusive relationships do exist.

We need hardly point out that even though Man is somewhat better than animals at doing more than one thing at a time (e.g. we may read a book or make notes while having our lunch), this too requires an effort; we too function best when we do 'one thing at a time' – either eat or concentrate on our work. However, this is not so because different activities are necessarily *physically* incompatible; many things that could be physically combined are not done at the same time: the mutual suppression of, for instance, feeding and love-making is a matter of central nervous competition between the two systems, not of incompatibility of the movements of the two systems.

The rule of 'one thing at a time' is not entirely hard and fast – thus we keep breathing during all our activities. But for the behaviours we shall be concerned with, mutual exclusiveness is the general rule.

(3) MOTIVATIONAL CONFLICTS

The last point leads us to the next step: exceptions do occur; in a number of situations an animal *does* combine at least parts of two normally exclusive behaviours – it may show what is called 'ambivalent' behaviour.

A gazelle may, for instance, neither flee nor feed but just eye warily a passing cheetah whilst at best still chewing what it has in its mouth. In general terms: it may neither perform *in full* the activities belonging to system A nor *fully* those of system B; the two systems will, so to speak, struggle for dominance, but neither succeeds completely in suppressing the other. As the simplest example of such ambivalent behaviour and of the way it has been interpreted (but by no means as the only type of such a motivational conflict) we shall discuss so-called agonistic or 'hostile' behaviour: the combination of attacking an opponent, withdrawing or fleeing, and performing 'threat displays'. The analysis is easiest in the case of an encounter between two males of the same species when they occupy adjoining territories (defended areas; Fig. 3.8).[23] In this, as in other types of ambivalent behaviour, three lines of analysis can be pursued, and they all lead to the same overall conclusion.

(a) In a territorial dispute, the behaviour of each of the two males upon meeting each other is dependent on *two sets of external stimuli*: first on those emanating from the neighbour (in fact from any other male that could be a rival for living space and a mate); secondly on stimuli from the place where the meeting occurs. When male A meets male B on A's territory, B's presence will provoke A to attack him and B will flee in

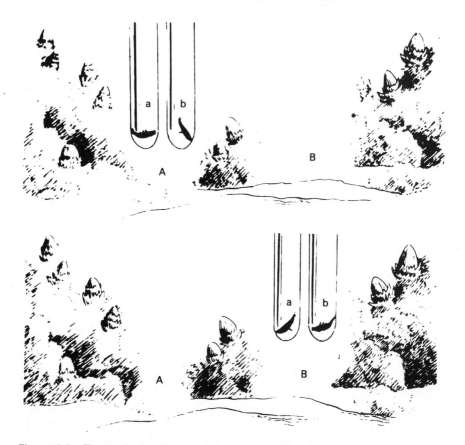

Figure 3.8   The territorial situation demonstrated by showing the behaviour of two male three-spined sticklebacks (a and b) occupying neighbouring territories (A and B). Responding to visual stimuli from their opponents, each male, contained and moved about in a test tube by the experimenter, attacks when he is on his own territory but flees when he is attacked on his neighbour's ground. From Tinbergen (1953a).

response. When on the contrary, the same two males happen to meet on B's territory, B attacks and A flees. Therefore, in such territorial males, whether each of them responds to one and the same rival by fighting or by fleeing depends on whether or not he is on home ground. Now, when two such males meet in the boundary zone just between the two territories, neither of them attacks nor flees, but both show 'agonistic displays' (most of which have the function of threat or intimidating signals – they repel the opponent, or keep him in check). Thus, from 'topographical' study, combined with recording of the types of behaviour shown on the two sides of the boundary, one deduces that, on the boundary, each of the males is in a state of motivational conflict – in this case a conflict between attack and withdrawal. The motivation underlying ambivalent behaviour is likewise ambivalent.

(b) If one records, every time one sees such a boundary display, which other behaviours *alternate* in quick succession with it, one finds that the systems shown are mostly either complete or incomplete attack, or complete or hesitant withdrawal – rarely, for instance, feeding, mating, nest building etc. (A complication is caused by the occurrence of so-called 'displacement activities', see below.) Since, unless forced by outside stimuli, animals tend to sustain any one type of behaviour once it has started, and to avoid quick switching from one type of behaviour to another, this quick alternation too points to the simultaneous activation, inside each of the two animals, of attack and withdrawal, again without either system becoming dominant.

(c) Thirdly, an analysis of the *form* of the actual displays performed sometimes reveals which systems are activated. Territorial displays often consist of recognisable combinations of those parts of attack and escape behaviour that are not incompatible. The classical example is the 'upright threat posture' of gulls and many similar postures in other animals and even Man (when, for instance, he is adopting the 'clenched fist' posture). A male gull will run towards an intruding rival, with neck stretched, bill pointing down (both the preparatory movements to one type of fighting: the delivery of pecks from above) and with the carpal joints ('wrists') raised (preparation for the other type of fighting: the delivery, with folded wing, of strong wing blows). But if the intruder does not withdraw but stands his ground, the first gull will stop, may turn sideways, sleek his neck feathers and pull his neck back a little – all components of fleeing behaviour. The resulting posture is, so to speak, a mosaic of components of the two behaviour systems. Another, equally widespread and equally revealing dual-component behaviour is the so-called 'pendulum duel' of, for example, territorial birds or fish: one of the two opponents makes a brief dash forward, which makes the other withdraw, but the forward dash stops before it provokes the defender to attack in his turn; then the roles are reversed, again for only a moment. The result is very much like one regularly swinging 'mobile' – the two males are connected by a 'behavioural' rather than a real wire, and in spite of oscillations stay roughly where they were at the start. (A very common human equivalent of pendulum movements is seen when a child tentatively moves his hands towards a tin of biscuits on the table, then withdraws it, then makes another intention movement, and so 'seesaws' back and forth until either the act of taking or that of not taking 'wins'.)

Thus the three independent lines of interpretative study lead to the same conclusion, and therefore support each other. As we shall see further on, this conclusion (viz. that a motivational conflict between attack and escape causes the various agonistic postures) has been confirmed in a number of experimental probes. Another important aspect of ambivalent behaviour is the fact that each species has at its disposal a number of different ambivalent postures; which one of these is actually shown depends on, among other things: (a) the *relative* level of arousal of the two systems (the same animal can show relatively more aggressive and relatively more defensive postures); (b) the *absolute* level of arousal, i.e. the overall intensity of the conflict; and (c) the environmental *context* (e.g. whether the mate of one of the males is present or not; whether the intruder happens to be near the owner's preferred nest site or elsewhere in the territory and other circumstances).

For our present purpose it is not necessary to discuss the question of *how*, in detail, the various conflict movements are caused (what physiological mechanisms control them); there is more than one theory about this problem, each of which probably contains part of the truth or applies to particular types of conflict behaviour. For the moment the first step – showing that many movements are due to dual motivation – is enough. What is important is the fact, already briefly noted, that we too can on occasion act under the influence of dual, conflicting, motivation – for instance, we have all at one time or another wanted to approach, say, a frightening animal or another person, yet have not quite dared to.

(4)   CATEGORIES OF CONFLICT BEHAVIOUR[24]

From extensive comparative studies we know that there are conflicts of many different kinds, and that there is also more than one category of resulting conflict behaviours. We shall first list the main categories of behaviours known so far.

'Inhibited intention movements'.   These are the initial, incipient parts of the full behaviour elicited; so called because they reveal, to the observer, what the animal is likely to do or is trying to do. The components of the gull's upright posture mentioned above are combining simultaneously into a 'mosaic' of such intention movements of both the systems that are aroused, forming a static posture. (As we have pointed out above, the human equivalent of this is the 'clenched fist' posture. Another example, again found in animals and Man alike, are the 'pendulum movements' already described.) There are even numerous cases (which have been described best in territorial fish) in which the front of each male (his pectoral fins) makes backwards swimming movements while its tail makes forward swimming motions, the two controlled with very clever precision so as to keep the fish exactly where he is.

'Redirected movements'.   In a hostile encounter (territorial or otherwise, e.g. in peck order disputes), one or both of the opponents will make (often violent) attack movements, but they aim them (as we do) at anything *but* their opponent (Fig. 3.9); if a less feared animal is at hand, this will be attacked. Similarly, a man who has been told off at work by his boss is likely to 'take it out' on his secretary or, at home, on his wife and children.

Figure 3.9 Two male herring gulls, occupying neighbouring territories, meet on their common border. The male on the left is 'grass pulling' (redirected attack); the male on the right is stopped from intruding. From Tinbergen (1953b).

An attack may even be aimed at an inanimate object: male blackbirds and other birds may peck vigorously at a leaf, a twig, at 'anything handy' when they dare not attack an opponent (Fig. 3.10). We ourselves may, 'in a fit of uncontrollable anger', kick a chair or bang our fist on the table. Such redirected movements are also known in the sexual sphere; males of some bird species whose advances are rejected by a female (either their own or a stranger), will copulate in front of her with a branch, or even with the ground. Needless to say, this 'fetishism' too is common in Man – perhaps even more common than in (wild) animals. The redirection (called 'displacement' by psychoanalysts) can, at least in Man, even be turned towards oneself – people bite their lower lip in extreme anger, they may bang their fist against their knees, pull out their hair etc. In the sexual sphere, many sexually motivated but socially inhibited people may masturbate. As we shall argue later, autists, who interact little with others and are as a rule far too timid to explore the physical world, are abnormally inclined to redirect a variety of behaviours towards themselves.

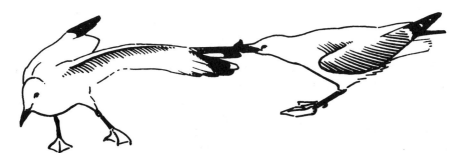

Figure 3.10 A male herring gull pulls at his neighbour's wing. From Tinbergen (1953b).

'Displacement activities'.   These, as we said, are not to be confused
with the concept of 'displacement' as used by psychoanalysts. As already
indicated, motivational conflicts between systems A and B often give rise
to movements that belong to system C. For example, male starlings
engaged in territorial threat will preen their plumage. Preening is also
regularly done by many male ducks before they dare mount the female
(Fig. 3.11) – the females of many species are no mean defenders of their
virtue when not in the mating mood. Male herbivore mammals that face
each other in dominance disputes will often scrape the soil with their front
feet; this is done even in species that hardly or never use their feet in actual
fighting, but that do use them in feeding, particularly when the ground is
covered with snow. Every countryman knows this 'pawing' in bulls.

Figure 3.11 Displacement preening before copulation by males of four species of
duck. 1, Sheldrake; 2, male garganey; 3, mandarin drake; 4, mallard drake. From
Tinbergen (1953a), after Lorenz (1941). Ritualisation consists of every species
touching its brightly coloured speculum with its bill (2, 3 & 4); the sheldrake rubs his bill
along the shafts of the wing quills and so produces a loud rattling sound.

People too may show excessive feeding behaviour as a consequence of 'nervous tension' (an everyday term for motivational conflict). Very common human (and, in general, primate) displacement activities are parts of our 'comfort' or grooming behaviour repertoire, i.e. behaviour that keeps our skin, hair etc. in order. Best known are scratching behind the ears, stroking one's beard or skin of the chin (done even by men who have never grown a beard), biting one's nails (originally no doubt the human way of nail trimming) etc. Finally, even the movements belonging to the resting system (from yawning to complete sleep), which are very commonly used as displacement activities in various birds and mammals (Figs 3.12 & 13); e.g. in dogs when reprimanded, also in lions who yawn so obligingly when visited by a car-load of safari-goers, are also shown by Man. Many of us yawn when embarrassed, children yawn when afraid but 'cornered', and under conditions of extreme but suppressed fear adult men may fall asleep, as has been reported on many occasions when soldiers had to take part in active combat, e.g. when they were expecting an order to 'go over the top' in World War I. Another effect of intense conflict is complete immobility ('akinesis', 'catalepsy' etc.); whether or not this is akin to displacement sleep is controversial, and for our present purpose of little concern.

Figure 3.12 Displacement 'sleep' posture (left) in an oystercatcher (watching its opponent) during an agonistic encounter. Tinbergen (1953b).

Figure 3.13 Displacement sleep (left) in a male avocet during an agonistic encounter. From Makkink (1936).

It has to be emphasised that redirected and displacement activities are two different expressions of motivational conflict: in the former, one of the aroused activities is shown but aimed at a substitute object; in the latter, a movement belonging to a totally different functional and motivational system is performed.

In a number of cases the movements produced in a state of conflict motivation are due to the activation of the *'autonomic'* system. Best known are, in birds, activities such as feather raising or flattening which are controlled by this system, and the primary function of which is temperature regulation; in many other animals, and in Man, panting and hurried breathing are other examples, coupled with the entire internal 'mobilization' process, and our blushing, turning hot and cold, sweating, hair raising, trembling, itching etc. may be related phenomena.

Finally, very intense conflicts in which fleeing is maximally activated but is in some way thwarted can give rise to *'protean' behaviour* or, as this type of movement is sometimes called, 'seizures'. (Because they were first discovered in laboratory mice in response to sudden, very loud and shrill noises, they are known under the somewhat misleading name of 'audiogenic seizures'. The descriptive name 'protean' is more general.) The characteristic of this type of conflict behaviour is 'systematic unpredictability', and in mice and other much preyed-upon animals a protean behaviour has considerable survival value, because it prevents a predator from anticipating what its prey will do in the next split second, and it is on such anticipation that the predator's success depends. Often it also repels the predator by its mere strangeness, or will make it pause. The most obvious human equivalents are the extreme forms of 'temper tantrums' and of course the seizures. In many cases, seizures and 'true' epileptic fits are partly caused by 'nervous tension' of various kinds. We shall return to this later.

(5) TYPES OF MOTIVATIONAL CONFLICTS

Having surveyed briefly what categories of conflict movements are common in animals and Man – what 'outputs' of an ambivalent nervous system we can observe – we must now consider the behaviour systems most often involved in such ambivalent states or motivational conflicts. There is a field of psychological research which lumps all such conflicts under the term 'approach-avoidance' conflict. Although we have initially, for simplicity's sake, used these same vague terms, closer study reveals that the use of the general term 'approach' is too simplistic, and can in fact be highly misleading, as the following (by no means exhaustive) list of examples will show.

Types of approach

We have already seen that conflicts between attack and escape or withdrawal are very common. It is worth pointing out that 'attack' (to be exact, approach in preparation for attack) means something more specific than 'approach'. For example, a hungry animal approaching a source of food, but inhibited by fear or suspicion, does *not* adopt an aggressive threat posture, but a posture revealing anxiety, in which the weapons used in fighting are not held ready, but preparations are made for withdrawal. On such occasions the animal is in a *feeding*-avoidance conflict, and its behaviour is different from that during an *attack*-avoidance conflict. Another common conflict situation, highly relevant to our topic, is that prevailing during *exploratory* behaviour. Many animals, particularly young ones and the adults of vulnerable species (e.g. small rodents such as mice), respond to any new (unfamiliar) object or situation with a mixture of approach and caution. The new object is at first avoided, though intensely studied from a safe distance, and is approached only hesitantly. The visual and sniffing reconnaissance from afar turns into touching, licking, contact-sniffing etc. once the animal is in touch with the object. After a period of such 'study' the animal loses this 'curiosity' and stops its exploratory approaches; it has familiarised itself with the situation and has either 'filed away' the information for 'future reference' or starts using the no longer suspect object without any hesitation.

In rats and mice this behaviour takes precedence over even intense hunger when a new situation is encountered; and the objects and situations most intensely explored and learned about are potential hiding places and their locations. The knowledge so gained enables the animals to run straight for the nearest cover when surprised by a predator, and on these (by no means rare) occasions this knowledge can mean the difference between life and death. The conflict underlying this hesitant approach – that between avoidance and *exploration* – is a third type of 'approach-avoidance' conflict.

Types of approach in children

The example just given is of special significance for our study. The reason is that, as everyone knows, human children are the champion explorers of this world. They begin to study their (social and physical) environment almost at once after birth, in particular those charming babies that we ourselves are used to calling 'lookers', who explore so strikingly with their eyes. Very soon the lips and mouth explore too; visual exploration of hands and feet appears early, and so does exploration by listening. It is important to realise that this exploration leads to *learning*. Thus, while still living in the cradle and in mother's arms, in fact from birth on and perhaps even earlier, a baby builds up an enormous store of learnt information 'for later reference': he learns, for instance, to recognise his mother by her smell as well as by warmth and touch; many babies even know their mother's individual voice at a much earlier age than commonly supposed, and all of them acquire a detailed and rapidly growing knowledge of their overall environment, such as for instance the rooms in their house, their own cot, and also the routines of the household in all its details.

When the infant begins to crawl, a relatively sudden change occurs. He will now begin to *approach* unfamiliar objects and from this moment on show the same caution as mice. Of course, this is and has always been of vital importance to the human child, for the world (even our secure modern world) is full of dangers, and the mother and older sibs, however observant and protective they may be, simply could not possibly protect the crawler from every wasp, scorpion, snake, or in modern conditions from every gas ring, electrical socket and other deadly dangers. It is in answer to this need that exploration always involves a conflict between, on the one hand, 'curiosity' or the urge to obtain as much information as possible from a new situation, and on the other a healthy proportion of fear. During every new encounter and exploratory interaction with something new, the balance changes only slowly towards the reduction of fear and the intensification of investigating until the child approaches and perhaps handles the new object, and then, after a thorough examination from all angles and with all senses, the avoidance element disappears altogether – the new situation or object has become familiar. After this, interest will not be aroused again until, on later occasions, the object is discovered to be usable in a new, more complex activity, which is then done with confidence – the once unfamiliar object has become known and accepted, and the new wave of exploration aims at trying out and learning ways in which the object can be used.

It is not generally recognised that fear or distrust, as an element of exploratory behaviour, has great survival value, indeed is an indispensable attribute, to an animal in its natural state, and likewise to Man; the outside world is full of potentially dangerous things and organisms. Any individual who, seeing an unknown object or situation, would blunder in without careful, step-by-step, alert and patient exploration, would have precious little chance of survival. The old saying 'curiosity killed the cat' reminds us of this survival value of the caution element in exploration. While this saying clearly underrates the vital importance of the positive, reconnaissance component of exploratory behaviour, it does hit the nail on the head with respect to the need for suspicion and caution. It is, of course, the innocently blundering, uncautious, in this respect ill adapted, kitten that is 'accident prone' and has a good chance of being killed. Similarly, as soon as the human infant acquires the ability to crawl and actively to approach objects, the tendency to do so cautiously, to be suspicious of anything new, appears as its (now vital) corollary.

The need for caution when faced with a new situation has led to another, extremely important adaptation of the social system or 'dyad' –

mother–(or caregiver in general–)infant. While the mother tends alertly and often more or less anxiously to supervise her child when he sets out on one of his expeditions, *the child from his side is boldest in his venturing out when he knows he is under such supervision, when he feels secure under the 'safety umbrella' provided by the presence of the mother or guardian.* Of course, there is a great deal of variation between mothers, in their skill in supervising without over-anxiously keeping their children with them, as there is between different children in the balance between their wish for security and their exploratory boldness; an over-timid child cuts himself off from many an instructive adventure, but over-bold children are accident prone and, under the primitive conditions of the past (as well as in rural conditions of the wilder parts of the world) end up in the stomach of a predator, at the foot of a cliff, or in deep water.

As we shall see later, this 'tightrope' characteristic of exploratory behaviour is of decisive importance for our understanding of why autistic children lag behind in their mental and intellectual development.

Exploration by autists

It used to be said, and is still said about autistic children even by specialists, that they do not explore, but rather ignore or withdraw totally from new situations, objects and people. This has been shown to be entirely wrong by the late Dr Corinne Hutt[25] who, in tests in which autistic children were faced with unfamiliar objects had the ethological (the *scientific*) good sense to refrain from breaking off after the standard time of the test proper, and to continue to observe for a considerably longer time. She found two things of the greatest interest: first, right from the start of each test the children, far from *ignoring* the new object, very carefully (a) kept their distance, and when they sat down seemingly unconcerned they would (b) do so invariably with their backs turned exactly towards the objects. Secondly, they *did* show the full investigation sequence, only it was stretched out over a much longer period than that of normal children, i.e. their distrust waned much more slowly. In other words, the difference between them and normal children was, in this context, one of degree. This shows that autistic children do little exploring because their anxiety wanes so slowly and because their timidity often holds them back altogether, but they want to explore all right; they actually do it only on those rare occasions when they feel secure. Dr Corinne Hutt's work illustrates clearly how futile many of the 'tests' are that many psychologists are so conscientiously carrying out (and use for purposes of evaluating children's educational needs) and how valuable, indeed indispensable for our understanding, are long periods of 'watching and wondering', not only of wild animals but of normal and abnormal children. This may seem (and *is*) 'elementary my dear Watson' but few researchers act on this insight.

Types of avoidance

Not only the 'approach' component of a motivational conflict, but also the counteracting motivation can be of more than one kind. A bird incubating its eggs has to get up occasionally, e.g. in order to turn the eggs (which is necessary for keeping them uniformly warm). The change from sitting to standing up requires a 'motivational struggle'. In order to stand up a certain inertia, and even the positive inclination to incubate, have to be overcome, and while the struggle between these two motivations goes on, i.e. before the bird actually stands up, it makes a number of conflict movements, in this case nest-building movements: first, in the form of merely looking at a straw, then of stretching its neck in its direction, then with increasing frequency and increasing completeness such 'intention movements' are performed until the bird picks up one straw after the other and arranges them into the nest's rim. After that the bird will get up.

We know a similar conflict, in which avoidance is likewise not really involved, in our own species: one needs only to observe social callers (including oneself) when it is time to take leave from their hosts. On other occasions, approach can be counteracted by the mere reluctance to enter into social contact. I remember observing a fellow professor during an examination of a student. He was just as nervous as the examinee, and he began to make (steadily increasing) rocking movements with one of his legs (a common human conflict movement – see Ch. 4) whenever he was working himself up to asking the next question. As soon as he actually 'fired' his question, his leg stopped, only to resume its rocking gradually while the student was talking. This type of reluctance to enter into contact with another person (and fear of making a fool of oneself) is a less overt but very common form of avoidance.

These few examples are representative of many, as every manwatcher can confirm. Manwatching opens one's eyes to innumerable types of conflict behaviour in one's fellow men and in oneself.

The genuine approach-avoidance conflicts

Of particular interest are those cases where the conflict is really between escape and *any* kind of approach or (in the conflict situation) staying where you are – the *real* 'approach-avoidance' conflict.[26] We call it 'real' because it does involve all kinds of approach, and this alone justifies the use of the general term. The so-called 'chin lifting' (a rhythmical upward tossing movement of the head) done by female eider ducks is an excellent example. We have seen eider ducks do this chin lifting in three situations: (a) when we approached them while they were foraging at a rich feeding site and were loath to leave; (b) when we approached a female with her small young, who could, or rather would, not flee as fast as I could approach; and (c) when females 'incited' their own mates to attack a strange male. This inciting is, in eider ducks, a dual movement: first an intention movement of attack is made, i.e. the female points her neck and bill at the stranger; then she makes a few chin-lifting movements aimed at her own mate. Both components have communication value: the pointing makes her own male hostile until he finally drives off the stranger; the female's chin lifting is most probably an appeasement gesture, informing the male that he must not attack her – an outcome of 'nagging' behaviour by females that in many animals (including our own species) is only too common. However, the point is that the sequence as a unit is an example of (a) a *succession* of the intention movements that reveal the dual motivation and (b) a movement (the appeasement part) that appears as a consequence of *any* approach tendency inhibited by escape. It is only in such rare cases, when it can be *demonstrated* that *any* type of approach when in conflict with avoidance gives rise to the same behaviour, that we are justified to speak of genuine approach-avoidance behaviour.

The list of types of motivations that can be involved in conflicts we have given is by no means complete. For example, R. J. Andrews[27] has shown that in certain song birds flicking movements of wings and tail occur, e.g. when the bird intends to move on, but hesitates between hopping and flying to the new destination. Once the decision has been taken these conflict movements stop. This is not an approach-avoidance conflict, but one between two types of approach. This conflict may be similar to that of the brooding gull in that an extra effort is required in order to fly.

'Triple conflicts'
So far we have been discussing conflicts between two systems only; but often three systems are involved. This is particularly common in the pair-forming and mating behaviour of many species of animals. This is worth discussing in some detail, *not* of course because we claim that sexual behaviour is involved in the autistic syndrome but merely because of the methodological aspects of studies of these more complicated motivational states.

We select monogamous species in which a personal bond between male and female is established at the start of the breeding season. Of this category, those species (numerous in at least four of the five main classes of vertebrates) in which the reproductive season begins by an upsurge of intraspecific agressiveness in the male are the most relevant. In most, though not all, of these species the male's aggressiveness is coupled with the development of an attachment to a particular site; these two phenomena together result in the occupation and defence of a breeding territory – incidentally, the concept so often rashly applied to human behaviour. In what follows it is again primarily the method, not the phenomenon itself that will occupy us, and the agression aspect rather than the site attachment (even though the latter is not entirely irrelevant). Our description will refer to a group of species to which we have devoted a lifetime of research: the herring gull and relatives, and the black-headed gull.

In these species the prospective partners go through a number of phases, of which the first, that of bonding long before actual coition takes place, will concern us here.

The results of these studies can here be sketched only in their merest outline; detailed facts and discussions can be found in Tinbergen (1959).[28]

In such species the establishment of a bond between male and female, which involves close approach and ultimately bodily contact, is facilitated by a tendency in both birds to approach each other, but it is initially greatly hampered by two other behaviour systems, each of which has survival value in its own right. The male responds to the approaching female by a predominantly aggressive response, due to the fact that she presents some of the stimuli characterising a rival male. Although this aggressive response is mixed with a tendency to approach (and allow approach by) the female, and to a lesser extent with a tendency to withdraw (colloquially: 'fear'), it is his aggression that, understood by the female, often blocks her early approach attempts, for she reacts very sensitively to his expressions of aggressiveness. In the female, aggression, though present, is far less pronounced, but she shows numerous signs of 'timidity' or outright 'fear' ('social avoidance'); her attempts to approach the male are mixed with a tendency to keep her distance, or even to withdraw and flee altogether. It is the female's behaviour that is most relevant to our present problem.

Two aspects have to be considered: (a) the momentary, fluctuating motivational state of the subjects; and (b) the way in which the behaviour of each of them is affected by that of the other – the signal functions of these behaviours; it is the outcome of this continuously varying interaction that determines what behaviour the female will show.

The resulting motivational state is expressed in terms of the degree of elicitation or arousal of the three major functional systems: that of aggressively motivated approach, that of sexually motivated approach and that of avoidance, and the same methods are used for identifying these three systems as have been discussed in the preceding analysis of behaviour in conditions of dual motivation. Their application leads to the conclusion that the great variety of behaviours shown by a female is due to 'motivational conflict', in this case approach to the male and withdrawal from him – the former mainly sexually motivated but mixed with slight aggressiveness.

What makes the analysis of the female's behaviour difficult is the fact that, as in children involved in a social encounter, the conflict within her does not remain constant. First of all, she is subject to short-term fluctuations: she oscillates all the time between more 'daring' approaches and incipient or even complete withdrawals. Such fluctuations are in part the consequence of the male's behaviour: a movement towards her, or even his looking at her may make her retreat; conversely his 'reassuring' gestures such as 'facing away' reduce her anxiety, and positively attracting movements and calls make her approach. The female's behaviour is also influenced by events in the rest of the environment, such as for instance a distant alarm call elicited by a predator, a slight movement of a neighbouring male, the approach of a rival female etc.

Secondly, one can observe in the female a slow, consistent and progressive change towards loss of avoidance tendencies and increase of the readiness to approach. This leads ultimately to close and uninhibited proximity, even involving mutual touching and, in the end, copulation.

Thus, by observing the behaviour of the female in steadily increasing detail we have been forced to describe her motivational state in terms of three specific behaviour systems, of which the sexual and avoidance systems dominate the struggle.

For our present purpose it is further of special significance that the male, in trying to overcome the female's timidity and make her approach him, takes into account, and reacts continuously to, the outward expressions of her fluctuating conflict state. He does so by, on the one hand, taking care not to frighten her (he is far less aggressive to her than to males and he shows the reassuring 'facing away' gesture more often to her than to males); and by, on the other hand, giving specific 'come hither' signals, of which he uses a variety.

In order to understand the female's behaviour fully, one has to remember that she is involved in mutual interaction with the male, and also reacts to other aspects in the environment. It is therefore not sufficient to observe the female only – one has to observe the male's behaviour and other outside events as well. This strains one's observational powers to the limit. The entire, highly complex overt pattern is illustrated in detail in the film by Tinbergen and Falkus (1969);[29] indeed the process can hardly be elucidated without *seeing* the behaviour. A substitute for seeing this film is to study our account in book form (Tinbergen *et al.* 1970). Our knowledge of the repertoire of indicators, checked mainly according to the correlation procedures discussed above but also by some experimental studies, is still increasing with continued observation and checking of predictions, even in the species that we have been studying for so many years. We need hardly remind our readers that human behaviour is infinitely more complex than that of gulls, yet has not been studied with these ethological methods for very long.

'Low-key' conflicts

Once one has understood the most pronounced but relatively rare cases of *strong* motivational conflicts, or 'intense nervous tension' that we have discussed, one discovers soon that *mild* conflicts or thwarting situations are by no means rare – and are in fact very common; animals and people alike are even more often in a state of mild conflict than exclusively motivated by just one system. When a gull wants to sit on its nest but is inhibited for instance by slight fear elicited by a distant disturbance, it will stand some metres away from the nest and continuously preen its plumage – a common displacement activity. A sign of even slighter unease in a gull, in fact that of the mildest conflict of this kind, is the so-called 'staring down', when the bird seems to look at its feet, or makes no more than a slight intention movement in this direction. This too is a displacement activity; its normal function is inspection of the feet, which is done (and followed up by appropriate action) when there are, for instance, irritating parasites on the toes, or when the toes have been slightly damaged. Other species display a variety of similar or different signs of slight 'nervous tension'.

Such signs of mild conflict or of frustration, caused by slight unease, embarrassment, a wish to be elsewhere and various other shades of avoidance motivation while another, much stronger motivation prevents withdrawal, are extremely common in human behaviour. I have already mentioned the case of the nervous examiner who made foot-rocking movements. While, on the whole, the resulting 'nervous movements' of animals are much the same for all members of each particular species (and practically 'innate'), human beings have an enormous variety of them, since learning plays a much larger part, and different people learn different things. We humans do have expressions, such as rest movements (from yawning to full sleep) mentioned above, and various grooming movements, that are so widespread that they are undoubtedly as near 'innate' as possible; but others, such as smoking, humming certain tunes etc., are influenced by previous learning, by habit. But even the latter have always an innate basis (e.g. oral stimulation in the case of smoking, vocalisation in the case of humming). As to the types of conflict involved, all of them contain either a form of avoidance (often apprehension, embarrassment) or some form of anger, or an element of thwarting. Many 'nervous' movements occur, for instance, when one is writing or talking and comes to a difficult passage, where one has to think hard. Some nervous expressions appear while one has to perform some difficult action (or more often just afterwards); thus most car drivers will either rub their chin or nose after a difficult and slightly risky overtaking, or their eye blink rate goes up, or they may start humming, or they clear their throat, pick their nose etc. In 'overawing' situations many people swallow 'needlessly'. Social avoidance is also expressed often by averting the eyes, by turning the whole head or even the body away, by hunching one's shoulders (even the most experienced politician reveals this when a question asked by a TV interviewer is inconvenient); by biting one's lips, by re-arranging one's tie, cuffs or (in women mostly) one's hair. Key jingling and similar manipulations, yawning, waving one's fingers, fiddling with rings or necklaces, and numerous other 'nervous' movements, are other conflict- or thwarting-revealing behaviours. Desmond Morris[30] has an apt name for all this behaviour: because these movements are much less easy to suppress than speech, he calls them 'non-verbal leakage'. Of what motivational state exactly each of these is the expression can be found out by the methods we have described above.

We have used so much space on these seemingly trivial types of behaviour and their interpretation because, while to be alert to them and to understand their significance is important in all our social interactions, they help us particularly when meeting autistic children, for they spend much more time doing these things than normal people.

The interpretation of many at first glance 'senseless' types of behaviour, first as social signals (which characterises their function, the way their effects contribute to success) and then as being due to motivational conflicts or thwarting of some kind (which describes how they are caused; what makes the individual perform them) is, for both questions, no more than the first step in their analysis. The further investigation of the specific function, and of the particular types of conflict, represents the next step. Of course ethologists have carried both the analysis of function and of causation further than we have done here, and there is a vast literature on both issues. However, for our present purpose a discussion of this more advanced work would lead us into needless detail, even though this may well become necessary in the future.

(6)   LONG-TERM EFFECTS OF THWARTED ANXIETY

When animals are artificially kept in a continuous or frequently recurring state of intense anxiety but are prevented from actually escaping, they will not only show a multitude of high-intensity conflict behaviours, but they will gradually change more or less permanently: they will become perpetually over-anxious, will withdraw and even panic at the slightest disturbance, will scream and make chaotic movements of the greatest intensity and, if cornered, will suddenly turn upon whoever approaches them and fight without the slightest inhibition – 'with the courage of despair'. On other occasions they will 'freeze', i.e. become motionless and sit for hours on end crouched in a corner, or as well hidden as the situation allows, showing not the slightest response to what goes on round them – behaving 'as if they were deaf and blind'. Often these long-term effects can have 'psychosomatic' aspects, such as for instance duodenal ulcers, high blood pressure and numerous other illnesses. There is considerable literature on this, centred on the concept of 'experimental neurosis', because much of this damaged functioning is reminiscent of what are often called neuroses in people. We do not particularly care for the word, but have to mention it because it is still widely used, if rarely well defined, in the psychiatric literature and certainly in practice.[31]

We shall argue later that this issue of lasting damage due to anxiety-dominated emotional conflicts is highly relevant to the problem of autism; whether we call the condition an 'anxiety neurosis' or not, we shall show that much of an autist's behaviour and even of his bodily characteristics consists of such long-term effects of an intense, anxiety-dominated emotional imbalance.

Ritualisation and formalisation

The recognition of conflict movements as such is often made difficult by two secondary processes. In animals, those conflict movements that have in the course of evolution acquired a secondary function as social signals (i.e. are 'understood' by other animals and reacted to appropriately) have become increasingly better adapted to this new function (Fig 3.14). The movements have become exaggerated, they may have acquired rhythmical repetitiveness; parts of the body that are prominently used in such movements may have evolved bright colours etc. – in short, a secondary adaptive process occurs of which the effects are to make the movement (a) as conspicuous as possible, and (b) as unambiguous as possible. The process is analogous with the signalling by means of waving of flags in a variety of ways and by giving the flags different, but clear and simple, patterns. This evolutionary adaptation to the new function as signals is called *'ritualisation'*.[32] Examples can be found throughout the animal kingdom, and are to us most striking in animals that use visual signals. Our own social, non-verbal 'language' contains some examples, of which perhaps the best understood is our smile. Comparative studies of facial signalling movements in apes and monkeys leave little doubt that our smile (a friendly, in technical terms an 'appeasement' signal) has been derived (as have so many appeasement signals in animals)[33] from what was originally a defensive threat posture, the baring of the teeth. The ritualisation has consisted of changes of degree of the movements of the lips, of the upward curling of the mouth corners, and of certain changes in the expression of the eyes, which we now interpret as 'friendly'. It would carry us too far to enter on a full discussion of this topic, and we refer to the existing summaries already mentioned.

Apart from this, however, we find that animals, and Man to an even greater extent, can develop their own, personal, *'formalisation'* of the conflict expressions of their species; this 'formalisation' leads to almost each individual having its own variants of the species-typical repertoire. For example, hyenas and wolves kept in confinement in zoos develop a habit of endlessly running in circles or figures of eight within the limited space of their enclosures. This happens most often in species that normally have to run a great deal as part of their hunting behaviour. The exact trajectory of their runs depends on the topography of the enclosure. Similarly, but (as we said) to a far greater extent, we ourselves develop individual forms of general, species-typical conflict movements such as touching our lips or nose when or just after having been in a 'tight spot', or in a conflict involving indecision or thinking out a problem. The infantile thumb sucking is rare in adults, but smoking gives us the same oral

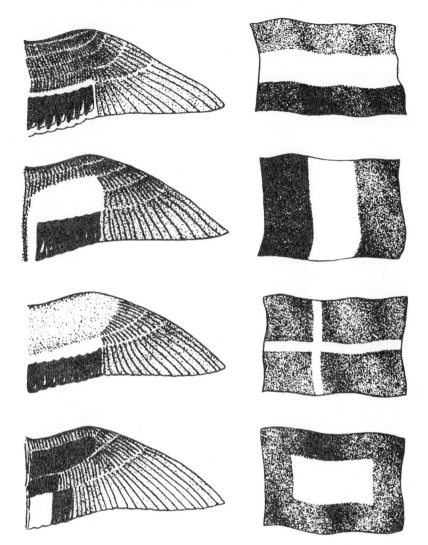

Figure 3.14 Morphological, differential ritualisation of the wing specula of different duck species, by which each recognises his own species in flight. *Left*, actual wing patterns; *right*, analogous signalling structure developed by Man. From Tinbergen (1951).

stimulation (as well as a stimulating nerve poison). Handling things 'nervously' is a common general pattern, but *what* we handle and *how* we do it differs between individuals: key jingling, or button fiddling, taking up and putting down things on our desks etc. are common though by no means the only 'formalised' patterns. Every person but the most unobservant knows scores of such individually characteristic conflict movements. The variability is greatest in mild conflict states; in severe emotional conflict states we tend to resort to the expressions typical of our species.

These individually formalised conflict expressions closely resemble the stereotypies that are so common in autists; in fact they *are* stereotypies in every sense of the world. That this is not generally recognised or, if realised, not considered of much importance, is once more due to the fact that the behaviour of normal children and adults has not been studied sufficiently, and that in particular *these kinds* of behaviours have not attracted more than occasional and rather fleeting attention, so that their particular causation is still ill understood, since they are so often disguised under a 'coat' of formalisation.

After this excursion into comparative ethology, we shall return to the behaviour of autistic and normal children and study it in more detail in the next chapter.

Notes and references

1   Ritvo, E. R. 1976 Autism: from adjective to noun. In Ritvo, E. R. *et al.,* p. 5 (see Ch. 1, note 4).

2   Rutter, M. 1978. Language disorder and infantile autism. In Rutter, M. and E. Schopler, pp. 85–104 (see Ch. 1, note 4).

3   Ricks, D. M. and L. Wing 1976. Language, communication and the use of symbols. In Wing, L. (ed.), pp. 93–135 (see Ch. 1, note 3).

4   Wing, L. 1976 (see Ch. 1, note 3.)

5   Hutt, C., S. J. Hutt, D. Lee and C. Ounsted 1964. Arousal and childhood autism. *Nature* **204**, 908–9.

6   The emphasis on perceptual and cognitive malfunctioning in autistic children is perhaps most pronounced in the writings of Hermelin and her colleagues. A key sentence in her recent writings seems to us: '. . . autistic children do not tend to integrate current experience with schematas and representations stored from previous sensory impressions' and again: 'The lack of integrated, rule-governed behaviour was found not only in regard to language, but also, though to a lesser extent, in perceptual motor tasks.' Hermelin, B. 1978. Images and language. In Rutter, M. and E. Schopler, p. 153 (see Ch. 1, note 4).

7   One of the main methodological characteristics of animal ethology as it developed, or rather, was revived in the late 1920s and early 1930s was the return to 'straightforward' observation of how animals behave, so that relevant questions could be asked as to 'why' they behave as they do. (For the four distinct meanings of 'why', see Tinbergen, N. 1951. *The study of instinct.* Oxford: Clarendon Press.) Representative works based on this new, yet old, approach are, for instance:
    Lorenz, K. 1935. Der Kumpan in der Umwelt des Vogels. *J Ornithol.* **83**, 137–213, 289–413;
    Tinbergen, N. 1953. *The herring gull's world.* London: Collins;
    Tinbergen, N. 1974. *Curious naturalists.* London: Penguin.
    A number of concrete examples of this approach to animal behaviour that has come to be called 'comparative ethology' are given in Tinbergen, N. 1973. *The animal in its world* (2 vols). London: George Allen & Unwin. See also Hutt, S. J. and C. Hutt 1970. *Direct observation and measurement of behavior.* Springfield, Ill.: Charles C. Thomas. In ethology, observer interference has in general been reduced and often

totally eliminated by either working with free-roaming, but tame animals who ignore the human observer or treat him as a conspecific, or by observing the animals from hides or 'blinds'.

8 We have ourselves seen quite clear examples of this. See also Axline, V. 1973. *Dibs: in search of self.* London: Penguin. Axline wisely refrains from labelling Dib's disorder, but her descriptions of his behaviour show that he was a striking example of the type of children we are dealing with in this book.

9 The admonition of P. B. Medawar, directed in 1967 in particular to psychiatry – 'It is not informative to study variations of behaviour unless we know beforehand the norm from which the variants depart' (Medawar, P. B. 1967. *The art of the soluble*, 109. London: Methuen) – has so far hardly been heeded by psychiatrists.

10 The literature on normal development of child behaviour and mother–infant interaction is growing rapidly. The following books, ranging from popular, in part very readable, overviews to works primarily written for professionals, give an impression of this growth.
Blurton Jones, N. (ed.) 1972. *Ethological studies of child behaviour.* Cambridge: Cambridge University Press.
Brazelton, T. B. 1969. *Infants and mothers.* New York: Delacorte Press.
(A very readable, month-by-month account of differences in the development of 'average', 'quiet' and 'active' babies and the correlated differences in the mother–infant interaction in the first year.)
Bruner, J., M. Cole and B. Lloyd (eds). *The developing child.* London: Fontana/ Open Books. (A series of up-to-date paperbacks to which we shall refer again in later chapters.)
Hassenstein, B. 1973. *Verhaltensbiologie des Kindes.* Munich: Piper.
Leach, P. 1975. *Babyhood.* London: Penguin. (This deals with the first two years of life.)
Lewin, R. (ed.) 1975. *Child alive – new insights into the development of young children.* London: Temple Smith.
Lewis, D. 1978. *The secret language of your child.* London: Souvenir Press. (A useful overview of expressive behaviour of children.)
Osofsky, J. D. (ed.) 1979. *Handbook of infant development.* New York: Wiley. (A major, up-to-date work intended for professionals.)

11 Darwin, C. 1872. *The expression of the emotions of man and animals.* London: Murray. Darwin's pioneering approach did not find emulation until well into the 20th century, when the ethological study of 'displays' and animal communication in general was taken up in earnest. Following the influential pioneering work by, among others, O. Heinroth in Germany and Julian Huxley in Britain, further analysis led to the recognition that dual or multiple motivation accounted for the vast majority of animal 'signalling' behaviour. The kind of work most relevant to our present subject can be found in the following.
Tinbergen, N. 1959. Comparative studies of the behaviour of gulls (Laridae): a progress report. *Behaviour* **15**, 1–70. (Reprinted in *The animal in its world*, vol. 1 – see note 7 above.)
Morris, D. 1977. *Manwatching: a field guide to human behaviour.* London, Oxford: Jonathan Cape/Elsevier (applied to human behaviour).
Morris, D., P. Collett, P. Marsh and M. O'Shaughnessy 1979. *Gestures.* London: Jonathan Cape.
A scholarly treatise on the application of studies of animal behaviour to the (social) behaviour of Man is:
Hinde, R. A. 1974. *Biological bases of human social behaviour.* London: McGraw-Hill.

12 The following incident describes one of many examples of non-verbal behaviour that, as far as we know, has not yet been described in the literature.

We had one of our daughters staying with us together with her husband and her three sons, the youngest of whom was four years old. During a meal this boy was sitting next to E. A., his grandmother, while both parents were seated at the other end of the table. The little boy was a little over-excited and, knowing himself out of reach of his parents, began to act rather too boisterously and slightly defiantly to his grandmother. Facing her and talking and laughing away, he was leaning over so far to her that she felt she had to restrain him, from perhaps grabbing her glasses or doing something else that could not be tolerated during dinner.

She did what she knew she and many other mothers often do under such circumstances when, for social and parenting reasons, a scene is to be avoided. She looked straight at him, mouth neither friendly nor cross, and 'stared him down'. After some seconds, the boy calmed down and, looking all the time at her, withdrew very slowly. When he had done this for a few seconds, a ghost of a smile appeared on his face. E. A. replied by an equally tentative hint of a smile. Thereupon, the boy's face lit up in a beaming smile, whereupon grandmother also smiled fully. The boy resumed his normal behaviour and then made some friendly gesture towards her. From there on he behaved calmly and in, if anything, an especially friendly manner to her. His parents, who were busy talking to other guests, had not noticed the incident at all.

When we talked this over, we both knew that E. A. had made, in functional terms, a very powerful non-verbal communication: 'Stop that, but I am not angry.' The boy's reaction had not been one to a threat, yet he was at the same time disciplined and momentarily more strongly bonded. We realised that, although we knew this way of disciplining and at the same time bonding a child, we had never analysed what was the expression by which E. A. had achieved this. The answer, after repeated further observations by N. T. and one of our daughters, was that E. A. (a) had kept her face completely neutral until the boy first smiled; (b) that she had not blinked but kept her eyes wide open and directed at him; (c) that *her upper eyelids, but no other part of the eyes or of the brows,* were raised approximately 1.5 mm (she described it initially by saying 'it felt as if my eyes were popping out of my head'). We are sure that every experienced mother or observer of mothers will recognise the expression we have just described, and will agree that E. A.'s behaviour is a seemingly slight, but in effect very powerful disciplining-cum-bonding signal. Other examples of the very rich repertoire of our species are given here and there in our text and, in more detail by Eibl-Eibesfeldt in his books on human behaviour.

Eibl-Eibesfeldt, I. 1972. *Die !Ko Buschmann-Gesellschaft – Gruppenbildung und Agressionskontrolle bei einem Jaeger – und Sammelvolk.* Munich: Piper.

Eibl-Eibesfeldt, I. 1973. *Der Vorprogrammierte Mensch.* Vienna, Munich, Zurich: Fritz Molden.

Eibl-Eibesfeldt, I. 1976. *Menschenforschung auf Neuen Wegen.* Vienna, Munich, Zurich: Fritz Molden.

Eibl-Eibesfeldt, I. 1980. *Grundriss der Vergeleichenden Verhaltensforschung.* Munich: Piper. (Sixth, revised edition with a greatly enlarged 18th chapter on human ethology.)

13   In using this expression, as he frequently did, Julian Huxley was referring to the contrast between the achievements of European brands of psychology and American behaviourism, which he considered fairly sterile, and those of the young science of ethology. While this 'fresh air' has led to enrichment of psychology, it has hardly yet reached psychiatry.

14   The estimate of some 5000 to 6000 autistic children in Britain, often extrapolated to other populations, or 'between four and five per 10 000 children' (L. Wing 1976, p. 71) is in essence based on the 'Middlesex Survey' of 1964 which involved 78 000 children, combined with the later Aarhus Survey of 1970, the Wisconsin Survey of the same year and the Camberwell Survey of 1971. The notion that these small samples are representative of whole populations is closely linked with the view that the

incidence of autism is totally independent of the environmental conditions under which the children grow up. As we shall argue in Chapter 5, we consider this view not only unfounded but definitely wrong. But these figures have begun to lead a life of their own. It is only recently that Victor D. Sanua of Adelphi University in Garden City, New York, has begun to collect data on the relation between the incidence of autism and particular cultural conditions (Sanua, V. D. 1979. *Cultural changes and psychopathology in children, with special reference to infantile autism.* Keynote address at the Congress of the World Federation for Mental Health, held in Salzburg, Austria, in July 1979). As yet, Dr Sanua's studies are not conclusive, due to the difficulty in obtaining reliable evidence, and he is finding it difficult to obtain the necessary funds for detailed study. We consider his programme to be one of great urgency; we shall return to the subject of autism and society in Chapter 5.

How persistent is the belief in the overall representativeness of the four samples mentioned above, and of the independence of autism from environmental conditions, is clear from the following incident. One of our colleagues who, in an attempt to find out whether present conditions in Northern Ireland might affect the mental health of children who have grown up under the tension of the civil war, asked the Health Authorities concerned for information and received the reply that the incidence of autism has been established by the Middlesex Survey!

15 The essence of the rationale of this section was already published in our 1972 papers – see Chapter 1, note 8.

16 The first summary in textbook form of what is now called 'Lorenzian' ethology was Tinbergen, N. 1951. *The Study of instinct.* Oxford: Clarendon Press. How far ethology has grown since can be seen by comparing this early work with modern texts such as:·
Manning, A. 1979. *An Introduction to the study of animal behaviour,* 3rd edn. London: Edward Arnold;
and the more comprehensive, though more psychologically oriented book:
Hinde, R. A. 1970. *Animal behaviour: a synthesis of ethology and comparative psychology.* London: McGraw-Hill.
Lorenz himself has recently published an updated textbook:
Lorenz, K. 1978. *Vergleichende Verhaltenslehre.* Vienna, New York: Springer.
This could be called the 'neolorenzian' approach to animal and human behaviour. An English edition will be published by Methuen.
A useful reference work in encyclopaedic form is:
McFarland, D. (ed.) 1981. *The Oxford companion to animal behaviour.* Oxford: Oxford University Press.

17 The basic ideas and evidence behind our views on motivational conflicts have been discussed briefly in the textbooks of Manning and Hinde (mentioned in note 16) which mention a number of the original studies. For our present purpose it is not necessary to discuss in detail the *mechanisms* which have been suggested to account for the various ways in which the motivational conflicts express themselves in behaviours of the various types we classify briefly in this chapter. There are various different views about these mechanisms and new hypotheses are still being generated, but they do not affect our main argument.

18 Norton-Griffiths, M. 1967. Some ecological aspects of the feeding behaviour of the oystercatcher on the edible mussel. *Ibis* **109**, 412–24.
Norton-Griffiths, M. 1969. The organisation, control and development of parental feeding in the oystercatcher. *Behaviour* **34**, 55–114.

19 Eibl-Eibesfeldt, I. 1975. *Ethology – the biology of behaviour,* 2nd edn. New York: Holt, Rinehart & Winston. (See p. 245 for a description of the nut-opening behaviour of squirrels.)

20 Tinbergen, N. 1951. *The study of instinct* (see note 16 above) contains the description of the reproductive behaviour of the three-spined stickleback, of which nest building

and the ventilation of the brood are parts. We refrain from listing the voluminous literature on this 'white rat of ethology' that has been published since.

Whereas for a long time the adaptedness of behaviour was taken as much for granted as the fact that most things fall unless supported, or (to take a behaviour example) as sneezing, laughing or eating, a considerable part of behaviour science is now studying in detail 'what is the use' of various behaviours of many species including our own, and also how such adapted behaviour has evolved in the history of species, and how it develops anew in every individual as it grows up.

21 Tinbergen, N. 1972. Functional ethology and the human sciences. *Proc. R. Soc.* B **182**, 385–410. Reprinted in Tinbergen, N. 1973. *The animal in its world,* vol. 2. London: George Allen & Unwin.

22 Tinbergen, N. 1965. Behaviour and natural selection. In *Ideas in modern biology,* J. A. Moore (ed.), 519–42. New York: Natural History Press. (Reprinted in Tinbergen, N. 1973. *The animal in its world,* vol. 2. London: George Allen & Unwin.)

23 Tinbergen, N. 1953. *Social behaviour in animals.* London: Methuen. Please note that we select agonistic behaviour from a great variety of other kinds of conflict-motivated behaviour; we do this merely because agonistic, and in particular the form known as territorial, behaviour is relatively easy to analyse.

24 A useful introduction to the kinds of behaviour resulting from dual or multiple motivation can be found in Chapters 16 and 17 of Hinde, R. A. (1970) *Animal behaviour* (see note 16 above), in Chapter 5 of Manning, A. (1979) – also mentioned in note 16 above – and in Tinbergen, N. (1959) – see note 11 above. For protean behaviour see Chance, M. R. A. and W. M. S. Russell 1959. Protean displays. *Proc. Zool Soc. Lond.* 132, 65–70.

25 Hutt, C. and S. J. Hutt (personal communication).
    See also Hutt, S. J. and C. Hutt 1970. Stereotypies and their relation to arousal: a study of autistic children. In *Behaviour studies in psychiatry,* 185. Oxford: Pergamon.

26 Most of the literature dealing with the so-called 'approach-avoidance' conflict is to be found in the work of the American 'behaviorist' school. In order to see this work in biological perspective, it should be noticed that the great majority of experiments in this field were done with animals (usually rats) whose approach was hunger motivated and whose avoidance was escape from a noxious stimulus such as an electric shock. When we distinguish between, for example, attack-motivated, hunger-motivated, parentally motivated approaches etc. we specify not merely approach behaviours with different *functions*, but also with different *causes*; the ethological analysis of types of conflict therefore carries us one step further than the (unwarranted) 'approach-avoidance' generalisations. Being at times compulsive manwatchers ourselves, we cannot help noticing – and being amused by – the various mild frustration movements made unwittingly by psychiatrists themselves when they are, for instance, doing their utmost to be patient with a person who keeps evading the issues these doctors, intent on helping, raise. We have found also that a conference of a society of psychiatrists (like other scientific meetings) provides one with so many instances that one soon begins to suffer from 'information input overload' and is in danger of missing a great deal of what is said in the scientific discussions!

27 Andrews, R. J. 1956. Some remarks on behaviour in conflict situations. *Br. J. Anim. Behav.* **4**, 41–5.

28 Tinbergen, N. 1959 (see note 11 above).

29 Tinbergen, N. and H. Falkus 1969. *Signals for survival.* A film originally made for the BBC's 'The World About Us', obtainable as a 16-mm film with soundtrack from McGraw-Hill's Film Division, 110 15th Street, Del Mar, California 92014, USA. The book with the same title by Tinbergen, N., H. Falkus and E. Ennion was published by the Clarendon Press, Oxford in 1970.

30 See note 11 above.

31 Masserman, J. H. 1950. Experimental neuroses. *Scient. Am.* **182**, 38–43.

32 For a concise account of ritualisation see Chapter 6 of A. Manning (1979) – see note 16 above. For the rationale underlying the reconstruction of the evolutionary origin of ritualised movements and the kind of changes brought about by this evolution, see Tinbergen, N. 1952. Derived activities: their causation, biological significance, origin and emancipation during evolution. *Q. Rev. Biol.* **27**, 1–32. In modern ethological research the emphasis has moved away from this subject, not because it is a dead end of no importance, but because attention has switched to other problems. See, however, McFarland, D. 1981 (note 16 above).

33 Tinbergen, N. and M. Moynihan 1952. Head flagging in the black-headed gull: its function and origin. *Br. Birds* **45**, 19–22. For a more recent and more comprehensive treatment of appeasement behaviour in a variety of contexts see Eibl-Eibesfeldt, I. 1975. *Ethology – the biology of behaviour* (see note 19 above).

4

Analysis of the autistic condition – the children's behaviour

In the preceding chapter we have shown how, in the study of animal behaviour, the application of the relatively simple notions of 'major functional systems' and of 'dual' and 'multiple' motivation has helped us to see order in behaviour that had initially seemed chaotic, and to reach a fair degree of understanding of what had long been puzzling. We tried, by the insertion of occasional remarks on human behaviour, to show that this kind of approach might well help us to understand certain forms of human non-verbal behaviour as well, in particular their underlying motivation. This seemed especially promising since, as Hutt and Hutt had first pointed out[1] it is just this kind of behaviour that is often so similar in autistic and non-autistic children.

In this chapter we shall discuss how we tackled this task and we shall present what we have learned so far. Although we cannot claim that we already understand autistic behaviour as well as the expressive behaviour of many animals – which has after all been studied by these methods for decades and by many workers – we believe that what we have so far learned is illuminating enough to warrant a plausible hypothesis about the nature of the autistic condition. Anticipating, we can say that autistic children show many signs of a motivational conflict between, on the one hand, the inclination to withdraw or stay away from certain social and physical situations and, on the other, the simultaneously elicited tendency to approach the same situations for the sake either of making social contact or of a closer exploratory inspection.[2] The main difference between autistic and normal children is one of degree; in autists avoidance, which in normal children appears briefly at the start of each encounter with such situations and is soon replaced by a less and less inhibited social or exploratory approach, remains dominant for much longer periods and is very often permanent. This forced us to conclude that *autists live in an almost continuous state of withdrawal- (anxiety-) dominated motivational (emotional) conflict.* Beyond this, we will argue that this aberrant emotional state is not just one out of many aspects of autism, but is at the very core of it and can account for many kinds of autistic behaviour that so far have been considered merely 'puzzling', 'odd' or 'bizarre'.

Direct signs of acute motivational conflict

In autistic children we can observe components of avoidance behaviour, of approach behaviour and also a number of movements that are due to the simultaneous activation of both avoidance and approach. Of these, the movements of avoidance and of approach proper are so commonplace that they are often either overlooked or, if they are mere intention movements, they are often so subtle that their connection with complete, overt approach or avoidance behaviour is not realised.

AVOIDANCE BEHAVIOUR

The most obvious form of these is of course actually moving away from persons or situations. This can be very conspicuous, e.g. when a child retreats or runs away when one approaches him, but usually it is far less conspicuous, for autistic children are masters in the art of quietly 'fading' away, of achieving an increase in distance in a surprisingly inconspicuous way. This is not accidental – they know by experience that this quiet withdrawal is less likely to make others approach them. Once one has noticed this fading away, one sees it time and again in autistic children when they are together with other children, or with adults. In fact, in such conditions they are continuously busy avoiding social proximity; and how effectively they do this becomes clear when one realises that they keep their distance all the time. It looks as if this distance-keeping is indeed their main concern in life; a thing to which they give constant priority.

Apart from this straightforward, complete withdrawal or distance-keeping behaviour, there are a number of slight signs, of low-key expressions, such as turning away without actually moving away, turning the head sideways or letting the head hang, or even merely looking away with the eyes only (gaze aversion, or rather gaze averting[3] in the strict sense), or looking 'blank', or even closing the eyes. It is also typical of an autistic child in a group that he is almost all the time standing or walking near the wall or fence, his back turned towards the others and his head hanging down.

Apart from these overt expressions of the tendency to withdraw, the child often fails to respond to stimuli that normally would make him approach but which his anxiety prevents him from actually acting on. Closing the eyes or (equally common) putting the hands over the ears is a mechanical means of achieving this 'cut-off',[4] but these children also protect themselves by a central nervous cut-off, by simply refusing to see or hear (without showing overt withdrawal) and perhaps even by actually not seeing or hearing. That all these phenomena are part of the withdrawal syndrome becomes clear when one realises that it is always the same external circumstances that cause them: encounters with people and with unfamiliar situations. The acoustic cut-off is so common that, as we have seen, autistic children are time and again judged, not only by laymen but by physicians and even psychiatrists, to be deaf. To see the fallacy of this one has again to get away from the clinical testing situation or the enforced contact with people or unfamiliar situations, and observe the child 'in the field', and without him realising one is observing him. Most autists will then soon show numerous responses to sounds that they consider not frightening: e.g. that of birds calling outside, of the wind, of sounds made by a pet,[5] etc; and also to sounds that are so frightening that they cannot ignore them, e.g. the sound made by a hoover,[6] or sounds – even that of distant footsteps – that they know by experience are likely to lead to social contact. A little persistent observation shows that autistic children can in fact be extremely sensitive to sounds: both to those that frighten them, and from which they either cut themselves off or withdraw in panic; and to even the slightest sounds that interest them without frightening them.

All these, and quite possibly many other signs, are parts of the one major functional system of avoidance; and one can see them come and go together. The issue is slightly complicated by the fact that they do not always appear in the same form; they can be ranked on a scale from mild to strong. To check this, one has only to observe – but patiently, and again and again. This has the additional advantage that one begins to notice what kind of conditions in the outside world elicit or increase this avoidance tendency in the particular child concerned. For instance, when a child is confined, as he usually is, by walls, fences, or by the unfamiliarity of the wider surroundings, strong stimulation of his avoidance (for example by suddenly and openly approaching and perhaps addressing him) forces him into the situation of a cornered animal, and it is in such situations that he may 'throw a tantrum'. Except when a child has, as some do, begun to use the trantrums as an operational tool to get his way, these tantrums could better be called *panic* tantrums than temper tantrums; they express, in subjective terms, extreme fear and despair at being unable to move away. When pressed further, the child may fight with the courage of despair and without any inhibition. (Such desperate defence must be distinguished from 'aggression'.[7]) Admittedly it is not always easy to find out what exactly has elicited withdrawal or even a tantrum in particular cases. The reason seems to us to be that no overt approach is required to make the child afraid; most autists can understand quite well a great deal of what is said by others, even though they may not overtly respond to it, and can take offence; they also anticipate quite well and may show avoidance when they are merely apprehensive about what *might be about* to happen and frighten them.[8]

From what little we know ourselves about this, we believe that in many autistic children there is a close connection between panic tantrums and 'fits', or 'seizures', which can be very similar to, and even grade into, 'true' epileptic seizures. It may be a matter of taste as to whether such children are said to suffer from epilepsis 'as well as' from autism, or that they are children in which tantrums develop easily into fits. Both tantrums and epileptic fits have much in common with what ethologists call 'protean' behaviour,[9] which (as we argued in the preceding chapter) is a recognised type of conflict behaviour which is often due to strongly elicited but thwarted escape.

It may well be that the term 'avoidance' is a little too crude to cover all the signs of a negative attitude to social and exploratory opportunities. 'Rejecting' may often come nearer the mark. Also, the anticipatory precautions, measures taken by these children to avoid even the creation of frightening situations – precautions that are not themselves overt avoidance behaviour – may not be very noticeable at first glance, but they are, in spite of their extreme subtlety, very effective in preventing the unwanted contact. Children with advanced autism are uncannily clever at this; everyone who has to deal continuously with such children knows only too well how time and again they manage 'somehow' to steer clear of the kind of contacts they do not want or dare not make. It is when one begins to notice that this avoidance of contact occurs time after time that one begins to realise that it cannot be accidental, and this makes one look more attentively for further signs of such precautionary behaviour; one begins to know, from the non-occurrence of contacts, that they *must* have such behaviours.[10] It is when one's perception has thus been alerted and sharpened that one notices, for instance, that these children avoid making the slightest gestures or sounds that could elicit contact behaviour in the adult – one step *better* than avoiding him themselves! 'Let sleeping dogs lie' is clearly their consistent strategy. But this does not become clear in a few standard tests – prolonged and repeated observation is the only way to discover it.

It is the result of this unwillingness of autists to make social contacts and their extreme reluctance to venture out into unfamiliar territory or activities that these children cling so rigidly to 'sameness', to the few situations, objects and routines that are familiar to them; even in many cases to a more or less limited range of foods ('food fads').[11] Another way of saying this is that they are totally, pathologically 'unenterprising'.

At first glance it would seem paradoxical that some autistic children sometimes 'run away' from home – a behaviour reported from quite a number of them. But we are convinced that 'running away from' is only half the story, for they seem always to end up at a place they have visited before and that, for whatever reason, has taken their fancy. This was first pointed out to us by a young woman (Olga, see Ch. 10) who had recovered from a long period of severe autism and who remembered such an occasion. Park (Ch. 9, note 1), and Beck (Ch. 9, note 6) give similar examples. What exactly triggers off such a quasi-exploration may vary from case to case, but it would seem to be the coincidence of (a) a peak of aversion to the home (never a completely secure place) and (b) an accidental introduction and sudden attachment to something novel, encountered under exceptionally favourable, non-frightening circumstances – for instance a children's playground. We need not elaborate this further; close observation reveals numerous indications of avoidance of persons and of unfamiliar physical situations in autistic children.

To every childwatcher it should be clear, however, that in this they do not behave fundamentally differently from normal children. Here too the difference is one of degree: social avoidance and withdrawal from, or resistance to the unfamiliar is merely much more intense and more frequent in autistic children; and, except when they are alone in their own little world, with their soother and not disturbed by what upsets them – rare occasions for autists – their lives can be said to be dominated by fear and apprehension.

APPROACH BEHAVIOUR

The observable predominance of avoidance behaviour in autistic children must not, however, make us believe that they show no trace of the opposite behaviour. That they do occasionally want to, and even do, approach either people or unfamiliar situations becomes clear when one knows what such behaviour looks like in normal children and when one creates the conditions under which approach behaviour appears. When in company, autistic children show little approach behaviour because it is largely suppressed by avoidance. This again is due to the fact that their avoidance is so easily elicited that 'company' almost always cows them. This is particularly clear when adults attempt to interact with the child. However friendly the way in which this is done, however effective their approach, smiling and speaking are with a normal child, even the friendliest of these overtures makes an autist withdraw.[12] Yet an experienced person can draw even an autist out of his shell. In order to do so one has to avoid any behaviour that, because it is directed *at* him, makes him withdraw, and (like the male gull described in Ch. 3) one must at the same time do something that positively kindles his interest. When one avoids looking at the child, speaking to him and even about him, he will sooner or later look at one. This looking, which can soon become an intensely investigative look, is the start, the intention movement, of an overt approach. With patience, one can see this develop into full approach (which comes usually from behind, for the child avoids face-to-face contact). This again can even lead to tentative interaction if the adult keeps doing something that positively attracts the child, such as, for example, playing with toys, talking about something that interests him, carefully not addressing him but rather seeming to ignore him. If one plays this well, even fairly withdrawn autists may approach and even touch one. E. A. has been able, even in demonstrations to specialist clinicians, to elicit not only contact making but playful interactions up to a quite intrusive peek-a-boo game, in which the child tolerated and, judging by explosive, no more than slightly nervous laughter, even enjoyed the (to many children fairly frightening) 'boo' part. On one occasion a boy, who at first glance seemed to shrink from any contact, approached her from behind, and feet first, until his feet actually touched her. We have found many teachers and caregivers (but hardly any physicians) receptive to directives about how to do this, how not to elicit fear yet at the same time to activate a child's interest, and many of them have reported back enthusiastically that the results were as we had predicted.

Apart from social approach aimed at people, the exploratory approach to new objects or situations, seemingly absent in autistic children with their obsession with 'sameness', can in fact also be observed. But, we repeat, for this one has to give the child time, and he has to be undisturbed in his preferred room or a corner so that he believes himself to be unobserved.[13]   It is not necessary to elaborate this; again, the signs of approach behaviour can be observed by any interested and patient observer. The point we stress is that even though autistic children live in *almost* constant dread and insecurity, they are not totally and continuously dominated by fear, but are under the surface willing and in fact keen to approach persons and unfamiliar objects and situations. But unlike normal children, autists show this approach behaviour only rarely. Also, what they show is usually incomplete: since they dare not actually approach, the only kind of approach behaviour is often the covert acts of looking and of listening.

Awareness of (a) the near-absence or the 'stunted' forms of the approach behaviour of autists, and of (b) the fact that they do socialise and explore, though almost always from a distance, is important for our understanding both of the overall retardation of the development of autistic children, and of the mysterious 'islets of good performance'. In order to understand the overall retardation we have to realise that the process of socialisation, which starts with and elaborates from early affiliation with the mother, leads to the formation of relationships with people from whom the child receives much of his education. Education, however, is not merely the result of being instructed, let alone of being instructed by adults other than a child's parents, of going to school.[14] We can in fact distinguish, in the 'programming' of each individual development, three quite distinct 'main channels of learning', each of which has its own function to serve, to wit: (a) learning by playful social interaction and observing what others do; (b) learning from exploration; and (c) learning from being instructed. Because the latter form of education plays such a large part in modern society we tend to forget that the other contexts for education are important as well and are in fact basic for a healthy development. The emphasis which is put on instruction in our modern society is largely due to the need for future members of this so exceedingly complex society to learn a vast number of different modern skills, for which specialist teachers have to be employed. But being instructed can be, and as a rule is being, overdone while playful socialising and exploration suffer and are in fact generally suppressed in all but a few of the most progressive schools. This leads to serious forms of under-development, even in many otherwise normal children. Even schooling itself is, as we all know only too well, not a simple matter of providing input for supposedly interested minds hungry for knowledge and understanding: the relationship of most children with teachers is different from that with parents; and the effectiveness of teaching is in part under emotional, non-rational control – children are clever at refusing to learn from teachers they do not like and respect. The modern under-emphasis on learning-by-observing-and-mimicking-what-adults-do is due to a number of conditions: the work done by the adults is nowadays much too difficult to imitate; the fathers work away from the home; domestic chores (in which especially girls love to take part at a certain age) are done by unintelligible and dangerous electric appliances etc., but however far the modern setting for education is from the ideal one, most modern children do on the whole learn that main skills they need in order to earn a living later and to fit into the adult society.

But an autistic child is not only at a disadvantage because he refuses to be instructed; by having failed to forge an adequate social bond even with his own mother and, as a consequence, with others as well (for all socialisation is an elaboration and extension of early affiliation with the mother) he also excludes himself from the playful social interaction with others which normal children use for learning by imitation of and participation in even quite complicated skills, as well as social *finesse*.

The playgroups of children serve this function of transfer of skills and attitudes not only when under the guidance of adults. As we shall discuss in another context later, they play an important part in the development of, among other things, mothercraft. Contrary to what many an animal ethologist of the past might have liked to believe, mothercraft is in our species not totally inborn; much has to be learnt, and this is done mainly in two ways: young children learn from seeing babies nursed and cared for in their own homes or in those of associated families; very soon they likewise learn observationally from seeing teenage girls in the group 'minding' the very young members of the playgroup; and when they approach their teens they learn a great deal by practice while they themselves are doing the childminding.

But it is not only social and motherly or parental behaviour in general that is learned in the context of playgroups and suffers when a child has not formed social bonds; another major consequence of failed bonding is that the essential condition for *exploratory* behaviour does not present itself.[15] In order to explore, to venture out into the wider world and to give free rein to curiosity and to investigate untiringly and alertly, a child needs to know that he is operating under the 'umbrella of security' that only a mother or other persons to whom he is emotionally bonded can provide; a basis to which he can return whenever exploration becomes too frightening or risky. Thus the autistic child misses out on exploration too.

Both learning from playing with others and learning from exploration are therefore practically impossible for the autistic child. Yet, as we have seen, even he does have, hidden under and suppressed by his overriding anxiety, the inclinations to socialise and to explore. Even autistic children do observe and mimic from a distance and on the sly; and even autistic children do at least some exploring.[16] But they do so only when they feel secure, and this means that they will explore mainly their own bodies or parts of the environment with which they are fully familiar; and they will explore only when they are in their accustomed room or corner, and when they believe themselves to be unobserved. This, we believe, is one of the reasons why so many autists do show 'islets of good performance'. A study of the kind of things that form these islets confirms this: they always concern activities for which socialising and/or exploration is not or hardly necessary.

In view of these severe handicaps it is in fact truly staggering to see how much some autistic children do manage to learn. It is at the same time an impressive demonstration of the strong urge, even in them, to learn from social contacts and from self-activity that there are many mute autists who can not only understand speech but who can read and even write, some of them in more than one language. We shall discuss this presently in more detail.

How exactly the emotional peculiarities of autistic children affect their intellectual development – for that matter how the normal emotional state controls the development of skills and intellect of normal children – we neither intend nor are competent to discuss. What we try to drive home is the fact *that* and to how great an extent much of our intellectual development is under the control of our emotional state. This is an aspect of child development that does not seem to receive enough attention in the literature, yet it seems to us that it is exactly to this emotional basis of mental growth that the damage is done which leads to autism, and probably to some other developmental aberrations as well, which are usually given other labels.

This brief sketch should be enough to support our claim that autistic children exhibit innumerable, directly observable signs of the major behaviour systems involved in their motivational state, and of which avoidance is so pathologically predominant. A special form of approach motivation, viz. that of truly aggressive behaviour, seems to develop in older autistic children, who are often clearly resentful of the way the world treats them. As we shall argue in Chapter 9, this is not to be confused with the occasional uninhibited all-out fighting that an autistic child can do when he is 'cornered', i.e. when he desperately wants to flee from a frightening person or situation but cannot do so. This it, as we have argued before, an expression of extreme but thwarted fear.

CONFLICT BEHAVIOUR

Not all autistic behaviour can be classified as either incipient or thwarted avoidance or as tentative approach behaviour; many movements of autistic children are direct expressions of the conflict itself. In order to recognise them as such, our experience with conflict behaviour of animals is valuable because it has opened our eyes to the variety of such movements one can expect and to their origin. The animal studies have also given us practice in the methods of detecting the motivational state underlying the movements. Many of the 'mannerisms' or 'stereotypies' belong in this category. But to recognise them for what they are requires an understanding of a few complications. We have seen that in animal studies the recognition of the origin of conflict expressions is often made difficult because they have been 'ritualised' in the course of evolution; that is, when they have (as many though not all have) acquired a secondary function as social signals, they have, in the course of adaptive evolution, been slowly modified in the direction of conspicuousness and unambiguity. Comparison between closely related species often helps in 'peeling off' that 'secondary veneer' because the degree and the kind of ritualisation differs even between closely related species.

The expressions of conflict that we can observe in autistic children are also often obscured, but by different processes. Firstly, the movements change as the child grows up, and become increasingly stereotyped. In order to distinguish this from the evolutionary process of ritualisation, we call this distortion of conflict movements *formalisation*. This formalisation can involve simplification of the movement and/or exaggeration of parts of it; it also loses its variability and becomes a 'stereotypy' or 'mannerism' and, because the state of conflict is often of very long duration, such movements are as a rule almost endlessly repeated. We shall presently discuss some concrete examples. Another obstacle in the way of understanding the origin of mannerisms has to do with the retardation of the child's overall behaviour development. This retardation expresses itself not merely in a lagging behind of the acquisition of skills, but also in that of the emotional development. This is most easily appreciated when one forgets for a moment the physical, structural aspects of the child, which by and large do keep pace with his physical age. Because we have ourselves been programmed in such a way that we judge a child's age largely by his physical appearance, we often find it difficult to recognise behaviour of, say, a 14 year old as being almost identical to that of, say, a five year old or even a younger child. And yet we have to do that in order to 'peel off' this type of distortion. When a big teenager wants to be hugged or even cuddled by his mother and tries gently to sit or lie on her lap, a normal mother's reaction will be, she understands the situation and recognises the child's behaviour as regression or retardation, to reject him, often very strongly so, and to show signs of emotional disapproval. (This incidentally can contribute to the downward spiral of the mother–child dyad, because the child feels rebuffed and the mother cannot adjust.)

The method by which we can recognise both formalisation and retardation and see through their effects so that we can recognise the origin of these movements is not interspecies comparison (although the comparing of young and older and of more and less severely affected autists can help) but, because they are individually acquired distortions, through tracing the origin and the subsequent formalisation of the movements by following the behaviour of children from a very early age. Because, as a child recovers, it will often reverse the formalisation process and 'deformalise' the mannerism, one can sometimes discover its origin by watching recovering autists. We have often been able to recognise the movements that belong to a much earlier stage of development, by looking at the behaviour of normal but much younger children than the autist under observation – another argument for studying normal development alongside the autistic derailment.

Before we are going to scaffold these general statements by a discussion of some examples, we shall first harden our interpretation of the dual motivation of autistic children by relating how one can check it by a variety of experimental manipulations.

Experimental testing of the conflict hypothesis

As in many ethological studies of animals, experimental checking can be done in a step by step procedure. The first step (1) is often the use of 'natural' or *unintentional* experiments, e.g. the recognition that certain changes in behaviour often follow, time after time, the same kind of changes in the environment that occur without the observer's intervention. This can be illuminating, for it gives one, for instance, a first idea – a hint – of what kind of events in the outside world will, for example, elicit avoidance behaviour and what kind of events will make the child approach a person or an object. An observer even slightly trained in ethology cannot help seeing such 'experiments by nature' happen all the time to autistic children. Parents, visitors, strangers met in the street, and last but not least doctors perform them, but usually without being aware of it. Every time a doctor sees an autistic child, with or without his mother, in his surgery or clinic, he unintentionally intimidates the child, often literally scares him 'out of his wits'. The more perceptive doctors do try, sometimes successfully, to put such a child at ease, but we know that the majority do not even notice that the child is subdued or even panicky; they merely notice that he does not respond – that, as it has been phrased, he 'behaves like an empty vessel'; or, in Bettelheim's words, as an 'empty fortress'; or that he 'is asleep' (DesLaurier).[17] We repeat that, although the many different 'tests' which psychiatrists and psychologists often apply to these children have an aura of much greater scientific respectability than the observational technique we advocate, they fail to show up much of what the child can do; they elicit the one thing that could be of use in arriving at a diagnosis and that yet is so often ignored or merely noticed, viz. increased and often bored withdrawal, sometimes all the way to panic tantrums and 'seizures' or 'epileptic' fits. This too is a flaw of method which prevents such scientists or doctors from obtaining relevant factual information, and which can lead to totally wrong or at least unhelpful conclusions. At the same time, the examining specialists often brush aside the reports of parents and tutors, which admittedly may sometimes be garbled or unreliable, but which are sometimes quite informative. Thus they cut themselves off from yet another source of information, which, with the use of a little critical perception, could sometimes be of great value. 'Cut-off' is a behaviour that is by no means confined to autistic children – in this less excusable form it is even exceptionally prevalent among physicians!

In our 1972 paper we described how we had systematically studied the effects of outside events controlled by ourselves on the behaviour of both normal and autistic children, and we gave a few examples of this procedure. (Incidentally, although we made it quite clear at the time that the facts we presented were *samples* of a much larger material, several reviewers and critics have misrepresented us by writing that *our entire work* was based only on these few samples (e.g. Wing & Ricks 1976, Schopler 1974).[18] We shall return to this and to other flaws in the current literature on autism in Chapter 7.)

(2) However, since 1972 we have steadily expanded our store of such observations on many children, and have *deliberately* caused behaviour changes both (a) towards an *increase* of the dominance of avoidance and/or an *intensifying* of the conflict, and (b) towards a lowering of the anxiety level, of a reduction in the domance of avoidance, and so a weakening of the conflict. Again, we shall describe a few representative examples. We want to emphasise two methodological aspects which we consider of great importance.

(a) We refrain from listing figures and tables etc: first, because the field is as yet in the state of qualitative observation and of preparation for the selection of factors that are worth counting; and secondly, because all these observations and experiments can be done by any one among our readers literally every day – it is not as if we have to do it with carefully bred and carefully manipulated laboratory animals or require costly apparatus to which only the experimenter has access. So, instead of asking our readers to trust that whatever figures and tables *we* would give were not faked (the basic trust on which any scientific endeavour is based), we urge our readers to use their *own* eyes and to *check* our observations for themselves. As Desmond Morris wrote recently, such 'manwatching' is a fascinating pastime, and 'can make even the most boring social occasion into an exciting field trip'.[19] In fact we have done some of our most interesting observations in the family, in supermarkets, buses, in doctors' waiting rooms and in hospitals, in the lounges of large international airports and similar places.

(b) Some of the interactions that we are going to describe between ourselves and either normal or autistic children upon our first meeting are genuine and extremely illuminating *experiments*, for throughout such meetings we act as 'dummies'-and-observers-in-one. Since meetings are a *series* of signal–response sequences that travel back and forth between child and us, every meeting is in reality a *series* of experiments. Further, because each subsequent step in the part we play has to be based on what we see the child do (in fact we *monitor* such a child continuously), and because the behaviour of the child is in no two meetings exactly the same, the records of such meetings are extremely variable in their details. This is an additional reason for not (yet) forcing these, initially qualitative, data into the straitjacket of simple tables. Of course, at a later stage quantification of data will be required, but for the moment and for some time to come, *premature* tabulation is likely to restrict our field of vision.

Again, what we are going to describe are a few samples which we know from long experience to be typical.

REDUCING THE ANXIETY

With regard to a *lowering* of the anxiety level, we have already mentioned C. Hutt's observations on the slow adjustment in this direction that autistic children made in the course of as short a period as an hour when confronted with a new object.[13] Even richer are the experiments we ourselves do with children on meeting them; moreover, they concern social rather than exploratory behaviour. This procedure has already been described in our paper of 1972 (see Ch. 1, note 8) and we need not do more here than quote the relevant passage.

> What we invariably do when visiting or being visited by a family with young children is, after a very brief friendly glance, to ignore the child(ren) completely, at the same time eliciting, during our early conversations, friendly responses from the parent(s). One can see a great deal of the behaviour of the child out of the corner of one's eye and can monitor a surprising amount of the behaviour that reveals the child's state. Usually, such a child will start by simply looking intently at the stranger, studying him guardedly. One may already at this stage judge it safe to now and then look briefly at the child and assess more accurately the state he is in. If, on doing so, one sees the child avert his glance, eye contact must at once be broken off. Very soon the child will stop studying one. He will approach gingerly and will soon reveal his strong

bonding tendency by touching one – for instance by putting his hand tentatively on one's knees. This is often a crucial moment: one must *not* respond by looking at the child (which may set him back considerably) but by cautiously touching the child's hand with one's own. Again, playing this 'game' by if necessary stopping, or going one step back in the process, according to the child's response, one can soon give a mildly reassuring signal *by touch*, for instance by gently pressing his hand, or by touching it quickly, and withdrawing again. If, as is often the case, the child laughs at this, one can laugh oneself, but still without looking at the child. Soon he will become more daring, and the continuation of contact by touch and by indirect vocalisation will begin to cement a bond. One can then switch to the first, tentative eye contact. This again must be done with caution, and step by step; certainly with a smile, and for brief moments at first. We find that first covering one's face with one's hands, then turning towards the child (perhaps saying 'where's Andrew?' or whatever the child's name) and then very briefly showing one's eyes and covering them up at once, is very likely to elicit a smile, or even a laugh. For this, incidentally, a child often takes the initiative (see, for example, Stroh & Buick 1971). Very soon the child will then begin to solicit this; he will rapidly tolerate increasingly long periods of direct eye contact and join one. If this is played further, with continuous awareness of and adjustments to slight reverses to a more negative attitude, one will soon find the child literally clamouring for intense play contact. Throughout this process the vast variety of expressions of the child must be *understood* in order to monitor him correctly, and one must oneself *apply* an equally large repertoire in order to give, at any moment, the best signal. The 'bag of tricks' one has to have at one's disposal must be used to the full, and the 'trick' selected must whenever possible be adjusted to the child's individual tastes. Once established, the bond can be maintained by surprisingly slight signals; a child coming to show proudly a drawing he has made is often completely happy with just a 'how nice dear' and will then return to his own play. Even simpler vocal contacts can work; analogous to the vocal contact calls of birds (which the famous Swedish writer Selma Lagerloef correctly described in 'Nils Holgersson' as 'I am here, where are you?'), many children develop an individual contact call, to which one has merely to answer in the same language.

'The results of this procedure have been found to be surprisingly rapid, and also consistent *if one adjusts oneself to the monitoring results*. Different children require different starting levels, and different tempos of stepping up. One may even have to start by staying away from the child's favourite room. It is also of great significance how familiar to the child the physical environment is. Many children take more than one day; with such it is important to remember that one has to start at a lower level in the morning than where one left off the previous evening. We have the impression that the process is on the whole completed sooner if one continually holds back until one senses the child longing for more intense contact.

It is interesting to compare this 'taming' of a timid child with the behaviour of the males of the birds described above that are trying to 'win the confidence' of a female. The assuaging of her fear is achieved by the male's use of a very similar procedure, including the monitoring and continuous adjusting (of course not 'deliberately') of his behaviour to the changing level of what the female can just tolerate. In those animal species that we have studied ourselves, there are numerous occasions on which the male does not adjust with sufficient sensitivity, scares off the female, and has to start anew. Many mammals are undoubtedly more subtly tuned, and we ourselves can, and have to, 'play' a timid child with much more *finesse* than a gull treats its partner.

We have found that the same procedure as here described for winning the confidence of young children works very well with many dogs too. Taking into account the different forms of social behaviour of dogs, the course of interaction is basically the same, and by ignoring a dog while engaged in a friendly chat with its owner one soon causes it to put a forepaw upon one's knee, and by avoiding too early eye contact while giving the right touch and vocal stimuli one achieves (even without providing the doubtlessly equally important chemical stimuli) the same 'clamouring for attention' as shown by children, including the presenting of toys.

Once one has developed a feeling for the details of the intricate signalling systems that lead to bonding, it is striking to see that what we have sketched here applies not only to toddlers. We know, for instance, a cello teacher who, once aware of these facts, discovered that with shy pupils up to the age of 14 one can avoid inhibitions by timidity (and consequent stiffening up), by making it clear to the pupil that one is not looking at the face of the pupil when one observes the movements and positioning of the left hand (which a cello player holds, of course, close to the head). This, incidentally, illustrates another point of interest: it is the gaze aimed at the subject's eyes which is intimidating; much more so than gazing at just any part of the body.

There are undoubtedly many differences between individual children, not only in the relative and absolute levels of dominance of timidity, in the speed of bonding, in aversions to individual adults etc., but also in the ranking of sensory stimuli that make a child draw back. There are children who do not want to be *touched* (and distinguish between where and how they are touched, by which sex etc.); other children object more to (specific) *vocalisations*; others (the majority) to certain *visual* signs. All this too has to be quickly assessed for the purpose of successful bonding. Further, the intimidating signs are not only very specific but have in addition to be distinguished from other withdrawal-inducing signs. For instance, some children (and adults) avoid very strongly non-social sounds such as that of a vacuum cleaner, a violin or a pressure cooker. Or, conversely, they may accept the most fantastic noises, but object specifically to particular but not necessarily frightening ways of talking to them. This shows that not all the withdrawal-inducing stimuli are fear inducing, but it is of course with fear-inducing stimuli that we are mainly concerned here. (Tinbergen & Tinbergen 1972, pp. 29–31).

INTENSIFYING THE ANXIETY

Our knowledge of conditions that can *increase* anxiety and – if withdrawal is impossible or not wanted by the child – intensify the conflict state is more detailed. This is of course because almost every contact of an autistic child with approaching adults and with unfamiliar surroundings, including visits to the clinic, invitations or instructions to do or undergo tests of various kinds etc. has this effect. Any even moderately perceptive observer cannot fail to see such increases in autistic behaviour every time he or she visits a class of autists, and Figure 4.1 gives an example of a child who made a perfect half-circle round E. A., keeping distance (and at the same time increasing the rate of his stereotypy). We further described in 1972 how an observer's looking at an autist, even in a friendly way, almost invariably makes him withdraw and show the usual correlated behaviour. This is the reason why over the years, when we became more and more sensitive even to the slightest signs of distress in such children, we became more and more cautious and less intruding, even when observing normal children. We realised that intrusive and even cautious observation and certainly too sudden interaction with children can in effect be *cruel*, and we have therefore refrained as much as possible from experimentally increasing anxiety and conflict levels.

This experience makes us view with a mixture of incredulity and horror more ruthless forms of 'behaviour modification' that one sometimes reads about in the psychiatric literature. Although we shall have to say something in favour of certain forms of behaviour modification in Chapter 7, we want to refer here to one of the recent studies in which, of all things, electric shocks were applied over long periods to a child who showed 'self-destructive behaviour' in the form of 'forcefully thrusting the back of her hand or wrist into her upper front teeth (hereafter referred to as *hitting*)'.[20] Electroshocking this five year old immediately after hitting (during the child's one year's (!) stay in hospital) resulted in a 'near zero rate'. 'After nine months in the home the subject was rehospitalised due to self-destructive behaviour, and the electroshock programme was reinstituted' (p. 243). This second period, however, was less successful and even (as, of course, to be expected) harmful: although the rate of the penalised form of self-destruction did go down, other forms of self-mutilation increased, resulting in a 'net increase of self-destruction'. Incredibly, the shocking was then extended to cover severely self-injuring 'jabbing' but was discontinued after 1½ weeks because '(1) jabbing increased; (2) hitting reappeared and increased; and (3) Elaina completely stopped eating, resisted entering the dining room, and hit and kicked at the presentation of food'. She was then 'restrained' and given tube feedings twice a day. It was only after this disastrous and unbelievably cruel as well as unintelligent series of maltreatments that 'an extinction program utilising noncontingent social isolation was chosen subsequent to the failure of the electroshock program'. This consisted of two daily two-hour sessions in an 8 × 10 foot isolation room, with a supply of toys. As a result, as given in a graph of the number of jabs and hits observed during 24 weeks of such daily sessions, both conflict movements extinguished. This means, to us quite obviously, that the child, in spite of hospitalisation and in spite of being without any social contact during the isolation sessions, became more normal than she had been even in the home in which she had

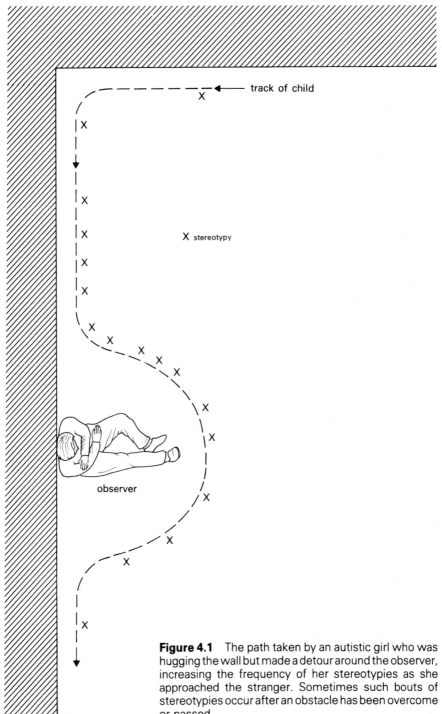

track of child

X stereotypy

observer

Figure 4.1 The path taken by an autistic girl who was hugging the wall but made a detour around the observer, increasing the frequency of her stereotypies as she approached the stranger. Sometimes such bouts of stereotypies occur after an obstacle has been overcome or passed.

lived between these two sessions – in our opinion a sad demonstration of the lack of insight, and of compassion, in those who had been in charge and those who were treating this child; they clearly had no idea that an isolation room is still far from an optimal environment!

We trust that our readers will understand why we refrain from presenting more accounts of deliberate experiments that result in an increase of autistic behaviour.

Concluding, we submit that experimental manipulation of autistic behaviour is possible in both the directions of decreasing and of increasing the underlying anxiety (in normal and autistic children alike), and that these experiments conform with our hypothesis that the autistic state is primarily an anxiety-dominated motivational imbalance.

Long-term effects of the motivational conflict

INTRODUCTION

Many characteristics of autistic children are best understood as the consequences not of a momentary emotional conflict, but as those of having lived for a long time in such a severe conflict state. Here too, animal examples may open our eyes to the significance of seemingly common-place events. We have already mentioned briefly that wolves, hyenas and similar mammals whose feeding (hunting) behaviour normally includes long periods of running or trotting, keep up this behaviour when confined in the, for them, tiny runs in which they are kept in zoos. Invariably, such animals develop a pattern of highly stereotyped near-circular or figure-of-eight shaped 'trods', to which they adhere with such precision that the worn-out paths stand out as hardened 'highways'.[21] Many animals even fail to change such locomotory habits after the physical barriers have been removed. N. T. remembers a wild long-tailed mouse that had been kept by Dr G. Manley for feeding experiments in a box of less than 30 cm high and covered with a piece of small-mesh wire netting. The mouse made itself at home and did feed, sleep etc. normally, but when disturbed by an observer would run round and would jump up until it touched the wire roof. It soon developed a highly stereotyped way of somersaulting, turning itself on its back when jumping up, touching the roof with its four legs and landing normally on the bottom of the box. After some two weeks, Dr Manley decided to let the mouse go. When he lifted the roof, his captive jumped as expected, but instead of making its way out, it continued to somersault under the now absent roof and made a number of identical jumps before it did make its escape. A large number of such 'accidental' long-term effects of confinement and other conflict situations have been reported from zoos.

Situations that elicit motivational conflicts have also been deliberately created and maintained with various laboratory animals, mainly dogs, cats, goats, sheep and monkeys. There is a vast literature on this work on 'experimental neurosis', in which animals were trained to expect food and so were 'approach motivated' but were given an electric shock which caused withdrawal.[22] As N. T. has been able to observe long ago in Howard Liddell's laboratory in Cornell University, all the animals showed at the start of the treatment a variety of 'conflict movements', similar in nature to those listed above as 'direct signs of acute conflict', though the actual motions differed of course from one species to another. Soon the animals showed these movements before the shock was actually given; they anticipated the expected shock, and were 'apprehensive'. After having been subjected to such conflict-producing tests for weeks or months, the animals would become abnormal in many respects for periods of months and remained so even after the actual experiments had been stopped. These long-term effects (described as 'neurotic') have not always been as fully described as a modern ethologist would want, but it is clear that some of them were behavioural (e.g. over-excited behaviour, stereotyped behaviour, withdrawal, rest behaviour and even sleep) but others were *somatic*: raised blood pressure, hair raising, gastric disorders all the way to gastric ulcers, even tumours in the pituitary gland of the brain.

All these animals had lived in motivational states ('moods') very comparable to those we have observed and analysed in autistic children. Like these children, they had been repeatedly, often continuously, subjected to stimuli that drove them to approach behaviour as well as to stimuli that induced escape – which, however, was prevented. As a result, they showed initially straightforward conflict behaviour, mixed with attempts to break out, or they gave up trying to escape. In the long run they developed one set or another of symptoms related to those commonly called 'stress' – more correctly, the responses to (psychosocial) stress.

A full analysis of the autistic state has to take into account that many of the direct expressions of the motivational conflict described above soon become changed, and supplemented by the effects of the long-lasting, almost permanent existence of this very intense conflict state. In accordance with the exceptional degree of individual adjustability to different environments that characterises our species, the variety of such secondary effects is much greater than that found in animals; in fact each child formalises his conflict movements in his own way, different from that of others. Yet there is enough underlying uniformity to make it possible to categorise them to a certain extent. In what follows we shall not attempt to give an exhaustive list of the variety of autistic behaviours; rather we shall try to demonstrate with a few selected examples how we can 'peel off' the secondary modifications and find the original movements as they were before these secondary processes changed them so much that they became 'puzzling' and 'bizarre'. We should add at once that we are not yet in a position to find the pre-formalisation origins of all the typically autistic behaviours; what we want to demonstrate is in what way one can find such origins, and check whether the findings tally with our claim that an anxiety-dominated conflict is at the root of the autistic condition.

RECOGNISING THE ORIGINS OF AUTISTIC BEHAVIOURS

Returning now to the detailed interpretation of specific forms of autistic behaviour, we shall apply the 'peeling off' procedure to some concrete cases and see where it leads us. As we have said, the two most important secondary effects of prolonged autism are the formalisation of conflict movements and the retention, sometimes over years, of infantile behaviour, which in a normal child is shown at a very early age and often for only a short period. Both these secondary effects can best be discovered by studying the genesis of a case from a very early stage. Unfortunately, this is often difficult or even impossible just because such early beginnings do not strike one as 'bizarre'; parents do not begin to worry about their child's strange behaviour before it has become too abnormal to overlook. Yet we can present some evidence that seems to us to support what we have said so far about the nature of the autistic condition. In discussing the secondary changes that have distorted originally straightforward movements, we cannot of course avoid overlap with the next chapter in which we examine the genesis of autism.

The fullest, yet undoubtedly still far from complete, list of 'mannerisms' has been given by Richer,[23] and we shall use his terminology. However, we will not confine ourselves to mannerisms but discuss some other examples of autistic behaviour as well. We shall arrange our examples under the same headings as we did with examples of animal behaviour in the preceding chapter.

Inhibited intention movements

We have indications that the incessant turning round on the spot or *twirling* that many autistic children do (*'pirouetting'*, Richer) is in origin a successive combination of the first stage of approach and the first stage of turning-round-and-walking away. We understood this suddenly when a girl of 10 years of age who had always shown this pirouetting when she was on the verge of entering shops, began at the same time to enter more readily, and to confine her twirling to making just one complete circle, ending up as she started, with her face towards the door. This made us realise that what the child did in reality was make a turn away (the intention movement of leaving), and then making a turn towards the door followed by the rest of the approach behaviour; incidentally, an exact analogue to the pendulum movements of animals in an ambivalent state. We then asked the home tutor (who told us this without knowing what it meant) whether the girl had at any moment in the full circle perhaps stopped, however briefly; and the expected answer came promptly: 'Yes, at the point where she had completed the first half-circle', in other words, just where avoidance switched over into approach.

We have seen this change from continuous twirling bouts to the completion of just one circle in a second child, likewise while she was gradually recovering from her more severe autistic condition. In both children the twirling always occurred at a moment of tension, of hesitation before a decision was taken (usually the decision to do an emotionally difficult thing). (The reason why the child, instead of turning back, went on in the *same* direction may be no more than a mere inertia phenomenon; our prediction is that in some cases such children may well turn back instead of twirl on in the same direction.) After we wrote this, Dr J. M. Richer showed us a photograph of a girl who did this 'alternating pirouetting'.

Rocking to and fro ('rock', Richer) while sitting or standing on the spot, is likewise a clear example of a succession of intention approaches and intention withdrawals. The only formalisation is its repetitiveness and monotony. It is again comparable to the pendulum movements so common in many animals (and in a less extreme way in normal children and adults when they hesitate between approach and withdrawal). It is worth emphasising again that the differences between 'normal' and 'autistic' behaviour are often differences of degree. When a normal man in, say, a pub brawl does a few steps forward towards another and then a few steps back, and perhaps even repeats this a few times, we find this perfectly normal, if perhaps a little over-excited. But if a child shows (a) merely the very first parts of moving forwards and backwards, and (b) repeats this for a shorter or longer time in a formalised way, we call it a 'stereotypy'.

This may not be the only origin of rocking. In a sitting child it may be due to an alternation between wanting to get up and wanting to remain sitting; also, the orientation of the rocking may lose its connection with the spatial arrangements in the environment; for instance, a child may at a very early age do 'side-rocking' (Richer: 'a rhythmic side-to-side movement of the body, usually with the feet slightly apart'). We suspect that the origin of side-rocking is roughly the same as that for forward–backward rocking. It is also possible that side-rocking is an infantile form of dancing; it is striking that it is often done when the child hears music – a subject to which we shall return in Chapter 6. Rocking movements of various kinds are also observable in many otherwise normal children, and even in adults when faced with a difficult mental task without being able to walk back and forth, for instance when one is tied to a book or working paper on the desk in front. We also have known more than one 'normal' child to do what Richer calls 'rolling', in which a child lies on his side and rolls back and forth. We think it likely that this too is a succession of two alternating intention movements and reveals ambivalent motivation, for it is often done when a child has gone to bed but cannot sleep. We must admit though that we cannot claim to understand the origin of all the various forms of rocking and rolling.

We have observed one autistic child who, when ill at ease, alternated forward and backward movements in a differently formalised way, viz. by proceeding towards some goal in a *series of two steps forward followed by one step back*, and so on.[24] This is even more analogous to the behaviour of the adult in the pub we described above.

Autistic children may endlessly *swing their legs* back and forth when they are sitting with their feet off the ground ('swing legs', Richer). We do not know the origin of the forward swinging and the backward swinging components, but we have observed this very often in normal children and in adults, and always in a state of (relatively mild) conflict, e.g. when facing unpleasant tasks or waiting impatiently for the conclusion of an unpleasant or embarrassing, i.e. avoidance-inducing, situation. Again, the autistic child does this merely in more prolonged bouts. We suspect that this (and also 'bouncing') is a form of formalised walking on the spot.

A very early form of autistic behaviour, in fact one of the earliest signs in the autistic derailment apart from refusal to make contact or resisting being taken up from the cradle, is a *'no' shaking* movement of the head ('head shakes', Richer). Whenever we have seen it, it was clear that the child either did this occasionally when showing apprehension in other ways as well, or permanently at least as long as other people were around. It seems fairly clear that this has the same origin as our normal 'no' shaking, viz. an alternation of two ways of turning the head only (rather than the entire body), away from a rejected situation, now in one direction than in the other. This is an interesting example of a movement that is at the same time genetically ritualised (for shaking 'no' is a movement common to very many human cultures) and an individual formalisation (which consists merely of far longer repetition of the shaking).

We think that a number of mannerisms are in origin *inhibited intention movements* of *exploratory behaviour*, often belonging to a much younger stage of development. For instance, 'hand regard' (Richer) – holding the hand(s) in front of the face and gazing more or less at it, often moving the hand(s) slowly – strikes us merely as abnormal because (a) it is done by a child much older than the baby in his pram or cradle (who does a lot of this early visual exploration); and (b) the eyes often do not actually look at the hand – a type of formalisation (loss of orientation) which is a very common feature of many mannerisms.

Some of the various ways in which autistic children can touch or tap objects briefly but repeatedly or near-endlessly seem to us to be formalised forms of incipient exploration by touch. Whereas a normal child will touch a large number of unfamiliar objects, and after a few touches begin to handle them and perhaps use them for a thorough exploration and even for building, an autistic child goes no further than the first, for him daring, step of just touching. While the normal child will use the exploratory behaviour for gathering all kinds of information about the object, the autistic child seems to learn little or nothing from this incipient mere-touch, and, not daring to carry his explorations further, becomes 'hooked' on tapping the same (by now familiar) object time and again, so forming a 'senseless' mannerism. Knowledge of the passing stages of exploration in normal, very young children allows one to recognise quite a number of such infantile exploratory movements, always consisting of an intention movement followed by withdrawal. For instance 'finger/object in mouth' (Richer) reminds one of the early stages of oral exploration so common in babies; some autists also sniff a great deal, for instance at rubber objects, and get stuck at this stage for weeks or months on end; the spinning of objects is obviously likewise a manipulating movement that has got stuck and has become a tension-expressing mannerism. Because an autist hates venturing far afield, many mannerisms also develop from infantile self-exploratory movements. If these offer in addition a powerful reward, such as the manipulation of the genitals, the autist becomes a compulsory masturbator. The range of inhibited, incomplete and end-lessly repeated locomotion and exploratory movements that develop into mannerisms is indeed very large, even though they are almost invariably done with a few familiar objects or parts of the child's own body.

An intention movement which we have so far not seen mentioned in the literature but have observed in several autistic children is the 'spoon tongue'. The lips are slightly parted and the tip of the tongue protrudes in a special way, assuming the shape of a spoon: the sides are curled up and *so is the tip* – a tongue position that we ourselves are unable to copy any more. We found however that this tongue 'posture' is typical in babies in the brief moment when they are put to the breast, just before they actually get hold of the mother's nipple with their lips. This preparation for taking the nipple in the mouth is done only centimetres from the breast, at the very last moment, and so is not easily seen by the nursing mother herself. This normally brief, fleeting intention movement, seen only in babies of the suckling stage, is retained, 'frozen', in some autists and so has become a typically stereotyped, in origin juvenile, behaviour that has been retained. This is another example of the value of comparing autistic behaviour with normal behaviour of much younger children than the autist under observation.

Tension postures
We know a number of forms of autistic behaviour in which the intention movements of the two aroused behaviour systems are not shown in alter-nation but, like the upright posture of gulls or the simultaneous forward-backward swimming movements of the different fins of fish, are com-bined in a tension posture which is a mosaic of 'frozen', simultaneously

performed movements. The most common example is the *overall muscle tension* often shown by autistic children. We have obtained some very revealing information about this from an 'Alexander teacher' (a kind of teacher–therapist whose finger tips are, as part of her particular skill, specialised in localising muscle tensions) who had a series of sessions with a severely autistic and mute child (Carla) from the age of nine years whom we know personally from a number of visits spread out over years. In the beginning, the girl hardly ever allowed the teacher to touch her, but she soon accepted fleeting contacts during 'rough and tumble' play (in itself an infantile form of play). But once the teacher could make sufficient contact for exploring the state of tension of the area round the neck and head, she found that, whever the child was about to make one of her typically autistic 'moans' or other noises, her chest and throat muscles began to tense up. It seems likely that, as such a mute autist grows up, it becomes increasingly difficult for her to bring herself to speak; that this reluctance to speak or even to make non-verbal noises becomes a very deeply ingrained habit. In fact, as we know from what this child told us (in writing), this is how she herself experiences it.

As observers of autistic children have undoubtedly seen in many cases, some of them often hold their hands in a rigid, curiously bent position: the 'body' of the hand is pulled back and up, sometimes at an angle of almost 90 degrees to the arm, while the fingers are half curved inward (flexed) and held almost like claws. This posture (*'wrist bend'*, Richer) puzzled us for a long time, but as happens so often, we understood its origin when E. A. T. observed the behaviour, under certain very specific circumstances, of very young normal children. The first time E. A. T. saw this in a normal child was in a girl of 18 months who was sitting, guarded by her grandmother, in a hospital waiting room while her mother, an out-patient, was with the doctor. In the large waiting room (where more patients were present) there was a rocking chair, a toy intended for just such children. This girl began to walk up to the chair from a distance of a few metres and in doing so stretched her arm towards it. As she approached the chair she hesitated and at that moment her right hand, which was nearest the chair, had assumed the pulled-back, fingers-flexed position we knew from autistic children. The left arm was likewise lifted a little, but it was not stretched towards the chair, and it and its hand were quite relaxed. The grandmother noticed the child's hesitation, bent over and steadied the rocking chair for her. Hereupon the child's right arm relaxed, she grasped the sides of the chair, and climbed in.

As so often with this kind of observation, E. A. T. was certain that she had seen this hand position before in children of this size but had not paid attention to it. Equally typical, just the next day she saw the same happen in another small child in a similar situation, and since then she has found that it is in fact a very common hand posture. The (almost inescapable) conclusion is that the autist's rigid hand position is a tense,

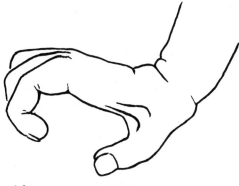

(a)

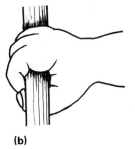

(b)

Figure 4.2 (a) The autistic ambivalent hand posture as seen, 'frozen', in a number of autistic children, very often in both hands at once, and without orientation towards any specific object. (b) The hand posture of (a) as seen, fleetingly, in its normal functional sequence in a toddler. *Top right*, ambivalent, 'hesitant' start; *centre*, on the move towards the desired object; *left*, grasping it. *Below*, the left hand, not involved in the grasping, remains relaxed.

'frozen' version of this infantile movement (Fig. 4.2). It is so difficult to recognise because you normally see it only in a toddler's hand, and in a much older hand it looks weird and is, until you have seen the infantile behaviour, almost unrecognisable. As we remarked earlier, the hand posture is clearly a direct analogue to the 'upright (threat) posture' of gulls (described above) in that it is a static 'mosaic' of components of approach and withdrawal – in this case and more precisely, of wanting to grasp something and not daring to.

Among the 'mosaic' movements must also be reckoned the *sideways orientation* of the whole body that autists often show when approaching someone. This is in animals a very common compromise attitude between facing towards and facing away, combined with locomotion. Whenever an autistic child is drawn out of his shell by skilful indirect contact-eliciting behaviour of an adult, he will walk round the room in a seemingly random way, but close observation shows often that he walks in a rather irregular but clearly discernible spiral with smaller and smaller radius; the approach component gradually wins over the hold-back component, and sooner or later the child ends by making contact with the adult from behind. The sideways orientation together with the gradual decrease of distance-keeping account for the great length of the path actually followed. One of us (E.A.T.) has demonstrated this repeatedly in various clinics with children who had never met her before but whom she usually could lure towards her in a matter of at most 15 minutes.

More easy to understand are the various *displacement activities* that 'belong' in the 'grooming' system – the behaviour that serves to maintain the body surface in good condition. Best known, and shown not only by children but also by adults, are the various skin-scratching movements, and also nail biting (which probably evolved in a world still without knives or scissors as the natural nail-trimming behaviour). A well known, disturbing aspect of these movements is that, to a minor extent in normal, simply nervous or tense people, but excessively in autistic children, they are carried on to the point of self-mutilation. The autistic child who either scratches himself or bites his fingers to the point of serious self-damage behaves as if he does not feel the pain caused by the damage; this seems to be one out of many examples of 'cut-off', of ignoring sensory input. It may be that some of these movements develop this self-mutilating aspect as a consequence of an admixture of a degree of redirected aggression; aggression elicited by frustration, or humiliation (often unwittingly inflicted by adults, for instance when they speak in a derogatory way within the child's hearing) and which, since the child does not dare attack the person concerned or an unfamiliar object, he directs against himself. This is only one example of the frequent phenomenon of two or even more expressions of the conflict or the frustration fusing into what we see as one single behaviour. We have more than a suspicion that head-banging and perhaps 'back bang' (Richer) and similar movements may well take their origin in redirected aggression or perhaps (inhibited) defence of the 'cornered animal' type.

Thus the 'self-destructive' behaviour known in so many autistic children may have a variety of causes. Displacement scratching at the ears may often result in sore patches and open wounds. Another quite common form of self-damaging behaviour such as biting a finger till blood is drawn seems to us more likely to be a self-directed form of aggression, analogous to a normal person's biting his or her lower lip.

Autists who are not quite mute but have a limited, though largely 'negativistic' vocabulary, may, when put under social pressure, utter what can only be called 'verbal stereotypies', which sound as if the needle of a gramophone has got stuck in a groove. We give an example in note 25.

Not all consequences of the conflict state lead necessarily to overt movement. The reported fact that autists often show electroencephalogram patterns that point to *over-arousal* (Hutt & Hutt – see Ch. 3, note 25) likewise fits into the picture. Research on animals suggests that over-arousal occurs as a consequence of a motivational conflict rather than, as Hutt seemed to suggest for autistic children, as the central cause of the autistic syndrome. The former hypothesis would fit in better with the other known aspects of autism, whereas the weakness of the latter idea is that, while it would make the occurrence of 'nervous' movements such as stereotypies and sleeping difficulties understandable, it would not shed light on, for example, the speech anomalies, on overall retardation, on the 'islets of good performance', or on the avoidance of unfamiliar social and physical situations.

Furthermore our hypothesis, that the anxiety-dominated emotional imbalance is primary, seems to us to make sense of one of the most serious aspects of autism, viz. the *absence, regression or defectiveness of speech*. Far from, as for example Rutter does, considering this the core of the autistic state (which, as we said would not help us in understanding the rest of the syndrome) we submit that an autistic child does not talk because his over-anxiety and the suppression of his sociality prevent him from wanting or daring to speak. Since speech is a form of social contact, speaking is quite understandably inhibited when the entire system of social behaviour is suppressed. After all, the autist rarely if ever makes non-verbal social advances either.

This notion, that autistic children are mute because they do not want to speak rather than because there is something structurally wrong with their speaking apparatus (or because parts of the brain involved in the nervous machinery of speech are damaged), receives support from the facts that (a) the occasional bits of speech that autists do produce can (unless taught to them by most forms of speech therapy!) be highly competent, and that (b) mute autists who recover often reveal a surprisingly good command of language.

We need not elaborate again the fact – one that has long been ignored in the literature – that autists usually have a very good *understanding* of speech; this too can be checked by anyone. What does support our hypothesis is that autists who recover emotionally need not really have any speech therapy as such (although certain non-intrusive forms of help can speed up the emergence of speech), but begin to speak 'of their own accord'. We shall discuss this in more detail in Chapters 6 and 9.

Another source of information about this and other aspects of the autistic condition are the reports of children who have recovered and whose retrospective statements must not be entirely ignored; and, even more interesting, the written testimonies that some seriously autistic children have given their tutors. We are personally in occasional contact with two mute autistic girls, one of 12, the other 17 years of age (Carla), who are both not only accomplished readers (in more than one language!) but who also write and/or use the typewriter. One of the things that crops up time and again in their writings is the excellent understanding of all that is and has been said in their hearing; and of deep resentment at being treated as if they cannot understand speech. We refrain here from discussing these two children in more detail; we have been assured that their histories will later be fully written up.

The non-development or poor development of speech further fits in with a much more general aspect of autism, viz. the *overall retardation* of autistic children. In order to understand this, we have to know how most children normally acquire the knowledge and skills they do. As we described earlier, children learn only a small part of knowledge and skills from deliberate instruction by adults. The over-emphasis on this form of learning is a fairly recent cultural phenomenon. As we have said already, much basic knowledge and many skills are developed during playful activities, by which children learn a lot from observing others, from practising for themselves, and from exploratory play. Now, if over-timidity or fearfulness suppresses both socialisation and exploration, it is not only understandable, it is to be *expected* that autistic children fail to learn an enormous amount that normal children learn during normal play. In fact, it is a near-miracle that in spite of their enormous emotional handicap, many autists teach themselves so *much*! When one investigates in detail what such children learn to do and what they do not learn, one discoveres an interesting rule: they learn on the whole a number of things that they can do without venturing out, without even their hands venturing away from their own body, and without requiring instructions by adults.[26] There is a remarkable correspondence between the inhibiting of social and exploratory behaviour and what is not learnt. If this simple fact is remembered when encountering any particular child, unique as he may be in detail, the *'islets of good* (and even excellent) *performance'* are easily understood. For example, musical children who have the good fortune to have access to a gramophone will, however autistic and clumsy they may be in other things, be able to place the needle in the groove with astounding accuracy and delicacy. A similarly interpretation seems valid for the drawing achievements of Nadia, the musical abilities of Joe Carter, the writing and reading skills of others, mathematical talents etc., which will be discussed in Chapter 9.

In this type of activity, many autistic children become the *opposite* of retarded, and this has, we suggest, to do not *only* with their concentration of effort and time on the relatively few activities on which they can safely indulge, but also with the powerful rewarding feedback which they receive when they are not distracted by having had to venture out too far, or irritated and humiliated by social disapproval, or even, paradoxically, by too much praise, which is often offensive by being given in a condescending way – like all other children, autists are entitled to respect for their dignity. This too will be discussed in more detail in Chapter 9.

The skilful behaviours of which autists are capable are as a rule rarely shown, viz. exclusively during the rare times and in the rare situations in which they feel at ease. This is a point that deserves some reflection, for much depends on how one interprets these rare flashes of competence. Much of the interpretation of autism depends on whether one attaches more value to the 'islets of good performance' or, conversely, to the usual overall poor performance of the child. Contrary to what many experts, and in particular neurologists, assume, we are convinced that the occasional good performance suggests very strongly that poor perfor-mance is not caused by defects in the executive mechanisms responsible for behaviour but that a deep, in our view 'emotional', malfunction pre-vents the 'deployment' of in themselves healthy 'behaviour equipment'. This view receives support from the fact that, when an autist has the good fortune to recover, he rarely has to learn his skills from scratch; while he may run through developmental phases, emotional and intellectual, that belong to a much younger age than his physical age, he can behave more capably than his initial clumsiness led one to expect.

Of course, the longer a child has been autistic, the more he lags behind. If or when he then begins to recover, he will not only have to unlearn a number of abnormal behaviours but will also have to go through the many social and exploratory activities that he has missed out on; as we shall discuss in more detail in Chapters 6 and 9, this has to be taken into account (and can also be used for monitoring a child's progress) during attempts at curing.

Closely related to the refusal to speak and its consequences is the habit of so many autistic children to respond to social approaches or even the mere presence of others by assuming a *'poker face'* and even a *'poker body'*. This very striking (and for caregivers very frustrating) behaviour is in our opinion an expression of the tendency and ability of autistic children alluded to before, viz. to avoid not only social contact itself, but to refuse to make movements that might be construed by others as expressing a willingness towards social contact, and so could lead to approaches by others that the child does not want. The poker behaviour of autists is in our view in essence a ploy, one out of many, to protect themselves from social contacts.[27]

Finally, one may ask whether autistic children show, at least on occasion, the equivalents of the category of conflict behaviour that we know from animals as *protean behaviour*. In our view there is little doubt that the tantrums in their worst form are just that. Like many other cases of protean behaviour they are shown when the child has an extremely strong wish to escape yet cannot do so (this is not true of all tantrums, because many autists learn soon that by faking a tantrum – and even a 'seizure'! – they can get their way). Also the form of an intense tantrum is as irregular, as 'systematically unpredictable' as protean behaviour in animals.

We repeat here that in our view there is a close relation between such tantrums and the 'fits' or 'seizures' that resemble and grade into 'true' epileptic fits in so many autistic children. Our interpretation of this is that children that have a somatic, 'organic' predisposition towards epilepsis will be likely to develop seizures in circumstances where other autistic (and normal) children throw a panic tantrum. We personally know one child fairly well who had frequent epileptic fits whenever she had been frustrated, unhappy or humiliated and who stopped getting such fits, or showed at the most brief 'startles' when she was treated, with considerable success, by the method to be described later, of forced holding by the mother (a therapy developed by Dr Martha Welch of New York which, as we shall describe, results in real cures through the re-establishment of an emotional bond between the child and his mother).

A few words may be added about aspects of retarded development that are at first glance not so easily recognised because most observers are not really informed about the normal development of children's behaviour. For instance, *walking on tiptoe*, so often shown by autists, can be observed as a passing and often very short phase in children who, a little further advanced than 'toddlers' are perfecting in a kind of exploring way the details of locomotory control. It may well be that there are children who skip this phase, but we doubt it. Tiptoe walking has one other aspect: even in normal children and also adults, it is occasionally shown when they do not feel quite secure; this can be done quite unconsciously. Other aspects of retarded behaviour are, in the domain of speech, the well known but ill understood *echolalia* and the so-called *pronoun reversal*, of which in our opinion the literature on autism makes far too much.[28] Echolalia is, in our experience, a phase of normal speech development, and every normal child goes through a period in which, when switching from 'Andrew wants this or that' to 'I want this or that', he uses 'you want this or that'. It would in fact be surprising if a normal child did not now and then reverse his pronouns, because he learns speech after all to such a great extent from mimicking the speech of adults (from echolalia in fact) and it takes quite an intellectual achievement to cotton on to the fact that when the adult says 'I' he means what the child would have to call 'you'. What does distinguish autists from normal children is that they get stuck, for long or for ever, in the phases of echolalia and/or pronoun reversal – again a difference of degree between normal and autistic.

Although, as we said before, this list of autistic behaviour is not complete, we believe that we can claim that our way of trying to discover the origin of so much seemingly senseless, often 'bizarre' behaviour of autistic children leads to results that do make sense in terms of our hypothesis. There is certainly good reason to predict that further study will show that all autistic behaviour fits in with the idea of the primacy of an anxiety-dominated emotional conflict, which forces the child to make movements of some kind, in particular the types or movements that we know from many animals in similar conditions. The 'senselessness' of so much autistic behaviour seems to be due to formalisations of several types, to the overall retardation of autistic children, and in part to the cunning ways in which such children succeed in not inviting social contact, an aim in which they often succeed so very well. In other words, 'senseless' or 'functionless' behaviour often serves this negative function so well that we adults are literally 'conned' into leaving the child alone.

RECONSIDERATION OF O'GORMAN'S DIAGNOSTIC POINTS

Because it will be helpful to see once more *in concreto* how our analysis applies to the syndrome as we have characterised it in Chapter 2, we shall now return to O'Gorman's list of diagnostic points (even though it now seems clear that they are not very logically arranged) and check whether and how our hypothesis can make sense out of the various symptoms. This will inevitably entail a certain amount of repetition, but experience has shown us that some readers prefer this slightly different approach to our earlier, more abstract argumentation, and the issue is so important that it deserves to be discussed from a variety of angles.

(1) 'Withdrawal from, or failure to become involved with, reality . . . etc.'

This is of course substantiated by innumerable facts but, as we have seen, it can be specified a little: the children withdraw from persons and situations that are, *to them* (with their pathologically over-sensitised anxiety and their consequent failure to learn from exploration), *unfamiliar*. The term 'reality', however, is neither helpful nor completely true: most autistic children do not withdraw from, for example, their own parents as long as they leave them alone; nor from their preferred room or corner in the room, and certainly not from, for instance, their special toys, or a comforter, etc. – most autists do have some exceptionally strong ties with 'reality'. It is with (part of) the reality *as we see it* that autistic children do not become involved.

(2) 'Serious intellectual retardation with islets of higher, or nearly normal, or exceptional intellectual function or skills.' Again, we can now make a more specific and more plausible amendment. As we have seen, the retardation concerns those aspects of the autist's development which in a normal child develop as a consequence of social intercourse and exploration but from which an autistic child shies away. The islets of good performance always concern skills which they can learn or practice on

their own. Among those 'islets' (so different from one child to another because of different innate talents and different opportunities) are such things as expertly handling a gramophone, a radio and a television set (and learning a surprising amount from this); expertise for instance in working jigsaw puzzles, in most autists the understanding of speech, and in some even of a 'second language'; in some children reading and even writing (which they acquire by 'observational learning'); in others such high-level activities as building with blocks or Lego, composing music, and producing quite extraordinary art work. The better we get to know autistic children, the better we can understand their islets of good performance and the clearer it is that to speak of 'cognitive defects' as essential aspects of autism, let alone as the primary cause of the other symptoms, is simply not in accordance with the facts. We submit that surprisingly many autists have even *better* than normal cognitive powers, but that they choose not to use them except when they feel secure.

(3) 'Failure to acquire speech, or to maintain or improve on speech already learned, or to use what speech has already been acquired for communication' (to which we must of course add regression of speech).

The deficient speech of autists in its various forms (either no speech at all, or regression of initially developing speech) is likewise understandable, and even to be expected, once we realise that speech is a form of social contact and that, in autists, the wish for such social contact is continuously inhibited. While (as a number of recovery cases show) a surprising amount is learnt by mere listening to speech (and in some children by reading), the under-development of speech is of course exacerbated by lack of practice. The idea that these children *can*not speak as a consequence of damaged executive neuro-motor apparatus, and the suggestion, based on this, that this apparatus should be examined neurologically in mute autists, is clearly due to a misconception. Not only is such an examination in the absence of other indications unnecessary (and in view of the complexity of the speech apparatus, quite probably extremely difficult), this type of examination, like any test, is positively harmful to an autistic child.

The deficiencies of speech in those children who are not totally mute are in many respects at first glance baffling, but they become understandable when they are compared with the way in which normal children acquire speech. First of all, such 'typically autistic' behaviours as echolalia, pronoun reversal, 'negativistic' expressions (such as saying 'no' much more frequently than 'yes') and undoubtedly many other peculiarities are well known to occur in certain relatively short early phases of normal speech acquisition. Further, every interested observer can notice that fluctuations in an (autistic or normal) child's mood cause temporary, often short-lived, advances and regressions; a setback in a child's general condition makes it return to the younger stages and *vice versa*. It can even be observed quite commonly that any effort that a child has to make for a non-linguistic purpose expresses itself in a momentary backsliding into younger ways of speaking. We cannot pursue this fascinating issue in detail, but submit that a better knowledge of normal speech development can make sense out of quite a number of the allegedly 'typically autistic' aspects of speech.

(4) 'Abnormal response to one or more types of sensory stimulus (usually sound)'. (We might add: to stimuli of any other modality as well, such as visual, touch etc.)

Here again our hypothesis can provide satisfactory explanations, and we can add numerous new facts which help to throw light on this issue. Briefly, an autistic child *over*-reacts to stimuli (and not only to sounds) that are to normal children either neutral or mildly withdrawal-inducing, but that are *to an autist* much more frightening and make him withdraw, either cautiously or in veritable panic. At the same time the autistic child usually *under*-reacts (to the extent of not overtly responding at all) to all stimuli that are unfamiliar or even disagreeable to him. Again, 'unfamiliarity' applies to both the social and the physical surroundings, and the criterion is not whether *we* think the child *should* be familiar with it 'because it has seen, heard etc. it so often', but whether the *child has acted* on this repeated exposure by familiarising *himself* with the situation. For both under- and over-reacting one has to distinguish between what is familiar or unfamiliar on the basis of 'innate', non-learnt or pre-learning 'knowledge', and what is dependent on having learnt or not learnt. For instance, the general statement that an autistic child 'does not react to danger' is demonstrably untrue: autists are often very good at avoiding an abyss (e.g. when they climb onto the sill of an open window on the second or third floor) and they may withdraw promptly from an aggressive dog, or from a scolding or even merely looking parent. But the same child will fail to respond to a fast-approaching car. The point is that the latter is a thing *that has to be taught*, and as we know, an autist resists being instructed. Much of this is understandable once one knows that these children are in many respects retarded. A large number of seemingly puzzling inconsistencies in their reactions to stimuli have nothing to do with damage in the sensory periphery; remember that the diagnosis 'deaf' is often made when a child does nothing but 'cut off', which is a central, motivationally controlled *refusal to respond*. Of course, whether a child is really deaf can easily be checked: if his peripheral acoustical apparatus is faulty he will respond to no sound at all, but if he is 'autistically deaf' he will fail to react to only part of the total available varieties of sound, but will react strongly and negatively to, for example, the vacuum cleaner or even to very slight sounds announcing the approach of a dreaded intruder, and also clearly but positively to, for example, bird song outside, or to laughter, or to the sound of a sweet being unwrapped behind his back.

Of course, the painstaking research that is being done on perception by autistic children (Hermelin and others) will one day become valuable and understandable as part of the overall syndrome, but this will only happen if perceptual peculiarities of autistic children as revealed by tests are seen in their proper perspective, viz. (i) as possible consequences rather than causes of the autistic emotional imbalance and its secondary consequences; and (ii) as peculiar to the test situation in which, as we have seen, many children underperform because they are cowed or hostile.

(5) 'Gross and sustained exhibition of mannerisms and peculiarities of movement, including immobility and hyperkinesis . . . etc.' About this we need say little more than we have done already; our main text explains sufficiently that these are due initially to immediate expressions of conflict (basically non-learnt, but elaborated and 'formalised' by personal habit formation, which leads to the development of different stereotypies by different children). The formalisation can go so far that we do not easily recognise the origin of the stereotypy, and merely see that it is 'bizarre' and 'without function'. We hope that the few examples we have given of the tracing of such origins will encourage others to study other, as yet still merely bizarre, stereotypies and either confirm, expand or replace our interpretations.

(6) 'Pathological resistance to change' ('adherence to sameness' of other authors).

This again is not only understandable, but demanded by our hypothesis. O'Gorman mentions four types of this, on which we comment as follows.

(a) 'Insistence on observance of rituals in the patient's own behaviour or in those around him.'

Rituals, like familiar environments, are reassuring. Many children want a certain amount of order and ritual, e.g. the reading of a bed-time story, meals at certain times etc. The autist in his resistance against change is again different only in degree. He can, by being mismanaged (e.g. by being 'humoured' too much) become a 'super-ritualist', an extreme 'stickler for (his) protocol'. This cannot (nor need it) be tolerated; how to cope with this will be discussed in Chapters 6 and 9.

(b) 'Pathological attachment to the same surroundings, equipment etc.'

In general terms, these can best be understood as mis-(re-)directed socialisation, which becomes both exaggerated and narrow because, to an autist, so few objects are available that are not frightening; and yet, as we have seen, even an autist very much *wants* to form attachments. The misdirection is of course the consequence of the inhibition of the normal social response. It is not rare for autists to become strongly attached to a pet; among dogs, boxers are said to exert a powerful attraction to autists.

(c) 'Excessive preoccupation with particular objects . . . without regard to their accepted functions' ('obsessions' in the terminology of other authors).

The high arousal caused by the neurotic conflict drives an autistic child on occasions towards over-activity. But here again: so few non-frightening opportunities, so few outlets for this urge are available, that the child is forced to occupy himself with those few, secure situations or objects presented. He dares perform so few activities that he performs the few 'safe' ones again and again; he becomes 'obsessed' not only with objects but also with these movements. Incidentally, it is inconsistent not to call a chain smoker 'obsessed' with cigarettes, or not to call a house-proud housewife 'obsessed' – many normal children and adults have equally 'bizarre' obsessions as autists. As so often, when we assume that these 'obsessions' of autists are invariably abnormal, we measure with two yardsticks.

(d) 'Severe anger or terror or excitement, or increased withdrawal, when the sameness of the environment is threatened (e.g. by strangers)' (The 'temper tantrums' of other authors).

When pressed, an autistic child readily throws a 'temper tantrum'. As we have explained, these are very often not 'temper' but 'panic' tantrums. Real 'temper' tantrums, in which the child takes the initiative in order to get his way, develop as a consequence of first giving in to his whims, then – inconsistently – trying to withold consent. As we mentioned above, some of such 'spoilt autists' have their whole family dance attendance to their most fantastic whims. When such 'tantrums' develop into 'seizures' and assume the character of epileptic fits, doctors are inclined to look for 'physiological' non-psychogenic aberrations. Although we realise of course that epilepsy is due to multiple causation, we want to stress once more that epileptic seizures in autistic children need not point to serious physiological dysfunctions, but may be largely the effect of the motivational conflict state; they can disappear entirely if and when the basic emotional imbalance recovers.

Concluding, it seems clear to us that the assumption that the autistic condition is primarily an anxiety-dominated emotional imbalance makes quite good sense when applied to the various symptoms, provided we recognise the many secondary developments of this initial imbalance as such.

Conclusion

Despite the condensed form in which we have presented our methods of study and our hypothesis about the nature of the autistic state, we hope to have made it clear that the ethological approach to autism leads to an overall picture that, however simplified it still may be, makes sense and has internal coherence. We emphasise that this is not because we have presented so many new facts (although a number of our facts had not hitherto been recorded), but because we have looked at the facts and marshalled them according to a type of approach that, although it has already proved its value in animal ethology, has so far not been applied as stringently or as comprehensively in child psychiatry. (Pioneering ethological work in children had been carried out much earlier, initially by J. B. Bowlby, M. Ainsworth and others, later with special reference to autism by S. J. and C. Hutt, and recently by J. M. Richer; and studies of normal child development are now appearing at a rapidly growing rate.[29])

The picture we present is in essence simple and straightforward: due to factors that we shall discuss in our next chapter, autistic children are primarily suffering from a motivational (emotional) imbalance, in which social avoidance and, as its corollary, avoidance of unfamiliar situations and routines dominate. Instead of playing a useful and passing part in every encounter, such avoidance has become almost permanent and suppresses the child's readiness, indeed its keen and vital urge, to form social bonds and to explore the outside world. This conclusion is based on the fact that the observable behaviour (including the absence of certain responses) is clearly made up of expressions of withdrawal (from persons and situations), expressions of its opposite – approach (likewise both social and exploratory) – and expressions of the conflict between these two strongly aroused motivations that mutually inhibit each other. The picture is complicated because the longer the child has been following this deviant course, the further his autistic state develops and the less well he fits in a normal society. In this chapter we have mentioned only those aspects of the development of the autistic condition (notably formalisation and retardation) that were necessary for our interpretation of 'being autistic' at various stages in this development; in the next chapter we shall discuss more of these secondary aspects of autism as part of the aetiology of the disorder.

We have to emphasise that we do not want to claim that *all* children who have been labelled 'autistic' necessarily suffer from the condition we have described here. It remains quite possible that there are children who show a syndrome similar or even identical to the one we have dealt with but whose internal condition is different. We cannot know for certain, but in our opinion such children must be extremely rare. Conversely, however, it seems to us quite possible, and even likely, that there are many children who suffer from a very similar emotional disturbance, but who express it in a syndrome that happens not to be called 'autistic'; we shall return to this problem in the next chapter.

We must also stress once more that, while we claim that the anxiety-dominated emotional imbalance does carry in its wake the many malfunctions that are characteristic of autistic children, we do not know the link, the details of the malfunctioning mechanisms that determine *why* and how the emotional imbalance has these autistic effects. We merely claim that recognising the emotional foundation of autism will guide future research into more profitable directions. We still have a long way to go before we can even come near to a 'full' explanation.

Finally, there are children who suffer not merely from autism but have other abnormalities as well. As we hope to show in the next chapter, there are at least sometimes connections between two such seemingly unrelated conditions. As we said, we realise that at the present stage of psychiatric research a hypothesis cannot be rigidly 'proved' or 'refuted'. We present it as, in our opinion, the most plausible overall interpretation, in which quite a number of reported findings, that at the moment are isolated parts of information that cannot yet be placed in context, may well later be found to fall into place. At any rate, we trust that our presentation may make other workers at least attempt to show either that their facts are in accordance with our views, or that they cannot be reconciled with them, and if not, why not. Our understanding of autism can grow only if we enter into a genuine dialogue.

Notes and references

1 Hutt, S. J. and C. Hutt 1970. In *Direct observation and measurement of behaviour*, 147. Springfield, Ill.: Charles C. Thomas.
2 Indications of the existence of an anxiety-dominated motivational conflict, in which approach is a component, can be found scattered throughout the literature – see not only Hutt and Hutt (1970) but also the many case histories in books such as Bettelheim (see Ch. 2, note 7) and in monographs (see Ch. 9).
3 A minor semantic correction is required: strictly speaking 'gaze aversion' refers to the subject who is responding negatively to *being looked at* by another person, while 'gaze averting' describes the subject's own *turning his eyes away* from somebody. As a rule, autistic children show avoidance when being looked at and avert their eyes from a variety of outside objects, including staring or even smiling persons.
4 Chance, M. R. A. 1962. An interpretation of some agonistic postures; the role of 'cut-off' acts and postures. *Symp. Zool Soc. Lond.* **8**, 71–89.
5 The following is one of our many experiences on this issue. A mother was shopping in a department store with her (very mildly) autistic son of three and a half years and her little daughter of two years, who was held on reins. Suddenly the boy had disappeared. After a frantic search he was found three storeys down listening to gramophone records that were being tried out. Though herself a pianist, the mother had not heard the music from where she was. Later, at school, this boy was judged to be deaf!
6 See our quotation from Ornitz (Ch. 5) about autistic children often being frightened of the vacuum cleaner.
7 The terms 'aggression' and 'aggressive' are often loosely used; most higher animals, and Man, have more than one form of aggression, each with its own function, and quite possibly with different causations. Much of the debate about the validity of Lorenz's book – *On aggression* (1966, London: Methuen) – arose not only from his claim that Man's aggressiveness is 'innate' and 'spontaneous' but also from the ignorance of many critics about the diversity of forms of aggressive behaviour. See also Tinbergen, N. 1981. On the history of war. In Valzelli, I and I. Morgese (eds), 1981. *Proceedings of the Conf. on Aggression and Violence: a psychobiological and clinical approach*, 31–9. St Vincent: Edizioni St Vincent.

8   The most relevant and perceptive work on this issue is that of J. M. Richer, see his: The partial noncommunication of culture to autistic children – an application of human ethology. In Rutter, M. and E. Schopler 1978 (see Ch. 1, note 4), 47–61.

9   See Chapter 3, note 24.

10 The ethological literature abounds with examples of the fruitfulness of this approach to the task of 'finding the function (or selective advantage)' of behaviour. Two approaches are used: one is to start from observed *behaviour* and ask 'what is its use?'; the other is to trace the behaviour that must have caused an observed *effect*. For examples of the former, see:
    Tinbergen, N. *The animal in its world* (mentioned in Ch. 3, note 7);
    The other is best illustrated by Von Frisch's famous work on the function (and causes) of the honey bees' 'dances':
    Von Frisch, K. 1967. *The dance language and orientation of bees*. Cambridge, Mass.: Belknap Press.
    This work started when Von Frisch observed that when a rich food source was visited by one bee, large numbers began to visit this particular source soon afterwards, which meant that the first visitor *must* have communicated with these followers in some way.

11 About 'food fads' and a way of treating them, see:
    Clancy, H. and G. M. McBride 1969. The autistic process and its treatment. *J. Child Psychol. Psychiat.* **10**, 233–44.

12 We have described this more fully in Tinbergen, E. A. and N. Tinbergen 1972 (see Ch. 1, note 8). Compare also the behaviour of good teachers such as Hedda and Miss Jane described in Axline's *Dibs*, (see Ch. 3, note 8) p. 11.
    For those who are alert to signs of approach behaviour, they are surprisingly obvious and the literature, especially the case histories written by 'laymen', abound with examples.

13 We refer again to Hutt, C. and S. J. Hutt in their *Behaviour studies in psychiatry* (1970) (see Ch. 3, note 25), p. 186.
    The following describes the kind of observation that can be made almost daily in, for instance, play schools, provided one refrains from interfering too much with the children. E. A. once spent 45 minutes observing a boy (aged, as she was told later, four years) whom we shall call John, who had been accepted in a normal play school even though he had all the characteristics of a relatively mild autist. He had not been officially examined or diagnosed. He was not totally mute, but during the first half hour or so spoke to nobody and avoided or ignored the other children and the observer. E. A. was later told that John's mother had, after her husband had left her, gone through a period of deep depression and had only just resumed taking John to and from school.
    When the observation began, the children just started to enter the school. All of them soon settled in the classroom, which was approximately 9 metres long and 5 metres wide, with tables along both sides and a central aisle, and in the adjoining playroom, to which an open door gave access. E. A. was sitting at one end, near this door; at the other end was a rocking horse, on which John climbed even before he had been relieved of his coat. The children moved about freely, although it was soon obvious that they were used to a certain degree of routine and discipline. One of the teachers helped John to take off his coat and talked to him in a friendly way, which John tolerated without replying and without looking at the teacher's face. He held, clutched in his hands, a piece of wood, to which he held on even while his coat was taken off. This done, he immediately resumed his rocking on the horse, and the teacher left him to himself. None of the other children took any notice of him.
    After about five minutes John climbed down from his horse and, still clutching his piece of wood, made some hesitant steps down the aisle in the direction of the playroom door, but stopped soon and hurried back to the horse to mount it. During

the next half hour he repeated these sorties, going a little further every time, but always returning to the horse, though gradually in a less frantic way than at first. Towards the end of the half hour, he stopped mounting the horse; he just stood next to it for a while.

When at long last he passed E. A., seemingly ignoring her, he reached the playroom door and stood there for some time, looking in; then he returned once more to his horse. This time he put down his piece of wood, carefully and lovingly, next to the horse and, with a few backward glances at it, started on a new excursion towards the playroom. Returning from such trips several times, he would every time look at the wood and pat it before setting out again. Each sortie lasted a little longer than the previous ones and he behaved in a less hesitant manner. Not far from E. A., at a desk on the other side of the aisle, a boy was making, in a hurried and compulsive way, parcel after parcel of crumpled-up paper, which he tied with a string, then setting out to try to find someone to give the parcel to. The children approached by him accepted his gift without a glance and put it down; no one opened his parcel; they were obviously used to his routine.

When, on his next trip to the playroom, John passed this boy he just happened to have a parcel ready, and he held it out to John. John came to a dead stop, as if dumbfounded, took the parcel in his hands and said, loudly and clearly, 'For me?' The parcel maker, already busy with the next one, simply nodded, whereupon John ran back to his horse where he put the parcel down next to his piece of wood.

When next he passed E. A., he stopped near her and, without looking at her, began to tell her, in a mumbling way, what had happened. She could hardly make out what he said, but his gestures and his looking at the parcel maker and at his horse left no doubt as to what he was speaking about. Having told his story, John took a painting easel nearest to E. A. and began to paint, his back towards her, but looking at her briefly now and then and talking, again indistinctly and unintelligibly, but clearly addressing her. Soon after this, the play school routine put an end to the sequence and John joined the rest of the children for some communical activity.

14 This point has been worked out in some detail by Tinbergen, N. 1975. The importance of being playful. *Times Educ. Suppl.* 10 January (reprinted in brochure form by The British Association for Early Childhood Education, Montgomery Hall, Kennington Oval, London SE11 5SW).

15 This dependence of exploration on having a firm attachment to a mother, who acts as a secure home base and so supplies a 'security umbrella', has also been described and analysed in rhesus monkeys – see, for instance, Hinde, R. A. 1974. *Biological bases of human social behaviour,* 185–9. New York: McGraw-Hill. A key sentence is 'Fear of novelty and of strangers could in principle well bring an end to the infant's behaviour' (p. 188). (The social behaviour of rhesus monkeys is in many respects convergent to that of Man.) See also Anderson, J. W. 1972. Attachment behaviour out of doors. In Blurton-Jones, N. (Ch. 3, note 10), pp. 199–217.

16 See note 13 above. Also Tinbergen and Tinbergen 1972; and, for a beautiful example, Axline's *Dibs,* p. 62.

17 See Chapter 2, note 7.

18 See Chapter 1, note 8.

19 Morris, D. 1977. *Manwatching* (see Ch. 3, note 11), p. 8.

20 Jones, F. H., J. Q. Simmons and F. Frankel 1974. An extinction procedure for eliminating self-destructive behavior in a 9-year-old autistic girl. *J. Aut. Childhd Schizophrenia* **4**, 241–51.

21 Holzapfel, M. 1938. Ueber Bewegungsstereotypien bei gehaltenen Säugern I and II. *Z. Tierpsychol.* **2**, 46–72; and III (1939) *Zool. Garten* **10**, 184–93.

22 See Chapter 3, note 31.

23 Richer, J. M. 1979. Human ethology and mental handicap. In *Psychiatry and mental handicap,* F. E. James and P. Snaith (eds), 103–113. London: Gaskell.

24   This boy was doing this (at school) for long periods, in fact practically incessantly when he was not engaged in such specific activities as eating, climbing a rack and a few others.

25   It is often emphasised that those autistic children who are not completely mute do still not use their speech 'for communicative purposes'. We believe that such 'non-communicative speech' too can be understood if we consider social avoidance to be the core of the autistic state. We have listened carefully to reports on an autistic boy of approximately 10 years of age, and have studied tapes of long conversations between him and one of his teachers. This boy's islet of good performance was his ability to design and construct (up to a point) various kinds of fancy machinery. He could talk fairly sensibly about his plans and about some other subjects, but had a standard, and in our view revealing, sequence of reactions when his teacher pressed him for answers which (because they had touched his anxieties) he was unwilling to supply. On such occasions the boy always began by replying with a reluctant 'hmmm'; then, when pressed for a clearer answer, by saying 'I don't know' (which, though undoubtedly not a truthful answer, was a clear communication). When prodded further, he said (again communicatively) 'You must not ask me that'. When then pressed still further, he began to speak rapidly, in long series of words, about things that had largely to do with his 'work'; but this was done in a non-communicative way – at least the contents of what he said was, to his teacher, his father and to us, incomprehensible. Much of what we could hear was repetitive and spoken in a monotonous voice. In our view, this can be best described by saying that when the boy was under social pressure, his speech turned into a meaningless 'verbal stereotypy'.

A similar case has been described by M. MacCracker (1975) in *A circle of children*, p. 97 (Philadelphia: Signet), and in more detail in the book *Lovey* by the same author (1977) and same publisher. This case was, however, different from our example in that, when the tape's 'verbal stereotypy' was played back slowly, much of what this child had been saying turned out to be understandable and communicative.

The subject certainly requires more study, both for finding the origin of this kind of formalised stereotypy and for coming to a better understanding of the autistic 'cognitive-cum-language handicap'.

26   See for some examples, once more, Axline's *Dibs*, pp. 147, 153–4.

27   One of the mute autists (Carla) whom we know well and who can type (showing an exceptionally good command of English) has described to us how, during her stays in a hospital ward, she deliberately 'played dumb' so as to be considered an imbecile and so discouraging the staff from seeking contact with her.

28   An autistic child who persists in using a great deal of echolalia has clearly got stuck in the phase in which a normal child says 'you' instead of 'I' only when echoing. Axline describes in *Dibs* (on p. 43) how Dibs suddenly began to refer to himself as 'I'. See also Max's remark in the contribution by Dr Welch (App. I): 'Thank you for holding you'. We know of other examples.

In Bartak, L. and M. Rutter 1974. The use of personal pronouns by autistic children *J. Aut. Childhd Schizophrenia* **4**, 217–22, the authors report on tests designed to find out whether 'spontaneously (sic) echolaliac autistic children' would echo the personal pronoun 'I' more often than 'you' or other pronouns; they found that this was not the case. By the very nature of the tests this paper does not, of course, throw light on the use of pronouns when autistic children are not echoing specific phrases but speak 'non-echolaliacly' in a test-free situation. Quite apart from the real nature of 'pronoun reversal', echolalia is itself a normal phenomenon; only in normal children it is a passing phase and happens intermittently and less persistently than in autistic children.

29   The crucial role of the mother and of mutual mother–child attachment in the development of the child was brought to the attention of psychiatrists, psychologists and ethologists by J. Bowlby's pioneering study (1951) *Maternal care of mental*

health, Geneva: World Health Organization; London: HMSO; New York: Columbia University Press – abridged version (1965) *Child care and the growth of love,* 2nd edn. London: Penguin. This work demonstrated in particular the long-term effects of mother deprivation in early life. Other milestones in the ethological study of mother–infant relations were the publications of C. and S. J. Hutt, already referred to; papers by M. Aynsworth (referred to in Bowlby's triology *Attachment and loss* (3 volumes) 1969, 1973 and 1980, published by the Hogarth Press and the Institute of Psycho-analysis in London); various contributions by N. Blurton Jones and his collaborators (see Blurton Jones, N. G. 1976. Growing points in human ethology: another link between ethology and the social sciences? In *Growing points in ethology,* P. P. G. Bateson and R. A. Hinde (eds), 427–51. Cambridge: Cambridge University Press). In the modern literature on autism, the contributions of J. M. Richer arrive at interpretations very similar to our own, and are in several respects penetrating into more detail (e.g. see notes 8 & 23 above). We have already referred (Ch. 3, note 10) to the series of summarising paperbacks *The developing child,* edited by J. Bruner, M. Cole and B. Lloyd, in which many aspects of normal child development are explored.

5

What makes children autistic?

Introduction

When earlier we argued that it is helpful to distinguish conceptually between the autistic condition (being autistic) and its genesis in the individual (becoming autistic), we did of course not forget that autism is not really a static condition but a process, a development that deviates, or 'derails', from the 'norm' (which, of course, is itself not *identical* in all normal children but encompasses a range of developments, yet a fairly narrow range, with variations that are intuitively[1] regarded as falling within the norm). In order to understand the nature of the autistic condition, at various stages in this development, we had (in Ch. 4) to anticipate by taking into account two of the dynamic aspects that belong strictly in the present chapter, two types of change in the basic condition. First, we studied the *short-term fluctuations* in the severity of autistic behaviour that each autistic child shows, often under the demonstrable influence of fluctuations in his environment. Secondly, we had also to examine a *long-term trend*, one of consistent change. Long-term change leads either to a certain degree of recovery or (allegedly much more frequently) to a gradual deterioration of the condition, characterised by a steadily increasing degree of retardation, and a set of such severe and deep-rooted handicaps that the patient is doomed to dependence on others for the rest of his life. What we tried to do in the previous chapter was to interpret the primary autistic condition, and its short-term fluctuations, and the long-term downward trend as being characterised primarily by an anxiety-dominated emotional imbalance, by a failure to develop social bonds, and a failure in developing a state of feeling secure and self-confident. This emotional imbalance, we argued, expresses itself in (a) behaviour directly due to this conflict state (itself fluctuating all the time, with short-term ups and downs) and (b) a set of secondary, long-term consequences. It was when we discussed the 'primacy' issue and some of these changes in the basic condition that we had to overlap with the problem that we are now going to discuss: how are we to understand the aetiology, the genesis, the ontogeny of autism? We shall concentrate on two aspects of this: (a) what can set off the autistic deviation or derailment in the first place? and (b) what can cause the further deterioration that is supposed to be the inevitable sequel?

To begin with the question of the origin, we shall first consider the descriptive aspects: how and when the switch towards abnormality can be recognised and characterised. After that we shall ask, and try to answer, the question of what makes this switch occur. The ultimate aim of this attempt at understanding will of course be the practical one of controlling, perhaps even of preventing, the derailment. For this we shall have to answer such questions as: how deeply rooted is the disorder? is its course reversible or not? and if it is, how could we bring such a reversal about? This we shall discuss in Chapter 6.

Description of onset and development[2]

Although considerable numbers of case histories have been published, the knowledge we can extract from them about the onset of autism is meagre. This is not only due to the variability of the syndrome, but also to the fact that in the first years of a child's life it is extremely difficult for parents to distinguish incipient autistic trends from variations in the normal course of development; every parent knows that some children talk, or walk, early and others late; that some children are more outgoing and others more self-contained etc. Such behavioural peculiarities may occur even when the 'physical milestones' of bodily growth are passed at normal enough times. This means that even observant parents, who may, for instance, have noticed an unusual placidity (or the reverse) in their young baby, will not really begin to worry until their child is about two or three years old and still does not, for instance, stand or walk, does not babble or utter even incipient speech and also fails to develop social attachments in general, and perhaps begins to make stereotyped movements such as rocking, head shaking etc. It is only when the child begins to strike the parents as too abnormal for comfort that they will take him to a specialist, and by that time the illness is usually far advanced. Even then it is unlikely that an immediate diagnosis can be made and therapeutic action can be taken.

First of all, many family doctors are not, and cannot yet really be expected to be, fully conversant with the early signs of developing autism; and even if they have their suspicions, they may want to avoid upsetting the parents unduly and perhaps unjustifiably – reasoning, and perhaps sincerely believing, that the child 'may well grow out of it' (a belief that, as we shall see later, is indeed more often justified than is apparent in the literature on autism). Or the doctor may be reluctant to pass on the case to a psychiatrist or a social worker because he knows that this offends some parents.

Even if contact with a knowledgeable child psychiatrist is made, he too might find it difficult to make the correct diagnosis because, as we have seen, an autistic child will either shut up completely in the consulting room (or even if the strange doctor visits him at home); or he may throw a tantrum. And since these responses are not at all rare in perfectly normal children, an investigation and proper assessment of a young autistic child is often hardly possible. This again forces doctors to rely to a large extent on what the parents can tell them, often about events that have happened long before. Naturally – inevitably – such second-hand, and in addition retrospective, information is often neither reliable nor very enlightening. For these and various other reasons the confusion illustrated in Rimland's table about first and second opinions (Table 2.1, p. 8) is not at all astonishing, in fact rather to be expected.

Since information about the early phases of autism is not only important for our general understanding but also because remedial measures are likely to be more successful if started early, attempts are being made all the time to obtain such information, so that attempts at rehabilitation can be started as early as possible.

Every doctor goes about this in his own way, but the information he collects depends not only on his own approach but also very much on the perceptiveness and the reporting abilities of the parents. Perhaps the most objective method used so far is the study of 'home movies', on which the parents may unwittingly have recorded much information that may be of value to the doctor. H. N. Massie,[3] for instance, reports that he has been able to find in such films, even in the most amateurish ones, quite unmistakable relevant indications of beginning autism or other 'psychoses' (and also of certain peculiarities in the behaviour of parents or caregivers), details that had been recorded long before contact with the specialist had been established. This contact had usually not been made until the child was three to four years of age, whereas some of the films had been taken in the child's first year, even the first few months of life. Such much more reliable retrospective information has been collected by Massie for children for whom the diagnosis, given later, was either 'autism', or 'symbiotic psychosis', or 'childhood psychosis', or 'childhood schizophrenia', or 'the mixed forms' (all lumped together by Massie because 'the diagnostic distinctions made by therapists and institutions are often unclear' and are 'possibly representing different illnesses', Massie 1978, p. 30). However, this method can of course be applied only in relatively few cases, and only in affluent societies, and helpful though it is, it cannot be expected to provide massive evidence.

Nor would it be realistic, at least at the moment, to expect more than incidental information from *forward*-looking ('longitudinal') studies, starting at birth and containing enough detail, of thousands of mother–infant dyads, in the expectation of finding later that one or a few of those children became autistic; for such a study to be feasible, the incidence of autism is (fortunately) far too low, even if we take into account the evidence, to be given presently, for the conclusion that temporary autism is in reality much more common than the medical profession knows. Therefore, without underrating the value of such large-scale longitudinal studies for a variety of other purposes, we cannot expect them to contribute significantly in the near future to the study of autism.

It is not only difficult to obtain retrospective information about the child himself and his behaviour, it is even more difficult to collect relevant evidence about either the history of mental health or illness in his parents and ancestors, or about his early environment and experiences. With regard to the latter: for information about the child's early environment and experiences to be remembered and recorded, the parents and the doctor must have to be at least open-minded enough to think that such evidence might possibly be relevant, and (for reasons to be discussed later) few people believe in this possibility. We shall argue that this rejection is premature and hinders our search.[4]

We shall conduct this search in two stages, beginning by giving a brief overview of the factual information about the genesis of autism that has been collected by various investigators, including ourselves. Based partly on this, partly on observations we made in some depth on some autistic children and their families we have come to know, we shall try to find a pattern and, we hope, at least suggest an explanatory hypothesis.

On the factual, purely descriptive level, there is no doubt that while a number of autists have indeed been 'odd from birth', others derail later. According to Ornitz,[5] who has published perhaps the best review of such descriptive evidence, the most vulnerable period for becoming autistic after an initial period of normal development ends at about age 30 months. Of course, the older a child is when he becomes autistic, the more conspicuous and recognisable are the symptoms. An 'odd-from-birth' baby may have struck the mother merely by his unnatural placidity, his unco-operativeness when taken up for a feed or when put to the breast, or even his active resistance against contact (such as arching his back, screaming and kicking). Other odd-from-birth babies cry almost incessantly while they are awake (which they may be for 20 out of 24 hours); and there are also babies who go through a phase of crying followed by one of placidity. At a later stage the 'blank' eye expression and the disconcerting way of looking 'through' or past people, even the mother, appear sometimes in children who at first had been normal; stereotypies such as head shaking and various kinds of rocking movements can be seen, and speech does not develop, or regresses after a promising start – all abnormalities that are less easily overlooked or ignored than mere placidity, which is often interpreted as 'contentedness'.

Several authors have described how the syndrome changes as an autistic child grows up. To quote Ornitz verbatim: during the first half year 'the child may continue to be "undemanding" but it soon becomes apparent that he is failing to notice the coming and going of the mother. Responsive smiling does not occur or is delayed. At four or five months, the normal anticipatory response to being picked up does not occur. Often a baby who is unresponsive to toys such as a bird mobile, rattle or crib gym may be paradoxically over-reactive to sounds produced by the vacuum cleaner, the washing machine or the telephone. The earliest vocalisation – cooing and babbling – may not appear or be considerably delayed.'

During the second half year 'the baby often shows an unusual response to the introduction of solid foods . . .' he refuses 'to accept, retain, chew or swallow foods with rough texture such as chopped meats. Without intervention some autistic children remain on pureed baby food for several years.' Toys are flicked away or dropped; the 'motor milestones such as sitting, crawling, pulling to a stand and initiating walking occasionally are accelerated but are more likely to be delayed'. There is a 'wide scatter in developmental profiles'. In this second half year the baby is 'unaffectionate'. He often 'fails to show the normal eight months "stranger anxiety" . . .'. Speech may start but become lost again, and 'there is no nonverbal communication'. 'At times the autistic baby may become agitated or panicked by the same unexpected or loud sounds as those to which he is completely oblivious on other occasions. Changes in other sensory modalities . . . may also evoke distress.'

'During the second and third years, the child seeks stimulation (sic) in all sensory modalities and often engages in peculiar mannerisms which seem to provide such stimulation. For example, there may be noisy and vigorous tooth grinding or the child will scratch surfaces and listen intently to the sounds that he creates.' He will continue to look intently at his own hands and finger movements. 'The normal transient toe walking . . . may become a permanent behaviour.'[6] Numerous stereotypies appear, 'toys are ignored or used without regard to function or meaning'. Play is not imaginative and takes the form of, for example, spinning objects. The child may take the adult's hand and move it towards a desired object instead of grasping it himself.

'Most of this behaviour continues into the fourth and fifth year, after which the severe reactions to sensory stimuli and the bizarre motility patterns may abate. Then the focus of clinical attention may be the unusual speech. The child may remain mute or speech may be limited to a few inconsistently used words . . . Echolalia may be pronounced, and along with this "you" or "he" or "she" is often substituted for "I" or "me".

'After the fifth or sixth year, two types of progression of the disorder occur. Some of the children may continue to manifest most of the symptoms already described. In others there may be a gradual change in the clinical picture . . . new features develop, suggesting either alternative or secondary diagnostic considerations . . . The disturbed relating (to others) is more likely to continue beyond the sixth year . . . The same is true of the language disturbances, and if language has not been used consistently for communication by age five years, then it is extremely unlikely that more advanced speech development will ever occur. When this is the case, intellectual development remains at a standstill . . . and the child begins to look less autistic and more and more retarded.' (Ornitz 1973, pp. 23–4.)

We have quoted Ornitz at some length to show that on the one hand descriptive knowledge about the onset and course of autism is not altogether non-existent, but that on the other hand there is still a great need for more, and for more reliable, information. It is also clear that the information is not always purely descriptive but is sometimes mixed with inferences (e.g. when it is said that the child seeks 'stimulation' which is said to be provided by mannerisms) and with assessments of the prognosis (which are of course based on what treatments given to autistic children have achieved *in the past*, and which may have to be changed if and when more effective educational procedures are applied).

It seems to us a fair statement of fact to say that even at the descriptive level the picture of the early stages of autism is still far from clear; masses of details are reported, but it is difficult to discern more than the merest outline of a general story, and more reports are clearly needed.

Interpretation

DIFFERENT VIEWS

In view of the scarcity of information on the genesis of autism, it is not surprising that many authors, at least the most recent ones, declare themselves still baffled. Nor is it unexpected that, even though there are authors who have expressed more or less clearly pronounced ideas and preferences for particular views, we cannot really discern any really well defined theories; in fact no two authors seem to hold exactly the same views. Rather than try to review all the opinions expressed we could refer the reader to some summarising works, such as Ornitz (1973) (Ch. 1, note 4) and Wing (1976) (Ch. 1, note 3). But this will not be of much help, for the discussions of the various possible theories on the genesis of autism suffer from a lack of clarity. Before presenting our own views we shall therefore first try to clarify the various issues at stake.

When mapping out possible explanations, the most profitable course is to think in terms of alternatives. Although this is not always clear in the literature on autism, three such sets (each of two alternatives) are often being considered. The difficulty in judging their merits is that these three sets are not always seen as distinct from each other. Yet they are of a different nature and, if any progress is to be made, we have to see this clearly. The three sets of alternatives are as follows.

(a) The 'nature–nurture' issue. Is autism due to a genetic or 'innate' defect, or to upbringing – more exactly, to the environment in which the child has grown up – or, better expressed (for this is not really an either–or issue), *to what extent* is autism due to a genetic defect and to what extent to the early environment?

(b) A totally different issue is at stake when people speak, as many workers are now inclined to do, of an *'organic'* cause of autism. The difficulty here is not only that an 'organic' defect can be due to either a genetic or an acquired defect (i.e. that this second categorisation runs across the first one) but also that a clear conceptual alternative to 'organic' is hardly ever mentioned. We suggest that by 'organic' these workers mean 'structural' and that they think of this as something opposed to 'non-structural', i.e. to a merely 'functional' defect of an organically or structurally sound equipment or set of mechanisms. The implication contained in the use of 'organic' is that the damage is of a rather more permanent, irreparable nature than a mere, temporary malfunctioning. The difference may be illustrated by considering why in a given case a child does not come when his name is called. This 'disobedience' may be due to the fact that he is totally deaf, i.e. that his hearing equipment (ear and/or the nerves and parts of the brain that usually pass on and process auditory stimuli) is structurally defective, in which case we would call his abnormal behaviour due to an 'organic' defect. But it is just as often the case that the child does not come because he 'does not want to' – for instance because, although he hears perfectly well that he is called, he is otherwise engaged; his brain has taken the decision to ignore the sound stimulus. Most people would call this non-organic, and would consider this just one out of several kinds of temporary malfunctioning of his auditory equipment.

The confusion to which failure to distinguish the different nature of the two sets of alternatives (nature–nurture and organic–functional) can lead is that people then tend to think in terms of false opposites such as 'autism is not due to early traumatisation by the environment *but* to an organic defect'. As we said, an 'organic' defect can be due to either a genetic or an environmental agent, and so can occasional or frequent malfunctioning.

We have another objection to the term 'organic'. It says clearly what is meant only as long as we think of large structures and of gross structural damage, and usually also of such damage being of a lasting nature. But we know that even when a person is 'hearing', i.e. responding to the class of mechanical stimuli that are perceived as sound, temporary but structural changes at the microlevel, i.e. of a biochemical or biophysical nature, do occur whether the behaviour is normal or not. If we could scan the molecular events involved in the hearing tract when a child does respond and when it does not, we would find 'structurally' different processes in both cases. The distinction between form and function is of a certain practical value when we are thinking of major systems, but even there we are in reality always considering *functioning structures*. Thus the 'organic' label is for more than one reason not a very helpful one. Its use can lead to quibbles that tempt us away from the real problems involved. For instance, it is now known (and in our 1972 paper we did not have that information at our disposal and so failed to recognise it) that children whose mothers have had rubella (German measles) during their pregnancy have a slight but significantly higher chance of becoming autistic than children of mothers who have not had rubella at the critical time.[7] Such children are said to have had 'congenital rubella'. Even with this knowledge we are still far from understanding what in such cases sets off the autistic deviation. In his review of the book by Chess, Korn and Fernandez (1971) – the main experts on congenital rubella and autism – Rutter (1973) pointed out that according to the authors' information it was only those children who were born deaf who developed autism.[8] This suggests that, although the derailment in such cases is primarily 'organic', the critical link with autism could be the fact that the deafness made it more difficult for the children to affiliate with the mother, since one of the channels of communication between them was not available (we shall discuss the relevance of this later). It cannot be entirely excluded that, now that expectant mothers are likely to know that contracting rubella may harm their child in other ways, this causes them anxiety, as we shall argue further on, and we cannot rule out the possibility that this has a damaging effect even on the unborn child.

(c) Among therapists and among some research workers we have seen evidence of still another set of alternatives in their views of autism, even though this is, as far as we know, not always clearly formulated, let alone put clearly in print. This is the distinction between *'peripheral'* and *'central'*. There is a trend of opinion that ascribes autism to defective sensory perception or to 'cognitive' defects; other workers who notice the clumsy way in which autists often move either their limbs, their entire body, or their hands think that there is something wrong with the motor control of these special parts of the body, with parts of the 'motor periphery'. The logical opposite to this has nothing to do with 'nature–nurture', or with 'organic–functional'; the opposite of 'peripheral' is 'central'. We found ourselves actually at variance with such views about the peripheral base of autism when we stressed that autism is 'primarily' a matter of emotional (i.e. central) imbalance and that the peripheral signs, both perceptual and motor, often disappear when the central disturbance is remedied. We anticipated this and the previous point to some extent in our earlier chapter because our examination of the autistic 'state' overlapped to a certain extent with the present one, but we shall have to say a little more about this peripheral–central issue later on.

The fact that the three sets of alternatives are often discussed as if they belong to one group of different possibilities, and the frequent failure to mention clear alternatives to a favoured theory are the main causes of the present confusion on the vital question of 'what makes children autistic?'

It is no wonder that the more critical authors still hesitate to express a definite opinion[9] even though certain preferences are being expressed. Among them one finds the (incidentally not very illuminating) conclusion that autism is due to a 'physical disease of the brain' (Ritvo *et al.* 1976).[10] There is also a widely prevalent opinion that 'the basic handicaps of early childhood autism are produced by organic, not emotional (sic) pathology. They are not caused by the personalities of the parents, nor by their child-rearing practices.' (Wing 1976, p. 381, where the findings of the Committee that met in 1970 under the chairmanship of Leon Eisenberg are summarised).[11] This itself was a reaction (as we now know an over-reaction) to the views adhered to by psychoanalysts, and voiced in its most extreme and crude form by Bruno Bettelheim, viz. that autism is largely due to the personalities of the parents involved. This notion was originally broached by L. Kanner[12] and sometimes unkindly described by saying that parents of autistic children are 'refrigerator parents'. Clearly, bias has made its contribution to the confusion; this bias is obviously due to a mixture of detached, objective opinion and emotional involvement and prejudice.

This brief introduction demonstrates that the issue must be considered to be still wide open, so that we have to reconsider it anew. From what we wrote in the preceding chapter, it will be clear that we think of autism as primarily a functional rather than an organic affliction (even though organic aspects may be involved as the consequence of the (psychological) malfunctioning and vice versa) and that we consider it a matter of central, 'emotional', 'motivational' rather than peripheral malfunctioning. Although we shall have to return to these two aspects in what follows, our main discussion here will be concentrated on the nature–nurture issue. We shall argue that, although genetics may enter into the picture as having an influence on the vulnerability of children to autism-producing influences, the deviation is very largely due to environmental factors, and although we recognise the possibility of some organic agents such as rubella and 'minimal brain damage' (which we consider an otherwise pretty useless term), we ascribe autism mainly to the 'psychogenic' influences among these external agents.

We have to stress that this seemingly 'theoretical' discussion is of more than merely academic interest. As we shall see, our conclusions about the nature and genesis of autism are relevant to the problem of how to treat autistic children, even though empirical, trial-and-error therapeutic procedures and their results are of no less importance and may even force us to review our theoretically derived views. As it happens, we found that on the whole our 'academically' derived views conform very well with the nature of empirically found therapies.

AUTISM AND HEREDITY

The notion – admittedly no longer adhered to generally, yet hardly ever explicitly rejected – that autism may be due to a *purely* genetic defect, with whatever influences of the environment being at best secondary developments of this primary abnormality, does not in our opinion receive support from the evidence. This evidence could be of three kinds:

(a) As far as we know, there is no direct evidence of chromosomal abnormalities or other kinds of abnormal genetic equipment.

(b) Another possible source of evidence of genetic peculiarities, which is often available to students of animals and plants, could be the results of large-scale planned breeding experiments. It is not necessary to point out that such evidence is neither available nor obtainable for human beings. (If an illness is, as the expression goes, 'running in families' – which autism is not, at least as far as is known, partly because severe autists do not, or hardly ever, reproduce – this would of course not necessarily be an indication of a genetic peculiarity. Parents and children may both show the effect of a similar environment – suntans 'run' in farmers' families – or a characteristic may be passed on by tradition or example – children of teachers, doctors, farmers, miners, may follow in their parents' footsteps.)

(c) A third approach to the problem is feasible however: the comparison of identical with non-identical twins. The rationale of this is simple: if a deviation such as autism were *purely* genetic in nature, identical twins should always be *concordant*, that is, show it in equal measure. But if identical twins could be found of which one develops autism while the other grows up normally, this points to environmental contributions to the deviation. It is important to realise though that *the converse argument does not hold*: when identical twins are found to be more often concordant than non-identical twins, this need not at all indicate a purely genetic origin of autism, though it would reveal a genetic base for the *degree of vulnerability*. It has further been well documented (most clearly by J. & E. Newson 1963, 1968, 1976) that parents adjust themselves to their individual children and as a consequence treat no two of their children exactly alike.[13] But since identical twins behave more similarly than do non-identical twins (and certainly more so than children of different ages), identical twins tend to be treated more similarly (and not only by their parents) than non-identical twins. The existence of a number of pairs of concordant identical twins is therefore no indication of a purely genetic basis of autism, and it is even to be expected that, if autism were largely due to the early environment (part of which is the parents' rearing regime), a higher proportion of identical twins would be concordant than of non-identical twins.

In fact, seven pairs of identical twins are known who are discordant, i.e.

pairs of whom one was autistic and the other not (Folstein & Rutter 1978).[14] Of course these data are still meagre and evidence of this kind is bound to remain very scarce, but it has to be stressed that strictly speaking the hypothesis of a *purely* genetic cause of autism does not tolerate a *single* case of discordance among identical twins. Moreover, only four concordant autistic pairs of identical twins have been reported.

What cannot of course be denied is the possibility, indeed the likelihood, that different children are not equally vulnerable to whatever conditions may initiate autism. Just as for any other illness, so for autism some children are undoubtedly more vulnerable or predisposed than others, and since no two children (except identical twins) are genetically identical, part of this difference in vulnerability may be due to genetic differences. But since the early environment of different children, from the moment of conception on, is also different, the environment can also contribute to the differences in vulnerability, and the proportional contributions of 'nature' and 'nurture' to even these differences are not known.

All this means that, until and unless evidence to the contrary were to be found (e.g. if Folstein & Rutter's material were to turn out to be unreliable), we have to conclude that autism is unlikely to be based on a purely genetic defect. As we remarked before, this is, as far as it goes, encouraging for the prospects of curing and prevention, since damage due to genetic defects is undoubtedly more difficult to undo or prevent than damage due to environmentally induced aberrations.

As long as a purely genetic basis of autism is so unlikely, it is futile to discuss whether, if future research were after all to discover an underlying genetic defect, this would have to be considered to be of an 'organic' or a 'psychogenic' nature. As we shall see, such a discussion is far from futile when it comes to tracing possible effects of environmental aspects.

AUTISM AND EARLY ENVIRONMENT

If a genetic basis of autism is likely to be restricted to causing differences in vulnerability, we have to conclude that the responsible agents for the onset of autism are largely to be found in the environment. When re-opening the discussion about this issue (a sensitive one because 'environment', while of course not exclusively meaning 'parents' and certainly not 'mothers', does *include* them), we should like to state first of all that in our 1972 paper we may have underestimated environmental agents that have an 'organic' effect, and over-emphasised the importance of 'psychogenic' factors. While we maintain that at the moment there are no indications for *genetically* determined organic causes of autism, we do of course accept the new evidence showing that children of mothers who have had rubella during pregnancy have a greater chance of becoming autistic than have other children. However, we must see this in proportion – very few mothers of known autists have had rubella at the decisive time during their pregnancies, so the contribution made by rubella is clearly relatively small. We must not forget, as we have already said, that organic and psychogenic aspects can be related, in this case by some rubella children having been born deaf.

Before going into specific detail we have now to discuss briefly a few issues of a conceptual–terminological nature that we have not yet mentioned.

First, we feel that the use of the term 'congenital', as for instance in 'congenital rubella', is a little confusing, since (rightly or wrongly) it is taken by many to mean 'genetically determined', whereas it means no more than 'present from birth'. There was a time when it was assumed that at least behaviour that was shown immediately after birth had to be 'innate' or purely genetically determined. This justified the equation of 'congenital' with 'innate'. We know now that a child can be harmed by conditions in the womb, i.e. his (very early) environment.

Secondly, we have noticed that sensory malfunctioning, such as not responding to sounds, is often assumed to be due to defective functioning of the sensory periphery (as when an autistic child is said to be deaf) and, similarly, that motor malfunctioning (seen, for instance, when an autistic child moves his legs or hands clumsily) is thought to reveal defects in the motor periphery. As we have seen, a proper behavioural analysis shows that such forms of faulty performance are parts of a much more comprehensive syndrome and are likely to be due to a much deeper, viz. a central nervous (in fact a 'motivational', 'emotional'), malfunctioning. The degree of sensory dysfunction and of clumsiness of movement fluctuates, even in the short term, with the child's degree of fear, apprehensiveness or unwillingness. We stress this point once more because of its therapeutical implications; as we shall argue in Chapters 6 and 9, treatments have more success when they are aimed at restoring a child's emotional balance than when (as we have seen in a number of cases) they are centering on sensory stimulation as such or on the manipulation or practising of clumsily moving limbs.

Thirdly, 'neurological' evidence is often – and, we submit, rashly – interpreted as proof of structural damage. It should not be forgotten that the vast majority of 'neurological' tests carried out on such children (and on others) demonstrate no more than mal*functioning*, and that the conclusion that such malfunctioning is due to structural damage (either in the brain or in the sensory or motor periphery) is no more than an inference. To base a hypothesis of *structural* brain damage on evidence of mal*functioning* is jumping to conclusions – it is like saying that a very sleepy or a very drunk person is brain damaged. The term, now so fashionable, of 'minimal brain damage' seems to be a (clumsy) effort to gloss over this difficulty.[15]

With regard to the thesis that autism is due to 'organic' defects, we have therefore to conclude that what evidence is available suggests that, although this is obviously part of the story, it is in all probability only a minor part. (The question of whether structural abnormalities can occur *as a result* of having been autistic for a considerable time is of course a different one, not relevant to the problem of what sets off autism, although it is highly relevant to our understanding of its further development – see below.)

It is worth repeating once more that the likelihood, in our view near-certainty, that, bar possible but relatively few exceptions, gross organic defects play at best a minor part in starting off autism, has likewise hopeful implications for the therapeutic prospects, since organic deformities, while not necessarily as irreversible as genetic defects, are in many cases fairly resistant to treatment.

It is because the various notions of a purely genetic or a purely organic origin of autism fail so clearly to account fully for the onset of autism that it is necessary to re-examine the possibility of non-genetic, and in particular non-organic, psychogenic factors. As we mentioned before, this idea of a direct behavioural response to aspects of the early environment has been proposed repeatedly in the literature – tentatively by Kanner, in its most pronounced and assertive form by Bettelheim and other analysts (Ch. 2, notes 2 and 3) – but it has met with little acclaim and has occasionally been emphatically, almost vehemently, rejected. Before we consider the possibility in more detail, we must remember that many people have non-scientific, non-rational reasons for rejecting the psychogenic hypothesis. As we shall discuss in a moment, part (*though by no means all*) of the psychogenic factors *are* to do with the behaviour of the parents, in particular the mother. It is of course extremely painful to have to believe that one may have contributed to the catastrophe that has hit one's child; even if there is no question of *blame*, the awareness or even a suspicion of such a possibility inevitably gives rise to feelings of guilt. These make it emotionally almost impossible for parents of autistic children to accept the theory of a psychogenic origin of autism, even in the face of quite suggestive evidence. Not only is there such non-rational resistance against this idea particularly, and a wish for either a genetic or another accident to be at the root of autism, but parents, again quite naturally, feel that adherents of the psychogenic thesis are cruel to them. As Dr L. Wing has told us several times: 'you are hard on mothers'. When we nevertheless publish what we consider to be a good case for a mainly environmental, and mainly psychogenic, origin of autism, we do this because the children's chances of recovery – or of being protected from even becoming autistic – are enhanced by therapies derived from this insight; *and the children's interest must come first*. If we have to choose between hurting *some* mothers and refusing to rescue *many* children from the disastrous downward spiral we feel we have no choice but 'to be hard on mothers'. It must not be forgotten that whether or not a mother feels hurt by being faced with the 'psychogenic' notion depends largely on *her* – we know a number of mothers each of whom have chosen to overcome their feelings of guilt, or rather to sublimate them into making a great effort to help their child, and in a number of cases with outstanding success. Such mothers have told us of their happiness after this achievement, which they would have missed had not we, or they themselves, been 'hard'. Details of such cases will be given in Chapter 10.

The idea that direct influences on the environment on a child's behaviour might to a large extent account for the development of autism[16] occurred to us first when we found that short-term fluctuations in the behaviour of autistic as well as of normal children were not only correlated with certain changes in the environment, but could be produced at will by controlling those changes. As we discussed in the preceding chapter, we found in fact (a) that under certain, very specific circumstances, almost all normal children could show slight or even intense autistic behaviour, and (b) conversely, that severe autists could under certain circumstances behave, at least for limited periods, like normal children. Contrary to the claim of many experts on autism – that the temporary autistic behaviour of normal children (which they call 'autistiform') is irrelevant for the understanding of 'true' autism, which is often stated to be 'fundamentally different' (a claim that we find nowhere substantiated) – our experience tells us that *there is in reality a continuum*, all the way from normal, through merely 'shy' or 'timid' or 'apprehensive' children, through very mildly and less mildly autistic children, to severe autists. Yet the notion that there is a sharp distinction between 'real' autists and 'normal' children who merely behave autistically on certain occasions, is not wrong but has only limited value. The idea of a sharp dichotomy is based on various circumstances. Firstly, many child psychiatrists to whom we have talked or with whom we have corresponded have simply no idea of the (very large) numbers of 'true' autists who are never taken to the doctor and who recover under the intuitive but expert care of their exceptionally competent, almost 'supernormal' mothers (see Ch. 10). Yet in our experience such cases of successful 'do-it-yourself' treatments are common. (In fact they may well outnumber those cases that make up the official figures of 5000–6000 autistic children in Britain,[17] or approximately four per 10 000 of all children, which are more or less matched by similar figures for a number of the few other countries for which figures are available). Secondly, although there is in *very young* children a gliding continuum between normal and autistic, a dichotomy does appear, as a secondary development, between those who recover and those who enter the downward spiral and become more and more severely autistic. It is these advanced cases that the psychiatrists see.

Increasingly impressed by the short-term and passing effects of changes in the environment on the degree of autistic behaviour in both normal and autistic children, and realising that genetic and organic defects were not likely to have caused the vast majority of cases reported in the literature or known to us, we began to pay renewed attention to possible long-term effects of similar origin. This made us look once again at the early history of autistic children. For this purpose we used, as well as was possible in view of the limited reliability and completeness of the information available, data to be found scattered in the literature and, with more confidence, the evidence we had ourselves seen at first hand or could collect retrospectively from parents and others who had known individual children well, some of whom kept records, either in the form of notes or of home movies. In the course of this work we began to discern a highly interesting and in our view more than merely suggestive pattern in these histories, and the rest of this chapter will be devoted to a summarising account of what kind of conditions can, in our view, make a child autistic. For details we refer to the case histories given in Chapter 10.

As we have said, we are not the first to investigate the possible influence of early experience on autism, but earlier authors have not, in our view, looked for the relevant aspects of the environment. Nor are the procedures followed in such attempts always above criticism. For instance, when Rutter and Bartak found no significant correlation between the progress of autistic children and the type of educational regimes of the schools they attended,[18] we submit that this is hardly surprising since we know only too well that the environmental conditions that we consider relevant have little or nothing to do with how the schools are labelled. Admittedly there are great differences between the three types of schools in the social environment in which children and teachers operate, but in any kind of school or unit one can find teachers who approach children in ways which tend to aggravate autistic tendencies and those who actually contribute much to the recovery of autists under their care. We submit that this seemingly neat and easy way of approaching the problem is far too crude and unsubtle for our purpose.

Before listing the conditions in a child's early environment that can lead to autism ('autismogenic' factors) we want to make clear that we know full well that we are offering no more than fairly incomplete clinical evidence, without critically selected 'matched controls'. But this is a limitation that, at least for the present, we have to accept, and that anyway no psychiatrist has so far been able to circumvent, nor does it seem likely to us that the procedure can be significantly improved in the near future. But this does not mean that we are *entirely* without controls. However, these are not to be found in hospitals or clinics, nor are they available only to the privileged few who deal with these children professionally. *We emphasise once more that 'controls', i.e. normal children in normal families, are everywhere around us, for all to see who care to observe the human scene.* We have met quite a number of people who do this, and it is our experience that *persons with the required knowledge and understand-*

ing of the norm are more common among the non-experts than among the child psychiatrists, quite possibly because the latter concentrate so much on the mentally abnormal. (Fortunately, many paediatricians and some psychologists are now becoming quite knowledgeable too.)[19] Another point we have to make is that, of the various autismogenic factors we will specify, by no means all are necessary to make a child autistic. *For susceptible children, even a few of them can tip the balance, and these few can be quite different for different children.* Which particular set is decisive in any given case depends on the child's nature and on the conditions he happens to face (see Fig. 5.1). It must also be remembered that there may be degrees of damaging conditions and of the responses to them.

Further, we have incorporated in our list factors for which damaging effects have been clearly demonstrated together with those which are merely more or less suspect but deserve closer attention, and there may well be gaps in our list, factors which we have overlooked. Finally, we have left the question open as to what extent individual factors have to be called 'organic' or 'psychogenic'; as we said, the distinction is neither sharp nor, for the moment, very important.

We often hear the objection that many children are or have been exposed to a set of what we claim to be potentially autismogenic factors without becoming autistic. We answer this by reminding such critics of the fact that even during severe epidemics of infectious diseases such as, say, influenza, or even smallpox, large numbers of people do not catch the disease. Of course this does not prove that such diseases are not due to infection, nor that the healthy persons have not been exposed to infection; it merely shows up differences in vulnerability between persons. We discuss this aspect with regard to autism in the section where we consider which children are vulnerable.

We have to admit that the 'list of potentially autismogenic factors' that we are going to present is based on in part tentative, even intuitive rather than 'hard' evidence. Yet, short of trying to produce, in deliberate experiments, 'statistically significant' numbers of autistic children, we shall have to rely on the accumulation of 'incidental' data. So far, few people have bothered to look at the aetiology problem in our way, and the main purpose of this chapter is to urge colleagues to do so.

List of potentially autismogenic factors

We shall consider these more or less chronologically, following the development of a child.

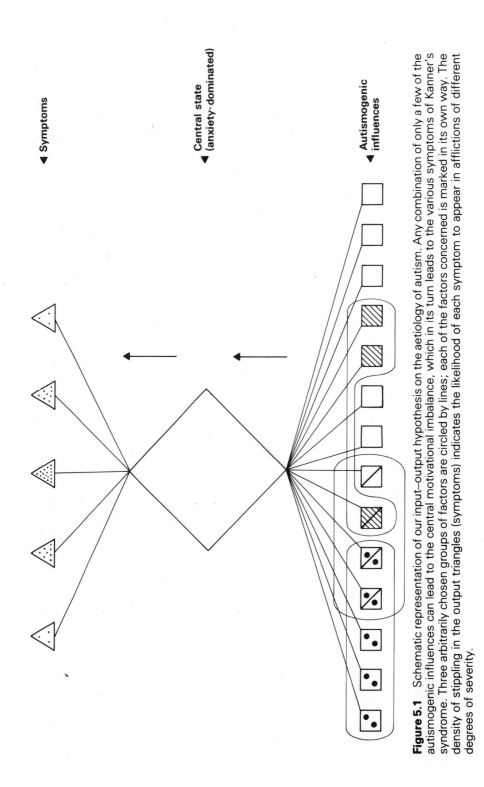

Symptoms

Central state
(anxiety- dominated)

Autismogenic
influences

Figure 5.1 Schematic representation of our input–output hypothesis on the aetiology of autism. Any combination of only a few of the autismogenic influences can lead to the central motivational imbalance, which in its turn leads to the various symptoms of Kanner's syndrome. Three arbitrarily chosen groups of factors are circled by lines; each of the factors concerned is marked in its own way. The density of stippling in the output triangles (symptoms) indicates the likelihood of each symptom to appear in afflictions of different degrees of severity.

PRENATAL INFLUENCES

Of the external factors that might predispose a child to autism, some act while the child is still in the womb. We have already mentioned rubella contracted by the mother during pregnancy. Since Chess[7] first demonstrated that among children of such mothers there are more autists than among other children, research on this has continued and sooner or later it will become clear how this effect comes about. (As we mentioned before, Rutter has pointed out that it seems to be those rubella babies who are born deaf who become autistic and, as we shall see, deafness itself may have a profound autismogenic effect – showing, incidentally, how organic and psychogenic processes can be intertwined.) It may further be relevant to remember that, in common with what is now being discovered about certain other viruses, the rubella virus can remain present, alive,[20] in a child for years after the original infection; thus a baby with congenital rubella could well remain 'under attack' for years.[21]

However, since the vast majority of mothers of autistic children have not had rubella at the relevant time, congenital rubella is clearly only one, perhaps even a minor one, of the factors involved.

It seems to us that a further search for other possible prenatal autismogenic circumstances may well produce more. A great deal begins to be known or suspected about the harmful general, somatic effects on the unborn baby of such material factors as food (more attention should certainly be given to vitamin deficiencies) ;[22] the mother's smoking or drug taking – including medically prescribed drugs – and a variety of other factors. Even less is known about possible psychological influences on the unborn baby, some of which might well in turn have 'organic' effects as well. The gaps in our knowledge of such psychological influences could well be due to a paucity of research efforts in that direction, and this again may be due to the still-lingering idea that the mind of a newborn is a 'tabula rasa' – an outdated notion which we now know to be untrue and even biologically bizarre. The fetus *in utero* is in fact now known to respond quite strikingly to a number of circumstances in his environment and is further suspected (on good grounds) to suffer noticeable after-effects of some of these after birth.[23] We even consider it quite conceivable that, for instance, the pushing and even thumping by mothers of awkwardly moving fetuses (maternal behaviour which is far from rare) might well be slightly traumatising to some babies. Similarly, it seems to us worth investigating whether depressed or anxious mothers (and mothers who report that they 'knew' from the moment of conception that 'something would be wrong with the baby'), or mothers involved in frequent violent quarrels with their husbands, or a continuously strained relationship between the parents, or a bereavement in the family, may not unsettle a baby before birth and predispose it, however slightly, to emotional imbalance. Again, such effects need not be purely psychogenic;

the accompanying humoral changes that are typical of stress could form part of the fetus's sub-optimal environment. However, we shall not press this point, but it has to be stressed that, until such questions have been further studied, firm statements to the effect that the prenatal environment has little or no autismogenic effects cannot possibly be taken seriously. Our point is that babies who are 'odd at birth' may already then be victims of non-genetic environmental conditions – for the embryo, the womb *is,* of course, the environment.

EVENTS DURING BIRTH

We are on firmer ground when we consider the effects of being born. To see these in proper perspective it may be useful to realise two points. (a) Even the most normal birth is for each child such a drastic, almost revolutionary change that it is a near-miracle, one of the great wonders of the human, indeed the mammalian, life style, that children survive this revolution unscathed and embark upon their extra-uterine life with such relative ease and indeed eagerness and zest. (b) Further, we must not forget that at least we urbanised members of modern industrialised nations have until recently been hardly aware of the artificiality of giving birth in the way that has become usual in our kind of society.[24]

At least in the upper and middle classes, certain obstetric–paediatric practices have until recently been taken rather for granted. Yet comparison with the conditions surrounding childbirth in the past might well show that modern practices, resulting in reduced infant mortality and reductions in discomfort to mothers during delivery, have not *all* been to the good, and certainly the psychological vicissitudes of the mother–infant dyad under modern conditions have been under-investigated and their influences probably underrated. Finally, the relatively scarce but important evidence that *has* come to light has not been sufficiently taken into account, at least in studies of autism.

We ourselves are neither competent nor prepared to swell our account by an attempt at an exhaustive review of the differences between more 'natural' childbirth practices and present-day procedures in hospitals and even at home in the various modern societies, but we suggest that the relation between autism and certain details of the birth of the children concerned deserves close scrutiny.[25]

We believe that, for instance, a deep *forceps delivery* may not only cause occasional though perhaps not very important bodily damage (although the head may be vulnerable), but that such a delivery might well on some occasions frighten the baby very badly. Similarly, the various manipulations by which a newborn baby is *stimulated to breathe* must be considered potentially frightening and perhaps traumatising. We further think it not impossible that, however well the baby is adapted to tolerate a certain degree and time of oxygen deprivation during birth, exceptionally long and difficult deliveries may well overstretch this tolerance and either damage the brain through *oxygen starvation*, or *frighten* the child, or both. Apart from these few obvious aspects of possible relevance to our problem, there may be a variety of others that in the present technologically minded phase of obstetrics (and indeed of society in general) may have been given insufficient attention. To mention only one: how far would maternity hospitals have gone in recent years with the application of *induction* (so as to have as many babies as possible born on weekdays between 9 a.m. and 5 p.m.) if the public had not protested?

EVENTS AFTER BIRTH[26]

Even when the birth itself has proceeded without any of these hitches, much can go wrong at later stages. Ornitz (Ch. 1, note 4) stresses that there is no doubt that children remain at risk of becoming autistic until they are 30 months old.

The first of the obstacles a mother–baby dyad has to meet presents itself immediately after birth. From the moment of birth onwards, mother and child begin to, and have to begin to, interact with each other, and this early interaction is now acknowledged as being of great psychological importance for both. We have reason to believe that certainly a *general anaesthetic*, and quite possibly some of the *local anaesthetics* that are, or in some countries were, almost routinely given to mothers in labour, may well affect the dyad significantly and so contribute towards predisposing a child to autism. It is known that some of these really quite crude chemical treatments make both mother and child 'dopey' for a certain time after the actual birth. It is now also known that it is natural for mother and child to begin interacting in a variety of ways in the first minutes, even seconds, after birth. The mother's mood becomes one of intense and almost exclusive interest in her baby, who is at first literally the centre of her universe (when given their babies immediately after birth they will stroke, kiss and pat them eagerly); from his side, the baby is for the first hour or so after birth remarkably awake and alert, is eager to make the first attempts at sucking, and is even remarkably competent in actively moving in a variety of ways that assist the mother in handling him. This reciprocal interest and activity is not of mere momentary significance: it begins to become clear that even these first minutes, certainly the first hours, of interaction have a *lasting effect* on mother and child; both partners of the dyad *learn* from such interaction; in fact each of them at the same time learns from *and* teaches the other; i.e. this early interaction is the start of *mutual programming*, a social process that leads to the growth of an increasingly complex and intimate *relationship*. All this should alert obstetricians and midwives to the need for compensatory, contact-promoting measures whenever a birth by Caesarian is necessary, in particular when the baby is premature and has to be put into an incubator.

There are indications that if this early interaction is made impossible (as it is when baby and mother are 'dopey' and as it is when the baby is taken away at once to be washed and dressed, to be returned only when the mutual, alert interest has abated and the baby's clothes prevent the mother from handling and exploring its 'appetising' naked body) the establishment of this relationship, the 'affiliation' or 'bonding', is made more difficult. We shall return to this presently, but we want to stress here that several things may 'go wrong' in these first few minutes, certainly in the first few hours, that could account for the 'placidity' or other deviant behaviour of some newborn babies, that can in turn bewilder the mother and impair affiliation in this way. Such dyads may be at risk, predisposed for, or perhaps already on the way to autism, or to another disturbed course. We must also stress once more that, although a 'dopey' mother may contribute as much as the doped baby to poor initial affiliation, no one would dream of 'blaming' the mother for this, any more than one would blame the baby. Rather, both are victims of conditions not of their making. When in what follows we will discuss some other parental autismogenic influences, we urge our readers to keep in mind this essential difference between 'having contributed to' and 'being to blame for' the illness of one's child.

Apart from being made impossible or difficult, the early interaction between mother and child can be positively converted into its opposite: a child can be made to *refuse contact*. A striking and perhaps not rare example has been described long ago by Mavis Gunther.[27] When babies have difficulties with sucking, e.g. by being unable to hold the nipple, the mother, or the nurse or the midwife, might attempt to help or force him by pressing his head against the mother's breast. Gunther describes how this may push the baby's nostrils against the mother's breast, so preventing the baby from breathing, and how this makes the baby resist. In a surprisingly short time such a baby can become conditioned *against* being put to the breast. This in turn cannot but affect the mother adversely, and for both parties the normal feeding session, which as we now know is not only vital for feeding the baby but also for the mutual bonding, becomes instead a highly upsetting occasion for struggle. Not surprisingly, this must interfere with, and even definitely predispose both against, the collaboration which is so necessary for proper bonding, on which so much of the child's further development depends. We keep emphasising this because it cannot be stressed too much that proper early affiliation is necessary for proper socialisation later and so is of vital importance for a child's future emotional and also for his intellectual development. We must remember that poor affiliation and consequently poor socialisation can affect a child's mental health in another, secondary way. It hampers not only healthy social development but, as we have said before, also, in its wake, the self-educating process that is based on *exploratory behaviour*. Since a child will explore well only when he is sheltered by the 'security umbrella' that only the safe home base – primarily his mother – provides, poor affiliation also damages the many learning processes that normally take place during exploration.

It may be thought that the seemingly subtle and minor temporary setbacks in the early stages of affiliation are unimportant because both partners will have later opportunities for catching up, and are adjustable enough to do so. Fortunately, this is often so; often these later opportunities are used properly, but only if mother and baby are capable of extra effort and only when the environment is suitable. But when, as is not rare, the mother is easily disappointed by the lack of her baby's co-operation, or when there are additional upsetting circumstances, the repeated mutual disappointment, the non-fulfillment in both partners of the *expectations* which they have of each other, all this together can have the opposite effect: instead of readjustment and compensation for early failures, both mother and child, or even only one of them, enter a self-reinforcing downward spiral; either or both learn to withdraw from the other and so to protect themselves against even more disappointments. We have gradually become firmly convinced that in a great variety of ways the modern environment affects unfavourably the resilience, the adjustability, of both mother and baby.

To continue our list of possible autism-facilitating environmental conditions: it need hardly be said that illness and, in particular, *hospitalisation*, either of the mother or of the child, in its many forms, can be, in fact is almost certainly as a rule, traumatising for both, and hence for the smooth development of the mother–infant relationship. Even though this is now widely recognised and many hospitals do offer facilities for mothers to be with their children as much as possible, even the best arrangements cannot remove entirely many aspects of the unfamiliar situation and procedures. This may apply more to occasions when the baby is hospitalised than to those when the mother is absent from the home, but both forms of environmental discontinuity are upsetting and, as everyone knows who has been involved in such cases, can have lasting effects which can only be undone if and when both mother and baby are exceptionally resilient and/or adjustable. And we have to remember that this resilience can already have been weakened by separation during the first week or so after birth.

Another circumstance that stands out in the history of many autistic children is the *birth of a sib* too soon after their own birth – say, within 18 months or so. Every observer of mothers and children knows that the older child, particularly the first-born, finds it difficult to accept the inevitable and indeed necessary switch of part of the mother's attention to the newcomer and that, unless the first-born is prepared for the expected arrival of 'our' new baby, the chance exists that he resents the loss of his mother's attention and feels abandoned, even betrayed. That this effect of the too-early arrival of the next sib is not so easily discernible in a comparison of the early history of autistic and non-autistic children is undoubtedly due to the fact that it is obscured by the effect of good or poor preparation of the elder child for the expected event, and of the differences in the way in which parents make or do not make the elder child take part in the 'welcoming process'. Here again, the effect of the arrival of a new baby may be greatly influenced by the overall situation; we believe that many pressures are at work in modern society which make parents neglect the time-and-attention-consuming tasks of preparing the elder child and of 'roping him in' as a welcoming elder sib.

Yet another factor that can traumatise a child and, under some circumstances, facilitate autism, is *moving house*, in particular when it is done while the parents are under stress. Financial worries; the need for meeting a deadline or else separating for a period; worry and tension about the new job that led to the need for the move, and innumerable other tensions that are part of both house-hunting and of the actual move into an entirely new environment; the loss of contact with friends and relatives – all this together can nowadays amount to a set of considerable pressures. The trauma that this can cause to a child of the age at which he is most prone to develop autistic tendencies (up to 30 months) can be considerable (see some of our case histories in Ch. 10). But here, too, much depends on how the parents prepare their children for the move; on whether they have both the gift and the time for making the move into an adventure to be looked forward to rather than an unhappy break in a hitherto secure life.

With the development of better means of transport and a consequent almost explosive increase in *travelling*, a danger has appeared that is very similar to those created by moving house. In our experience, with normal children and with some autistic children, a period of too frequent visits, particularly to unfamiliar environments and even abroad, including of course to people who are strangers to the child and perhaps speak a different language, and with a tight schedule involving frequent moves to new 'places and faces', is often emotionally disturbing and may produce quite long phases of autistic behaviour even in normal children; it certainly has adverse effects on autistic children. (The fact that they often become withdrawn and 'no bother' under such conditions may make parents believe quite wrongly that they are 'getting better'.) Ever since we have ourselves 'overworked' one of our own children in this way we have seen not a few examples of this aspect in our affluent and restless society.

We cannot say for certain, but we suspect that often repeated, habitual overlong weekend *car drives* for the sake of the drive itself and not as a means of getting quickly to friends or relatives, or to a place in the country suitable for carefree play, must have effects on children that may well be similar. In modern society children need freedom and a chance to live their own lives rather than being dragged around and exposed to restless 'information input overload'.

In yet other cases, one serious frightening *accident* seems to switch a child from 'normal' to 'autistic'. The report of Copeland and Hodges,[28] which they mention in passing, about a two-year-old boy who suddenly became autistic after he had fallen into a river in spate and had been discovered and rescued only after he had hung on desperately (and, from his point of view, abandoned) for a considerable time, may not be unique; we have heard of similar cases.

We further believe that insufficient attention has been given in the literature on autism (though it is well known to social workers and educators) to the highly unnatural *social conditions* in which children of small families in urban conditions, especially in isolated flats in 'high rise' or tower buildings, grow up. There are various aspects to this. First of all, a mother of one or two children living in this kind of isolation, and with modern mechanical domestic devices at her disposal, may be lonely, bored and depressed. She may solve her problem by taking a job and leaving the children to others – 'child minders', day nurseries or, in the relatively most favourable cases, to a stable mother-substitute. Or she may sit at home and transmit her sense of boredom and lack of purpose, even depression, to her child. Or she may on the contrary become over-involved with the child(ren) and force her attentions onto them, prodding them into activities of *her* choice and whenever it suits *her*, so leaving them far too little time to occupy themselves. In addition, the children in such high-rise flats and similarly isolated conditions have far too little oppor-tunity to become members of mixed-age neighbourhood playgroups, a social setting which is now becoming recognised as being conducive (and, we believe, even essential) to healthy mental development, but which, within our lifetimes, have become a rarity, especially in cities where the playground in which we ourselves grew up – the street – has become too dangerous. This change too has 'crept in' on us, and we tend to forget how different the modern situation is from what it used to be until less than half a century ago. As we shall discuss presently, the disappearance of the mixed-age playgroup is also important in other respects.

Apart from these 'non-parental' environmental, potentially autis-mogenic influences (which we have indicated only very briefly and superficially), there are a number of ways in which the *behaviour of the parents* is clearly relevant to the aetiology of autism. We know of course that opinions differ about this, and that the notion that, to say it as neutrally as possible, the parents of autistic children are not a random sample of the population, while expressed by a number of authors and characterised in a variety of ways, has been rejected, sometimes with great vigour, by some modern writers on autism. In our opinion, this rejection is scientifically unjustified, irrresponsible and not altogether rational.

It is in the nature of the subject that it is difficult to obtain unequivocal evidence either way, but quite clearly the problem is being under-explored. This may have to do with the notion, brought up in so many discussions, that if parental and family characteristics had any influence, the presence of more than one autistic child in a family should be much more common than is the case. But this argument fails to take into account (a) that no two children in a family, except identical twins, are genetically identical and equally vulnerable; and (b) that, as has emerged so clearly from the studies of J. and E. Newson mentioned above, no two children even in the same family are treated in exactly the same way; in fact the parents adjust to a very great extent to the different personalities of their children. It is in fact amazing that so many of us, most of whom have experienced this in our own childhood, seem to have forgotten this simple fact.

From a study of the case histories mentioned in the literature (including the home movie studies by Massie referred to above) and from what we have seen ourselves, we suggest that the following family characteristics can facilitate autism, and certainly deserve closer study instead of being shrugged off.

First of all, it seems to us that every alert 'manwatcher' who studies children and their parents cannot help being struck by the effect that the *inexperience* of young mothers can have on their children, particularly on the first one. In order to appreciate fully the importance of this we have to realise in what respects modern urban family life differs from that of even less than a century ago. Until then, most families were 'extended families' in which young mothers were helped and instructed as a matter of course by the women of the older generation. There used also to be close contact between families living close together; neighbours helped each other mutually, and children grew up only partly in their own homes, partly in informal playgroups of up to approximately 20 children who knew each other intimately and who were of different ages, between about 3 and 15 years of age. As we pointed out before, the importance of this was not only that much was learned, by both boys and girls, without formal school instruction, but that girls grew up in a setting where they could not help seeing babies being nursed, and where at a later age they were roped in to supervise and guard younger children. From these activities girls learned numerous details of mothercraft which many modern girls never get the chance to learn. This knowledge can to a certain extent be acquired by following 'classes in mothercraft', but these are at best only very poor substitutes, even though some modern methods may be more efficient or more hygienic than those of the past. The modern inexperienced mother cannot fully catch up on this missed education, and we are convinced that in the modern urban setting the number of inexperienced mothers is considerable. (We emphasise the role of the mother, risking the wrath of 'women's lib' advocates because, whether we like it or not, it usually is, or ought to be, the mother who has the milk and feeds the baby, with all its consequent opportunities for affiliation. The father is important,[29] but in a different way.) Inexperience of the mother leads to innumerable gaps and malfunctions of her motherly behaviour. Incredible though it may sound to some, we have known young mothers who had to be told to do more with their babies than just feeding and cleaning them, who for instance never said a word to them, or sang, or played, or joked with their babies! One of those poor mothers, when told that her baby would like this, countered by saying in astonishment: 'But surely he can't yet *understand* what I say?' Such mothers not only miss a great deal of happiness, but they deprive their babies and unwittingly hamper their normal development.

(It is in our view of paramount importance that the degree to which mothercraft has to be learnt, and in what way this non-genetic programming is effected, is more generally recognised. The emphasis that comparative ethology has – rightly – put on the extent to which not only animals but even Man is equipped with 'innate' behaviour, has led to the false notion that ethologists claim that *all* human behaviour is simply innate. This has of course never been claimed and to ignore the fact, often stressed by ethologists themselves, that Man is the most adjustable species in the world, is to fall into the trap of believing that mothers can be effective by 'just being natural'.[30] An over-reliance on 'super-Spockian' dogma, a failure to see that 'natural' motherly behaviour in Man depends to a very great extent on the types of experience we have briefly indicated above, can be a danger to children. It is ironical that we, as ethologists who have so often been criticised for over-emphasising the 'innateness' of behaviour, now find ourselves forced to tell child psychiatrists to give more attention to the part played by learning in the programming for parenthood! We shall return to this later.)

Closely related to inexperience, and in fact often a corollary of it, is *over-anxiety*, uncertainty, hesitancy in so many young mothers we have seen. Such uncertainty is of course to be expected in women who have been insufficiently programmed in the natural way. Curiously enough, it is often strengthened rather than reduced by the opportunity for consulting *too many* books on mothercraft – conflicting advice, often given with irresponsible confidence, makes an already insecure mother wonder continuously 'whether she does it right'. The mechanism whereby such over-anxious mothers, or mothers lacking in self-confidence, may affect their children may well range from hormonal influences during pregnancy to a variety of psychogenic influences after birth; without entering into details, we submit that further study on this is required, particularly because we have often spotted this lack of self-confidence in mothers of autistic children. *That* over-anxious and uncertain mothers affect their children adversely and make them in turn uncertain of themselves and even over-anxious seems to us beyond doubt. No observant person can fail to see that what the mother does or does not do, either on her own initiative or in response to unexpected and, to her, puzzling or upsetting behaviour of her baby has an effect on how the baby in his turn responds to *her*.[31] Babies are now known to be far more perceptive than was formerly thought, and when a mother, in response to, for instance, a 'colic' baby or to other unexpected behaviour of her child, either turns her back on him or fusses overmuch or, at the other extreme, tries to 'discipline' him or even batters him, this can of course lead to severe trauma.

We suspect that there may still be many autismogenic factors to be discovered in the early relationship between mother and child. For instance, *post-partum depression* of the mother must make affiliation extremely difficult, and we suspect that it may be more common in the early history of autistic children than would appear from published case histories (which are often incomplete).

Related to this are the cases in which a mother keeps *working* up till the last minute, and then finds that when the congratulatory visits are over she is suddenly all alone with her baby, and very lonely. This not only depresses her but may make her lose interest in playing with her baby at the appropriate times, and even blame the baby for tying her to her home. Such playing (in moderation and especially after feeds) is probably important. The following are a few details which we feel should be mentioned.

Many mothers who *bottle feed* their babies do not realise how important it is to mimic as much as possible the natural breast-feeding situation. In this, baby and mother face (and touch) each other, and while the feed lasts, innumerable little adjusting movements are made by both. If bottle feeding is necessary, it is important to hold the baby in the same position as a breast-fed baby, the teat must be held as near as possible to the mother's nipple, and the bottle preferably held against the mother's body. All this is neglected when the baby is fed in an impersonal, mechanical manner and certainly the use of 'bottle props', which leave the child alone while sucking, creates a tremendous gap, perhaps very harmful, in the necessary interaction between mother and child, in particular if the mother fails to hold the baby afterwards and to 'play' with him, and instead just takes the bottle away or at best replaces the baby's nappy and tucks him in 'efficiently' and without losing time.

To deprive a baby of regular face-to-face and skin-to-skin interaction may, we believe, reinforce the early tendency (reported of the 'odd-from-birth' babies) to direct their attention away from the mother, and perhaps to 'imprint' them on sounds, as so many autists are whose 'comforter' is either music in general or one particular record of which the incessant playing has become an obsession.

Another, and we are sure very important, contributing cause of autism is the situation that can develop when *both parents* have *intellectually demanding* and interesting jobs, although some such parents manage to avoid causing stress to their children. Even mothers who, by the usual standards, take good care of their babies, cannot, even if they have interrupted their intellectually interesting job for, say, six months, keep their minds entirely off their work and as a result their attention and care given to the baby suffers. Although we now begin to acknowledge what really good parents have known intuitively since time immemorial, that even very young babies are sensitive to very slight signs of inattention, we ourselves are convinced that our scientific knowledge of the uncanny perceptiveness and vulnerability of babies, from newborn ones onwards, is still so fragmentary as to make us underrate seriously the importance of proper and undivided attention to the job of mothering and parenting. Merely going dutifully through the motions of the bodily care of the baby is not good enough.

In many such families where father and mother have stimulating jobs, the mother is in addition placed in an unfair position by still being expected to do the bulk of the domestic chores. Those who favour equal rights for women in the fullest sense and who advocate a return to a full-time job by the mother as soon as the baby can be cared for, either in a day nursery or by a succession of substitute mothers (rather than by a stable mother figure), forget that it is not only the time spent in the home that is important but the *quality of the parental behaviour* shown during that time. Modern society is placing mothers, especially those who have been educated so that they can have intellectually stimulating or demanding work and who yet try to be fully satisfying mothers, in a difficult position. For career women it is hardly ever possible to combine the two tasks successfully. In our experience, either the work suffers or the children, or both, and in addition the mother may succumb to nervous breakdowns. From the point of view of the mental health of children, such women should, ideally, decide either to work or to have a family. But this is a cruel choice and many women will remain unfulfilled when they give up either their work or reproduction. An ideal solution may well be impossible.

It is probably this type of parents who have been mentioned under various terms in many places in the literature, as being 'too serious', 'too intellectual', 'cool' or 'cold' ('refrigerator parents') and similar terms. We believe that none of these terms hits the nail exactly on the head; *'serious'* or *'preoccupied'* comes perhaps nearest the mark. A shortcoming of these parents and their families that has not by any means been emphasised enough is precisely this seriousness: it is their inability to joke and to engage in 'fun and games' that in our opinion does a great deal of harm to their children, emotionally and intellectually. The fathers have to come in here too: 'rough-and-tumble' play, later 'horseplay' of a physical nature as well as in the form of joking is largely a father's job. At any rate, fathers and mothers do this in different ways.

In our experience, the tremendous importance (even to small infants) of a cheerful atmosphere in the extended family and the neighbourhood group, of joking and laughter, even of mutual teasing, leg-pulling and the quick exchange of jokes and witticisms (however 'silly') is far too little realised. To the vast majority of people in modern Western society who have grown up in a world in which it was important to 'do well' and to find themselves a place in the face of fierce competition, it is hardly known how much more relaxed and how much more cheerful and unstressed even the urban world was of two generations ago. This world, in which we ourselves grew up, was already much more serious and geared to 'efficiency' and competitiveness than the world to which 'human nature' has been adapted in the first place: that of small groups of hunter–gatherers, which has been the social and ecological setting for at least 100 000 years and probably very much longer, and which changed to agricultural communities less than 10 000 years ago, and to a modern industrial society, so to speak, only yesterday. We shall return to this in a moment.

It is hardly necessary to stress the profound traumatising effect that the circumstances surrounding the *divorce* of parents can have on even very young children, particularly when it is preceded by a period of serious bickering or suppressed hostility or even indifference between the parents, and when the children are assigned to a father or a mother who does not remarry, or whose new partner is not to the child's liking. The resulting emotional disturbance of the child need not be autism in the full sense of the term as used here, but autistic traits are far from rare in such children, can last for a long time, and may be combined with other symptoms. As with other autismogenic conditions, the ultimate disorder may take a variety of forms.

Like some kinds of divorce, a *bereavement* through the death of a parent is well known to have profound emotionally disturbing effects on most children, and should be considered as a possible contributing factor in the examination of all case histories. Bereavement may be autismogenic in particular when the surviving partner him- or herself responds to the loss by neglecting or even rejecting the child(ren). Such *de facto* rejections are highly significant, for they create the situation which we believe to underly so many cases of autism: the continuous presence of the parent, which elicits in the child attempts at socialisation, *combined with* the disappointing experience, time after time, of not receiving the response he yearns for – of being *in effect* rebuffed time and again.

A contributory condition which, like moving house, has not been recognised as a potentially very upsetting factor, is the absence, in only too many families we know, of any consistent *routine*, of order and regularity, which by its reliability provides security for children. Children do not like to live in a chaotic, *unpredictable* home.[32] The time when it was thought that children must not be 'inhibited' and must be left free to develop their own life style and potential is fortunately over, but we feel that it is not sufficiently realised that a minimal set of rules is not only not harmful, but is positively beneficial to children. The rules required may be different from one family to the other; for instance bed time may have to be adjusted to the needs of every particular child, it may have to vary with circumstances; it need not be a particular clock time but be linked with other events in the family's life. Also, certain things simply have to be disallowed – such as playing with electric sockets, hot water taps and many other things in a modern home that can be dangerous even to under-exploratory children who are not kept in check. Without recommending a highly structured, very strict regime, we do agree with those parents who know the need for a number of 'do's' and 'don'ts' and who consistently adhere to those they impose. Of the greatest importance to a child is that the parent be consistent and just. We are convinced that very many parents either do not realise the self-defeating effects of inconsistency, or cannot make the effort (which on crucial occasions may have to be considerable) to be consistent. It is our experience that living under a well-known and reliable set of reasonable rules, far from harming a child, provides much-needed security. Conversely, we have noticed in some families with an autistic child the totally chaotic living conditions, when the child can at no moment predict what is going to happen next, and we know from one autistic child (Carla) who, though mute, can write quite lucidly that this chaos is resented. Visiting social workers do not always spot such chaos in the 'timetable' because many mothers of this type will pretend to be in charge and well organised whenever they have visitors. (The fathers often remain in the background or are 'strict' in fits and starts.)

Another circumstance which can act as a pressure on a child, make him feel insecure and prevent him from performing with confidence is the tendency (which we have seen in the parents and particular the fathers of some autists) to show that they are *ambitious* on behalf of their children, especially their sons, who even as toddlers are expected and even required to show enterprise, courage and intelligence (and later, at school, to 'do well'). This ambition is nowadays not merely a – presumably quite natural – wish of many fathers, it has come to be seen as fully justified and 'for the child's own good' in the highly competitive society which we have created, and which he has to enter as well prepared as possible. That is why even the most unselfish, personally not particularly ambitious fathers often feel that, society being as it is, the best service they can render their sons is to make them profit as well as possible from whatever opportunities for 'education' (read: training for a future job) their boys can be offered. In practice, this often leads to overstretching a boy's abilities, to continuous prodding, and too much 'keeping him at it', i.e. at doing his homework. But it would be a mistake to think that such pressurising by ambitious parents does not begin until a child goes to school: we have often seen parents who put their young babies under pressure by requiring too much of them. This kind of pressure is different for boys and for girls. We often say, colloquially, that the worst defect (in the parents' eyes) of boys is to be either dim or unenterprising; and that the worst defect of a girl is to be plain, or to be a messpot. Certainly, even very young children may well feel such expectations and be hurt if the parent shows his disappointment. If a child yields to such pressures, he may lose his playfulness, imaginativeness, independence and freedom of thought, and it may stunt the growth of his mind and of his social experience. If he does not yield he may become a 'negativistic' rebel and perhaps fail. Only in rare cases do children shrug off this kind of pressure and make their own way in a constructive sense. Of course this pressure is not always autismogenic; it is a stress to which innumerable children in our society are exposed without really succumbing, and in the debate on education that has been going on for scores of years, and has been revived time and again with constantly changing attitudes and ideas, we believe that insufficient attention is given to the overall mental growth of children and too much to 'preparation for society' in the sense of fitting children for future niches in production. This is a problem usually discussed with regard to older children, but it is very relevant for much younger children as well. This is not the place to say more about this general problem, but we consider it important to realise that this pressure on potentially autistic children, like so many others, has to be seen in the much wider context of the overall developments in our explosively changing society.

Finally, we have been alerted by our colleage Dr F. Hall[33] to the fact that schools for the educationally subnormal (ESN and SSN) are attended by a high proportion of emotionally disturbed, not necessarily subnormal children. She also told us that even babies can become confused and upset when their fathers and their mothers speak two different languages, and have no command of each other's language. This, together with the fact that we have noticed an 'autismiform' setback in young children after emigrating with their parents, suggests to us that a *language discrepancy*, either between the parents or between the child and his new environment, might well on occasion be a contributing autismogenic factor. With the increase of cross-cultural mobility and migration of 'labour', especially from poor to rich countries, this might well apply more often than it did a generation ago; it certainly deserves closer examination. At any rate, in England children of *immigrants*, especially of West Indians who speak a version of English quite their own, feel at sea when taught, and required to express themselves, in 'English English'. Whether this is the right interpretation or not, it is a fact often commented on that far too high a proportion of West Indian children, at least in London, are in ESN schools, and that they behave surprisingly normally when allowed to use their own English.

We have no doubt that, once the possibility of environmental traumatisation is investigated more thoroughly, the above list may well have to be expanded, and that the way in which autism-producing factors already mentioned exert their influence will then undoubtedly become better understood.

'Consequential' autism

In the foregoing we have confined ourselves to those children whom we consider potentially normal, though more vulnerable than other children through either genetic predisposition, or very early experience, or both. But we believe that there are a number of children who become autistic as a secondary consequence of some other, in their case primary, defect. We have already mentioned that especially those 'rubella children' who are born deaf are at risk; rubella children who have good hearing rarely becoming autistic. (Quite apart from the rubella issue, we believe that a very *small* proportion of autistic children who are officially diagnosed 'deaf' are really deaf.) The case of the rubella children does show, however, that it is possible that some structural sensory defects can give rise to autism, carrying it (so to speak) in their wake. (We use the term 'consequential' rather than, as originally intended, 'secondary' because the expression 'secondary autism' is already being used in a different sense.)

Although we have found other reports of autistic children who would fall into this category (such as the boy Pino described by Zappella[34] who suffered from the rare De Soto syndrome), we believe that 'consequential' autists in our sense are rare, and that many psychogenic cases are, without justification, considered to be due to some (merely inferred) structural defect.

As we have discussed before, even in those children who are described as 'autistic and *in addition* epileptic', the epileptic behaviour may be a consequence of the autistic state, one for which the child may be predisposed but to such a minor degree that the epileptic fits disappear completely with even slight improvements in the child's emotional balance.

Nevertheless, consequential autism as defined above does occur, and this is one of the reasons why we are not claiming that our hypothesis applies to all autistic children, or rather that it offers the complete explanation. We do claim, however, that our interpretation is valid for very many, if not the vast majority, of autistic children now pronounced to be 'organically' or in other ways irreparably damaged, and who are being given a poor prognosis. In the next chapter (Ch. 6) we shall discuss the implications of this for the issue of education and rehabilitation.

The downward spiral[35]

So far, we have discussed exclusively the onset of the autistic course. Certain aspects of the further development of the autistic condition, such as the formalisation of stereotypies, and the various ways in which the behaviour development can be held back so that autists of long standing become increasingly retarded, have been discussed in the previous chapter. Here we must discuss another aspect of the long-term development of the severe autist. A severely autistic child makes it increasingly difficult for the parents and others to maintain normal social intercourse with him. Most families of autistic children, and in particular the parents, become in their turn profoundly affected *as a consequence* of having an autistic child and of not knowing how to cope with him. The majority of such parents give up attempts at educating this child (and it is of course hardly possible to interact fully with an unresponsive child). Other parents give in to their children's every whim and so literally 'spoil' them by a process of unwitting, but very effective, operant conditioning: the children learn soon that even the slightest threat of a tantrum may get them their way. Other parents, or the same parents on other occasions, either cannot help becoming angry with their children or they exclude them from activities and occasions where they would be an embarrassment, or a danger to themselves; and many parents of autists do not hesitate to explain or mention, either more or less apologetically or by way of warning, that their child is autistic, and do this within earshot of the child, not realising that this may deeply hurt him. Even if the parents are willing to try to educate their child, it becomes increasingly difficult for them to get through to him, and certainly in such a way as to allow or encourage him to take part in play of any kind. Finally, there are parents – we know more than one of them fairly intimately – who relate to their autistic child in an intensive love–hate manner in which hatred can be surprisingly strong. Such parents (those we know are mothers) commit in effect a kind of 'psychological child battering'. They treat their child at times with a measure of love and patience, but revert at other times to indifference, to treating the child so to speak, as a piece of furniture, or at other times even with contempt and anger. But it is not easy to discover this hidden hostility because such parents are usually clever at concealing it when others are present. Also, this kind of mother assumes not infrequently the attitude of showing 'how bravely they bear their cross'. All this is often noticed by their children, who are deeply hurt time after time, and (understandably) keep withdrawing into themselves or become destructive and aggressive. It is almost impossible not to become angry with parents of this type, but those cases we know a little better are themselves pitiable victims of their own upbringings and other circumstances. In fact, as we shall see in the next chapter, even such parents can sometimes be helped and be 'roped in' as co-therapists and even ultimately become the principal therapists.

It is this phenomenon of mother and child mutually damaging each other further which makes us speak of 'the downward spiral'; initially, either the baby or the mother may be the unresponsive partner of the dyad, but in most cases of severe autism it is really the dyad, soon the triad in which the father is included, and very often the entire family that may become damaged. This is often the cause of the quite common ultimate disaster: for the sake of the well-being of the parents and also of the other children in the family, it often becomes necessary to give up and hand the child over to an institution. In the past such children often received a new label when this happened: they were called and treated as schizophrenics. Nowadays, thanks to the activities of the various national societies for autistic children, a number of such children are accepted in special schools. According to the reports of the British Society for Autistic Children, these schools, while undoubtedly much kinder to the children than the old institutions in which they ended up, seem to be run on the basis of the notion that the majority of autists have to remain dependent for their whole lives. As it was put in a fairly recent BBC television programme about autism, which was largely concerned with the Society and its activites, autistic children are 'ineducable'. Even as recently as late 1978, we heard Miss Sybil Elgar, the concerned and devoted founder and first Principal of Somerset Court (a home for adolescent and adult autists) say about autistic children: 'You can't make them relate but you can teach them simple skills'. We shall take a critical look at these views (and challenge them) in the next chapter.

We must repeat that this brief sketch of a number of environmental conditions which in our experience can contribute towards the 'derailment' of a child's development towards autism must not be understood to mean that any single one of the factors we mentioned can *by itself* make a child autistic – although with very severe traumatic experiences and with highly vulnerable children this may occasionally happen. When we study the environment of an autistic child attentively and patiently at first hand, we often see aspects that the doctor in his interviews or brief contacts with child and parents never sees, and which will not appear either in answers given to even quite sophisticated questionnaires. Such collecting of as full first-hand information as possible, such 'reconnoitring fieldwork', is of course time consuming and requires considerable sophistication from the observer. But we claim that it *has* to precede or at least to accompany the conventional methods of interviews, tests and questionnaires. If done competently, it reveals very clearly, even at this preliminary stage: (a) that an autistic child has been exposed to a number of the conditions we have listed, though by no means to all of them; and (b) that the particular set of such conditions and the particular form in which they prevail can be very different from one child to another. Add to this that different children are also genetically different from each other, and it becomes understandable, even to be expected that the syndrome varies so widely from child to child. In fact it is surprising that, with these qualitative differences in the conditions and in the nature of individual children, as well as with the quantitative aspect of the degree of severity of the set of pressures and of the resilience of each child, the syndrome of early childhood autism can be as (relatively) clearly delineated as, by and large, it is!

As a matter of fact, the unity of the syndrome is of course not as striking as the popularity of the term suggests. On the one hand, as we have already stated in Chapter 4, and as we can now understand a little better, there is enormous quantitative and qualitative variety in the syndrome, and as a result different authors differ more in their opinions as to what is 'true' autism and what is not than is really justified or necessary. But on the other hand, we believe that it is insufficiently realised that the same, or very similar, sets of environmental conditions that we made responsible for the frequent occurrence of autism are widespread, and that they often lead to emotional disturbances with syndromes rarely recognised as being related to autism. It is this conviction that makes us feel that a better understanding of autism may well turn out to have a bearing on a number of other forms of emotional disturbance; and this again may help us to adopt a more critical, more scrutinising and more questioning attitude to what our present society is really doing to our children and grandchildren, and so to the citizens of the future, those who, within decades, will be moulding the further evolution of their society.

As we shall presently argue, there are good reasons for considering autism a true civilisation disease, and this has been to us (and, we submit, ought to be to many) an additional spur to take a detached and more general look at the ways in which our society is changing, indeed at where the human species is going. Autism is, in our view, one little expression of the very many extremely complex and far-reaching changes which are taking place in our environment. In fact, the 'autismogenic' factors that we have indicated must be considered as expressions of genuine *psychosocial pollution*, which itself is only part of the overall process of disadaptation to which our civilisation is subjecting us.[36] While it may well be impossible to undo a number of other aspects of our disadaptation, there is no valid reason and therefore no excuse to accept meekly the traumatisation of so many of our own children.

Which children are vulnerable?

Finally, at the risk of being accused of imagining things, we want to call attention to an aspect of autism of which many of the scientists concerned may not be aware, but which occupies the minds of many others who are in intimate contact with autistic children. To them, and to us, it looks as if a disproportionately large number of autistic children are in one way or another exceptionally gifted. Some of them have had the chance to demonstrate these gifts: Nadia[37] was – but is, sad to say, no longer – an astonishingly gifted artist as a very young child; recently, the apparently outstanding autistic pianist Joe Carter made the headlines in the British national press.[38] The famous case of Dibs[39] (who, although Axline wisely refrained from labelling him, fell well within the range of autism as defined here) reveals another aspect of autists that may well be far from rare. As we have mentioned, we know personally two mute autistic girls who (as is evident from what they *write*) have exceptional linguistic and literary gifts. Paradoxically, such gifts can contribute to these children's isolation. We know 'normal', but in many respects mildly autistic children in our own environment who have exceptional social sensitivity and are easily hurt by the merest of snubs or even lack of empathy, and other children who are profoundly poetic in the way they respond to, for instance, pets, flowers, cloudscapes etc.[40] Others again have such an intense interest in music that their most generous act of friendship is to play over and over again their most cherished gramophone record to visitors. All such children are continually in danger of being met, by other children and by adults, with incomprehension, with ridicule, and even with hostility, and this makes them withdraw even further into themselves. Additional autismogenic conditions such as we listed above may have much more serious effects on such children than on less sensitive or less gifted children. We are convinced that many (though not all) autistic children have this combination of social perceptiveness of over-sensitivity and exceptional intellectual or artistic gifts. There may be a connection between this and the fact that one very often hears concerned adults say (as we do) that the autistic children they know are such exceptionally 'attractive' or 'touching' children. This again is why many teachers who have dealings with them have a stubborn belief that their charges can be saved, and therefore refuse to give up. Such patient, loving optimists are known to all of us and we can recognise them in many published accounts of autistic children.[41] We believe that, even though the educational efforts of such people fail only too often, or at any rate do not cure the children in their charge completely, their judgement has an important core of truth in it. It seems to us (and we urge all those concerned to consider this seriously, and to observe autistic children with this 'hunch' of ours, and of so many others, in mind) that there is a correlation between exceptional gifts of some kind – great perceptiveness, strongly positive social attitudes, exceptional intellectual and/or artistic gifts – and exceptional vulnerability to the autismogenic influences we have listed. In other words, we believe that autistic children are not a random sample of the population, *but that some or perhaps even many of them have been and still are children with an above-normal potential* – quite contrary to the notion that they are inherently below the norm. But in order to test this idea we need researchers of far greater sensitivity and perceptiveness, with better eyes and more patience, and without the intrusiveness that is marring so much of the research that is now being carried out and published under the banner of objectivity and scientific detachment. We repeat what we said at the start: the phenomena of deviant development of the human behaviour machinery are so complex that we are only just beginning to find suitable methods for their study.

So the question 'which children are vulnerable?' cannot yet be answered *in concreto*; although, in view of the work summarised by Folstein and Rutter (see this chapter, note 14), it is likely that genetic differences between children co-determine the degree of vulnerability, and that the intra-uterine environment is also involved.

Autism and society

We have argued that neither differences in susceptibility nor 'organic' defects can alone account for making children autistic; that they play in fact only a minor role. We claim that the environment, in particular psychogenic aspects of the early environment, is much more important than is usually assumed. This view was based mainly on case histories, and on direct observation of short-term responses of children to events in their environment. Is it possible to check the validity, or at least the plausibility, of this hypothesis in other ways? We believe that this can be done – up to a point – by placing the problem in a wider context. To explain our attitude towards this and related problems we have to discuss once more a few matters of method.

The most direct way of testing the influence of early experiences would of course be to set up an experiment, i.e. to compare the development of two groups of children: one that would be deliberately exposed to the allegedly autismogenic conditions, while the other – as well 'matched' as possible in all other respects – would be raised under an allegedly non-autismogenic regime. Apart from the fact that this would require very large numbers of 'guinea-pigs' (and quite an array of better-than-average researchers), such an experiment would, as in so many fields of medicine, be ethically unacceptable from the moment we began to suspect that it might harm one of the groups. The deliberate withholding of possibly beneficial treatments is rightly considered morally wrong.

The next best way would be a 'clinical' comparison of the early environmental conditions of children who have become autistic with those of healthy, non-autistic children. This could be done: (a) retrospectively by digging into the history of autists and non-autistic children; or (b) by following large samples of children from birth and seeing what conditions turn out to be correlated with the development or non-development of autism. We have applied the first approach (admittedly in rather an exploring, sampling, not really systematic way, but we could not yet go beyond this reconnaissance stage). The first results certainly suggest that a more systematic and more penetrating clinical study is well worth doing, even though the complexity and subtlety of the relations between child and environment, the variability between children, and the attitude of parents, would make such a comprehensive clinical study an extremely difficult task.

Since (in view of the relative scarcity of autists) the second approach would require the involvement of many thousands of children, this would no doubt have to be a co-operative effort, involving many researchers. Because of this, the value of the total information that would be collected would be impaired by the fact that no two observers would record *exactly* the same kind of data. For these and other reasons we are still very far from having a solid, reliable body of this kind of 'forward looking' information, nor are we likely to obtain it in the near future; for such massive enquiries to have any chance of real success the science of psychiatry is still far too young, too much in a groping stage.

In the absence of such more or less direct information, could we test our hypothesis in other ways? Although it is not really possible to obtain strict 'proof' or 'disproof' of this kind of hypothesis, we can indeed come nearer to an understanding in other ways, which deserve at least a brief discussion if only to alert psychiatrists to the relevance of developments in some other sciences.

AUTISM IN DIFFERENT SOCIETIES

Since there is such a huge variety in the nature of human societies and in the environments in which children grow up, it would in theory be possible to compare the incidence of autism in these different surroundings and to look for correlations with the conditions in which children grow up. Unfortunately, we are still very far from having this kind of information. The difficulty is that absence of reports from many countries might be due to regional unawareness of autism just as well as to real non-occurrence of the illness. We suspect that the truth lies somewhere in the middle, and that autism is not only more widely reported, but is actually more common in modern, industrialised, urbanised and highly competititive societies such as our 'Western' society (and also in ethnically different, though environmentally similar societies such as that of modern Japan, and perhaps the Negroes in the US). But until we have more reliable information of this kind, the evidence will remain no more than suggestive. What is known, however, would seem to point in the direction of our hypothesis.[42]

AUTISM IN DIFFERENT TIMES

Another way of studying the links between society and autism would be to compare the incidence in the course of history. Here again there are no really indisputable data. We do know that there have been autistic children in the past – the 'wild boy of Aveyron'[43] is considered to have been one – but for various reasons we have no idea how common they were. For one thing, no relevant records have been kept until recently (and even our present figures about the incidence of autism are far from reliable); for another, many autists would in the past probably have died without being officially recorded; finally, autistic children, had they occurred, would undoubtedly have been given different 'labels'.

However, it may be significant that, when Kanner described the syndrome in sufficiently clear and objective terms in 1943, he found, when he inquired among colleagues, that the condition was at that time hardly known. In view of the fact that he described the syndrome rather than inquired about 'autism', and because it seems hard to believe that severe autists such as we all can see now would at that time be unknown to the majority of doctors, we consider it likely that autistic children are now reported for modern Western and westernised societies in such large numbers not merely because the condition is now better known (even though this is so as a consequence of the recent explosion of publicity) but because it reflects a genuine increase. The truth about changes in the incidence up till now will never be known with certainty; however, a careful watch on developments in the future could reveal whether or not the situation is (as we fear) changing for the worse.[44]

With so little reliable *epidemiological* evidence on hand, it must be admitted that for the moment our view of autism, as being largely due to a sub-optimal early environment, cannot be considered firmly based. However, it gains in plausibility when we look at the problem in wider context of *the overall relationship between Man and his environment;* at the way in which our species fits in it, is adapted to it; and at *recent changes in this 'ecological' relationship.* In this respect Man is, compared with all other animals, in a unique and anomalous position. In order to understand this position, we have to look at our evolutionary history, from at least a million years ago right up to the present. We have to do this in two steps, first by looking back, very far, over the very long period in which our hereditary characteristics were moulded in and by our natural habitat – by evolution by means of natural selection – and then by studying the recent, much shorter period of 'cultural evolution' in which we created, and had to live in, a greatly changed (and still changing) world.

We have referred to some aspects of this in the preceding pages but, at the risk of being found repetititve, we shall now attempt to place these incidental remarks in a more comprehensive context.

LIFE STYLE AND ENVIRONMENT OF ANCESTRAL MAN[45]

Our knowledge on this subject has grown considerably in the last few decades. It is true that the fossil remains of our ancestors and their works tell us less about their behaviour than about their structure and the material aspects of their cultures, but the recent, truly impressive joint efforts of paleo-anthropologists, archaeologists, geologists, zoologists, botanists and many other specialists, has led to a surprising number of quite plausible inferences about the way our ancestors lived. We can deal with this only in the briefest outline.

The *hominid* line – the evolutionary sequence of generations that was to lead to the emergence of Man – branched off from ape-like stock several millions of years ago. Of all the different pre-human fossils known so far, it is not quite understood who are our direct ancestors and who represent sidelines that since have become extinct, but it seems that approximately one million years before Man began to conquer the Earth, his ancestor *Homo erectus* (himself the descendant of populations who had already evolved the upright stance and had left the forest habitat to live in more open country, in tropical Africa and perhaps also further to the east) had begun to spread out over the temperate zones of Eurasia. *Homo erectus* had also inherited from his ancestors the way of life and the ecological niche of *hunter–gatherers*, i.e. they had a mixed diet of vegetable matter and of animals on which they preyed. The fossil remains of *erectus* and the traces of his activities show beyond doubt that he had already come quite far on this new road; numerous finds reveal that he was an accomplished maker and user of tools, including weapons; that he knew how to use fire; and above all that he was a formidable hunter who was capable of killing prey animals much larger than himself – up to the size of horses and even elephants. This he could do only because, like the present-day lions, wolves, spotted hyenas, and African wild dogs, he hunted in packs – in his case, packs of adult males. Though at a less advanced stage, his way of life must have been very similar to that of the few tribes of modern Man who even now – or at least until they changed under the impact of our modern civilisation – have not all made the step towards agriculture, let alone towards modern industrial life, but still live as hunter–gatherers: the bushmen, the Australian Aborigines, the Eskimos and a fast-dwindling number of other peoples.[46]

As in these contemporary hunter–gatherers, there was in early Man a division of labour between the sexes, which was reflected in their build: much of the gathering of vegetable food such as leaves, roots, fruits and nuts, and much of the catching of small animals, was done by the women and children not very far from their base camps, whereas the hunting of large game was done by small groups of the more strongly built adult men, sometimes quite far from home.

As in modern hunter–gatherers, each group had to live in a circumscribed, although possibly large, area; they were not true nomads. The reason was that *in order to earn a living they had to have, as have modern hunter–gathers, an intricate knowledge of where, at any time of the year, they could find the food and game that was in season. Within* their total living range they had to move around, following the game wherever it went. Although the size of the range of each group varied, depending on how rich such a range was (on its 'carrying capacity'), it usually had to be very large compared with even large modern farms. Also, the limitations of the action radius of even these tough hunters, as well as the limited 'carrying capacity' of the range of each group, made it impossible for these groups to have a range large enough to support life for very many individuals. So, until the development of agriculture (which allowed a much more intensive use of the land) the groups of people must have been on average small, and they would have to live fairly far from each other. It is estimated that groups were rarely larger than a couple of hundred people, and usually much smaller – as with the surviving groups of hunter–gatherers, groups might on occasions fuse or split up.

The point that interests us is that *the hunting–gathering style,* which our ancestors had evolved and improved over such a very long period – a couple of million years (i.e. from well before they had evolved into *Homo erectus) – carried with it a social organisation suitable for this life:* like other pack-hunting mammals and like most apes and monkeys, they *must* have lived in so-called 'closed' societies or 'in-groups', in which every member knew every other member individually – quite different from the large 'anonymous' societies such as a herd of reindeer or of wildebeeste, or winter swarms of starlings.[47] In fact, it is highly probable that Man has for at least a million years, and his ancestors probably already much earlier, lived *in groups that* – although there may have been occasional fusion and breaking-up of such groups, and exchange, for marriage, of young men and women between groups – *consisted of a small number of 'extended families',* i.e. families together with close relatives, including for instance widows, in-laws, grandparents and the elderly in general.

It is true that not all modern 'primitive', i.e. non-westernised, people are hunter-gatherers, and that the social structures of various populations differ a great deal amongst themselves; thus there are, for instance, vegetarian societies and also matriarchal societies, and long before Western civilization began there have been peoples who lived in much larger, undoubtedly anonymous, societies. However, the vegetarian societies as found, for instance, on some Pacific islands, while demonstrating the flexibility of our species, are sidelines that have branched off from the mainstream. And the larger, 'anonymous' societies of other than Western civilisations were later developments, dependent on, for instance, agriculture or pastoralism, trade, the founding of cities and improved communication and administration – all fairly recent developments. Also, as until very recently even in our present society, the basic social unit remained the (extended) family or the small settlement. The main point to remember is that the way of life of the hunter–gatherer, living in small in-groups, evolved during at least a million years and probably much longer, and that many of the ecological and social relationships that we ourselves have grown up with have developed only in the last 10 000 at most 15 000 years, some of them 'almost yesterday', i.e. in the last century.

In such primitive societies children grew up in a setting quite different from that of our society. Babies and toddlers (i.e. the relatively few who survived) were in the care not only of their own mothers and fathers but, to quite an extent, of other adults and even teenagers as well. But these were all known and trusted persons; the 'stable mother substitute' was a group of friendly persons of all ages. In these in-groups young mothers could draw on the experience, advice and help of older, experienced women; and as babies grew up to toddlers, they lived increasingly not only with their parents but spent a large amount of their time in playgroups composed of children of all ages. In such communities, parentcraft developed almost imperceptibly: all children not only saw how babies were nursed and older children cared for (and occasionally disciplined), they learned a lot from such observation. Also, older children, perhaps especially girls, were often in charge at an early age of younger members of their group, and so learned mothering by practising it. The role of fathers had to be different; they were the providers of game and often had to be away on long hunting trips. In the base camp the adult men also played a slightly different parental role from the women. Young boys undoubtedly observed and imitated a number of typically masculine occupations (while young girls were drawn to female company and occupations). The men were undoubtedly responsible for a different kind of parenting than the women, as they are now in modern hunter–gatherer societies, and even in our present society, e.g. they would engage children in rough-and-tumble play, in hunting games, in the more masculine kind of joking etc.

Everyone who has lived among modern hunter–gatherers has seen how much children in such societies learn without being sent to school, and how refreshingly light-hearted and cheerful the atmosphere in such societies is as a rule. *Few members of modern Western societies realise how uncheerful, sour and efficiency-oriented, how much less happy the atmosphere in modern societies is!*

In all learning that has to be done, in the old societies as well as in ours, the accent has changed rather drastically. Whereas children in more primitive societies learned and learn relatively little from deliberate instruction and more from observation, imitation and practice in a playful atmosphere, children in modern societies have less opportunity for observational learning and practice, and are increasingly forced to rely on being instructed. This is in part inevitable: modern children simply have to learn more in order to become competent breadwinners. But the amount, and above all the subtlety, of what has to be learned by children in 'primitive' societies, and what modern Man has simply lost, is far from negligible. Our institutionalised way of teaching is neither so necessary for every sort of education nor is it in all respects more effective than the old ways. Many (though by no means all) modern attempts at reforming institutionalised teaching make sense when seen against our evolutionary background; and an awareness of the changes in the course of our history can help us look at autism in a new, more informed way.

OUR BEHAVIOURAL HERITAGE

What we have sketched about the life style of our ancestors is more relevant to an understanding of the behaviour of modern Man than is as yet recognised. What it teaches us is that, as one of our prominent biologists expressed it, somewhat over-cautiously, 'the human behaviour repertoire is of some evolutionary depth'.[48] We believe that we can be a little more specific.

Like all animal species that have ever existed, so our ancestors must, at every stage in their long evolutionary career, have been built and been functioning in such a way that they could 'make a living' (and reproduce) in the particular ecological niche which they occupied – most recently, in that of a pack-hunter-cum-gatherer in relatively open terrain. Just as all other animals, our ancestors had to be 'fit', i.e. adapted to their habitat. To realise the full significance of this seemingly commonplace fact, one has to remember that survival does not just happen: every animal is continuously doing a sort of balancing act, it has, as we said before, to do a 'multi-dimensional tightrope act';[49] it is engaged in a struggle against innumerable difficulties that the habitat puts in its way. Living is in reality the execution of a continuing series of extremely sophisticated efforts and skills; those needed to find a good habitat to obtain and utilise food, water and other essential resources; to get rid of waste products; to defend self and often offspring against such dangers as extreme weather, predators, parasites and so forth. This adaptedness is a characteristic not only of bodily functions but also of behaviour; we repeat that behaviour – more precisely, the living machinery that produces the behaviour – is just as much part of an animal's 'equipment for survival' as are its liver, its kidneys, and all the other vital organ systems. Since each animal develops and grows from a fertilised egg, this being fit or adapted is the consequence of the adaptedness of its *development* – the process of growing up is 'programmed' in such a way that it will lead to a 'fit' adult.

Development, not only of the body but also of its behaviour machinery, is largely determined by hereditary factors, by the genetic 'blueprint' embodied in the chromosomes of the fertilised egg from which most animals start. Especially in 'lower' animals (the descendants of old forms of life that appeared early in evolution), much of the behaviour is largely 'innate', i.e. it develops normally without receiving much supplementary instruction from the environment, more precisely from learning by experience that is gained in interaction with the outside world. Not only do such animals learn little, it is even difficult to distort their behaviour development by raising them in abnormal conditions – they *resist* being 'taught'. Such animals behave in fairly rigid, inflexible ways; if conditions are abnormal, they 'break' (i.e. die) rather than 'bend' (i.e. adjust). Hoever, as evolution produced ever new and different animal forms, a trend developed towards more complex nervous systems and towards a greater ability to adjust to variations in the environment. Although there are differences between species, the more recent, 'higher' animals are on the whole those whose programming of the behaviour machinery during development is increasingly supplemented by learning. This makes for flexibility, for the ability to adjust better and better to a wider and wider range of environmental conditions.

Among all the animal species, past and present, Man is by far the most adjustable. He is the opposite of a narrow specialist, rigidly set in his ways. New conditions do not easily 'break' him, he bends; as has often been pointed out, he is a specialist in non-specialisation.[50] He has 'intelligence', a propensity which includes not only the ability to learn extremely well, but also curiosity, inventiveness, imagination and creativeness.

But we human beings ourselves – even, and perhaps especially, those impressed by the achievements of science and technology – have admired the intelligence of our species so much that we have often failed to notice that our adjustability is not unlimited, but that, as in all animals, the learning processes themselves are subject to rules; they are genetically constrained on the one hand, and prescribed on the other. The idea, based on the view of Man's unlimited adjustability, that a newborn's brain is a *tabula rasa* on which all the instructions for his future behavioural development will, so to speak, be engraved by his experiences with the environment, is a myth. We carry with us in our genes a rich heritage of our long, evolutionary past. First of all, we all develop a number of 'innate' behaviours. The simplest examples are a baby's crying, its smiling, and a number of other activities and attitudes which enable the mother to feed him and to care for him. Many other behaviours such as, for instance, walking, are partly programmed genetically, but require various kinds of learning to reach their full efficiency. But even where learning enters into our development, it does not happen in a random way; it is part of our heritage too that we learn certain things more readily than others.

Thus we learn more readily and preferentially to walk on our hind legs than on all fours; we can learn to eat a number of things that we would not eat without being taught, but no normal people learn to eat, for instance, stones or faeces. With respect to the rewards we expect ('reinforcing feedback'), we all have a preference for social approval over, say, a penny or a Smartie (something so often not appreciated by psychologists who submit children to discrimination tests, even though already decades ago the prominent psychologist Donald Hebb described how one of his chimpanzees began to offer *him* one of the slices of banana he had given her as rewards for correct choices).

Most behaviour is neither completely learned nor completely innate, but develops under the control of both genetic and learned instructions. Thus, while our tendency to want to learn to speak is genetically inherent in us, which one of the thousands of existing languages we shall learn is determined by the language spoken around us. The extent to which behaviour is innate or learned varies: thus many of our non-verbal expressions with a communicatory function, such as facial expressions and 'body language', are to a much greater extent innate than speech (and are therefore roughly the same in all people, anywhere in the world); the cultural (i.e. learnt) variations, while present, are relatively minor. While one could say that body language is innate to a greater extent than speech, it is less rigidly innate, a little more flexible, than the crying of a baby.

Our intelligence expresses itself also in other ways, e.g. in an almost irrepressible tendency to explore (to investigate and to learn as much as possible about) any object or situation that is new to us. Many other species are exploratorily minded, but none even approaches Man in the width and depth of this self-teaching.

In short, we are genetically programmed to develop some practically wholly innate behaviour, to learn certain things rather more readily than others and, by means of our exploration, to seek or even to *create* the right conditions for learning.

Those biases in favour of learning certain things and against the learning of other things have one thing in common: in the natural habitat this genetic control of what will be learned and what will not is *an adapted trait*: it leads to success; in other words, *learning is part of the programming for survival*; it supplements, refines, polishes the 'sketchy' results of the basic genetic programming. Further, the few 'purely' innate behaviours we have are those that have to 'work' immediately when needed, for which the spending of time on learning would be to our disadvantage, perhaps even lethal.

This interplay of nature and nurture in development (of which we gave no more than an extremely crude sketch) expresses itself also very clearly in the differences between people, even those who grow up in roughly the same environment, who have the same 'opportunities'. As we all know, there are (a) quantitative differences between 'brighter' and 'dimmer' children, but also, and more interestingly, (b) qualitative differences, in 'gifts' and their opposites – 'blank spots'. Such differences can be either enhanced or smoothed out to a certain extent by the way children are brought up. Further, we should in this context not think merely in terms of intellectual endowment and development but also (and we submit, in our highly rational, rationalising, technically thinking times, *especially*) in terms of emotional gifts and weaknesses, among them differences in resilience against pressures of a psychological nature.

While we begin to see these principles of the nature–nurture interaction at work in incidental cases, we are still very far from having an overall, concrete knowledge of how nature and nurture contribute to the normal human behaviour development as a whole, and of where exactly the limits of our adjustability are to be found, i.e. in what particular respects and how exactly an abnormal environment can impair a child's development.

In spite of innumerable studies of children and their ways, our knowledge of what a child needs and what damages him (either bodily or psychologically) is still very fragmentary and the subject of much dispute. But few are unaware that damage *is* often done; for example, many people are quite ready to consider disturbed children of many kinds as victims of a 'bad home background', even though it is not possible to pinpoint exactly what it is in this background that does the damage. In this kind of climate of thought it is remarkable that the environmental and psychogenic origin of autism is still so emphatically rejected. As the reviewer said, speaking of the proceedings of the 1978 conference of experts, held in Switzerland: 'The psychogenic school are the "baddies".'[51]

How very necessary and illuminating it is to see the nature–nurture aspects of human behaviour in the light of our evolutionary history becomes clear when we proceed to examine what *effects* our extreme yet limited adjustability and our superior intelligence have had on more recent periods of our history. These effects have been unprecedented; they have not been foreseen and are still ill understood; in fact we are only beginning to realise what has been happening to us – what *we* have made to happen – and what is still happening with ever-increasing speed: the exclusively human, literally new type of evolutionary change – the cultural evolution.

GENETIC AND CULTURAL EVOLUTION

In the several millions of years in which our ancestors gradually became the species Man, they evolved a characteristic that helped them to 'cash in' on the growing capacity to learn: the period between birth and adulthood, that of growth and development, became very long. Consequently the human young had increased and prolonged opportunities to learn, and although part of this learning took place, as it does now, within the children's own playgroups, children also learned a great deal from adults. This was partly done by accepting their leadership and observing and imitating what they did, and partly by being deliberately instructed, by adults and by their sibs. In this way a second type of inheriting *savoir-faire*, of transfer of instructions-for-development, came into its own: that of non-genetic, cultural transfer, of transfer by means of individual learning. Inventions were made by creative individuals, then handed on, and so became part of collective and cultural knowledge. This cultural transfer differed from genetic transfer not only in the way it was handed over but also in the size of the evolutionary steps it made possible, either steps forward (gains) or regressions (losses). Mutations and recombinations in the genetic constitution have to be very small because too large a 'jump' upsets the growth so much that the embryo is not viable. But things such as the inventions that led to the making of increasingly sophisticated tools, to the use of fire, to better housing and clothing, to agriculture, to the use of the wheel etc., were enormous yet viable jumps or 'saltations'. It was this that allowed this new type of evolutionary change – the change by means of culture – to proceed faster and faster, for useful knowledge once acquired became incorporated in the total knowledge of new generations, and so cultural education became an accumulating and accelerating process. A second aspect, a corollary of this cultural evolution, was a change in the relationship of our ancestors to their environment. More than any other animal species, whose main aim is to *maintain* themselves in their environment, early Man began to take control over and to *change his environment to suit his needs.* Animals do that (thus birds build nests and beavers build dams), but even though young may learn part of their future behaviour from adults, or by practice, such rapid cultural transfer of an *accumulating* nature is not found in animals – except, in an incipient form and under exceptional conditions, among monkeys and apes. But in Man the process that had started perhaps a million or more years ago at a pace that may not have been greater than that of his genetic evolution, became gradually faster, and so our cultural evolution (with its effect: the changing of our environment to suit us rather than the other way round) began to outpace the speed of genetic evolution. And since a healthy life, or fitness, depends in any organism on being adapted or fit, i.e. on doing what the environment requires us to do on penalty of failure, the man-made changes in the environment affected our fitness. Of course, by and large, the changes we made were (as they were intended to be) of such a kind as to make life easier, to reduce or eliminate altogether many of the pressures that reduced our viability. Up till very recently it has been obvious that the growing control we have over our environment – by means of our increased knowledge and understanding and by means of our technologies – has indeed on the whole been beneficial. But it is now becoming clear also that our 'conquest' of nature has not been wholly to our advantage; we begin to discover more and more harmful 'side-effects' (i.e. effects we had neither intended nor foreseen). In a nutshell, what has happened is this: our medical technology has made great strides in beating off parasitic and other illnesses. As a result, a higher and higher proportion of children survived until they could reproduce and beyond, and so our numbers, instead of oscillating round an average, have for many generations been growing consistently, though with many ups and downs. Now we live in a period in which this population growth has become so rapid that we speak of an explosion. Unprecedented and increasingly larger masses of people have to be fed, clothed and housed, and agricultural and other technologies are struggling to keep up with the growing demand.

But with the growth of all our technologies, and the giant industries to which they give birth, we have unwittingly called up a host of new harmful processes, new 'pressures' that reduce the quality of our habitat. Very briefly, these new pressures amount to: over-exploitation of our natural resources ('renewable' ones such as our forests, the fish and whales in our oceans, fresh water, even agricultural soil; and 'non-renewable' or exhaustible ones such as fossil fuels); and pollution of many kinds. With regard to energy (needed not only for making our machines, for making them work, and for transport and innumerable other tasks, but also for making the fertilisers on which high agricultural yields depend), complete depletion of some of our non-renewable resources is in sight.[52]

The pollution of our habitat takes many forms; we have not only to think of the poisoning of air, soil and water that is fast becoming a world wide problem, but also of such things as soil deterioration, desertification, and the creation of strains of parasites and pests that are resistant to some of the very drugs that were made to combat them.

GROWING UP IN THE MODERN WORLD

It is in this context that we have to look at our social environment too, for many of the new pressures are of a 'psychosocial' nature; we have created *psychological forms of pollution* which form a serious threat to our well-being and to that of our children.

Our modern societies, in particular in the ever-growing cities, have become very different indeed from those in-groups of extended families in which, for innumerable generations, the human young used to grow up until the more recent, in evolutionary perspective extremely short, phases of the cultural evolution changed the social structure. Greatly simplified, these changes have been twofold: (a) to an increasingly extent, modern children grow up in large, dense, 'anonymous' societies, at its most extreme in large cities and 'megalopolises', and (b) as already stressed, behaviour programming is less and less done in the informal but effective context of playgroups and the family, and more and more in schools and other institutions, where the emphasis is on being instructed and on having to learn a large, and still growing variety of new skills.

There are a number of consequences of these two trends that are harmful to normal development. These again fall under two headings. First, an increasing number of children are faced with conditions which overstretch their adjustability. They meet innumerable strangers; they grow up in an atmosphere of 'work' rather than play; their tendency to play and explore is not given free rein, and organised instruction, involving a certain degree of regimentation, has come instead, leading only too often to loss of interest and even rebellion. Secondly, the developing of parentcraft is suffering from what the American–Russian educationalist Urie Bronfenbrenner has called the 'virtual break-up of the family' (and we would add: from the reduced opportunity for seeing babies nursed and/or having to be in charge of younger children in the context of the closed in-groups).[53] There was a time when there was great confidence in 'human nature', in the sufficiency of 'innate' growth of mothercraft. Now we begin to realise that for the development of full behavioural efficiency (in our particular context, of good mothering and parenting) a great deal of 'polishing' by learning is required. We must emphasise again that with the disappearance, in the most 'anonymous' parts of our society, of the main settings for this programming-by-experience, *a very dangerous process has started*: that of *loss of parentcraft*, a truly *cultural loss, for which it will be extremely difficult, perhaps impossible, to compensate.* The institution of 'mothercraft classes', of organised instruction, is seen by many as a form of progress, of better health care. And even though this is true in some respects, we should see it rather as an attempt to *correct* for *losses* of efficiency in the raising of our young, and we believe that such correction, far from leading to better parenting, is at most a second-best to the original natural way of learning how to raise our children – a substitute that falls short of the optimum. We are convinced, although of course there is no 'proof', that the number of parents, especially mothers, who rear disturbed children because they themselves were not optimally parented is large, and that a number of autists are victims of this type of culturally caused disadaptation, one of a host of harmful 'side-effects' of the cultural evolution.

When now, in the light of this wider view of 'human nature' and the changes in the human condition, we look back at our list of 'autismogenic factors' we will see that many of them are, directly or indirectly, related to the deterioration of certain aspects of our social climate. Rather than running through the list once more, we rely on our readers to see this for themselves.

Conclusion

Our argument in this chapter on what makes children autistic involved three steps. After recapitulating what begins now to be known about the course the autistic derailment can take, we turned to its causation. Following some methodological comments, we argued that the contribution of heredity is almost certainly far less decisive than it is in the disorders that are known to start with a fault in the chromosomal endowment of the fertilised egg, and that the genetic aspect of the problem is rather one of causing differences between children, of whom certain types are more susceptible, more vulnerable than others. (How to characterise the susceptible children we do not yet know, but there seems to be a correlation between being highly perceptive, socially sensitive and intellectually or artistically gifted and being at risk of falling victim to autismogenic external conditions.) Our second step, based on scrutiny of the developmental histories of autistic and non-autistic children, was the enumeration of a large number of outside conditions of which, for such susceptible children, a limited number, different from one case to another, can trigger off the derailment. Many of these conditions are of a psychogenic nature. We stress once more that many of these outside factors are not necessarily the 'fault' of the parents, and that even those that are aspects of their parenting can be traced to conditions, often of many years ago, to which they themselves were exposed and by which they were damaged. In this context, our conscience forces us to be 'hard on mothers' (as some mothers see it) in order to help children, of the present and of the future. The third step in our argument was to see if and how our view of what causes autism fits in with the wider, overall view of the present condition of civilised humanity. We submit that a balanced view of the history of Man shows us that recent developments in social conditions are in part disadaptive. In this social aspect of our overall disadaptation, autism is one of perhaps many unhealthy, faulty types of development.

To recapitulate our views on the extent to which 'nature' (genetic predisposition) and 'nurture' (influences from the environment) causes a child to become autistic: while we do not deny that there may well be hereditary components in the causation of the autistic derailment, we assert that these components do no more than determine the *degree of vulnerability* to pressures exerted by the environment. There is of course no either/or to this; what we claim is that environmental autismogenic factors are at the moment being greatly underrated, indeed hardly given any attention. We further suggest, more specifically, that the responsible environmental factors are largely of a social nature. And since they act primarily through sensory inputs that affect the child's motivational state and through this his behaviour, our interpretation must be classed as being largely 'psychogenic' – 'organic' (structural) defects seem to us to be of minor importance.

We are of course not the first to propose a psychogenic aetiology; we merely revive the notion expressed, in rather simpler forms, by authors such as Kanner, Bettelheim and Zaslow.[54] But our interpretation differs from the earlier ones in that we mention a much larger range of environmental factors than these predecessors and in that we ascribe a far less important role to the personalities and behaviour of the parents; certainly we avoid apportioning *blame* to them; apart from being in many cases unfair, this is counterproductive because it tends to increase rather than reduce their unhappiness. We will return to this issue in the next chapter because it is highly relevant to the design of treatments.

We realise full well that, with the present state of our knowledge, our views cannot but be tentative. But so much seems to make them plausible, at any rate more plausible than other attempts at understanding what makes children autistic, that it seems to us highly desirable that much more research be aimed at testing them. As we shall elaborate in Chapter 7, not just the quantity but rather the *nature* of such research is of vital importance, and what we in fact advocate is a less conventional medical, even a less conventional psychiatric approach. We need a broader approach, one in which other disciplines concerned with the biology of Man are incorporated. In such a broad attack of the problem, ethology and ecology can render useful assistance – are indeed of crucial importance.

Notes and references

1 Of course even in the finest statistics on the frequencies of various degrees of deviation 'from the norm', the decision as to what percentage of the population is to be called 'normal' is arbitrary and subject to disagreement. This is true of very many populations of data, but even more so in psychiatry than almost anywhere else.

2 Case histories can be found in many of the summarising books mentioned in Chapter 1, notes 3 and 4, and Chapter 2, note 7; further, in the monographs on individual children listed in Chapter 10. The difficulty in making use of them is that they are usually (a) very fragmentary and (b) often biased by the authors' theoretical views. Neither can be avoided; thus the case histories we ourselves will give in Chapter 10 pay quite some attention to each child's early experiences. We consider that, in the light of our analysis of the aetiology of autism, and in order to restore a kind of balance in the evidence published so far, this is necessary, for ever since Bettelheim over-emphasised the role of parents in causing autism it was not only his particular views which were rejected but, with them, the possibility of any psychogenic influence of the early environment. As Wolkind wrote (see Ch. 1, note 6), 'The psychogenic school are the baddies'.

3 Massie, H. N. 1975. The early natural history of childhood psychosis. *J. Am. Acad. Child Psychiat.* **14**, 683–707.
  Massie, H. N. 1978. The early natural history of childhood psychosis. *J. Am. Acad. Child. Psychiat.* **17**, 29–46.

4 See note 2 above. An additional reason for distrusting many case histories is that statements such as, for instance, 'birth was normal' may fail to mention such things as that the baby had been blue (i.e. had for some time been starved of oxygen) or that forceps were used. Such, often quite relevant, details have to be dug up from records, if such records are at all complete enough. Again, the term 'normal' often reflects personal views of those concerned rather than a generally agreed view. Much of what is usually called normal is considered abnormal and harmful by workers such as Leboyer (see note 24 below).

5 Ornitz, E. M. 1973 (see Ch. 1, note 4).

6 As we said before, toe-walking may form part of autistic behaviour of people of all ages, but is also a passing phase in normal development. In autists we believe that it can be either an example of regressive or retarded behaviour or, quite possible, part of anxious behaviour – or both.

7 Chess, S., S. J. Korn and P. Fernandez 1971. *Psychiatric disorders of children with congenital rubella.* New York: Brunner/Mazel.

8 Rutter, M. 1973. Review of Chess *et al.* (1971). *J. Aut. Childhd Schizophrenia* **3**, 276–7.

9 O'Gorman's book (see Ch. 1, note 4) stands out among the summarising books because of its open-mindedness.

10 Ritvo *et al.* 1976 (see Ch. 1, note 4).

11 Wing, L. 1976 (see Ch. 1, note 3).

12 Kanner, L. 1943 (see Ch. 2, note 3).

13 Newson, J. and E. Newson 1963. *Patterns of infant care*. London: Penguin.

Newson, J. and E. Newson 1968. *Four years old in an urban community.* London: Penguin.

Newson, J. and E. Newson 1976. *Seven years old in the home environment.* London: Penguin.

As sociological reports on child-rearing patterns in urban families of six social classes (Class III is subdivided into 'white collar' and 'skilled manual'), these books have a deserved high reputation, but when the authors pronounce on the nature of autism and the treatment of autistic children (e.g. in *What is an autistic child?*, prepared for the National Society for Autistic Children) they show in our opinion a lack of understanding and insight. (See also Ch. 9, note 25).

14 The most recent and most thorough comparison of monozygotic ('identical', M Z) and dizygotic (D Z) twins with regard to the concordance or discordance of autism in the members of each pair is that by S. Folstein and M. Rutter (1978) in Rutter, M. and E. Schopler (see Ch. 1, note 4), pp. 219–43. They found that in 11 M Z and 10 D Z pairs, four of the former were concordant. The occurrence of four concordant pairs among the M Z twins, while of course not necessarily due entirely to genetic factors (being so similar, they may also have been treated similarly by their social environment, see note 13 above), suggests a genetic component in their vulnerability to autismogenic conditions from the moment of conception onwards, i.e. either while living in the womb, or during birth, or afterwards or during all these phases. Although the total numbers studied are (inevitably) still small, the fact that 7 pairs of M Z twins were discordant, far from disproving our contention that autism is to a large extent induced by the environment, shows of course that the environment exerts a great deal of autismogenic pressure. We feel that the authors underestimate the importance of this high proportion of discordant M Zs.

(In a review in *Monitor*, the magazine *New Scientist* of 3 March 1977 adds to the confusion by writing, under the heading 'Autism linked to genes and brain damage', the prize sentence 'So the answer to the question is autism genetically predetermined or environmentally induced seems to be yes.' And, completely unwarranted: 'The most unlikely cause seems to be psychological trauma – which can explain neither the mental retardation associated with autism, nor the differences between the twins' (p. 515). The least we can say is that in order to see this issue in perspective, we have of course to avoid thinking in such either/or terms.)

15 But see Hauser, S. L., C. R. DeLong and N. P. Rosman 1975. Pneumatographic findings in the infantile autism syndrome – a correlation with temporal lobe disease. *Brain* **98**, 667–88 – a reference to which Professor L. Weiskrantz kindly drew our attention. Since there is no agreement, either on the selection of subjects for this work or on the exact significance of this sort of evidence (see *Lancet* of 25 September 1976, 668–9), this and, we submit, all other reports on real or alleged structural abnormalities of the brains of autistic children must be regarded as unconvincing. Even if brain damage were generally correlated with a section of the autistic population, the old question of what is cause and what effect remains (see Ch. 7). Quite apart from this, the test is 'not without risk' (*Lancet*, p. 668) and is also said to be highly unpleasant for the person tested. If our view of the autistic condition is correct – and at least the over-anxiety of autistic children seems to be a fairly generally accepted fact – this alone should make any doctor think twice before using 'pneumo-encephalograms' as diagnostic tools. Autistic children are not only *interesting* subjects for study, they are also *sufferers*.

16 In studying this part of our argument, we ask the reader to remember that we do not claim that the environment is *alone* responsible for autism. Autism is, to use a fashionable analytical term, undoubtedly 'multifactorial' (i.e. due to a very complex interaction of influences). For a thoughtful discussion of this and related issues see Dixon, B. 1980. Reconciling health and disease. *Encounter* **54**, 64–8.

17 The generally accepted and continuously repeated statement that autism is found in

around four per cent of the population (implying of *any* population, at least in the Western countries, and unchanging) is based on no more than four censuses, viz. one done in Middlesex, one in the London district of Camberwell, one in Aarhus, Denmark, and one in Wisconsin, U S A (see Wing 1976 – Ch. 1, note 4 – pp. 65–71, 292–3).

18 For a summary of this study, see Bartak, L. 1978. Educational approaches. In *Autism*, M. Rutter and E. Schopler (eds) (see Ch. 1, note 4), pp. 423–38. 'Three units were selected. One was primarily a psychotherapeutic unit with little emphasis on teaching, one provided a structured and organised setting for the teaching of specific skills, and one used a more permissive classroom environment in which regressive techniques and an emphasis on relationships were combined with special educational methods' (p. 426). See, for details, Bartak's references to the reports published in 1973 by himself and Rutter.

19 See Chapter 3, note 10.

20 Chess, S. (1971) mentions that Desmond *et al.* (1976) have found live virus in the cerebrospinal fluid of rubella babies of up to 12 months of age. *J. Aut. Childhd Schizophrenia* **1**, 33–47.

21 We consider this an additional reason for not subjecting such children to 'more stimulation' in general. It is an accepted procedure to treat polio, glandular fever and hepatitis patients with *rest*; the same might well be recommendable for rubella children.

22 See Macfarlane, A. 1977. *The psychology of childbirth*, 12–13. London: Fontana/ Open Books, who also refers to earlier work; and Brackbill, Y. 1979. Obstetrical medication and infant behaviour. In *Handbook of infant development*, J. D. Osovsky (ed.), 76–126. New York: Wiley. Valuable new work is reviewed in Herbinet, E. and M.-C. Busnel (eds) (1981) *l'Aube des sens*. Paris: Editions Stock.

The importance of diet and especially (mega)vitamin supplementation in relation to some mental disorders is now beginning to be recognised. See, for instance, Pauling, L. 1974. On the orthomolecular environment of the mind: orthomolecular theory. *Am. J. Psychiat.* **131**, 1251–7. For a specific example of work on megavitamin treatment of autism, see Rimland, B. 1974. An orthomolecular study of psychotic children. *J. Orthomolec. Psychiat.* **3**, 371–7.

Rimland, B. 1976. The successful megavitamin treatment for 300 autistic children. In *Supernutrition*, R. A. Passwater (ed.), 67–8. New York: Pocket Books.

Rimland, B., E. Callaway and P. Dreyfus 1978. The effect of high doses of vitamin B6 on autistic children: a double-blind crossover study. *Am. J. Psychiat.* **123**, 472–5.

With these and relatively few other exceptions, the effects of diet on mental health and on health in general are not receiving the attention they undoubtedly deserve. Of course, we do not believe (as will become clear in Ch. 6) that drug taking, smoking and eating 'junk food' *alone* can 'cause' autism, but merely that abstaining from smoking and drug taking and adhering to a balanced diet (by both parents) may well reduce the chances of a child's derailment, since it is likely to increase his resistance against this and other assaults on his health. We need not stress either that healthy parents are bound to enjoy parenthood more and to be more alert to early warning signs than sick parents.

23 For a brief summary of the sensitivity of the unborn baby to a variety of sensory stimuli, see Chapter 1 of Macfarlane's book, mentioned in note 22 above, which describes work done since the early 1930s by Sontag and others. Of particular relevance to our subject is:

Sontag, L. W. 1966. Implications of foetal behaviour and environment for adult personalities. *Ann. NY Acad. Sci.* **134**, 782.

24 Under the influences of the work of Sontag and, more recently, of Leboyer (e.g. 1975, *Birth without violence*. London: Wildwood House) awareness has grown of the

very real possibility that prevalent practices of obstetrics in modern, especially Western, societies may well be far from optimal, and possibly be harmful to children. Interesting work on this is also being done by M. Odent, see Gillett, J. 1979. Childbirth in Pithiviers, France, *Lancet* **ii**, 894–6.

25 Although little attention is paid to this in the literature on autism, the disturbing effects of 'missteps in the dance' are often mentioned in the literature on mother–infant relations. The term itself is used by D. Stern in his book (1977) *The first relationship: infant and mother*, in the series *The developing child*, J. Bruner *et al.* (eds) (see Ch. 3, note 10). The book *Studies in mother–infant interaction*, edited by H. R. Shaffer (1977), London: Academic Press, has no special chapter on bonding failures, although Gordon's chapter gives some information on abnormal responses to sound in 'autistic-like' children. We find Stratton's discussion of the difficulties encountered in assessing long-term effects of the circumstances prevailing during and shortly after birth especially helpful. He stresses, in our opinion correctly, that a broad range of factors has to be considered and that 'missteps' in the interaction between child and either mother or caregiver may mutually reinforce each other and so involve both in a downward spiral. (Stratton, P. M. 1977. Criteria for assessing the influence of obstetric circumstances on later development. In *Benefits and hazards of the new obstetrics*, T. Chad and M. Richards (eds), 139–56. Lavenham: Lavenham Press.)

26 Apart from D. Stern's introduction mentioned in note 25 above, we refer to some more technical works.

Report on the CIBA Foundation Symposium 1975 on Parent–Infant Interaction. Amsterdam: Associated Science Publishers.

Shaffer, H. R. (ed.) 1977. *Studies in mother–infant interaction.* London: Academic Press.

Kennell, J. H., D. K. Voous and M. H. Klaus 1977. In *Handbook of infant development*, J. D. Osovsky (ed.), Ch. 23. New York: Wiley. Solnit, A. J. and S. Provence, ibid., Ch. 24.

A more anecdotal but very readable and interesting book is: Brazelton, T. B. 1969. *Infants and mothers, differences in development.* New York: Delacorte Press.

27 Gunther, Mavis 1961. Infant behaviour at the breast. In *Determinants of infant behaviour*, B. M. Foss (ed.), vol. 1, 37–44. London: Methuen.

28 Copeland, J. and J. Hodges 1973. *For the love of Ann.* 87. London: Arrow Books.

29 Hale, N. C. 1979. *Birth of a family.* Garden City, NY: Garden Press /Doubleday.

30 The well known book by Spock, B. 1973. *Baby and child care.* London: Times Mirror, New English Library, while containing much that is valuable, is certainly in many respects dated and perhaps a little misleading in its 'trust yourself' attitude.

31 See, for instance, Blurton Jones, N. and G. M. Leach 1972. Behaviour of children and their mothers at separation and greeting. In *Ethological studies of child behaviour*, N. Blurton Jones (ed.), 217–49. Cambridge: Cambridge University Press.

Leach, G. M. 1972. A comparison of the social behaviour of some normal and problem children. Ibid., 249–85.

Main, M. B. 1977. Analysis of a peculiar form of reunion behaviour in some day-care children: its history and sequelae in children who are home-reared. In *Social development in children: day care programs and research*, Webb, R. (ed.) 33–78. Baltimore: Johns Hopkins University Press.

Ainsworth, M. D. S. 1964. Patterns of attachment behavior shown by the infant in interaction with his mother. *Merrill-Palmer Quarterly* **10**, 51–8.

32 We have seen a most striking example of this but are not at liberty to describe the case history of the persons concerned.

The mute autist – Carla – whom we mentioned before, was sent, at age 17 years, to a children's home during her family's holiday. She later commented in writing that she had enjoyed her stay there in spite of her inability to speak with anyone, 'because I was always clearly told what I was expected to do, had three well-cooked meals at more or less fixed times each day' and in general 'knew where I stood'.

33   Dr Fae Hall (personal communication).

34   Zappella, M. 1976. *Il Pesce Bambino*. French translation (undated): *L'Enfant Poisson*, 158–80. Paris: Petite Bibliothèque Payot.

35   Dr J. M. Richer has independently arrived at views very similar to our own, and will himself deal with this in more detail than we do. We heard him explain his views to a group of visiting colleagues from Japan in October 1979, but feel we are not entitled to quote from his off-the-record talk.

36   The reports on psychosocial stress that we have seen on this subject issued by the Laboratory for Clinical Stress Research (W H O Psychosocial Center), Fack, S-104 01 Stockholm, have so far not given much attention to this aspect. The many works on the damaging effects of our rapidly accelerating cultural evolution and the resultant changes in our environment concentrate largely on material aspects and say little about what amounts to 'psychosocial pollution'. For recent introductions to the problem as a whole see:
Ward, B. and R. Dubos 1972. *Only one Earth*. London: André Deutsch.
Ward, B. 1979. *Progress for a small planet*. London: Penguin.
See also the publications in the form of separate 'papers' and books that are being produced, since 1975, by the Worldwatch Institute, 1776 Massachussets Avenue N W, Washington D C 20036, U S A, which are available at low cost.

37   Selfe, L. 1977. (with an Introduction by E. Newson) *Nadia – a case of extraordinary drawing ability in an autistic child*. London: Academic Press.
Unfortunately, Nadia's artwork deteriorated when she was given the kind of education that has been advocated so long by those who believe in the limited educability of autistic children, though no one can say whether the loss of the quality of her drawings was due to this education. We shall return to this in Chapter 6 (see also Ch. 9, note 25).

38   Adamson, L. 1978. Striking the lost chord. *Guardian*, 6 October 1978, p. 6. Joe, the third of three children, showed already in the first months lack of response and of sociability. At three years he was (as many autists are) 'a wizard at the most complicated jigsaw puzzles' and although he now can still speak only in single sentences, he 'can play Bach to prize winning level' and gives occasional performances.

39   Axline, V. 1973. *Dibs* (see Ch. 3, note 8).

40   Rimland, B. 1978. Inside the mind of the autistic savant. *Psychology Today* August, 69–80.
Rimland reports that out of 5400 case histories of autistic children on file at the Institute for Child Behavior Research in San Diego, no fewer than 531 describe 'extraordinary abilities . . . musical and mechanical, artistic, mathematical', some displaying highly unusual feats of 'memory, geography, pseudoverbal, co-ordination, extrasensory perception', or a combination of such abilities. Since, in Rimland's opinion, the view that 'autistic children suffer from an emotional as opposed to a neurological disorder . . . has been abandoned by all but a small minority of professionals', it is not astonishing that he looks for an explanation in terms of abnormalities in the brain, particularly (on the basis of neurological tests and one *post mortem*) in the right hemisphere. Interestingly, and to us highly suggestive, he also mentioned that a normal psychology graduate who studied twin autistic savants who both had an 'amazing ability to make calculations based on the calendar', discovered suddenly, after long practice, that he could match their speed for quite a long time! Since intense concentration and long practice (in other words, an 'obsession') could produce this effect in a non-autistic person, the question arises again: were the brain abnormalities reported causes or effects of being autistic? Apart

from this, our own experiences suggest that among the 5400 children whose case histories are on file in San Diego, considerably more than the 531 mentioned may well have 'islets of good performance' that have either not been allowed to develop or have not been reported, or have been seen merely as 'obsessions'. Rimland's evidence also makes us wonder once more whether autistic children are a random sample of the population or whether (in some way) exceptionally gifted children are perhaps more at risk.

41 See, apart from the books we mention in Chapter 9: Rothenberg, M. 1977. *Children with emerald eyes*. London: Souvenir Press – a book which radiates the loving optimism of the author. We cannot follow her rationale (and believe that she proceeds largely by intuition) but she does elicit remarkable responses in some of the children in her care.

42 In a personal communication to us, Dr Tsuneo Taguchi of Tokyo has expressed his suspicion that autism and other forms of emotional disturbance in children may well have sharply increased in Japan in the last two decades or so, but he stresses that reliable figures about the situation 20 years ago are hard to come by. Because of the suddenness of Japan's transformation into a modern industrial nation and the undoubtedly strong pressures under which many Japanese families live now, reliable surveys would even now be important for purposes of comparison with the few data available for Europe and the USA (see note 17 above).

V. D. Sanua is collecting what little information is available on the incidence of autism in different cultures – Sanua, V. D. 1979. Cultural changes and psychopathology in children. Keynote address to the *World Federation for Mental Health,* Salzburg, Austria, July 1979 – and on the incidence of autism in the different social classes within cultures – Sanua, V. D. 1980. Socioeconomic background of parents of autistic children: a critical review of the literature, presented at a *Symposium on Enigma of Infantile Autism,* Montreal, September 1980.

43 The 'wild boy of Aveyron' is often thought to have been what we now call an autistic child: see Wing, J. (1976) in Wing, L. (ed.) (Ch. 1, note 3), p. 4, where he refers to the famous book by J. M. G. Itard (1801, 1807) *The wild boy of Aveyron*, English translation by G. and M. Humphrey 1962. New York: Appleton-Century-Croft.

44 Why Wing and Ricks (see Ch. 1, note 8) object to our statement (1972, p. 9) that 'autistic behaviour is either more common than originally realised or is actually on the increase' is difficult to see, for there seems to be no third possibility.

45 For life of early man, see:
Lee, R. B. and I. DeVore 1968. *Man the hunter*. Chicago: Aldine.
Washburn, S. L. (ed.) 1966. *Social life of early Man*. Chicago: Aldine.
See also the first five volumes of the series *The emergence of Man* (1972–5). New York: Time-Life.

46 For the Bushmen, see Marshall Thomas, E. 1969. *The harmless people*. London: Penguin.
Eibl-Eibesfeldt, I. 1972. *Die !Ko Buschmann-Gesellschaft: Gruppenbildung und Aggressionskontrolle*. Munich: Piper.
For other modern hunter–gatherers see:
Coon, C. S. 1974. *The hunting peoples*. London: Jonathan Cape and Book Club Associates.
For Eskimos: personal observations by ourselves during our year with the Angmagssalik Eskimos of East Greenland, 1932–3.

47 Eibl-Eibesfeldt, I. 1975. *Ethology, the biology of behaviour*. New York: Holt, Rinehart and Winston.
Wilson, E. O. 1975. *Sociobiology*. Cambridge, Mass: Belknap Press.
Lorenz, K. 1978. *Vergleichende Verhaltensforschung*. Vienna, New York: Springer.

48 Medawar, P. B. 1973. Foreword to N. Tinbergen: *The animal in its world*. London: George Allen & Unwin.

49   Tinbergen, N. 1972. Functional ethology and the human sciences. The Royal Society Croonian Lecture. *Proc. R. Soc. Lond.* B. **182**, 385–410.
50   Lorenz, K. 1978 (see note 47 above).
51   Wolkind, S. 1979 (see Ch. 1, note 6).
52   The best recent sources of information are: Ward, B. (1979) and the publications of the Worldwatch Institute (see note 36 above).
53   Bronfenbrenner, U. 1974. *Two worlds of childhood.* London: Penguin.
54   After we had handed in our 'final' text to the Publishers, Professor Robert W. Zaslow of San José State University in California kindly sent us a copy of Zaslow, R. W. and M. Menta 1975. *The psychology of the Z-process: attachment and activity,* 2nd edn. Spartan Bookstore, San José State University, in which he devotes a chapter (pp. 214–42) to outlining a psychogenic theory of autism. This chapter 'follows exactly' Dr Zaslow's much earlier presentation (1967) to a meeting of the State of California Psychological Association in San Diego. Apart from a brief mention of this 1967 paper (without bibliographical details) by L. Wing (1976), who dismisses on p. 73 its thesis, together with some other psychogenic hypotheses, as being based on 'anecdotal' rather than 'experimental or epidemiological' evidence, we have not seen Zaslow's views mentioned in the literature; an omission that reflects the bias underlying the present unpopularity of environmental and in particular psychogenic views of the aetiology of autism. From Dr Zaslow's former pupil Dr J. A. B. Allan we also received some valuable reprints, of which we mention only: Allan, J. A. B. 1977. Some uses of 'holding' with autistic children *Spec. Educ. Can.* **51**, 11–15 (in which he also mentions earlier work of great interest). Allan's therapeutical methods seem to be even more similar to Welch's technique than Zaslow's, although Welch is more insistent than either that the child's mother must, if at all possible, do the holding. See further our remarks on this in the next chapter.

6

To what extent can austistic children recover?

In this chapter we turn from an analytical approach aimed at the scientific understanding of autism to the practical exercise of trying to find a cure for autistic children. If some of the points we made earlier are repeated in the introduction to this chapter, it is for the benefit of those more practically inclined readers who may have found the first half of the book to be less suited to their immediate needs.

Different views

When one reads the many published summarising treatises on autism, one might get the impression that there is a fairly general consensus of opinion on this issue; time and again one reads that 'only a small proportion of autistic children recover' and that 'the prognosis for autistic children is poor'. But this impression of a generally held gloomy view is deceptive; it is due mainly to the fact that it is expressed, and repeated so often, by a relatively small group of prolific writers on autism who claim, with remarkable confidence, that their opinions are nearer the truth than those of others. A little reflection is sufficient to see that any final conclusion on the potential of autists cannot possibly be justified. First, as we have stressed at the start, the phenomena of behaviour development of children are so extremely complex that their scientific study cannot possibly be said to be beyond its infancy, and without better scientific understanding there is no theoretical basis for any opinion about educability or ineducability of autists – what the experts offer as a final answer is a *fashionable* view rather than a *well founded* conclusion. Secondly, if we proceed by the principle of 'the proof of the pudding is in the eating', and go by what empirical basis there could be for either a pessimistic or an optimistic outlook, we have to keep in mind that the basis for *any* prognosis is the outcome of therapies that have been tried out in the past. In the case of autism this is a very shaky basis indeed, for what O'Gorman said in 1970 ('our efforts in the past have been largely empirical' – a euphemism for haphazard – 'and largely ineffectual')[1] is as true now as it was then.

In view of this, one would not expect a well founded 'consensus of opinion'. Indeed, when one casts one's nets wider and takes into account whatever evidence one can find about what people who have dealings with autistic children think on this issue – psychiatrists who do not agree with the 'generally agreed' opinions, many therapists, teachers and parents – one finds a wide *variety* of opinion, ranging from the very pessimistic to the very optimistic, and one also finds evidence of treatments with effects that seem to belie the gloomy view held by so many.

It will help if we go a little into the reasons for this variety of opinions. There are a number of them.

First of all, the *children* that receive the diagnostic label 'autistic' differ very much amongst themselves, and they may not all have the same chances of recovery. We know very little of what might be the inherent differences in susceptibility that predispose one child more to autism than another, but it seems very likely that there are such differences and that they are due either to genetic influences or to intra-uterine experiences, or (most likely) to both. Also, it seems now to have become more generally accepted than when we wrote our first paper in 1972 that there are differences in degree of autism; that a child can be mildly or severely autistic. The only pronouncement about the chances of different children seems to be a kind of rule of thumb: children who by the age of five years have not acquired (or resumed) speech and who have been found to have 'a low intelligence quotient' are less likely to recover than children who have at least some speech at five years and are considered to be of normal or high intelligence (Ornitz 1973).[2]

Opinions about prognosis also differ between the *psychiatrists* concerned. Their opinions seem to be determined by what they have learned in their medical–psychiatric training; by the methods of examination they apply; and by the sample of children they see. For instance, it is no accident that psychoanalysts such as Bettelheim and Ruttenberg[3] have rather more optimistic expectations than most other psychopathologists: attaching, as they do, great importance to early traumatisation and tending to believe that what the environment has done to a person can be undone more easily than purely genetic or severe and irreversible 'organic' damage, they are bound to expect autistic children to be curable. The results they have so far obtained with treatments based on their views do seem to give some support to their confidence (although, as we shall argue, we believe that their therapies can probably be further developed into even more effective ones, treatments that are based only partly on a better understanding of the causes of autism, and rather more on intuitive insights into what these children need).

The more pessimistic views so widely canvassed at the moment (at least in the English-speaking world) are in our opinion biased both by the nature of the research methods applied and by the fact that the children seen by most experts are not a representative sample of the total population of autists.

Most of these experts rely either on office interviews and tests done by clinical psychologists or, if they spend time on observation, they look at children in clinics or special schools. Hardly any of them do real 'field work', i.e. observe the children to any extent in their home environments. Yet anyone who has done such field work and knows how normally, intelligently and sensibly many autistic children can behave when they are at ease in their own environment can testify that tests done by or in the presence of a stranger and/or in strange surroundings give a distorted idea of their true potential.

Closely related to this methodological shortcoming – in fact a direct consequence of it – is the fact that most psychiatrists are acquainted only with the more serious cases of autism. Because they rarely observe children in their family environment and as a rule wait until patients are 'referred' to them, they do not see the considerable number of autists who recover. What these doctors see are the children who, often at two, three or even four years of age, have lagged so far behind and have become so clearly abnormal that their parents begin to insist that there is really something seriously wrong with them. Thus the clinic-based psychiatrist naturally sees a slanted sample of the total population of autists, and it is not surprising if his experience with predominantly severe autists leads to pessimistic expectations. He may not *wilfully* close his eyes to the less severe cases; he does not know of their existence or, if told about them, is inclined to believe that they are not 'true' autists. Many parents do indeed report that the doctors to whom they turned did not take their observations and worries seriously.

Another methodological source of bias is the fact that almost all psychiatrists, never having had any training in the observation of (non-verbal) behaviour, are inclined to look for 'tangible', 'biological' or genetic, or 'organic' causes of autism and even if they do not find such 'tangible' defects, tend to believe that they will be found.

All this together goes far towards explaining why most psychiatrists believe that autism is an incurable illness; and this belief in turn leads to a biased attitude towards the significance of the relatively rare occasions on which even a severely autistic child behaves normally or even exceptionally well: such incidental events are not considered of great importance but are on the whole regarded as 'flukes'.

We believe that those who, on the contrary, attach special importance to such incidental good achievements and believe that they reveal the child's true potential are, while perhaps equally biased in this opposite direction, rather nearer the truth.

However this may be, the existence of these different and, in extreme cases, so diametrically opposed views reveals that opinions on the issue of educability of autists, like so many other opinions held in science, are not as objective and rational as they might seem, but are partly moulded by (often not conscious) subjective, non-rational thinking. This is of course neither surprising nor to be condemned, but it is just as well to be aware of it.

Different views about the educability of autists are also held by *therapists and teachers*. A considerable number of them are strongly influenced by the opinions of the scientists they know or whose works they have read. It is striking to note the difference between those who believe a pessimistic psychiatrist and those who are followers of optimistic scientists. Therapists of a pessimistic bent are responsible for the kind of statements already quoted – that autistic children are 'ineducable' or that 'you can't make them relate but you can teach them simple skills'. Another reason for pessimism in therapists and teachers is failure: if you find that you have little or no success with your charges, it is only human to ascribe this to *their* low potential rather than to possible inadequacy of your own procedure. And pessimism based on failure is of course only too easily reinforced by authoritative statements by experts that autists are ineducable. In view of this, it is in fact astonishing to find that there are so many therapists and teachers who keep trying to help their charges, who never give up hope, who 'believe in them'. These stubborn optimists among the therapists and teachers have an attitude towards the occasional glimpses of normal behaviour they see in their charges that is diametrically opposed to the one to which we referred above: far from shrugging off the few incidents of unexpectedly normal behaviour as flukes that can be ignored, they consider them to be highly significant glimpses of the 'true' nature and abilities of the child. In more scientific terms: they are convinced that the few occasions of normal behaviour show that the neural 'machinery' is there all right but it is most of the time, in some admittedly unknown way, prevented from working properly.

Finally, very similar considerations apply to the *parents* we know. Among them too one finds all shades of pessimism and optimism. In our experience it is on the whole the parents who have not succeeded in lifting their children out of their autistic state, who are (as is only natural) pessimistic, i.e. emotionally predisposed to believe in ineducability, while, equally naturally, parents whose children have recovered are optimists. It is unfortunate and a serious block to progress that the National Societies for Austistic Children[4] in a variety of countries are influenced so strongly by doctors of the pessimistic kind, and so, inevitably, attract almost exclusively parents whose children have not recovered.

In view of all these differences – between the children concerned, between methods, between patients studied and between opinions held by the psychiatrists involved, between the experiences of therapists, teachers, and, last but not least, between different parents – it would seem to be unjustified, and not quite responsible, to present dogmatically a – quite possibly temporary – 'majority opinion' as more than just that: as the final verdict. It is quite clear that the problem of educability is still wide open, and that we have to look at it anew. This is what we have tried to do, and as a result we have become convinced that there are good reasons for more hope. Those reasons we shall now discuss in some detail. The reader must not expect a cut-and-dried case for all we shall suggest, with well substantiated 'verification'; as will have become clear in the course of our arguments, we claim that work on this issue is still in the stage of qualitative analysis; that what is needed is new exploratory thinking. In this we are not alone – in fact there is a growing ground-swell of thought and work which is based on similar convictions.[5]

Educability – the nature of our argument

Our opinion that many autists can be educated and become normal, in some cases even outstanding persons, is based on considerations of three kinds, two of them conjectural, the third more directly factual, but all pointing in the same direction.

First, if one accepts, as we do, that the autistic condition is primarily an emotional imbalance, and that this imbalance is to a very great extent due to the environment, i.e. to upsetting experiences in early childhood, it would seem plausible to assume that what the environment had caused to become 'derailed', can be guided back onto the right track by a corrective change in the environment – a therapy. Such a correction of the developmental course would seem to be more difficult if autism were due to purely genetic or to 'organic' defects such as 'gross' (or even 'minimal') brain damage, which could be expected to be more serious defects, less easily remedied than an emotional imbalance.

Secondly, we consider it fruitful to look at autism in the light of modern Western, or rather, industrialised and urbanised, acquisitive and competitive society. We have argued that this society, while in many respects beneficial, does create at the same time a number of conditions which require a greater degree of adjustment than even our exceptionally adjustable species is capable of. Although epidemiological evidence concerning changes in the incidence of autism is practically non-existent, and facts on the geographical or societal distribution are still tentative (but see V. D. Sanua's recent work),[6] it looks very much as if quite a number of our 'autismogenic' factors are typical of our modern society. What begins to be known of the types of social conditions to which our species has become adapted in aeons of genetic evolution, and in which the young of our species can be moulded by experience of the kind that their genetic constitution requires or tolerates, indicates clearly that modern conditions offer on the one hand too much and on the other too little opportunity for fulfilling the human child's developmental potential. This consideration leads one likewise to expect that appropriate manipulation of the child's environment might well either prevent or undo the autistic derailment.

Both these inferential arguments are reinforced by our third point, which is based on a body of more direct, straightforward evidence, evidence of the typically medical and empirical kind, based on the saying 'the proof of the pudding is in the eating'. Empirical comparison of the effects of the many different therapies that are being tried out suggests strongly that *those that concentrate on the restoration of the disturbed emotional balance are the ones that have the highest degree of success.* In other words, our attempts at understanding autism and the empirically discovered results of various therapeutic regimes lead to convergent conclusions. *In our view this means that they mutually strengthen each other.* This is a weighty argument, since the workers concerned came to their conclusions independently of each other. When we wrote our 1972 paper, the new therapies such as that of Dr Welch (see below) had not yet been developed, nor did *she* learn about *our* views until after she had developed her treatment – and when she read our paper she thought at first that her therapy ran against our view that 'adults should not intrude'.

When we began to sense that different treatments might well have very different success rates, we decided to try to find out what characterised those seemingly more effective treatments. For this it was necessary to collect as much evidence as possible about different educational regimes and about the results obtained. This may sound a simple task, but in fact it is, at least at present, a very difficult one. Indeed the difficulties are such that it is only too easy to shrug off the evidence now available as 'unreliable' or 'insignificant', and even to argue that it is vain to make a comparative assessment at all. However, we feel that this must not deter us at the start; rather it should compel us to subject the difficulties to a close scrutiny. The circumstances that hamper us most in making valid comparisons are the following.

(a) Although we do need a variety of treatments for our comparison, the actual situation offers rather too much of a good thing: the variety of regimes is too large; in fact it is no exaggeration to say that no two schools, clinics or even individual persons apply exactly the same procedures.

(b) An additional difficulty is that, although many therapists, teachers and parents involved describe, or at least give a label to, the educational methods they have applied, those labels and even the descriptions are rarely sufficient and unambiguous; one and the same label or description given by different authors can refer to very different realities. When you actually observe what two persons *do* rather than what they *say* they do, you may find that they proceed in fact in very different ways. For instance, one speech therapist may habitually try to hold a child's attention at all costs and may keep requesting or even ordering him to say a particular word, repeating it time and again ('Say "apple" '). In extreme cases such attempts may even involve forcing the child's head back to a position in which he faces the therapist so that his only defence against eye contact is to 'avert' his gaze. The therapist may show impatience or disapproval. At the other extreme, another speech therapist may adjust continuously to the momentary moods of the child, may primarily 'mother' him, perhaps play and joke with him – such workers bring, in an unobtrusive way, almost 'on the sly', some speech teaching into what are in essence playful socialisation attempts, during which the child may either copy the therapist's speech or may even say something of his own; often he may say loudly what he had for a long time said internally.[7] Yet both these treatments, however different, are often called 'speech therapy'. Individual speech therapists may (in fact do) differ in many more aspects of their behaviour – subtle and perhaps insignificant to *them* but quite possibly vital to the children concerned. Also, different children respond, of course, very differently to one person and way of teaching; as with normal interpersonal contacts, such imponderables as the 'personalities' of both, and of whether they 'click' with each other or not – perhaps even doing so on one occasion and not on others – all such things can and do vary. The same is true of almost everything a caregiver does: the way in which she speaks to a child, the degree of patience shown when a child misbehaves; the way and even the tone in which a child is disciplined or spoken to in general – all this may in fact vary, though they may well be *described* in the same words. And this matters, because children, even or perhaps especially autistic children, can be uncannily sensitive to such subtle, seemingly imponderable variations. It cannot be said too often that at the present stage of understanding of human behaviour, still an art or craft rather than a science, we can draw only approximate conclusions from what we are told about what a caregiver actually does. The least we have to do is to observe what is actually being done.

The same applies to the reporting of the effects of various kinds of treatment. What one therapist reports as a 'success' may be described by another as no more than a 'minor step forward'; thus the 'parroting' of a few words may be compared favourably or unfavourably with an occasional meaningful utterance, depending on what the therapists concerned see as their aims.

If reports by therapists must be treated with caution, it certainly is uncritical to go by what different *parents* report about their interactions with their child. In particular many mothers, keen to meet with social approval, not only give very misleading accounts, but even behave much more lovingly to their children when they feel themselves observed than when they think they are alone.[8] It takes considerable sophistication (and patience) to pierce such a 'cloak' of (often probably unconscious) acting on the part of mothers, but the good observer can often notice the slight slips into the usual, non-acted behaviour that such mothers do make. Although we ourselves are of course far from convinced that we see all that is relevant, we submit that by taking these difficulties into account we do get a better impression of the real interaction of such children with their environment than if we were merely to go by interviews, questionnaires and tests, however impressive, 'controlled' and 'quantitative' the latter may be supposed to be.

(c) Reliable comparison of the success rates of different regimes is further hampered by the fact, which can be remedied only in due time, that each centre works with only a few children at a time, individual persons often only with one at a time. Therefore, almost all the reports, even those that contain enough relevant information per pupil, have so far been 'statistically non-significant' and are, and will for a long time be considered, by those preoccupied by the need for counting and measuring, to be of negligible value. Even when such reports concern a sizeable sample of children, the treatment they have received will not have remained constant but – if the therapists concerned are at all sensitive and adjustable – will have been gradually adapted to what they discover to be the child's real needs. In reporting, the worker may not be able to recall all those adjustments.[9]

(d) Another difficulty again is that of assessing the condition of a child both before and after a given time of treatment or education. Although there is now an extremely useful schedule (BRIAAC) designed by Dr B. Ruttenberg of Philadelphia for objectively scoring a large number of aspects of a child's behaviour,[10] this scheme has not so far been generally adopted, and for the time being we shall have to go by either lengthy descriptions of improvements in a child's behaviour, or by statements such as 'he was rather severely autistic when he arrived (with, on occasion, the addition of the name or standing of the doctor who made the diagnosis); now, after n years of treatment, he is attending a normal primary school'. Yet, however vague, even such a statement is of course of considerable value.

(e) If the information available is not ideal because it is incomplete, and only half reliable, comparison of the effectiveness of different regimes is hampered even more by the failure of many workers concerned to report at all on their procedures and their results. From personal experience we know only too well that many therapists (and parents) and those who are guiding their therapeutic attempts are overworked, and often involved emotionally to such a degree that it is unrealistic to expect them to provide such reports. Even so, the sad fact is that a great deal of potentially valuable information that could be of help in judging present procedures and in designing those of the future is available only to the workers involved.

In addition, what information is available suffers from a bias: publications of treatments and their remedies are not likely to come from those who have had little or no success, and most of the published case histories are in fact reports on more or less successful treatments. This (and the fact that these reports have been written by 'laymen') is perhaps why research psychiatrists, 'professionals' in general, are so reluctant to take notice of the (far from negligible) number of such reports that *have* been published about individual children. However, we have found that by reading these laymen's accounts critically and without bias, and with due appreciation of the usually simple, everyday language (often quite refreshing after one has read pompous, verbose and dry-as-dust 'scientific' treatises), and finally by sifting fact from theorising, one can extract valuable information from case histories of this kind.[11]

One may well ask whether these five obstacles, that make a sound comparison of different therapies difficult, do not make it totally impossible. We submit that to accept this would in fact be defeatist and that, under the present circumstances, it is better not to wait for who knows how many years, and instead to make at least an attempt to use what information we have, and see where it gets us. So, without forgetting about all the reservations we have mentioned, we shall now discuss what we have learned so far about the effects of different regimes that have been applied to autistic children and try to extract useful guidelines from them.

While very far from complete, the information we will use comes from a variety of sources: we have seen a number of individual tutors at work and/or have been more or less involved with their work; we have visited a number of schools and clinics, some in Britain, others in Holland, in Belgium and in the United States; we have looked at a variety of films and videotapes about educational procedures, among them the BBC television film that strongly advocated the 'ineducability' viewpoint, but also films on more or less successful treatments (which we shall presently describe). We have read a number of published reports, and we have had numerous discussions with colleagues in the countries mentioned above, with visitors from many countries, and with correspondents. We have studied several cases at first hand of cures achieved by parents, mostly without the knowledge of, let alone guidance by, doctors. Finally, we have also studied, at close quarters and for several years, some (so far) unsuccessful attempts, and tried to understand the possible causes for these failures – an exercise that, as we gradually discovered, can be quite revealing. Details of some, though by no means all, of the case histories of such children are given in Chapter 10.

From the evidence collected in this manner, we shall now discuss those treatments which have quite clearly achieved more than the pessimistic school would predict; we believe that they alert us to a number of principles that seem to be worth more study than they have been subjected to so far. We find this sampling of a variety of regimes also useful for another reason: we believe that many therapists who are applying more or less successful treatments are convinced that they have found *the* best way to treat autistic children. But not only might there be more than one way leading to success, we might also, by combining the seemingly best features of several treatments, be able to design a way of treating autistic children that is better than any single therapy so far developed.

Towards a successful treatment

THEORETICAL DERIVATION

As we have indicated before, one way of approaching this issue is to try to derive ideas for the education of autistic children from what we believe we understand of: (a) the nature of autism; (b) its aetiological origin; and (c) psychological stresses at work in modern industrialised and in general highly complex societies. This could lead to ideas as to what kind of education we would expect to be effective. If our theorising has had any merit at all, such 'thought-up' treatments should conform at least fairly satisfactorily with those that are found empirically to be in fact successful.[12]

In a treatment derived from an understanding of the aetiology, it would be logical to give top priority to a restoration of the child's emotional balance, i.e. to attempts at reducing the pathological over-anxiety and the resulting withdrawal that we consider to be the essence of being autistic. This means that we would expect the penalising of single undesirable behaviour components and the teaching-by-instruction of isolated skills such as walking, grasping objects, drawing, speaking, reading, writing etc. to be symptom treatments that would at best affect only these single, isolated expressions of the general autistic state, while leaving the underlying, basic, disorder untouched, or even (as in the case of penalising such things as the self-inflicting of injuries) aggravate it. The restoration of a sense of security would, of course, have to be done primarily by 'supermothering' (including the establishment of some degree of discipline, regularity etc.) but it should also include, as an aspect of this, the adjusting of one's parental behaviour to the emotionally younger state of the child. Yet, at the same time, the child would probably have to be treated as *more* advanced than his physical age with regard to his 'islets of good performance'. Symptom treatment might not be unsuitable as such but it would have to be done only when the child shows that he feels secure enough to co-operate. Even 'penalties' might have their use, again provided they did not increase the child's anxiety. In Chapter 4 we have explained how some (verbal and non-verbal) signals have the dual effect of making a child stop doing the unacceptable thing and yet making him seek bond-strengthening as well. Parental behaviour of this kind might well have its part to play.

From our analysis and from other theoretical considerations, we would further derive the idea that the use of drugs ('pharmacotherapy', 'medication') should be avoided as much as possible, or at least be used only in emergencies and for 'tiding over' exceptionally bad spells. It would also seem wrong to give in to a child's tantrums and so teach him in effect to become progressively demanding in the maintenance of sameness in the environment. Examples of such impossibly spoilt children, who impose extremely restrictive regimes on their familes, have been reported quite often. Likewise it would seem to be wrong to allow or encourage an autistic child to withdraw progressively more – a development that happens only too easily with placid babies, of whom the mothers think 'that's what he obviously wants'; 'when we leave him alone he is happy' etc. Our analysis would seem to indicate that, if at all possible, one ought to concentrate on helping the child *socialise*, and only as this succeeds, however slowly, to supplement this with a suitable, and only the really necessary, level and amount of skill teaching. As in normal development, such socialising should begin with helping the child to affiliate, i.e. to form the emotional bond with his mother, which, as we have argued, mother and child had failed to form at the proper time. How all this could be done in detail would, of course, have to be worked out for each individual child–mother dyad, or child–parents and even child–family system; we shall discuss some practical aspects in Chapter 9.

THE PROOF OF THE PUDDING

We can also approach the problem of curing from the practical, empirical side, and try to find out, not what kind of treatment we would theoretically *expect* to work best, but rather which ones of the many different therapies that are already being applied *do* work best. *A priori*, the two approaches need of course not lead to the same results; for theories, however plausible, may after all turn out to be wrong, but *if* theory and practice were to correspond, they would mutually support each other.

As we have said, we have paid quite some attention to how autistic children are being treated, and with what outcome, partly by making personal observations during our visits to clinics, schools, tutors and families, partly by studying the published and personally communicated reports, and we feel we are beginning to get a fair impression of what kinds of treatment work well, and which do not lead to much improvement.

Before we describe some of the most interesting of these treatments, we can say, with a fair degree of confidence, *that those that produced the best results do indeed conform in general with what we had derived from our analyses*. Even in cases where therapists stressed that they concentrated on the teaching and development of skills – perceptual, motor and cognitive – we noticed that success came with those regimes that, often unwittingly, did also improve their pupils' emotional balance. But, not surprisingly, we also found that several regimes we saw being applied made us either modify our earlier views to some extent or showed us elaborations of which, in our analytical preoccupation, we had not thought ourselves. In fact, it was fascinating to discover examples of imaginativeness and inventiveness that had obviously sprung from quite remarkable intuitive understanding of the children's world.

Restoring the mother–child bond

Under this heading we are going to list some of the types of therapy in a continuous series, irrespective of the sub-headings we have used so far.

(a) Of all the therapists we have seen at work or whose papers we have studied, the psychiatrist Dr Martha Welch of New York proceeds in a way that seems to us to be both theoretically sound and, as far as one can say now, more successful than any other procedure.[13]

Dr Welch makes *the mother* of an autistic child hold him on her lap in a face-to-face position, embracing him (even when he resists) and smiling at him, talking to him, stroking him over his head and back or patting him on the back – in essence, doing what a normal mother would frequently do to a much younger child, particularly when he is distressed. At the start, this is done in supervised sessions, but the mother is instructed to do this herself every day for certain periods (varying in length as the situation demands).

Dr Welch developed this procedure step by step and in a largely empirical way. She has allowed us to quote from a letter she wrote to us on 17 August, 1978, which we do at some length because this method of 'holding' turns out to be so impressively effective. We have changed the names of the patients concerned.

'As a Fellow in Child Psychiatry at Albert Einstein College of Medicine in New York, I was required to spend two years in the outpatient nursery for autistic children and their mothers. The staff watched these children without understanding much. Then a mother–child pair with a symbiotic psychosis presented.

Following Mahler's teaching, they did not separate them. However, when the pair came to the nursery, the other children, who had been seemingly unresponsive, began to protest vehemently. The nursery therapists then asked the other children's mothers to come too. The one child whose mother was not available had to be removed because of the obvious pain he was in at seeing other children with their mothers.

In 1974 when I entered the nursery, the children and mothers were there together but without much change. In fact, my case had been there two years without effect. I was told to try to get close to this very difficult mother who had carried a knife to the nursery for the previous two years. Somehow we managed to establish a close relationship in the two month period before I had to be absent with sick leave. While I was absent, the mother and child attended the nursery faithfully. Then when I was ready to return, the mother disappeared. I then called her mother (i.e. the child's grandmother) for help. The grandmother was reluctantly willing although she insisted that I come to her home for our meetings because she ran a day-care nursery for the City of New York in her apartment.

The child's mother was furious with me for invoking her mother's help but did agree to participate in weekly sessions. Later she was able to tell me that she was angry because my long absence had caused her to miss me and had made her realize that she wanted me to hold her. This realization opened the floodgate of feeling she had for her mother. In our sessions with the grandmother, the two women told each other how much they longed to be close, how much the daughter wanted her mother to hold her, how jealous she was of the babies in the day-care program who were getting the grandma's care and attention, and how much the grandma missed the babyhood of her six children and wished to return to that time. A breakthrough came when the grandma physically embraced the mother on Mother's Day. The mother finally experienced the holding she had been missing all her life. Within a day or two the autistic child uttered his first words, even though he had not been present at the session. Furthermore, from this time on the mother was able to face him when she was angry. Until then she had abandoned him until she had cooled off.

The next key case was the Henleys, whom you will see on the N B C film. Max was referred to our hospital by his nursery school at age three and one half because he was unrelated, bizarre, did not speak, only communicated by having tantrums, and was obsessed by flushing toilets. He worked hard to avoid gaze contact with anyone, especially his mother. The parents acted at first as though there was nothing wrong with Max. When the school suggested that there might be pathology (medicinese for "that he might be ill") they took him for hearing tests in case he was deaf. He was not.

When mother and child entered the nursery, the mother was profoundly shocked to see the severe disturbances in the other children. She asked if her child were as seriously ill. I said yes. From then on, I had her fullest co-operation. This has not always been so with the mothers of other children. Mrs Henley was able then to remember having stopped holding Max before his first birthday, maybe earlier. She took care of his physical needs only. After this revelation, Mrs H. picked up Max who was having a tantrum on the toilet (his usual place) and held him despite a tremendous physical battle. I held her to encourage her not to let go (this holding by the therapist of the mother is now no longer done by Dr Welch, who believes that it is wrong). This went on every day at the nursery at least for an hour, and at home she held him for up to five hours a day.'

Because this case has turned out to be fairly typical, we add what Dr Welch then wrote about the effects of this treatment of Max and his mother. (We might also add that we have seen both since, in May 1979, and found the boy by all criteria normal, just a touch shy of us, and academically in several respects at a level far beyond his age.)

'Within six or seven weeks, he began to speak. One day he said "Thank you for holding you". Subsequently his speech developed rapidly and his ability to establish and hold gaze (contact) gradually improved. I will never forget his joy when he ran over to his mother to say, "Look, mom, I'm fighting with the boys!" It was a sweet moment, for Mrs H. and me. Also in January he began to show reading readiness without having been taught anything. By age 5½ he was reading exceptionally well. He had been accepted at a private school with a scholarship for kindergarten this past year, but his mother and I felt that all day school was too much separation for a boy so recently emerging from complete autistic withdrawal.

This child is now warmly related to his whole family, also to his teachers, and of course to me. He has tremendous curiosity in all things, interest in art, a large vocabulary for his age, a joy in living, and an intimacy with his mother that surpasses most so-called normal children's ability to relate. He is also very mutual. He articulates his feelings extremely well.

Now in this case, the mother was willing to forcibly hold the child. In other cases, the mothers have to be forced or at least coerced.'

Of course, when seen in the context of our interpretation of autism and its origin, it would seem to make eminently good sense to give a child who has missed out on adequate mothering or has otherwise been 'hurt' a solid dose of 'supermothering', however belatedly, and to do this by treating him the way one would have done when he *began* to 'derail'; i.e. by behaving towards him as if he were a very young child, or treating him the way any mother would deal with even older normal children when they need support or consolation after moments of distress, or when ill or sickening for an illness etc. It would seem *a priori* plausible to base a treatment on the assumption, the hope, that an autist can in this way 'catch up' on a deficit at the very root of socialisation and exploration without which his development could not have made normal progress.

Dr Welch's great achievement is in our opinion that, at several stages of her search for a therapy, she has had moments of intuitive, flashlike, insights and has at once begun to act on them. We believe, and her results so far justify this belief, that her therapy reaches the core of what has gone wrong in this development of autists. What did surprise us and what we ourselves would certainly not have expected, is that the method works even when mother and child are violently aversive to the holding–being held procedure.

Having seen, and largely understood, the rationale and the effects of the Welch procedure, we now believe that our earlier critical attitude to the method applied by Zaslow and his co-workers[14] (in which the therapist does a kind of holding) was in part misguided (see Ch. 5, note 54). But we also believe that it is a crucial aspect of the Welch procedure that it is the *mother* who must do the holding, not the therapist. Dr Welch insists that the therapist must on no account 'usurp' the role of the mother (a point also made by Axline); also, the mother learns essential skills from doing the holding herself.

Dr Welch has now treated quite a number of children – autists and others – and she has prepared for us a brief report of four successes and one failure, which we print in Appendix I (p. 322). More patients are of course under treatment, and the prospects for the majority look very bright. Together with her mother, Mrs Jane Welch, Dr Welch has also established a 'Mothering Center', where group sessions are held under guidance and in which up to six mothers and children take part together.

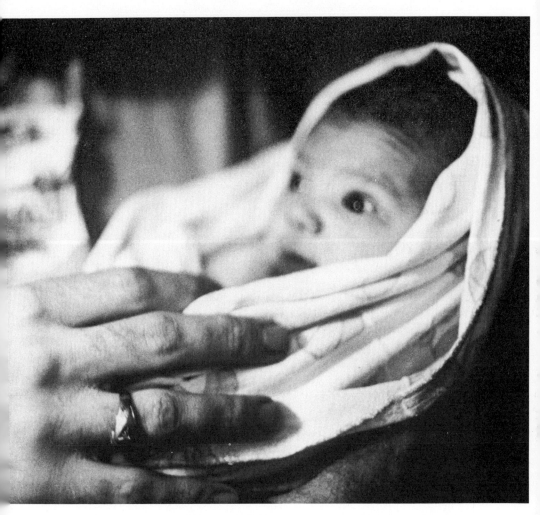

Plate 1 The alert reconnaissance of the world by a competent new born. (We once saw this expression on the face of a 12 year old autistic boy after his first holding session. For 10 minutes, he looked first at his mother and then at his father, who, deeply moved, remarked he had never seen his son look at anybody in this way.) From Hale (1979).

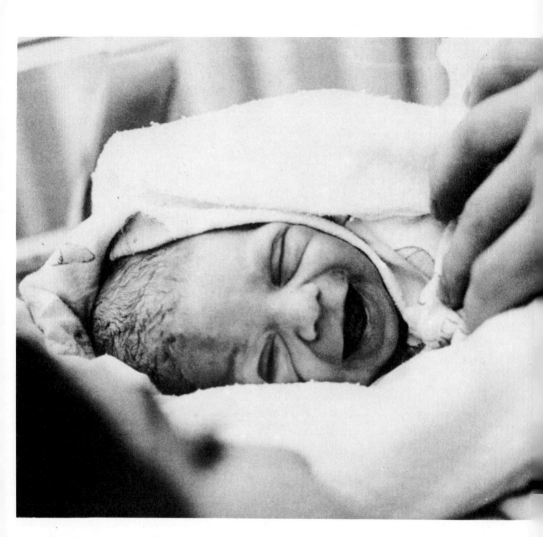

Plate 2   The smile of a newborn. (Many autistic children smile like this for the first time after a holding session.) From Hale (1979).

Plate 3 'Holding' in the natural setting. A normal three-year-old in distress is held by her mother.

With upset, tired or sick children it is often necessary to return to earlier stages of nursing such as 'holding', even suckling etc. This stops as soon as the child has returned to normal. With autistic children this principle of 'returning to square one' has been turned into the core of a new therapy by Dr Martha Welch MD of New York, as the sequences shown in Plates 51–58 inclusive (photographs by P. Elmhirst) show.

Plate 4 'Holding' in two
other natural situations.
Top: Father calms his
over-boisterous son.
Bottom: Mother hugs her
tired young son.

Plate 5   A 'Welch session' (1). The boy is still resisting.

Plate 6 The same 'Welch session' as on Plate 5, a little later. The boy begins to interact positively with his mother.

Plate 7 Another 'Welch session'. The start: the child resists; the mother's mother gives support to the mother.

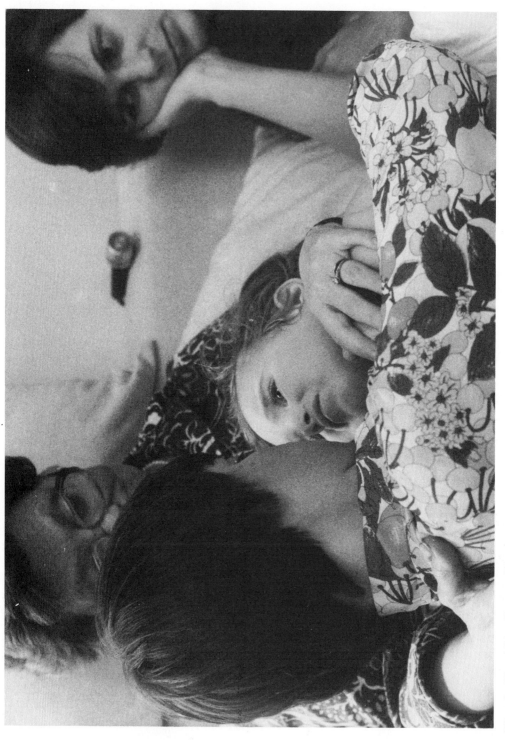

Plate 8 The child, still resentful, begins to make eye-to-eye contact with her mother.

Plate 9 Interaction with Grandmother.

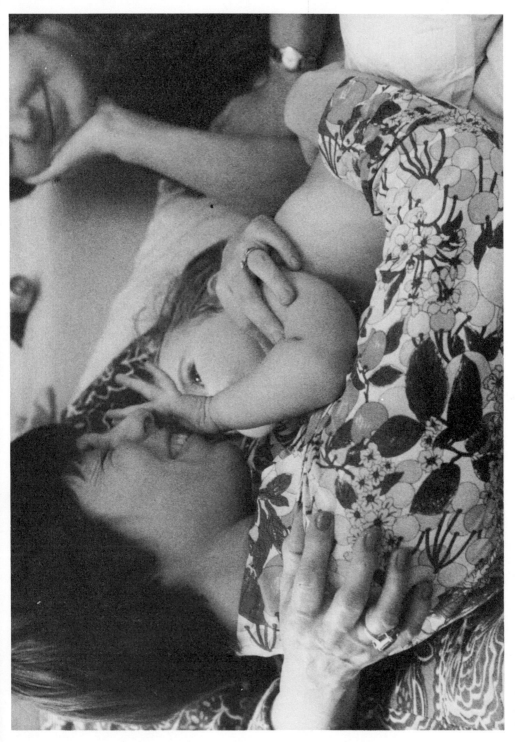

Plate 10 Exploring Mother's face.

Plate 11 Interacting with Dr Welch. Dr Welch's face reflects her response to the progress made during the session.

Plate 12 Exploring chess pieces elsewhere in the room.

We were allowed to sit in on a mothering session as well, and are convinced that here is at last, if not yet the best possible therapy, at any rate one that far surpasses in results anything that we have seen or read about so far.

Dr Welch emphasises that it is essential that the mother holds the child in each session *until the phase of resistance has turned into positive attachment behaviour.* As indicated in Max's case, this might in the beginning take hours. Unless a mother is prepared to abandon for a while everything else and never let go, the treatment might not only fail, but *lead to some opposite results*; if a child notices that it can get off by throwing a tantrum or biting his mother, or by urinating in her lap (a defence put up by some children) these disruptive behaviours are positively reinforced. During the struggles the mother must remain friendly and behave as a loving mother of a very young child – which *may* include berating him for particularly obstructive behaviour! With children above the age of approximately 10 years it is of course advisable not to take up the face-to-face position, but to hold the child at one's side.

Needless to say, all this demands a great deal from a mother, and also from her husband and other children. But once the holding sessions begin to lead to earlier and earlier switching to attachment behaviour, both mother and child enter a phase of providing each other with, and experiencing from each other, positive feedback instead of discouragement, and thus the downward spiral of autism is turned, *for both*, into an upward spiral. It is hardly necessary to emphasise that Dr Welch has noticed a profound change in the mothers, an intense realisation of happiness that they thought they had lost forever; and as this proceeds, the whole family begins to feel happier. After we had learned about Dr Welch's method and had seen her practising it, we have ourselves supervised such 'holding sessions' with various autistic children and their mothers (parents) and have also succeeded in persuading other therapists to begin holding courses. Although these courses have been completed only for a few of the dyads concerned, progress has already been made by all of them; it is too early to say more.

An interesting feature of this treatment is that the child often begins not only to talk, but to bring up memories of traumatising events of which the mother had no recollection at all. Some of these events may be seemingly trivial, but they have obviously been deeply hurtful to the child. For instance, one child (who remembers an astonishing number of details from experiences at age 15 months and even from 11 months on) recalled an occasion at about that age when, as had happened before, she was 'parked' with her grandparents for a day while the parents went house-hunting. In order to prepare for any eventuality, the mother had packed the girl's pyjamas in her little suitcase. It now turns out that the child had seen this and taken it to mean that the parents, contrary to their promise, would not return and might abandon her altogether. Evidence of such memories of events at a very early age are of course found in more children. (This incident also shows that parents need not feel guilty about 'having made a mistake'.)

On the basis of her experiences so far, Dr Welch is convinced that, as was obvious with Max Henley, once a mother–child bond has been successfully re-established the child will not only show how much, while in his withdrawn state, he had latently learned, unnoticed by his relatives and teachers, but will also, so to speak, take his further education in his own hands and catch up enthusiastically and rapidly. While our experiences with recovering autists confirm this to a large extent, we do believe that one qualification should be added: the longer and the more severely a child has been autistic, the more he will have missed out on the learning of those skills for which instruction is necessary, and the more helpful it will therefore be to provide him at least with some extra opportunities for belated acquisition of some abilities. However, we agree with Dr Welch in essence that a recovered child will be keen enough to take the initiative in finding such opportunities. Even so, such children may well be unable to fill completely the gaps left in the period when social withdrawal made them not only reject instruction but made them miss a great deal of playing with other children, and thus a number of things that are learnt best in a play context. Also, children who are recovering from autism may well remain vulnerable and easily discouraged for a long time, and may well need not only a continuation of short holding sessions but a great deal of sympathetic encouragement – 'moral support' or 'moral holding'.

The 'forced holding' procedure of Dr Welch differs in one important aspect from the 'holding' and 'rage reduction' treatment described in Zaslow and Breger (1969): Welch considers it essential that, if at all possible, the child's mother rather than the therapist holds the child. It is true that in their later publication Zaslow and Menta (as mentioned at the end of our previous chapter) put – at least in some chapters – more emphasis on instructing the child's parents to hold him, or at any rate to take over this task once the therapist has started the treatment. It is not quite clear to us to what extent and when this emphasis on the parents' role has developed, for the different chapters in Zaslow and Menta seem to contradict each other in this respect. But so much seems clear that there has in Zaslow's work been a gradual shift towards parental engagement. As we have seen, J. Allan's work has also moved in that direction. This shift may well have preceded Welch's very definitely mother-centred therapy. Rather than trying to settle the issue of priority it seems to us worth pointing out that different workers have, obviously independently, arrived at very similar ideas for a treatment of autism, and until we learned about Welch's treatment, our own approach has also developed independently and by the use of rather different methods of study. But, priority apart, we give the Welch procedure, so to speak, pride of place because of its biological consistency and plausibility, and because we have ourselves seen its effectiveness. We hope and trust that closer contact between the various 'psychogenically oriented' therapists will lead to refinements and elaborations that will make these treatments even more effectual.

One cannot help wondering how it is that these therapeutical approaches have not been taken more seriously and have not become better known. We suspect that this is due to *fashion*, and that this fashion has had its origin in the rejection and virtual ignoring of psychogenic theories of aetiology in the 'autismological' literature. In view of the favourable results claimed by those who apply one form or the other of 'holding', this rejection-by-shrugging-off seems to us unfortunate and not conducive to progress.

Other procedures

While we are convinced that the Welch method of 'holding' tackles autism at its roots and is best suited to be the core of its treatment there seem to be no *a priori* reasons for considering it the one and only or invariably the complete answer. In fact, various measures of success are being reported by therapists who proceed in different ways. In the search for the best possible way of treating autism, such reports must of course be given serious consideration – not because those treatments would necessarily be better than holding, but because they might perhaps be combined with it and, jointly applied, achieve more than any single one alone. Without claiming that we are in a position to give a final assessment of their value, we shall list and discuss briefly what information we have so far collected about such possibly subsidiary treatments.

Before we do so, we want to point out that some of these may not *at first glance* seem to have much in common with holding or other methods that aim at the restoration of a healthier emotional balance. But we believe that upon closer inspection most or all of them, by whatever name they go and even in whatever terms they are described, may well have a considerable emotional impact; that, whatever else they achieve, they help reduce anxiety and apprehension and enhance self-confidence, initiative and independence; and that it might well be this emotional impact that is the decisive healing factor.

(b) Thus a number of workers in California have been teaching autistic children a variety of skills for a number of years and obviously with considerable success. Schreibman and Koegel[15] have published a brief account under the revealing title *Autism: a defeatable horror*.[16] From their semi-popular account, which is especially valuable because the text is supplemented by a number of very instructive photographs of therapists at work, they show that the children in their care do tolerate a great deal of what we would in 1972 have called relatively instrusive skill teaching, including fairly conventional forms of speech therapy. They also apply some 'behaviour modification'. But it is equally clear, although the authors do not emphasise this much, that all this is done in a warm, loving, bonded atmosphere. The photographs show that the children are trusting and attached to the teachers, otherwise they would never tolerate a close face-to-face encounter in which the speech therapist not only demonstrates her mouth movements but is even allowed to manipulate the child's lips. While we appreciate the considerable degree of success these workers are reporting, we suspect that (a) their treatment works so well because they do in fact give priority to 'treatment at the emotional level', in particular to creating a secure environment for the children, and (b) part of the skill teaching might well be unnecessary because the children might have learned quite a lot of their own accord.

More recently, the authors associated with this group have emphasised in particular the behaviour modification aspect of their treatments, but in order to find out to what extent security-restoring aspects of their procedures are involved as well, we would want to observe personally what they do; this we have so far not been able to do.

What is interesting in this group is the extent to which the children's parents are engaged as co-therapists, though in another way than is done by Welch. But as with the Welch procedure, the impact may be felt not only by the children but also by the parents and, as we shall see, this aspect is considered important by other workers as well.

(c) Important work of a different kind (which deserves a fuller report than we can give here) is being done by Dr Geoffrey Waldon M.D., who operates the Centre for Educating Young Handicapped Children at Home, in Didsbury, Manchester.[17] In a circular about his Centre, Dr Waldon writes that 'the chronological ages of children accepted by the Centre range, with a few exceptions, from within the first year (the younger the better) to about ten years of age, at initial referral.' After 'a preliminary assessment and discussion of the child's problems and levels of functioning', Dr Waldon decides about a treatment. In this, his 'own sessions with child and parent(s) and/or teacher at fortnightly or in some cases four-weekly or weekly intervals' serve to instruct the adult(s) involved in the art of conducting daily sessions of approximately one hour. While we hope that Dr Waldon will in the not too distant future write his own treatise on his procedures and the rationale behind them, we are grateful for permission to print a brief account that our colleague P. Harverson has written on the basis of a series of interviews with him, and of her experience while watching him work with her own pupil, a girl whose tutor she has been for a long time. Miss Harverson is herself engaged in writing a fuller account; for details of this and also of the film that is being made of Dr Waldon's work, see note 17. Miss Harverson writes:

'Dr Waldon's work grew out of his many years' experience as a practising doctor working with "brain-damaged" and disturbed children, and as a lecturer in

Clinical Audiology in the Faculties of Education and Medicine at Manchester University. He has thus had the opportunity to examine and follow many hundreds of children with all kinds of problems. He now works privately as an educator of handicapped children, among whom is a majority of children with varying degrees of autism.

He has made a very close study of the development of normal children and compared it with that of the retarded, and has come to believe that the common basis to all normal growth of thought, understanding and behaviour is the child's own activity, starting from the day he is born. He is convinced that nearly all concept-forming activity (as opposed to specific-skill learning) is done by the child when he is alone or at least undirected by an adult. It is this normal exploratory "busy-ness" which is the foundation for all logical, spatial and mathematical understanding.

It is Dr Waldon's thesis that if there is *any* impediment to the child's activity (as, in the case of autism, an emotional withdrawal from the environment) the result is a growing "out-of-tuneness" (disharmony) between bodily growth, understanding and environmental expectation. For it is in activity that children develop their thinking and their powers of reasoning (as Piaget also contended): then lack of activity is bound to have a deleterious effect on these same general types of understanding, and on the expression of them.

Children at this sort of disadvantage are often made to feel inadequate and handicapped largely by the social pressures put on them. They therefore resort to defensive behaviours which further retard them and further discourage them from the kind of exploratory play which they need to engage in if they are to learn. Dr Waldon's practice then is to create in each lesson a situation as free as possible from social pressure but in which the child is encouraged – sometimes even at first physically manoeuvred – to be active at whatever level of competence he has reached. The aim is to get the child as soon as possible to provide all the effort necessary, to have him attend entirely to what he is doing and to ignore the teacher, except as a source of interesting things to do. The better his understanding, the greater his interest and the more readily he can disregard irrelevant features within his surroundings – including the teacher/adult.

The level of competence is originally assessed by observing the spontaneous reactions to different materials presented to the child (bricks, pegs, puzzles, objects to match and sort etc.). Once this has been determined, the teacher (whoever it might be) continues, in a neutral way, to put material and tasks in front of the child so that the child is as likely as possible to attend exclusively to what he is doing. To this end the teacher often stands behind the child, who is usually seated at a table, and assists, without comment, *only* enough to ensure that the child is always working either to the maximum of his physical ability or close to his "top" level of competence and understanding since it is at this growing edge that true learning takes place. Such "asocial lessons", as Dr Waldon calls them, require practice, keen observation and much self-restraint. Repetition is encouraged, but so is variety, effort and freedom of movement, because the final goal for the child is *adaptability* and *confidence*.

Dr Waldon frequently reminds parents and teachers that effort brings its own satisfaction and provides its own motivation once it has been fully tasted and enjoyed. This is why he thinks that, with this kind of activity, vociferous adult approval is not only misplaced but also misguided. The kind of spontaneous, varied and effortful activity in normal children which Dr Waldon tries to reproduce in the "lessons" is typified by the solitary child who (unaware that he was being observed by his mother) got on and off a sofa 37 times, varying his method slightly each time! So in the lessons Dr Waldon varies (1) the way he distributes the material or (2) the number of elements. Only gradually, as the child becomes more capable, will he raise the level of difficulty and sophistication. In all this his aim is to foster the confidence which comes from understanding and dealing effectively with the environment.'

In the autumn of 1978, Dr Waldon kindly allowed us (E.A.T. & N.T.) to visit him, to ask him questions about the background of his work, and to sit in on sessions with two of his pupils. While we cannot of course claim to have received more than a fleeting impression of his method, we add a few comments of our own, based on our reactions at the time. Needless to say that these comments are our, not Dr Waldon's, responsibility.

When engaged with a pupil, Dr Waldon clearly, as emphasised by Miss Harverson, refrained from 'instructing' him. After facing the child with a task, or rather a challenging situation, he confined himself on the whole to being a source of support and (largely silent) encouragement, adjusting (or so it seemed to us) his behaviour from moment to moment to what seemed to be required. There was very little, if any, coercion, but we would not call these sessions 'asocial'. When the child hesitated or faltered, Dr Waldon sometimes made a few subtle attempts at either reviving his interest or encouraging him; or he would for instance say 'You don't like this any more. Fair enough.' or words to that effect and face the child with a new 'task'. It seemed to us also that, by subtly and shrewdly modulating his behaviour in response to that of the child, he exerted a kind of quiet authority as well as moral support, which obviously appealed to the children we saw on our visit. We did not hear him praise the children in a condescending way (perhaps because, as we do, he believed that this could easily insult a child), nor did we hear him make disapproving remarks or discourage the child in non-verbal ways. There was a great deal of, again largely non-verbal, well timed *acknowledgement* of the child's achievement (or, on occasion, of his reluctance to proceed further). In this, Dr Waldon's behaviour reminded us very much of what Axline reported about her interaction with Dibs, although Axline seems to have verbalised more.

The children's attitude to the sessions was, in turn, very much dependent on Dr Waldon's behaviour. They obviously wanted him to be near them and to take notice of what they achieved, but they also tolerated his occasional withdrawal. We think that he deliberately tested and, we believe, enhanced their independence by now and then moving away from them, occupying himself perhaps behind a screen or a cupboard in another part of the room and, towards the end of a session, leaving the room for a short time, though without closing the door. The way we saw it was that, although the children were certainly practising what we would call skills (from simple manipulatory to sophisticated intellectual skills – we do not make the distinction made above by Miss Harverson but do not consider this important), the sessions seemed, so to speak, to float on Dr Waldon's emotional impact. His behaviour struck us as that of a good father, one who at the same time provides security, reassurance and encouragement by his mere presence and subtle interaction with the child, treating him at a level required by the child's sense of his dignity, and also challenging and so stimulating the child's initiative, inventiveness and creativeness. While seemingly aloof, Dr Waldon did exude a kind of fatherly charisma, and we felt that, behind the variety of tasks set or offered to the child (and behind the opportunity, given at the end of both sessions, for free creative activity of the child's choice) the emotional aspect of this fatherly attitude might well be of decisive importance in his procedure. We also agree that the self-confidence the child develops by coping with challenges likewise contributed greatly to his emotional growth; the relation between emotional and intellectual growth is clearly mutual, and far from simple.

As the name of the centre indicates, Dr Waldon treats children with a great variety of handicaps; in his own words: 'The majority of the children attending have delayed and slow development which might be associated with a movement disorder or a remote disposition. Among these are children referred to as being "autistic" or "spastic". Frequently children are referred as "not talking" or as having speech disorders. Reading disability and emotional maladjustment, including in children who are considered to have normal general abilities, are other reasons for referral.' In applying roughly the same kinds of treatment, with relatively minor adjustments to individual needs, to a very wide array of disorders or types of malfunctioning, Dr Waldon obviously acts on the belief that the various labels he mentions apply to symptoms rather than to deeper causes. In this his attitude is rather convergent with ours in that he too suspects that there is more affinity between autism and a number of other developmental 'derailments' than either the symptoms or the diagnostic labels suggest. We have seen, and shall see below, that he is not alone in this view, nor in its implications for the design of a therapy.

It is also worth pointing out that Dr Waldon too attaches great value to active participation of parents and teachers.

Finally, we believe that there is more compatibility between Dr Welch's holding method and Dr Waldon's procedure than is at first glance apparent. It seems to us likely that bodily holding is the first stage in a rehabilitation process of which 'moral support' without actual touching may well be effective once the relation with the mother and the rest of the family has been established. In other words, the 'baby stage' may well have to be followed by exposure to situations that normal children learn to cope with when bodily holding has either been superseded or required at most at moments of distress. Furthermore, since we believe that normal children learn a great deal from exploration in its widest sense, Dr Waldon's procedure would seem to have a role to play because it combines the more advanced forms of 'non-touch holding' with the healing influence of offering the child challenges of a kind and in a way that further fosters self-confidence. At the same time we believe that Dr Waldon's method might well be maximally effective with children who have 'graduated' from bodily holding, although the latter may well, as Dr Welch claims, be necessary at the start with most if not all autistic children. We shall return to this question of an integrated therapy in a moment.

(d) In 1979 we were invited to visit another centre which reports good results with, among others, autistic children: the Institutes for the Achievement of Human Potential, in Philadelphia, which were founded and are being run by Dr Glenn Doman and his collaborators, among them (initially) Dr C. H. Delacato (the author of *The ultimate stranger*).[18] This centre takes in a variety of children ('brain damaged, mentally retarded, mentally deficient, cerebral-palsied, spastic, flaccid, rigid, epileptic, autistic, adenoid and hyperactive') of many of whom Doman and his colleagues, not deterred by these diagnostic labels, believe that their brains, though malfunctioning, are potentially capable of working much better than they do, or even normally, but who have been in some way traumatised ('hurt' or 'brain injured' is the term Doman uses). We do not feel competent to judge the rationale of the treatment developed by Dr Delacato and Dr Doman (and with which, among others, Dr René Spitz and Professor Raymond Dart have also been associated) but include these institutes because of the impressive results their treatments produce.

Dr Doman's inspiration for this work came from personal experience with more than one case of near-miraculous recovery of fellow soldiers (he fought in the 'Battle of the Bulge' of World War II) who had been shot through the brain. He argued that if severely damaged adult brains could be coaxed back to near-normal functioning, the much more resilient brains of 'hurt' children must be expected to be even more capable of recovery.

The children treated in these institutes, many of whom had been pronounced incurable by their doctors, are first rated on a competence scale of 14 levels, running from '0' (no movement) through intermediate levels such as 'moving forward flat on abdomen without pattern' and various forms of crawling, creeping and walking to 'walking, cross pattern'. By various tests (for a rationale of which we must refer to Doman's book), it is then determined whether the potentially functional central nervous system malfunctions either in one or more of three sensory input systems (whether their incompetence is in their 'tactile, auditory or visual systems') or in one of the three main output or motor systems ('mobility, language or manual competence'). Then, according to the specific malfunctioning discovered or deduced, the child concerned is subjected either to a regime of intense sensory stimulation in the affected sensory sphere, and/or to a pattern of 'putting through', making him passively perform the movements he does not ('cannot') perform. These treatments start at the first of the 14 levels above the one the child concerned masters and move slowly up the scale. Doman stresses that a child is not and must not be 'entered' for a higher level until he has mastered the one he is engaged in. Another characteristic of the Doman–Delacato treatment, which it shares with those we have already mentioned, is that the children are mainly treated by their mothers who, in teaching sessions, are instructed how to proceed, and who come back to the Institute only for checkups and for instructions with regard to the next higher level. Of course, this roping-in of the mothers (and some fathers) enables the Doman Institutes to treat a great many children at a time and with a limited staff.

Whatever the merits of the rationale behind these treatments, the treatments themselves are obviously very effective, as is illustrated by the following figures, derived from a summary of results obtained with 76 children with a variety of abnormalities, who (after various forms of neurosurgery, the nature of which will not concern us here) received the suitable behaviour treatments over the years 1958 and 1959. At the start, 56 of these children did not walk; 40 did not even crawl. These children, whose ages at the beginning of the treatment varied from 12 months to 9 years, began treatment no sooner than 10 months after surgery. The duration of treatment ranged from 6 to 20 months, with a mean of 11 months. No child was refused treatment because of severity of deficiency in moving *per se*, or in crawling, creeping or walking.

The results were, briefly: at whatever level a child started treatment, it was performing considerably better at the end of the treatment than at the start, and the average improvement in terms of the 14 levels distinguished was 4.2 levels. The range of improvement was from 0 levels to 13 levels. For details we must refer to the original publications.[18]

When, after having read Doman's book, we visited his institute, we became convinced that there was more to the treatment than the published accounts indicated. It was striking that it did not consist merely of the various ways of taking a child through the stimulation and/or mobility exercises, but that the staff (so to speak) radiated a mood of affection, of love, and of confidence in and respect for each child and parent. In other words (although in a programme sheet for a full day's work for a mother only five minutes might have been allotted to 'loving' as such,) each child was actually lovingly attended to throughout every day. The reason for omitting any mention of this overall attitude was obviously that the attitude came so naturally to the Domans and their staff that it seemed not worth special mention. In our view it is in part because the 'skill training' programme was done in this quite strikingly favourable social context that so many of the children concerned made such astonishing progress. Our visit convinced us even more of the necessity to treat descriptions of treatments (and also labels) with caution and open-minded awareness of possible shortcomings in them (or positive qualities not explicitly mentioned) and, as a consequence, of the necessity of going and seeing what is actually being done. We also realised that if these treatments worked well with genuinely brain-damaged children, the question whether or not autism is due to structural damage does not seem to be so very relevant after all.

We cannot judge to what extent the Doman–Delacato procedure benefits autists of the type we are writing about. Because Doman's Institutes are not inclined to treat autism as a distinct 'entity' of nervous disorder, we could not find out, either during our visit or in subsequent correspondence, whether the treatment was adjusted to autistic and other conventional labels or whether the results with autists were different from those obtained with other children. We agree to a certain extent with the notion that autistic children have, in their emotional condition, a great deal in common with many other types of 'brain-injured' ('hurt') children in the Doman–Delacato sense, but feel that for the sake of overall assessment of their methods it might be helpful to break down the results according to the original diagnosis given, rightly or wrongly.

All in all, however, we believe that much in the Doman–Delacato treatment is of value for the treatment of autistic children, provided it is understood that the emphasis on mere skill-teaching as given in the published reports is not taken to mean that the treatment does not involve the promotion of socialising and the consequent emotional adjustment. In this respect, we have seen for ourselves that both the Waldon and the Doman–Delacato treatments involve these, seemingly imponderable, emotional aspects, the significance of which these outstanding educators may well have understated.

(e) Brief mention must be made here of the story of Raun Kaufman who was severely ill soon after birth, recovered, but began to show more and more autistic behaviour at the end of his first year, and became worse during the following eight months. His father's book is summarised in Chapter 10.

If one strips this book of theorising, it describes very convincingly how an intensive treatment by the parents according to the Delacato rationale, but clearly involving an intensive, continuous programme of socialisation, leads to striking successes (we wonder though whether the attempts of the parents to make Raun into a prodigy are well advised, but this issue falls outside the scope of our book).[19]

(f) A different procedure again is the one that has been applied and described by Helen Clancy, on which we have already reported in 1972.[20] Since we have not heard of recent developments of this treatment, we merely quote here what we wrote in 1972:

'Dr Helen Clancy and her husband Dr Glen McBride from Brisbane provide an example of integrated team work of a therapist and an ethologist.
They have concentrated not only on direct observation of behaviour but also on
research in causation; and their therapy is based on the *relationship* between
the autistic child and his family (in particular his mother) and on the *process* of
affiliation. They have studied mainly children who have shown deficiencies in
their social bonding behaviour from a very early age on. Their results lead them
to suspect that motivational disturbances may often be primary, rather than for
instance perceptual or speech defects as such. The effects of their therapy bears
this out: speech improvements occurred in all 16 children treated so far, none
of whom received speech therapy. The Clancy–McBride therapy is original: it
elicits the collaboration of the mother by beginning to explain their method and
requiring her active co-operation. All these children show initially a
pathological rejection of any but very few preferred types of food. This
rejection is broken by the therapist offering a very small quantity of a rejected
type of food on a dish of the preferred food. When, as is usually the case, this is
enough to make the child refuse the entire meal, it is simply taken away and no
other food is offered. The result is an initial period of actual starvation. This,
and the child's frustrated response elicit invariably increased solicitude in the
mother (as well as, in many cases, hostility to the therapist). However, once the
child begins to accept the new food, and makes up for its previous (food)
deprivation, operant conditioning is started with the object of facilitating social
contact, beginning with direct eye contact (between mother and child). This,
Dr Clancy told us, makes use of the intense interest of all children in soap
bubbles, and the mother's presentation of this reinforcer immediately after the
child glances in her direction is used to speed up, step by step, the establishing
of eye contact, and the entire process of affiliation.

The success of the method seems to depend, as expected, on the willingness
of the mother to cooperate, and so ultimately on the authority of the therapist
with the mother. This therapy (as that of Axline, the author of *Dibs*) differs
from our "taming procedure" with normal shy children in that, although a
strong bond can develop between the therapist and the child, she takes care not
to usurp the role of the mother. This suggests to us that, however useful our
"taming procedure" is as an experiment, it would not be a suitable start for a
therapy, except with children who have been given in residential care, or with
children whose mothers cannot or will not co-operate. Clancy, incidentally,
refuses to treat the children of uncooperative mothers.

On the other hand, Clancy's and McBride's procedure does involve, as they
stress themselves, a certain amount of "intrusion", and might well therefore
be open to improvement, e.g. by adjusting the speed of the conditioning to
slight signs of resistance in the child. (Tinbergen & Tinbergen 1972, pp. 43–5,
Ch. 1, note 8).'

We have little to add to this, except for emphasising that this treatment too
involves the mother and aims at re-bonding. As the therapist applies the
kind of deliberate mild 'torture' to the child, the mother is helped to
respond to his 'supernormal' distress signals (often to the extent of holding
him) which, in Clancy's experience, all mothers do. The use of soap
bubbles rather than the routine sweets or other food as reward to help the

child over his initial fears is a welcome inventive break away from conventional practices.

This, incidentally, could be extended and used in other situations by trying out a variety of other (including partly social) rewards. The cue for this can and must be taken from what one notices about the child's interest; if, say, a look at a passing bus, or a playtime with a pet, even (as used by the parents of Elly Park – see below) the use of a counter for scoring difficult achievements, or any other thing or event gives the child satisfaction and self-confidence and helps him in the socialising, the use of such reinforcers would seem to be commendable.

(g) David Park (the father of Elly of *The siege*) has described (1974) a method of operant conditioning that worked well up to quite an astounding level.[21]

When Elly saw that a mildly autistic son of her parents' friends used a wristwatch-shaped counter (such as golfers use to record their strokes), on which he could himself accumulate a score, so that he could count up all the occasions during a day when he had been 'good' and receive a reward for 30 points a day, she asked for a counter of her own. Then 'her mother made a great invention', as first Mrs Park, but soon mother and daughter together, worked out a weekly 'contract', which specified words, expressions and acts that were to be rewarded in the week to come. 'Faults' were soon deducted as penalties. Too difficult tasks were avoided (so that in effect this was a graded task regime). As old problems were solved, they disappeared one by one from the contract, and new, more ambitious tasks were added. Elly soon built up scores of hundreds, many more than were necessary for the standard reward of ice cream after dinner. 'When 1,000 points were offered for swimming the length of the pool, Elly, who had never before swum more than a few strokes, did it six times in one afternoon . . . The counter and contract provided by far the most successful experiment in behaviour modification that our family ever tried' (p. 191). Park further comments that 'The system utilised and turned to advantage the peculiarities of autistic children: their interest in systems, in counting, in ritual, and their literal honesty' (p. 190).

(h) In the spring of 1978, we were kindly allowed by Dr Bertram A. A. Ruttenberg to visit the Developmental Center for Autistic Children in Philadelphia, of which he is the Director and where he works with a staff representing a variety of disciplines.[22] The school specialises in what Ruttenberg calls 'clinical education' which rests on 'its capacity to integrate educational treatments and mental health therapies not usually provided in a regular educational program . . . The clinical approach allows children to accomplish relational and motivational goals or educational tasks slightly more difficult than those already mastered, regardless of level'. (This, we feel, is a principle which others, Doman excepted, have not emphasised as explicitly as it is done here.) Under the 'processes used in the model' (i.e. the procedure), the first mentioned by

Ruttenberg is a 'relationship-building process'; the second a 'motivation–development process', while perceptual retraining process and classroom behaviour management process are mentioned in that order. There is liaison between school and home, but only limited parent participation. At the time of our visit we saw the 16 children then attending and quite a number of staff, but there was not a strict one-to-one relationship, except for special sessions. Thus we saw a play session of one therapist with two children; and a session of one boy with one therapist of which the purpose was increased stimulation of the gravity and movement receptors in the inner ear; in view of what we have said before about inferences concerning perceptual malfunctioning, it will not surprise readers when we emphasise that, as this was done in a friendly playful fashion, its therapeutic value might in our opinion well lie in this individual, playful rough-and-tumble interaction *per se* rather than in the extra stimulation of the inner ear, which might have been incidental.

The rationale of the Center is based on psychoanalytic principles and it is beyond our competence to judge its theoretical validity. What we saw in practice seemed to us to conform on the whole to what we would expect to be effective. Thus, we saw a lot of informal socialising in the dinner hour and on the playground, and parts of the day were spent in communal singing with staff and children informally sitting in a circle. (Having seen Dr and Mrs Welch's 'Mothering Center', we wonder now whether mothers could perhaps be brought in during these kinds of sessions.)

Our impression was that the children responded on the whole well. However, we must leave the full reporting of this impressive educational experiment to Dr Ruttenberg.

(i) *Children as co-therapists.* In several schools for autistic and other disturbed children, and most explicitly and deliberately in the Yasuda Life Welfare Foundation's Nursery School in Tokyo (under the leadership of Dr Masumi Sasaki), the therapeutic value of interaction with normal children has been used by allowing autistic children, some of them fairly severely afflicted, to be integrated in normal school life.[23] Mr Hajime Yasuda kindly sent us, and several other workers on autism, a copy of the excellent 50-minute, 16 mm film which demonstrates this method with several children and documents the great advances in socialising and various skills that can be achieved. Admittedly, this requires the collaboration of exceptionally devoted and gifted teachers, one of whom we can see at work in this film. Dr Sasaki has written to us to say that another film 'on the integration therapy for pre-school children in their home and nursery school' is in preparation. Dr Sasaki stresses that, in his opinion, therapy must be started at as early a stage as possible. Certainly, the two little girls shown at the start of the film improved with remarkable speed. We shall return to this below, but remark here merely that the mention of the word 'home' indicates that Dr Sasaki is not exclusively concentrating on therapy by other children and by teachers but probably also the all-important part that can be played by the mother.

We need not repeat here that our knowledge of the social setting in which the human young have been adapted to grow up during hundreds of thousands of years, before the cultural evolution imposed the recent environmental changes on children, makes it understandable that co-operation of mother, father, other children (both sibs and in-group members of other families) and members of the 'group of extended families' who all play their parts in non-industrialised and less extremely urbanised societies, is still conducive and indeed very important to the normal behavioural development of children. During the very short life so far of our cultural, certainly of our industrial, evolution genetic adjustment has not had a chance; for this, an incomparably longer span of time would be required.

(j) *Animals as co-therapists.* In the autumn of 1978, we came into contact with Mr E. Royds of Glasbury, Hereford, England, Riding Advisor to the National Society for Mentally Handicapped Children, who specialises in using riding on horseback as a means of drawing out emotionally disturbed children of many kinds, among them autists, by giving them (carefully supervised) pony rides.[24] The following are verbatim quotations from Mr Royds' notes on a lecture he delivered at the University of Witwatersrand, Johannesburg, South Africa, on 21 August 1978.

> 'I am going to talk about riding and severely handicapped children and what riding may, and often can, do for them . . .' (I have been practising riding with) '. . . severely handicapped children (i.e. children who can only accept teaching from those specially trained to give it) and to (a few) moderately handicapped children (who can accept teaching from anyone who knows his subject) . . .' [Like Dr Waldon and Dr Doman, Mr Royds prefers not to be too specific about diagnostic labels, but the children he talks about include autists.] 'By riding I mean putting a child onto a horse, or pony, leading it at a walk for two or three minutes with a helper on each side, dismounting it, making it pat the horse as its "thank you" and then putting on another child . . .'

The horse must walk, not stand still.

A summary of the effects on children, written in 1975, mentions among other things:

> 'Data obtained from 3 different schools, hospitals etc. and a total of 86 children show that after regular pony rides 73–75% of the children whose general behaviour was rated "very poor" originally (and this is a euphemism for the real bottom of the barrel) improved to such an extent that life outside an institution might be considered for them. The greatest improvements concerned self-confidence, sociability, speech and relief of tension, the child becoming more relaxed and contented. Possibly the most remarkable improvement, almost certainly the most significant, is the improvement in speech. *There are*

27 cases I know of, 14 I have heard myself, of children speaking their first words ever from the saddle (emphasis ours).'

Mr Royds further mentions some interesting points about the interaction between the horse and the child. First of all, even fairly ill tempered and not fully reliable horses (and certainly more generally friendly horses) respond to a severely handicapped child with an extremely friendly 'concerned' attitude, clearly sensing that 'here is a being who is not going to boss me but who needs my help'. Our own interpretation is that the slightest signs of helplessness the child gives are perceived by the horse, and make it respond as to a young foal (Mr Royds himself rather feels that the child is treated like a mate). The extraordinarily fine perceptiveness of the horse, so well known to riders and epitomised by the famous story of *Clever Hans*,[25] is also revealed by the fact that as soon as a horse begins to show signs of irritation and unco-operativeness with a child, Mr Royds takes that as a first sign of the child's improvement, which presumably expresses itself in a slightly less dependent and a shade more dominant behaviour!

In Mr Royds' experience, the improvement in children's condition in the course of time follows a predictable course: 'with few exceptions . . . for the first six months, almost vertical, for the next two years, horizontal (great pleasure will be given but very little therapy) and then a steady rise to the child's ceiling, which is usually quite a bit higher than the experts suppose'.

(k) Whereas horses are no doubt of particular importance in assisting the first steps of socialisation in withdrawn children, a variety of other pets may likewise be used for this purpose. At the 105th Annual Meeting of the American Public Health Association held in Washington DC in 1977, Professor and Mrs Samuel A. Corson reported on their experiences with 'pet-facilitated psychotherapy' (PFP) in a psychiatric hospital, involving a variety of patients.[26] The pilot project on which they report was started when the barking of dogs which were kept (for quite different purposes) in a kennel near the hospital made some of the patients, especially adolescents (many of whom had been uncommunicative throughout their hospital stay), break their self-imposed silence and begin to inquire whether they could play with the dogs or help take care of them. In the subsequent work 'the dogs were introduced to the patients either in the dog kennels ("dog ward"), or on the patient ward, or on the patient's bed . . .' This was not done until the patient had expressed a wish to be allowed to care for a dog, and had been allowed to choose which dog. Later this was extended to other pets.

The PFP sessions were conducted with 50 patients. It was unsuccessful in only three patients ('because they did not accept the particular pets'). The patients selected for PFP were all

'withdrawn, self-centred and uncommunicative, some of them almost mute and psychologically bedridden. They lacked self-esteem and exhibited infantile helplessness and dependence . . . The introduction of a dog to a patient gradually developed in the patient a sense of self-respect, independence, and responsibility . . . This was at first confined to their relation with their dog . . . (but) . . . it turned out not to be a closed circle . . . On the contrary, the dog began to serve as a catalyzing socialization link on the patient ward . . . *the danger, initially feared, that attachment to the pet might preclude socialization with fellow humans turned out to be groundless* (emphasis ours).'

Although much of this and subsequent work was done with elderly patients, some of the case histories describe the beneficial effects on 'psychotic' adolescents. We mention this case of the therapeutic use of dogs and other pets because we have the experience that quite a number of autistic children, even those who are deadly afraid of some or most pets, can socialize with one animal or another. As with the Corsons' patients, the danger of a pet usurping the place of a human companion has to be considered, but is in our experience not great.

SPECIAL SCHOOLS

Partly through the efforts of the Society for Autistic Children, which includes greater publicity given to autistic children and their problems, a growing number of special schools or units have been set up in the last 15 years or so in which attempts are made to educate autistic children as well as possible. We have visited a few such schools and have some information about others. It was originally expected by the leaders of the Society for Autistic Children that special schools could make considerable contributions to the education of autistic children, but the initial fairly high hopes have on the whole not been fulfilled.[27] This, we believe, is partly due to the prevalent resigned attitude implying ineducability or very limited educability. There are indeed signs that if such units are motivated by more hope, better results can be obtained than has so far been the case.

The observations and discussions one of us had with the headmistress and staff of an exceptionally successful, now unfortunately abolished little school for autistic children in one of our large cities showed that here too the emphasis was on socialising (with the staff and the children amongst themselves, and less deliberately with the parents) and skill teaching-by-instruction was subordinate to this.[28] The children (most of whom were initially mute, and also were considered then by most experts to be unable to understand speech) were addressed verbally. This was used, for instance, for simple disciplining tasks such as explaining, usually without showing anger or indignation, why some specific behaviours were either wanted or unacceptable. For example, when one child joined another one engaged in drawing on a piece of paper and began to scribble over the same paper, she was given a paper of her own while it was explained to her that her scribbling would spoil the boy's drawing. When, during a meal, a child refused to hand over his emptied plate, he was simply told 'You know what will happen; if you don't pass your plate you can't have the sweet'. On both these and other similar occasions the children immediately responded appropriately to the verbal communication. The majority of the children concerned made considerable progress during the few years of their attendance.

The several other schools and units in which autistic children were being treated and which we have been allowed to visit repeatedly and which showed promising results involved a variable amount of skill teaching, emphasis on a warm, yet fairly well structured procedure, and understanding of the need to adjust to the children's retardations. In some of them there is rather an overlap with Dr Sasaki's and Dr Yasuda's procedure. *Unfortunately, none of the persons in charge of these schools have so far published particulars about their educational methods or their results, and we repeat once more that we hope that such reports will be made public.*

'Do-it-yourself' mothers (parents)

In the last five years we have been alerted to the fact that there is a category of persons who have shown themselves to be experts in the art of educating autistic children, but whose extremely important fund of expertise has remained almost entirely untapped. A few members of this group have described their achievements in books but, probably because of their popular style, these books have largely been ignored by the professional world. In addition, however, we have discovered that there are large numbers of parents who have not reported in print but have likewise had the misfortune of discovering that one of their children began to show the syndrome we have been discussing throughout this book and who have, without the help or even the knowledge of a doctor, managed to bring their child back to normality. Apart from parents of this type who have contacted us after they had heard us speak, or had read our earlier contributions, we know in our immediate environment several such couples who were not solicited by us, had not realised what ailed their children and must in our opinion be considered a fair sample of the many unrecorded cases of autism, at least in Britain and the Netherlands. But whether or not our sample is more representative than the census figures which have been published so far, we want to stress the importance of these 'do-it-yourself' parents as a source of inspiration in the search for successful education or rehabilitation procedures. While we refer readers to Chapter 10 for descriptions of some case histories in more detail, we mention here only the facts that (a) most of these children have been saved primarily by their mothers with either mere moral support from the fathers or the special, in some respects limited, fatherly contribution that is normally made to the education of young children, and that (b) the core of all the D I Y cures we have so far been able to observe has been of the kind we are advocating. That is, priority has been given to 'supermothering', to strengthening the bond between the child and his mother (and, in the process, the rest of the family); to adjusting, in innumerable details, to the level of performance of the child at any stage of his development, yet with due regard for the need for discipline; and, where special interests became obvious, to encouragement of achievements in the 'islets' of such good potential. We have thus found, much to our surprise and delight, that quite a number of parents *are* capable of impressive adjustment to the very great demands that autistic children impose upon them. We submit that, at least in the urban populations of our country, every observant and slightly knowledgeable person can discover more than one such case in his or her own environment. We believe that, with few exceptions, no professional therapy can equal what the best D I Y parents are doing. As unwitting instructors for other parents of autistic children, such D I Y parents are eminently worth observing.

However, to rope in D I Y mothers as tutors for children whose own mothers feel unable to cope with them carries a risk: the very gifts that make the D I Y mothers such outstanding therapists for their own children might well make them unintentionally usurp the role of the mother and bond the child to them instead of to his own mother. Perhaps this could be prevented by warning such tutors of this danger – as indeed all good tutors have to be warned not to *replace* the mother. Also a D I Y mother must not be asked to help other children *at the expense* of her own.

It is true that good home tutors can bring about a degree of improvement in an autistic child, but it looks to us as if even their hard and devoted work can lift the child to a partial recovery only, to a level below that of which the mother who takes part in a Welch treatment can reach. As far as we can see at the moment, all the treatments discussed under our heading 'Other procedures' must be seen as supplementary to the restoration of the mother–child bond.

'Hopeless' cases

By contrast to this selection of a variety of potentially beneficial forms or elements of the ideal therapy which we are trying to find, we mention briefly two cases of which we have a long personal experience and which illustrate the pernicious effects those parents of autistic children can have who, instead of having constructively adjusted to the needs of their child, have, either from the very beginning or soon afterwards, entered the downward, mutually damaging spiral we have described. In both cases the mother is the one primarily concerned, because the father has either withdrawn into his work or has left home altogether. What is striking in both cases, and in a number of other cases on which we have received information from, among others, Dr Martha Welch and Dr D. Jennings of Ottawa, Canada (who, as we have mentioned in our Preface, is one of those exceptional psychiatrists who makes long-term observations of autistic children and their parents in the latter's homes),[29] is the ambivalence of the mothers. In all contacts with outsiders they demonstrate what appears to be a warm, motherly attitude without giving the slightest sign of the other aspect of their response: a certain amount of hostility to their children. (In our experience, psychiatrists and psychologists are only too often taken in by the 'acted' warm and loving behaviour.) But the hostile component of the attitude of such mothers becomes visible when they believe themselves unobserved, or have become so used to the presence of an observer (either a friend or a relative, or a social worker, or an exceptionally patient, perceptive and tactful psychiatrist or psychologist) that they act, as they only too frequently do, when they are alone with their child. Under such circumstances they will often neglect their child, or they may even in a sense 'batter him emotionally' or torture him 'psychologically' – either by 'sending him to Coventry' or by treating him in callous or genuinely spiteful ways.

However, a number and perhaps the majority of these mothers have themselves grown up in unsatisfactory or unhappy circumstances, and hence need help as much as their children (though they themselves might vehemently deny this). Recently we have had some indications that such seriously damaged mothers can indeed profit from treatment, in particular from being made to play their motherly role as required in the Welch therapy. There is even not the slightest doubt that *all* the mothers following the Welch courses profit as much as their children – as, of course, they would be expected to do if there is truth in the 'downward spiral' notion. However, for this to have a chance to succeed with these very difficult mothers, one would need therapists who, besides having been trained in the Welch therapy, have also an acute understanding of the ambivalence of the mother's feelings and behaviour towards her child, and – last but not least – have enough authority to make the mother follow instructions if and when these have to be given. For there is, with such severely damaged mothers, a strong possibility that they cannot bear the treatment (with the concomitant exposure to themselves of their deeper feelings) and give up, and so in effect sacrifice their child by giving way to their own fears.

Conclusion

This review, of ways of treatment of autistic children that justify a more hopeful attitude than is at the moment found in most professional students of autism, is not intended to be exhaustive: we have selected what seem to us to be important samples. For reasons that we need not once more make clear, we have not always confined ourselves to what many experts would call 'true' autists but have included examples of a wide variety of emotionally disturbed children, and even withdrawn adults and elderly people. We did this because, while we acknowledge the value for diagnostic purposes of confining ourselves to observable symptoms (i.e. behaviour abnormalities), deeper probing into the nature and aetiology of quite a number of other mental disorders may well reveal closer affinities with autism than their diagnostic labels reveal; and a better understanding of any of them could well help us understand the others. We have further refrained from quantitative indications of the degree of improvement observed since, as we have seen, these are, if given at all by the different authors involved, expressed in terms that (inevitably) differ from case to case – uniform rating systems such as, for instance, B R I A A C are not yet in general use. We have had to go by what we have considered credible statements about the progress of the children, as well as by what we have, in a number of cases, observed ourselves. We want to emphasise the great need for the further development of a conceptual framework, of methods of research, and of communication about results of both research and different therapies. Until this has been done, comparison of therapies will have to remain at the present pre-quantitative level.

In spite of the under-developed state of the field, some guidelines do emerge from the treatments we have mentioned above. It seems to us clear that those regimes that have promising results apply fairly consistently what our analysis of the autistic state and its aetiology would make us require: they give priority to re-socialising and the consequent reduction of the predominant anxiety, social withdrawal and social rejection. When a more healthy emotional balance is re-established, a child will begin to make social contacts and will also engage in exploratory behaviour, from which he is then only too keen to profit by the variety of learning activities open to normal children, and necessary for a healthy development.

The many therapists who work along these lines – teachers, parents, psychiatrists – have with impressive inventiveness created not only a number of ways of achieving 'emotional rehabilitation', but also a variety of ways of aiding the urgent learning tasks facing an autistic child; we refer to Clancy's use of soap bubbles, Mr Park's use of a counter as an aid for Elly's self-teaching, the involvement of parents, other children and even animals as co-therapists, the stimulation and putting-through techniques of the Doman Institutes etc. There is no reason at all to assume that *the* best way of educating autistic children has been found. But we believe that Dr Welch's rebonding procedure should where possible be the core of treatment and that this treatment can be enriched and made more effective by incorporating the best, in principle and detail, of any other therapy that shows a promising degree of success. We have little doubt that we are only at the beginning of this process of elaboration and that we can learn a great deal from further careful study of how successful therapists proceed. We submit that this way of approaching the problem opens the gates for the development of treatments of still greater effectiveness than any of those applied now.

It may not even be premature to begin to think of the problem of prevention. Perhaps the most realistic way to approach this is by giving increased attention to 'early warning signs'. An over-placid baby, one that refuses social contact; over-anxiety or lack of experience in mothers; or traumatising events such as hospitalisation, frequently moving house etc. might, if their possible damaging effects are recognised, put the adults concerned on the alert, and special attempts at affiliation and socialisation could be initiated before the autistic course has gone too far. The indications are that the earlier such treatment is started, the more effective it can be.[30]

If funds were made available for the development of early treatment methods, a great deal of suffering could be ameliorated and considerable sums of money could be saved by rehabilitating children who would otherwise, as so often at the present time, have to be institutionalised, at great cost to the community. And although it is difficult to teach young mothers the subleties of good mothering if they have in some way failed to learn mothercraft in the 'natural' way, there are quite a number of simple, yet basic, 'tricks' that can be taught to adults of normal intelligence. Fortunately, young children are, so to speak, 'itching to grow up', mentally as well as physically, and will often take their education into their own hands.

Finally, we should remember what has been said about a possible link between autism – and many illnesses in general – and nutrition; in particular we refer back to Chapter 5, note 22, in which the first results of megavitamin treatment are mentioned. But it will be best to see all these aspects of treatment in their full context, and our present view is that the core of a therapy for autism lies in the restoration of the mother–child bond, on which further socialisation and emotional as well as intellectual development seems to depend.

This review, of the various ways that have come to our notice in which autists are now being treated with a certain degree of success, is of course unlikely to be complete. Even so, it shows that there are not a few people who, far from accepting the verdict that autists are ineducable, are trying to find ways of educating them. More: they are beginning to have rates of success that can no longer be ignored. True, what has been achieved so far falls far short of the ideal mass experiment, with 'matched controls', that is clearly desirable. But we submit that such a mass experiment will – for the reasons we have discussed earlier in this chapter – remain a pipe dream for a long time to come. Even if it were organised now, it would take so much time that at least a generation of autistic children would continue on the sad downward spiral in which so many are caught, or at best would remain the subject of research into the nature of autism rather than into ways of helping them. Therefore we owe it to those suffering children and their families to act on the evidence collected so far, for this is enough to show that the claim that autists are beyond help is unjustified and very probably wrong; it certainly was wrong for those who have recovered. It is therefore to be hoped that the work described in this chapter will inspire increasing numbers of therapists to apply these promising procedures; there is simply no excuse for not trying them out. Since what is needed is more evidence of the same critical standard as that provided by, for instance, Drs Welch and Zappella; such future work should not only be as carefully recorded as these workers do, but the proportion of successes – and therefore of failures – should be published as critically as possible, and attempts should also be made to explain the failures. Examples of this are given in the two appendices following Chapter 10.

Granting that the numbers of children treated so far are small (due to the fact that the continuous broadcasting of the gloomy view that autistic children are ineducable has understandably discouraged many therapists) we nevertheless predict that treatments in which the 'holding' is central, but which could perhaps be enriched by some of the other treatments that we have mentioned, will prove to be beneficial for many children, and will really cure quite a number of them as completely as some of the patients of Dr Welch and Dr Zappella, and as some of the children of the do-it-yourself parents who we shall describe in Chapter 10. Sceptics, who keep repeating to us that they 'don't believe in' or 'don't agree with' the procedures described, are invited to try at least to learn the essentials of the 'holding' method and to apply it, rather than repeating their negative opinions. Fortunately for the children and their families, a growing number of therapists have actually started to apply Welch's method, on which we first reported in public in the summer of 1981 at the meeting of Nobel laureates in Medicine in Lindau, Germany, and so far good progress has already been achieved in a number of their cases, while not a single failure has been reported. The main purpose of this chapter, in fact of our entire book, is to give this encouraging new development as wide publicity as possible.

Finally, we repeat once more that, in this context too, it is not important whether or not the children concerned were 'rea'' autists; as we have all the time been at pains to emphasise, we are speaking of children who show 'most or all' of the symptoms we have described in Chapter 2. The reaction we have heard *ad nauseam* to our reports on successful treatments, viz. that the children who have recovered cannot have been 'true' autists is in many cases not only at odds with what we know of their pre-treatment behaviour and with the diagnosis, given in many cases by professionals, but it is, as we have tried to explain, the natural consequence of taking 'ineducability' to be a proven fact instead of what it is: an inference based on having, *so far*, failed to rehabilitate such children.

Notes and references

1 O'Gorman, G. 1970 (see Ch. 1, note 4), p. 124.
2 Ornitz, E. M. 1973 (see Ch. 1, note 4), p. 34.
3 Bettelheim, B. 1967 (see Ch. 2, note 7).
   Ruttenberg, B. A. A. 1971 (see Ch. 2, note 7).
4 For readers who want to inform themselves, we give here the relevant particulars about the British Society for Autistic Children. Its address is: 1a Golders Green Road, London N W 11. One of the Society's founders, Dr L. Wing, writes about it in her book (1971) *Autistic children, a guide for parents,* p. 154, London: Constable – 'This Society . . . runs an information service and is in contact with all the other societies for autistic children throughout the world. It publishes articles, and a bibliography of relevant literature.'
5 We met this dissatisfaction with the entrenched, pessimistic, or rather resigned, view time and again in our many discussions with persons immediately involved with autists mentioned before. See also our comments on case histories in Chapter 10.
6 Sanua, V. D. (see Ch. 3, note 14 & Ch. 5, note 42).
7 We know of a very successful speech therapist who has told colleagues that her therapy consisted basically of 'playing with the children', but who refrained from saying so in public because she knew that this would not be considered a serious therapy, but 'almost a confidence trick'.
8 Among the parents we know well, there are several in whom we have seen this dual behaviour – one when in company and quite another when they believe themselves to be unobserved – time and again. We still have not been able to understand to what extent they do this deliberately and consciously, but the fact of their duality is clear enough.
9 This (quite natural and commendable) adjustment can be observed in almost every case history that covers a prolonged period, and in which both child and caregiver or teacher are closely observed.
10 Ruttenberg, B. A. A., M. Dratman, J. Franknoi and C. Wenar 1966. An instrument for evaluating autistic children. *J. Am. Acad. Child Psychiat.* **5**, 453–78.
   Ruttenberg, B. A. A., B. I. Kalish, C. Wenar and E. G. Wolf 1977. *Behaviour rating instrument for autistic and other atypical children (BRIAAC): scales and instruction manual.* Published by the Developmental Center for Autistic Children, 120 North 48th Street, Philadelphia, Pennsylvania 19139, U S A.
   B. Rimland has been using his 'Form E-2 Checklist' for a more than usually detailed classification of types of autism. In his 1971 paper (The differentiation of childhood psychoses: an analysis of checklists for 2218 psychotic children. *J. Aut. Childhd Schizophrenia* **1**, 161–74), he found that 9.7 per cent of these children do have 'true childhood autism. Form E–2 is effective in differentiating truly autistic from autistic-type children.' (p. 161). The checklist is very detailed and purely descriptive and covers aspects of a child's early history as well as (in particular) aspects of his abnormal behaviour. Copies of the form can be obtained from the Institute of Child Behaviour Research, 4157 Adams Avenue, San Diego, California 92116, U S A. The form has the advantage of relying on the parents for information rather than on tests in the laboratory, and asks 79 questions in Part 1. We suspect that our views are most relevant to the problem of 'true autists', but that they may well apply likewise, at least in part, to many of the other children on this list. For instance, the rating system used for evaluating each child may in part be based on what we would call differences in the severity of the deviation. Thus, *part* of the discontinuity in the scores obtained may be due to the secondary dichotomy that emerges as initially autistic children grow up and either recover or get caught in the downward spiral.

11   See Chapter 10, second section (Notes on published accounts).

12   Yet, as we all know, a successful treatment need not necessarily consist of reversing the process that caused the illness in the first place: as Dr Rimland once wrote to us 'The fact that aspirin makes a headache disappear does not mean that the headache was caused by an aspirin deficiency.'

13   The American N B C has made an excellent short 16 mm sound film of Dr Welch at work with two different autistic children and their mothers: *The bond that holds.* WNBC TV News, Center 4, Dr Frank Field's Special Report, January 1978, 30 Rockefeller Plaza, New York, NY 10020, USA. For a detailed report on some results and for instruction to therapists, see Appendix I (contribution from M. Welch).

14   Zaslow, R. and B. Breger 1969. A theory and treatment for autism. In *Clinical cognitive psychology*, L. Breger (ed.) 246–89. Englewood Cliffs, NJ: Prentice-Hall.

       Dr Breger has since written to us that he has dissociated himself from Zaslow's method.

15   Schreibman, L. and R. L. Koegel 1975. Autism: a defeatable horror. *Psychology Today*, March, 61–7.

16   In the article mentioned, they wrote: 'We can make some systematic report on 16 children who participated in our first experimental classroom during the years 1971 to 1973. All of them had been diagnosed by agencies not associated with our research. All were severely psychotic. Six were completely mute . . . all had been expelled from or denied access to regular public schools or special education classes . . .' (After treatment) 'Ten of the 16 children were discharged within 18 months and went on to regular or special education classes in the public schools. The other six still attend special schools for autistic children developed from our model. While their progress has been slow, we expect them to be able to attend regular classes one day' (pp. 66–67).

17   We are here quoting from Dr Waldon's handout received from Dr Waldon in the autumn of 1978, when we visited him and observed him at work. A forthcoming film on his procedure, called *'Understanding understanding'*, will soon be available from the Manchester Trust, 636 Wilmslow Road, Manchester 20.

       A colleague of ours, P. Harverson, is writing a book in which Dr Waldon's work is to be represented, to be called *The listeners – the story of some autistic children,* (details to be announced).

18   Doman, G. 1974 (see Ch. 2, note 7). The term 'brain injured' in the title of this book does not in all cases refer to known structural damage but includes functionally impaired brains as well.

       Delacato, C. H. 1974 (see Ch. 2, note 7).

19   Kaufman, B. N. 1976. *To love is to be happy with.* London: Souvenir Press. This is the British edition of the original American book called *Son rise.* New York: Harper and Row.

20   Clancy, H. and G. McBride 1969. The autistic process and its treatment. *J. Child Psychol. Psychiat.* **10**, 233–44.

21   Park, D. 1974. Operant conditioning of a speaking autistic child. *J. Aut. Childhd Schizophrenia* **4**, 189–91.

22   See Chapter 2, note 7.

23   Sasaki, M. 1978. A comment on the film 'All are friends – an integration remedy for autistic children'. Department of Neuropsychiatry, Faculty of Medicine, University of Tokyo, Japan.

       This film shows two pre-school girls and one boy in mainly playgroup setting who make remarkable progress and show the advantage of starting treatment when children are still very young. The (older) boy shown in the film is more severely withdrawn and, taking this into account, his progress is likewise good. But it is also clear from the film that, as with other treatments, the teachers concerned have special gifts for this type of procedure.

24 Royds, E. 1977. *The Beacon*, 46–51. Also Royds E. personal communication.

25 Pfungst, O. 1965. *Clever Hans: the horse of Mr von Osten*. New York, Holt, Rinehart and Winston.

26 Corson, S. A., E. O. L. Corson, P. H. Gwynne and L. E. Arnold 1977. Pet dogs as nonverbal communication links in hospital psychiatry. *Comprehensive Psychiat.* **18**, 61–72.

27 The last report we heard, as part of a lecture given by Miss S. Elgar in Oxford in the winter 1978–9, was resigned to the view that most autistic children cannot be educated but can learn to do simple manual tasks (see Ch. 1, note 2).

28 Since this experimental project was interrupted and the small school was absorbed by another school with a different attitude to the education of autistic children, there is no point in naming this initially very promising project.

29 Shortly before Dr Jennings had to break off his work in London and settled in Ottawa, we had several days of intensive discussion with him, in which much of what we knew or suspected about the family backgrounds of 'hopeless' cases was confirmed.

30 We describe a particularly striking case in Chapter 10 (that of Fae).

Kempe, R. S. and C. H. Kempe report on promising attempts at spotting 'early warning signs' of children who are at risk either of being abused or of suffering in other ways; see their book (1978) *Child abuse*, London: Fontana/Open Books. Much of what they say, though not directly applicable to the majority of cases of autism, does have a bearing on the problem of early detection of incipient autists.

7

Methodological comments

We shall now try to pull together a number of comments we have made, at various places in our text, on matters of research method, and we shall add to this a few more general methodological remarks. While our main concern has been to advocate the use, in the investigation and treatment of autism, of certain methods widely used in comparative ethology, some of the recommendations we shall make about method are not peculiar to this special field but apply to all biological, in part even to all scientific, research. Naturally, these remarks imply criticism of much that we consider imperfect or erroneous in child psychiatry. Indeed, as will by now have become clear, we feel that this field could with profit, without completely discarding the methods now in use, broaden its research strategy by incorporating methods of approach that have shown their potential in related sciences.

Since we have, where relevant, illustrated our comments with specific examples in the main text, we shall here confine ourselves to restating the main general points:

(a) Throughout the book it has been our concern to check the validity of hypotheses – our own as well as those of others – by examining *how wide a range* their explanatory power covers; for how many known facts they can account. This is of course an integral aspect of any research, but it is particularly important in studies of mental disorders in childhood which, as we have pointed out, are perhaps the most complicated phenomena we encounter in nature, and which yet have to be studied *in toto* as well as in detail. It is because of this complexity that any study of abnormal, and indeed of normal, child behaviour must, at least for the time being, have an exploratory character. We submit that this exploration must start by observation of the children's behaviour. It is by the *abnormal behaviour* that we recognise that the development is going wrong. Whatever we can infer or observe and measure of the underlying causative events that can be found to contribute to this dysfunctioning of the behaviour machinery is, and for a time will remain, less directly observable than the behaviour itself – the movements, postures and 'expressions' we see.

These extremely complicated events remain, to the investigator, chaotic until he can discern patterns, sequences and correlations. Concentration on any one particular part of these patterns or their underlying machinery without remembering that they are parts of the whole phenomenon will lead to storehouses packed with facts which will remain unrelated and meaningless until and unless their place in the overall pattern is understood. Many publications in this field fail to do, even to attempt, this and as a consequence the literature on autism has on the whole an atomistic character.

More attempts at testing the width of applicability of hypotheses or statements to all the facts so far known are urgently needed. To mention a few instances, the ideas of the centrality, in the autistic condition, of a cognitive and language disorder, or of over-arousal, or of retardation, or (in the development of autism in the individual child) of the importance of 'organic' and/or genetic aspects have, as far as we can see, not really been put to the test of overall plausibility. It is true that statements on these issues are found in the literature, but the supporting arguments, if mentioned at all, are far from convincing. Constant repetition of mere claims does not make them more valid. (It is perhaps in part because ethologists have themselves failed so often to pause and consider this 'plausibility aspect' of the many bold statements they made in the past that they have become particularly aware of its importance.)

(b) Closely related but nevertheless distinct is the need, in the search for causal relationships underlying observed phenomena, to distinguish clearly *correlations* from *cause–effect relationships* between events. Every correlation between events A and B can of course mean that either A helps causing B or B helps causing A, or that A and B have some cause in common. Because of this, we had to argue that the idea, suggested or at least implied by S. J. Hutt, that over-arousal might well be a primary aspect of the autistic condition, could be countered by the equally likely – in the light of other evidence, rather more likely – interpretation that high general arousal is a *consequence* of continuing strong conflict motivation. To consider abnormalities in the functioning of blood platelets as a possible causative agent rather than, perhaps equally possible, as one of the consequences of being autistic, is equally arbitrary. The same applies to notions, implied or explicit, that peripheral (sensory or motor) malfunctioning is a determinant or a component rather than a consequence of being autistic. Ultimately, experiments in which alleged causes are deliberately manipulated would of course be the best way to decide such issues, but in this field many experiments, even if they were possible, are of course ethically out of bounds. Fortunately, as always in applied science, where mastery over rather than understanding of natural events is the aim, we can replace decisive experiments by empirically inspired 'gambles' to support the general plausibility criterion; we can test whether therapies and rehabilitation attempts based on one theory work perhaps better than those based on others. This we have done as well as we could in Chapters 6 and 9.

We submit that it is in part because research has so far on the whole been less than impressive with respect to points (a) and (b), that the unfortunate and, in effect, defeatist view has taken root that autistic children are irreparably damaged; and this in turn has, as we know from personal experience of a number of cases, sapped the morale of many a parent.

(c) In ethology we have further learned the hard way how confusing it is, not just in the study of behaviour but everywhere in the science of biology, to fail to distinguish conceptually between the question of *function* or selective advantage on the one hand and that of *underlying causation* on the other; and, within this last overall question, to distinguish between (a) the causation of the moment-to-moment control or physiology of (in our case) the 'state' of being autistic; (b) the causation of the development, of the progressive change from early stages to the next, more advanced ones, or the aetiology of autism; and (c) the causation of the gradual change in the ontogenies of successive generations that leads to evolution – of the history of autism.[1] In our field it is at the moment in particular the problems of the nature of the autistic state and that of its development that are often thought of as one rather than as two distinct (admittedly interrelated) parts of the overall problem. In addition – not astonishing since psychiatry is a branch of medicine rather than of biology – the problem of controlling (containing, curing, preventing) the autistic development has often been almost blended with discussions of the other two problems, that of the nature of autism and that of its aetiology.

Apart from these three general aspects of method in which it can contribute to psychiatry as a natural science, ethology is in other ways specifically relevant to the study of autism.

(d) Undoubtedly because we have to do with a problem of behavioural malfunctioning, which is more difficult to describe in a detached way than, say, a temperature or a rash, confusion exists (as everywhere in psychiatry) at the very start – the stage of *diagnosis*.[2] There have been, and still are, many discussions about whether a child is a 'true' autist or, say, a 'negativistic', a 'reactive', an 'aphasic', an 'elective mute' or any other type of child – terminological wrangles which are due to vague, often unconscious disagreements about the delineation of the syndrome and which are for many reasons quite futile and are even hampering research. In addition, in some diagnostic statements and views, inferences (such as the idea of 'ineducability') have been mixed with observed facts. This leads to endless confusions. Even such an outstanding worker as the Dutch psychiatrist J. Foudraine (who has done much to modify old-fashioned views about schizophrenics and has modernised their treatment) concludes a report on a 46-year-old woman who had as a child been diagnosed as 'autistic' and who, under his treatment, recovered and belatedly resumed an independent life in society, with: she 'could not have been' a true autist *because* she recovered![3]

(e) It further strikes the ethologist, whose science owes so much to a return, however belated, to *non-interfering observation*, how the trend in modern psychiatry is to repeat the mistake that has held back the development of psychology so much in the past: the trend to pass over or run hastily through the observational–interpretative, the qualitative, exploratory or reconnaissance phase that every natural science has to go through (and to return to from time to time), and to resort prematurely to measurement and experiment.

As we have seen, experiments, even seemingly unobtrusive psychological tests, often make autistic children withdraw further rather than draw them out (or even, when their true abilities are underrated, anger or bore them). In such cases the results obtained do not reflect a child's full potential. Apart from this, many tests, focusing as they often do on special, limited aspects of a child's overall performance, tend to yield facts whose significance and relation to other evidence are likely to remain obscure and so remain isolated, disconnected bits of information until subsequent research will, with luck, enable us to see them in their proper context. Until that happens, it will of course be impossible to see how necessary the work was, and is, for our understanding. We have tried to explain in specific cases why 'watching and wondering' is often necessary for deciding what one wants to investigate and how it should be done, and also for assessing how fruitful the planned work is likely to be for the purposeful and economic future conduct of research. 'Mere' observation, often seemingly aimless and time consuming, may in fact turn out to be, in the long run, more economic and efficient than the carrying out of experiments before we are clear about their purpose. At the present exploratory stage of the work, it seems to us, for instance, of much more importance to unravel the conflict motivation underlying the observed behaviour of autists than to obtain E E G s or blood samples, to make brain scans or even to do neurological or psychological tests (many of which, as we have seen, merely show what a child *does* not do, and not necessarily what he *can*not do). We feel that, as so often in science (ethology itself not excluded), the sheer availability of fascinating techniques, of sophisticated apparatus, and of trained personnel, has too much say in the decisions about what kind of 'data' should be obtained. The preference for experimenting and for probing inside the bodies of autistic children has also a practical aspect; we shall discuss this under paragraph (k), p. 208.

(f) The most specifically relevant contribution from ethology to our problem was the combination of observation and interpretational and/or experimental study of behaviour that is due to *motivational conflicts*. Methods of study applied to this phenomenon *had* to be developed by students of animal behaviour for the same reason that they will *have* to be used in the study of severely autistic children, simply because neither of them speak. Because we have found, in many discussions with child psychiatrists and with parents, therapists and teachers in a number of countries, that these methods, however commonsensical and obvious they are to ethologists, are clearly difficult for others to appreciate, we have in this new account given so much space to a step-by-step introduction to the rationale of this type of study. We suggest that child psychiatry could profit greatly from application, and further development, of the methods applied by us – methods which, incidentally, are still being refined in comparative ethology.[4]

(g) Whenever we observed, saw films of, or read accounts of the way autistic children are examined, tested, assessed and taught, we realised that, as animal ethologists with special experience in the study of wild animals in their natural environment, we were particularly aware of the indisputable fact that, like wild animals, autistic children are prime examples of organisms – of functioning systems in general – that are highly sensitive to *'observer interference'*. Like most wild animals, autistic children respond to a stranger primarily by withdrawal, and this reaction is so strong that it suppresses all other behaviour. This is why field ethologists go to such lengths to apply, even more meticulously than good hunters do, 'field craft' and 'hide craft'. It is clear to us that the vast majority of researchers, teachers, therapists and even parents of autistic children are unaware of the imperative need for 'making oneself scarce', either by being really concealed or by waiting until one is ignored or at least no longer feared or resented by the child. (It took Dr Iain Douglas-Hamilton and his wife Oria – see their book *Among the elephants*[5] – four years to become accepted even by the less suspicious members of the elephant population of the Lake Manyara National Park in East Africa.) The result of incautious behaviour of the adults is that time and again they come to the conclusion that a child *'cannot'* do a thing simply because it *does not* do it; and that they overlook, and even fail to search for, the (often very considerable) abilities which the child possesses but does not dare, not want, or not deign to reveal. By their ignorance of this simple fact, and in many cases by an astonishing lack of perception, many workers miss a considerable amount of vitally important evidence. Ironically, quite a number of autistic children show a degree of perceptiveness that puts many an expert to shame!

(h) To ethologists it is second nature to observe not only sick animals but to look (even preferably) at the behaviour of normal animals. To them it comes as a shock to discover how pitifully little most child psychiatrists know of the normal behaviour development of children (as distinct from their performance in 'tests'). Medawar's admonition,[6] aimed at psychiatrists, and quoted by us in 1972, that 'it is not informative to study variations of behaviour unless we know beforehand the norm from which the variants depart' (1967, p. 109) has so far been heeded very little by child psychiatrists, perhaps under the mistaken impression that the normal development is known. We believe that we have given enough examples to show that this simply is not true and that even the rapidly growing science of normal child development has still by no means completed the task of describing, ordering and mapping (not to speak of understanding) the development of the behaviour of normal children. We trust that we have shown how fruitful the comparison with normal child behaviour has been for our understanding of autism as a *deviation* from the normal course of development. Indeed, it might be said that insufficient knowledge of the norm alone has been enough to prevent child psychiatry from really getting to grips with the problem of autism. This is why we repeat our recommendation to consult at least the literature on this subject.[7]

(i) In the study of the moment-to-moment control of behaviour, as in developmental studies, early ethology had a bias against (a) considering all behaviour as responses to outside stimuli, and (b) assuming that development starts from a *tabula rasa* mind, that behaviour develops through nothing but learning. Yet, because the environment could be manipulated so much more easily than could an animal's internal 'machinery', even the early ethological studies paid a great deal of attention to the relation between behaviour and the environment. The internal machinery of behaviour control had originally to be inferred, then to be reconstructed from isolated physiological 'spot checks', and it is only just beginning to be studied as a complex and integrated system. Even so, the early emphasis on responses to external stimulation has led to important discoveries about external control, which have greatly enriched our understanding. It was therefore natural for us to begin our study by paying attention to the children's responses to their continuously varying *environment*. In most psychiatric studies of autistic children, this too has not been done as well as it can now be done (that is: by paying attention to what is obviously relevant to the child; by taking into account the existence of a limited number of 'major functional systems', each of which is responsive to its own set of external stimuli; by paying attention to the inverse relationship between strength of motivation and minimum required stimulation etc.).[8] Yet we have seen that it is only through knowledge of this relation between behaviour and external influences that the interpretation of autistic behaviour as being the consequence of an emotional imbalance can be judged. Having done this, we cannot see how else the autistic state and its genesis could possibly be understood. Psychology is now absorbing a number of ethological methods, and it is to be hoped that psychiatry will follow.[9] (It is ironical that we ethologists, so often accused of being biased in favour of 'innateness' of behaviour and of its 'spontaneity', have now the task of stressing the importance, in the ontogeny of autism, of traumatisation by early experience.)

(j) The specific points that we have raised here can be supplemented by two more general considerations. If we look back on the emergence, or rather the revival, of ethology that took place from the 1920s on, we can, with hindsight, discern that it was started by a few, at first intuitive and vaguely expressed, later more explicitly formulated 'flashes of insight', or central, seminal ideas. The most important of these were: (a) that behaviour could be fruitfully considered as objectively as other life processes as the outcome of intricately functioning *organ systems* (involving sense organs, nervous system and muscles) on a par with, say, such systems as the digestive, the excretory and the endocrine system; and (b) that this system of behavioural organs is part of each animal's (and of Man's) 'equipment for survival' (ultimately: for reproductive success); that it is intricately adapted to this, and should be seen as the outcome of evolution – of genetic evolution by means of natural selection in animals, and by this type of change supplemented by 'psychosocial', 'exosomatic', 'cultural' evolution in Man.

We repeat here our claim (expressed in our Foreword) that in the research on autism no comparable flash of insight has so far happened; as we said there: 'what is being built up is a mass of disconnected facts in search of a theory', and we have argued in this book that our approach, while it has of course not yet led to the ultimate solution, does lead to a set of plausible hypotheses, which begin to find confirmation from the results of new therapies.

(k) As we have already adumbrated in point (e), there is, in the field of child psychiatry with which we are here concerned, a curious dichotomy of approach to the phenomena – a dichotomy, incidentally, that can be seen in many areas of medical research as well. It would seem self-evident that research should be considered a means towards the promotion of health, the curing of illness and the relief of sickness. Yet the impressive growth of medical and physiological research, the digging, in ever more detail, into the healthy and sick mechanisms involved, from the level of the body as a whole down to the biochemical, biophysical and even molecular level has carried with it a split in the interests of doctors, whether they be practitioners or research workers. For large numbers of medically qualified people, and increasingly for medically oriented biologists, chemists, pharmacologists and other scientists as well, the intellectual 'game' of *understanding* (initially started in the hope, tacit or openly expressed, of arriving at cures through such understanding) has more and more become a primary aim – numerous scientists engaged in medical research have to all intents and purposes divorced their work from the search for *cures*. A corollary of this is the increasing reliance of practitioners on the consultants and, through them, on innumerable laboratory tests and on hospital-based treatments. This again has led to what many outsiders consider a deplorable loss of 'clinical perceptiveness' (the 'klinischer Blick') of the good practitioner who is concerned with people rather than with symptoms and cases. Commentators from very diverse walks of life, such as Ivan Illich, Dixon, Kennedy[10] and others have called attention to this disturbing trend. Without subscribing to all the criticisms such authors express, we have (in our opinion) to admit that these modern developments carry great dangers with them. Nor are doctors the only persons qualified to judge these issues; they are a matter of *general* concern.

Hand in hand with this movement of the 'centre of gravity' towards research for research's sake, a growing prestige has become attached (not quite rationally) to what we could call the 'microanalytical' procedures. This has occurred at the cost of the 'input–output' approach; an approach – as respectable in science as ever – in which a complex system (in our case, the individual or even the mother–child dyad) is regarded as a 'black box' into which one 'feeds' input (a therapy) without for the moment probing inside, and observes what 'comes out' (a deterioration in health, an improvement or no discernable effect). We want to stress once more the urgent need for a more systematic application of the input–output approach side by side with the microanalytical probing. For one thing, we believe that our work on autism demonstrates its considerable potential; for another, it is cheaper and leads often much more quickly to therapies. The disadvantage of microanalysis, glamorous and fashionable though it may be at present, is that it leads easily to atomism, to not seeing the wood for the trees, and only too easily to abandonment or at least postponement of the search for a cure. Thus, we would suggest that for the time being detailed research into structural brain damage, into EEG's, into the abnormal functioning of blood platelets, even into the finer mechanisms of perceptual, cognitive and language development of autists may well be of less immediate importance to the problem of how to cure autistic children than the 'input–output' procedure. Better, detailed understanding of the processes will undoubtedly become important at a later stage and in other contexts, but our present point is that studies in these fields have so far contributed little to the problems of how to cure autism. (We shall discuss in a moment the lack of therapeutical motivation due to other factors, even more obviously non-rational than those involved in the dichotomy issue we have been discussing.)

At the risk of being considered presumptuous – and of course not forgetting that we are outsiders to medical science – we venture to suggest that the dichotomy of interest and effort is discernable in many areas of medicine outside psychiatry; we suggest that the fields of nutrition and of cancer research could do with a shift away from mere microanalysis towards an input–output approach aiming at curing.

We now have to return briefly to a point we have already mentioned: the fact that, particularly in our corner of medical research, *non-rational* (though often rationalised) considerations enter often into arguments that purport to be of a purely scientific nature. Two of these non-rational 'stowaways' in particular have to be seen clearly for what they are.

(1) No unbiased observer can fail to notice that there is, among parents, a (quite understandable but nevertheless unjustified) reluctance to give equal weight to indications that the environment is largely responsible for

autism as to indications of an 'inherent' (either purely genetic and/or irreversibly 'organic') cause for autism. In our text we have tried to help parents to overcome this bias, which we suspect is due to false feelings of guilt, but we accept at the same time that it is unrealistic to expect parents to be quite as detached and rational about this as the scientist can be, *has* to be. This non-rational bias is, however, also present in quite a number of psychiatrists who, likewise understandably, have wanted to avoid hurting parents by 'blaming' them as long as opinions about the aetiology of autism varied so much. But in the interest of autistic children, living and still to be born (for there is no reason to expect autism simply to disappear suddenly – on the contrary), it is our clear duty to help parents face the possibility, indeed the likelihood, that the early experiences of their child, *for many of which they cannot be held responsible,* can have made him autistic, and so to give them both more hope and practical advice.

Unfortunately, there is also a rather non-rational element in the attitude of many doctors, therapists and teachers who support the 'ineducable' myth: it is, of course, emotionally difficult to believe in the educability of autists when your attempts at educating them have so far failed so consistently.

(m) Finally, in this area of medicine as in others, we have noticed many signs of the well-known, deep-rooted, yet always astonishing trust in authority – either one's own or that of the established consultants – which is coupled so strongly with the hierarchical structure of the medical world. We have received a large number of letters and verbal communications from many countries which reveal quite a remarkable degree of 'grass roots' agreement with our views, but which express at the same time that 'it is no use trying to convince the experts'. Some of these reactions have come from doctors, even from psychiatrists! It is not just an opinion held by habitual grumblers, but a fact of modern life that there is, among the public, a widespread and growing feeling of unease and even of distrust of the medical 'establishment', which is felt to be conservative and even ill informed, technomaniacal and arrogant. Among the many reasons for this feeling we suggest the following. The busy practitioner cannot possibly keep up with the new developments; he has often to discard confused or false information given by patients; many patients expect and want their doctors to be authoritative; consultants are rarely informed about or even interested in, fields outside their own; established techniques tend to be employed just because they are there; but above all, the most vocal spokesmen of the medical profession are openly insisting, much more than other scientists, on recognition of what they consider to be their special status, on not being questioned about the validity of their opinions. We will not labour this point overmuch, but urge our colleagues in child psychiatry to become a little more open-minded, a little more *humble*, to acknowledge in particular, as some of them actually have done even in print, that they do not understand autism; that they can learn from non-medical disciplines; and that they ought to pay a little more attention to the successes that many 'simple' loving and infinitely patient parents and teachers have had in rehabilitating autistic children. By doing so, they might learn a great deal. The fates of very many autistic children and their parents may well depend on such a change of heart.

Lest we should antagonise our colleagues working in this field by appearing to be ruthless iconoclasts who condemn every single aspect of the work done and being done (an impression that the fairly aggressive tone of our 1972 publication has done much to create), we should like to repeat once more that we claim no more than that certain *methods* that were originally evolved in comparative ethology can be fruitfully applied in child psychiatry (and, we believe, in psychiatry in general). Such application does not necessarily mean a complete supplanting of all methods in use (although we do believe that much thinking in psychiatry is in need of more scientific vigour).

Nor do we feel entitled to claim that ethology has itself developed a 'complete' methodological equipment; it is a young science, in part even no more than a pre-science, and although certain of its methods have already proved their worth, it is quite likely, in fact to be expected that, given time and opportunity, new and better methods will develop which will allow greater contributions to be made to psychiatry. In fact, such methods are already used, even in child psychology and child psychiatry.

Even less should we ethologists claim that the traffic of ideas and methods we advocate should necessarily be one way; certainly much work that is being done now on animal behaviour has clearly been influenced by human psychology and psychiatry.

Notes and references

1 See Tinbergen, N. 1951 (Ch. 3, note 7); Tinbergen, N. 1963. On aims and methods of ethology. *Z. Tierpsychol.* **20**, 410–33; and, in a more popular representation, Tinbergen, N. 1965. *Animal behavior*. New York: Time/Life. The notion of 'the four why's' is now generally accepted among behaviour students.

   For a thought-provoking discussion of the relevance of ethology for psychiatry, see Kramer, D. A. and W. T. McKinney 1979. The overlapping territories of psychiatry and ethology. *J Nerv. Ment. Dis.* **167**, 3–22.

2 In fact we are convinced that throughout the entire field of psychiatry the classification 'differential diagnosis' of, and terminology concerning mental disorders is in a chaotic state. This may well be due to the (misleading) influence of areas concerning 'somatic illnesses', particularly those of infectious diseases, where in so many cases the parasite and the range of symptoms it produces are well known. A further 'red herring' across the path of the psychiatrist is that syndromes that are similar to those known to be caused by *demonstrable* brain injuries (as studied extensively since World War I) tend to be ascribed to the same kinds of structural damage when they are observed in intact people, about whose brains is known no more than what neurological tests – i.e. observations of *input–output relationships,* of *malfunctioning* – indicate. Certainly, in the literature on

autism there is, as we have pointed out in this book, an inclination to assume structural damage merely on the basis of neurological tests, even when we know that the symptoms are due to an emotional disturbance, and often disappear when treatment changes this disturbance, i.e. reduces the over-anxiety.

3 Foudraine, J. 1974 (see Ch. 2, note 8).

4 One of the best methodological introductions to the ethological study of child behaviour is that by Blurton Jones, N. (1972) – see Chapter 3, note 10. See also the chapter on human ethology in the new, sixth edition (1980) of Eibl-Eibesfeldt, I., *Grundriss der Vergeleichenden Verhaltensforschung*. Munich: Piper.

5 Douglas-Hamilton, J. and O. Douglas-Hamilton 1975. *Among the elephants*. London: Collins.

6 Medawar, P. B. 1967 (see Ch. 3, note 9).

7 See Chapter 3, note 10.

8 The most recent discussion of this can be found in *The Oxford companion to animal behaviour*, edited by D. McFarland. Oxford: Oxford University Press.

9 For more ethologically oriented psychological studies of child behaviour, see Lewin, R. (Ch. 3, note 10) and the series *The developing child*, edited by J. S. Bruner *et al.* (see Ch. 3, note 10).

10 It is not generally realised by doctors, and not even known to many of them, how strong the feelings are beginning to be among the general public about these attitudes of the medical profession. One need not go the whole way with either Ivan Illich in his *Medical nemesis* (1975), London: Calder and Boyars (though it deserves to be widely read), or Ian Kennedy in his (unfortunately titled) Reith Lectures of 1980, *The unmasking of medicine* (see especially lecture 5), published in the six issues of *The Listener*, starting on 6 November 1980, to know, as many of us do from painful experiences, how justified our comment is. This has nothing to do with the fact that Britain has a special form of National Health Service or, as Americans like to call it, 'Socialised Medicine'; doctors under any system are made to absorb these attitudes during their training. For Dixon, see Chapter 2, note 12.

8

Overall conclusion

As we have said at the start, the main contribution we intended initially to make to the problem of early childhood autism was to show how some methods of research, developed in comparative ethology, could and should be applied in order to understand the nature and the genesis of autism, and to design possible methods of educating autistic children.

When we began to apply these methods to autistic children we soon discovered that we arrived at conclusions – at first tentative and provisional then increasingly plausible – that differed widely from what is at the moment the prevailing opinion among the (relatively small and closed) group of professional child psychiatrists and psychologists who are involved in research on autism.

In particular it became clear to us that there is as yet no comprehensive hypothesis about the nature of being autistic. The views that are often advocated, for instance the one that is claimed to be widely accepted at the moment, viz. that autism is primarily a 'language-cognitive handicap', and several other attempts at a theory fail to explain some essential aspects of the autistic syndrome. If, to the contrary, one sees *the autistic condition* as an anxiety-dominated emotional imbalance, which leads to social withdrawal, and in its wake to failure to learn from social interaction and from exploratory behaviour (which is shown only when a child has successfully bonded with his mother), then a great number of symptoms become comprehensible.

As to the question of how children *become autistic*, we find the prevailing opinion (that mainly 'organic' aspects, certainly *not* traumatising experiences in early childhood, are responsible) confirmed only to a very minor degree. Despite the fact that, as S. Wolkind pointed out in his review of Rutter and Schopler's voluminous elaboration of the Conference Proceedings in St Gallen in 1976 (see Ch. 1, note 6), 'those who believe in psychogenic origin are the baddies', we develop here the view that, although heredity may be involved to the extent that genetically different children may well be different in their vulnerability to autism-causing influences, and although there is some evidence of the influence of congenital rubella and of the effect of nutrition, by far the most important autismogenic factors are of a psychological nature. In Chapter 5 we have given a provisional list of these environmental causes of the autistic derailment; these causes are in urgent need of renewed study.

With regard to *treatment* finally, we once more reject as unfounded the widely advocated view that 'autistic children are ineducable' or that 'you can't make them relate but you can teach them simple skills'. We quote evidence from a number of sources that shows conclusively that this is simply not in accordance with the facts, but is rather a counsel of despair, based on the failure of so many therapists to educate autistic children. We argue in Chapters 6 and 9 that the type of treatment one would expect to be successful on the basis of our analysis of the autistic state and of its genesis corresponds strikingly with the empirically derived therapies which are now being tried out in various parts of the world. We describe some of these in Chapter 6, and argue that an even more successful therapy than any of them might well be designed by combining the best elements of each of them.

We expect that, as in 1972, this (new, updated and elaborated) account of our views will be received by the professional child psychiatrists with suspicion and that once more sharp criticism will be expressed. This is no doubt in part due to the unfamiliarity of our approach. Our study of the literature on the subject and our contacts with many workers in the field have made clear to us that the research methods applied by this branch of medicine do not yet include all those applied in comparative ethology (and in biology, even in natural science in general). In Chapter 7 we have briefly summarised what we consider to be the main methodological shortcomings in this field of child psychiatry. To 'stir up' the rather stagnant 'pool' of work has been our primary objective.

Of course, we do not claim that we have found *the* solution to the many problems with which autism presents us, in particular to the problem of *the way in which* emotion affects intellectual growth. We have concentrated on this emotional basis of intellectual growth because the intellectual aspects of child development receive enough attention from students of renown, such as J. Piaget, J. S. Bruner and M. Donaldson.[1] But we do claim that the understanding of autism, and the ability to cure autistic children will be promoted if the methods of study we have discussed here, and the framework of our approach and hypotheses are more purposefully applied. Child psychiatry cannot afford to ignore developments in the biological study of behaviour, which is without doubt one of the most active growing points of 'the life science'.

A few remarks must be made here on the wider implications of our study of autism and on the overall context in which autism and related disorders must be seen.

If, as we and a growing number of people believe, it is becoming clear that many cases of autism can be cured and even prevented by a return to healthier forms of parenting, such a restoration of sound child-rearing would not be the end of the task facing us.

Everyone with a minimum of biological knowledge and insight who takes in only a small part of the massive literature on the emerging consequences of our cultural evolution must surely be aware that modern human society is not in an optimum state, is in fact literally sick, and is rapidly becoming still sicker. This sickness, of which autism is only one aspect, has been sneaking into Western and westernised societies and is now spreading into the 'communist' bloc and into the Third World. It is partly of a physical (somatic, organic) nature, partly of a mental nature, and in many aspects both.

Briefly, what has happened, and is still happening at a steadily accelerating pace, are consequences of our persistent striving for a more prosperous, more comfortable and therefore (we assume too easily) a healthy life. We do this in the mistaken belief that by following this course we will become *happier*. We have now begun to wake up to the fact that this is a utopian mirage. While we have admittedly made our lives more comfortable, we have at the same time created a host of damaging, potentially deadly new pressures. These new pressures can be classified in three main categories.

Populations in all but a few of the most affluent societies show an accelerating increase in numbers and in the consumption per head. By becoming more numerous and by demanding more per head, we are consuming the capital instead of merely the interest of the resources of the Earth, and as a consequence *we are reducing the world's total carrying capacity*, i.e. the capital of our resources. As a result, famines (with epidemics and the survival of ever more irreparably damaged children in their wake), shortages of even such elementary necessities of life as fuel to cook raw food, water, and innumerable other resources are becoming more serious. This depletion of our natural resources is not merely a matter of quantity, it is now well known (though it has hardly penetrated to the medical world) that modern food and other consumer goods for sale in our *affluent* societies are becoming *qualitatively* sub-optimal.

Apart from this over-exploitation there is widespread *pollution* of our environment, caused by waste that nature cannot recycle. This pollution begins to receive increased attention, and we know now, for instance, that we take up into our bodies more dangerous heavy metals than is healthy; that our industrial effluents pollute air, soil and water over wide areas, adding for instance sulphur, CO_2 and many poisons which kill off the life that our planet used to carry; that in Britain alone at least 1500 food additives are used to make our food look more appetising or to give it a longer 'shelf life'; that we use recklessly inorganic nitrogenous fertilisers which by destroying humus, cake up the soil, and of which ever-increasing quantities flow off into inland waters and the sea. In all this (as, to be fair, in many more positive developments as well) the United States of America is in the lead. Already ten years ago we have heard it stated that the average American citizen was, judging by America's own health laws, 'unfit for human consumption' – a 'sick' but thought-provoking flippancy.

This material pollution is serious enough, and it has led to an alarming loss of fitness. But less attention is being given to the many signs of *mental* or 'psychosocial' pollution, of the deterioration of our social environment. Urbanisation, growing competitiveness, growing acquisitiveness, the striving for 'efficiency' are all causing 'psychological pollution'.[2] The WHO Laboratory for Clinical Stress Research in Stockholm and a (limited) number of research centres elsewhere are trying to understand what is happening, but as yet our knowledge of psychosocial stress is still fragmentary.

It is in this wider context that autism and many other stress diseases of a psychological kind must be seen. In our understandable but in reality reckless pursuit of higher material prosperity we are not only damaging ourselves but, more alarmingly, our children. This is distressing enough for those who see this happen to their own children but, purely objectively, it is of even more far-reaching impact: *we are damaging the human breeding stock of tomorrow*. Quite apart from, for example, the effects of starvation, of lead poisoning etc. on children's brains, we cause, by breaking up the social context of 'groups of extended families' and even of family life itself, very serious long-term damage: we breed and raise women and men who have not had the chance to develop fully their potential for optimal parental behaviour. As we have seen, this has, in part, to be learnt, and the proper settings for this 'programming for parenthood' are becoming scarcer all the time. We thus cause, and are undergoing, a self-inflicted cultural loss which will be difficult to replace. *Guidebooks and mothercraft classes, however good, can never teach fully what is learnt in the natural social context during 15 years of childhood.*

The significance of this is that, even if we were to learn to control autism and other mental stress diseases, we would, in the context of human populations, still be practising symptom treatment. This is better than no treatment at all, but it is important, indeed imperative, for us to see the magnitude of the problem facing us. Without such a more comprehensive understanding of the disadaptation courses which humanity is now following, we can never hope to do more than minor patching-up operations. The problem of autism is with us because of the life style we have chosen, and it is this life style we shall have to change.

However, to return to autism: whether or not we are right in these general views on human society, we submit that we have made a good case for refuting the opinions quoted at the start of this book. Many autistic children *can* be cured, and in our opinion such cures can best be effected by an integrated therapy, in which Welch's 'forced holding' must form the core, but in which as many as possible of the other promising methods must be incorporated as well.

The great practical difficulty will be that, as we have seen for ourselves, it is not enough to have read about the Welch method, nor even to have been present for a while as observers (even though, as Dr Welch recently remarked: 'a little bit of poor holding goes a long way'). It will be of the utmost importance that Dr Welch be given the opportunity to train thoroughly a number of carefully selected, highly motivated and psychiatrically competent pupils, who can then start to spread the new therapy as widely as possible. It would be sad if, when so much effort and money is spent on relatively ineffectual research and therapeutic attempts, no strongly motivated candidates and not even the modest amount of money required for their training were forthcoming.

We do not want to be misunderstood as assuming, in starry-eyed optimism, that in this way *all* autistic children and their parents can be helped to recover. There remains a solid core of difficult cases, of parents who have not the means or who will keep resisting any treatment. Yet we know from a few such seemingly 'hopeless' cases that even in them the downward spiral *can* be broken, provided the psychiatrist concerned is well trained and has a strong yet sympathetic personality.

Finally, even in cases that remain resistant, there may still be a way out, namely the adoption (rather than mere fostering) of such children to loving, capable and permanent substitute-mothers, who might well be able to recall even such children to life.

Notes and references

1   Donaldson, M. 1978. *Children's minds*. London: Fontana/Collins.
2   The new scientific journal *Stress*, founded by Dr Hans Selye, may well become an important source of information about this issue.

9

Practical suggestions to parents and caregivers

This chapter has been written at the urgent request of a considerable number of parents, caregivers and others who are in daily charge of autistic children, but we have included it only after much hesitation. Some of the reasons for our caution are: although we feel that we have made good progress towards understanding autism, it would be foolish to claim that we 'know all about it'; even if our views on what makes a child autistic are right, it need not follow that we know the best way to cure him; the therapies discussed in Chapter 6, promising though they are, are still more or less tentative 'prototypes' of therapies that may still be much improved on in the future; totally new insights might emerge that could make fundamental changes in treatment desirable; a treatment that is suitable for one child need not be the best way of treating others.

Quite apart from that: unlike the many parents and caregivers to whom we are going to make these suggestions, we have not ourselves been in *continuous* charge of an autistic child, and have therefore not experienced the full pressures of living with a non-relating, non-speaking, oddly behaving, at times screaming, 'naughty', and in many respects 'eerie' child that can drive especially parents to despair. Yet we are not totally inexperienced: we have seen, heard and read a great deal about (and taken part in) the moment-to-moment interaction with autistic children; we have discussed a variety of practical problems with many parents, caregivers and clinical workers; and we have ourselves worked for longer or shorter periods with a fair number of autistic dyads. We have studied a number of therapists, teachers and parents in action, have witnessed and read about a number of successes and, above all, we have been assured time and again that our example and advice, and E.A.T.'s occasional demonstrations in clinics, when acted upon, have led to encouraging, sometimes to striking improvements in the children concerned. On balance we felt that our advice was more likely to do good than harm; and at least it might lead parents away from a totally resigned attitude, from meekly accepting the situation without even attempting to do something about it.

We have to stress that the following are no more than some general guidelines that we believe to be helpful, at least for a proportion of cases.

We have tried, by illustrating our general advice with specific examples, to give an idea of how to translate our general suggestions into action, but the decision about how to proceed, and especially about what is best at any given moment, has to be left to the adult in charge. There is no end to the surprises one meets in interacting with an autistic child, but the inventiveness and the speed of adjusting of the adults concerned can also be quite astonishing; time and again we have been amazed at the imaginativeness of which caring adults are capable.

The nature of the subject has prevented us from arranging this chapter in the form of a flowing, coherent argument; inevitably, it is more or less kaleidoscopic. We have also allowed ourselves a certain amount of repetition, partly because several suggestions could bear such repetition, partly because some readers will quite probably turn to this chapter before having read the first part of our book (although it would help if such readers would read Ch. 6).

The essence of our advice is to have hope and confidence. The fact that progress may at first be very slow and hardly noticeable makes it difficult to maintain an optimistic attitude, yet this is important, and can be crucial. It helps to form the habit of comparing your child's behaviour with that of a long time back – months or even longer – for this can remind you of how much worse things have been. To recognise even small signs of improvement not only helps morale but also the recovery itself, for a parent who notices improvement cannot fail to take delight in it and, often unwittingly, to show this delight to the child, who is then encouraged in his turn. Because it is the mother–child dyad that has become sick and has been caught in the downward spiral of non-socialisation, this mutual encouragement (the producing of 'positive social feedback' instead of 'negative social feedback') can turn the downward spiral into its opposite: an upward spiral. We have seen this happen in enough cases to feel justified in maintaining that the prognosis for many autistic children need not be as gloomy as it is so often said to be. Yet, recovery is rarely quick, and parents of an autistic child face a very demanding task – the more so the further advanced or pronounced the disorder is.

Before giving specific advice, we want to discuss briefly three general aspects of the attitude that it is most desirable for parents of an autistic child (or of an otherwise emotionally disturbed child) to develop and to foster in themselves.

Early detection

If we are right in considering autism to be the outcome of a gradually developing estrangement between a child and the people around him – a refusal to make social contacts and a self-isolation which may gradually become worse and worse – we would expect that recovery would be most likely if this derailment is recognised and treated at as early a stage as possible. As far as our experience goes (and that of, for instance, Dr Welch and Dr Waldon), this seems in fact to be the case. Our most general advice, to parents and especially to mothers (who are in the best position and also naturally inclined to watch their baby): do observe your baby intently (though of course without undue anxiety) and keep your eyes open for possible signs of incipient social aloofness. We do not intend to be alarmist; we merely urge mothers to be observant, and ready to act if such early warning signs are seen. In many cases, though by no means invariably, these signs are noticeable soon after birth. If a baby is clearly consistently withdrawn, on the whole over-quiet and undemanding, 'good' and seemingly contented and not reacting even to the most persuasive approaches by his mother, and even more so if a baby arches his back and resists being taken up from his cot and perhaps cries overmuch, it is best not to reason (as some quite sensible parents are known to have done) 'If our baby does not really want company, we will have to accept that he is inherently a loner'. Withdrawn behaviour *has* to be taken as a *possible* early warning sign.

The natural occasion on which to observe your baby is, of course, during and immediately after feeding. We should add that it begins to be more generally recognised that, for the growth of a healthy and warm bond between yourself and your child, it is important that you try to breast-feed him. It is especially then that mutual eye contact is almost inevitable; and it is more particularly the short period after the feed and before the baby falls asleep that free, cheerful and playful interaction happens almost automatically and certainly ought to be indulged in. If for some reason you cannot breast-feed your baby, do hold the bottle in such a way that it seems to come from your body and not from somewhere in outer space; certainly the mechanical method of putting the bottle in a clamp attached to the cot and leaving the baby alone is psychologically wrong – a normal baby needs intimate contact with his mother or at least with a human caregiver. If you feel unable to enter into such a personal relationship, you should at least try to force yourself to start it, and so give yourself a chance to wake up to the delights of receiving your baby's attention and interest in return. For, if all goes well, a baby is above all such *fun*!

Although many autistic children are reported to 'have been odd from birth', this is not always the case; autism can develop after an initial period of perfectly normal development. According to most experts, babies can be at risk till they are 30 months of age, although (largely because early stages are rarely noticed and certainly not always reported to the doctor) it is not really known whether the danger of withdrawal is the same throughout those early 2½ years. But it is advisable to remain alert to the possibility that a child withdraws even after an initially normal start. Some babies fail to develop 'babbling' and 'cooing'; or they may begin to show stereotypies (such as shaking of the head, rocking in one way or another, or over-frequent eye blinking); or they may assume too often the 'blank' eye expression, or look through or past their mother; a baby may fail, when you return after a few hours' absence, to raise his arms or he may show in other ways that he does not really want to be picked up; he may even begin to avoid you too often. Such regressions may be temporary, but they deserve attention because they may reveal a deterioration of his social behaviour, and in such cases it is *change* towards social withdrawal that can indicate the beginning of autistic tendencies.

It is because these early warning signs can be slight and subtle, and also because they often 'sneak in' so gradually that they may well escape notice if the mother is not observant (perhaps because she is too busy, or worried on other counts, or absorbed in other matters etc.), that we keep repeating our basic advice: observe your child as much as you can. Also observe the reactions of neighbours, relatives, health visitors and other outsiders, for they may see things that you yourself have not spotted, yet they may not find it opportune or tactful to remark on them. Examples of such alertness of outsiders can be found in, for example, the story of Elly Park,[1] and in Fae's case history (see Ch. 10).

Of course, whether seriously withdrawn babies will invariably become autists or will develop other types of aberrant behaviour (or will 'grow out of it') is another question. Our point is that abnormal social withdrawal always deserves close attention.

That we direct these introductory remarks specifically at mothers is intentional. The development of a warm and affectionate mutual bond with the mother is in our species the natural and the best starting point for the development of normal social behaviour in later life.

There are people who feel that to allocate this task of 'affiliation' primarily to the mother is unfair – a baby is after all her and her husband's joint responsibility. This attitude (which is based on the view that the division of labour between the sexes is a *purely* cultural phenomenon) is often expressed by extreme feminists, who want complete equality for men and women.

It will be clear from our earlier chapters that we think that this extreme belief – in the *complete* interchangeability of the roles of men and women – is misguided where the parts to be played by mothers and fathers are concerned. It is a simple biological fact that men and women are genetically different,[2] and there are many indications that this expresses itself not merely in the fact that it is the mother and not the father who produces milk and nurses the young baby, but also in the different parts to be played by fathers and mothers in the overall organisation of the family. We think that we have to accept that, however important the role of the father is, it is at the start mainly a supporting one, one of provider, protector and moral supporter, and that his *direct* interaction with their child comes later, and is *different in kind* from (though not less important than) that between child and mother. To attempt to give the father exactly the same role as the mother would be impossible as far as breast-feeding is concerned, and would at the most be a second-best as far as the first steps in affiliation are concerned. Admittedly, this second-best solution is often forced upon a father, and it often works because it is fortunately possible for him to adjust and modify his parental behaviour, at least in some details and to a certain extent. Yet, because a baby's first intimate contacts have to be with his mother, it is primarily her task to initiate whatever corrective course is necessary if early warning signs become apparent.

In modern society this may leave a mother with a difficult choice: she may have to give up her outside job or preoccupation, irrespective of whether she finds this fair or not. This is admittedly a hard decision to make for a mother whose intellectual interests and satisfactions have been found to lie in such outside activities, but we consider it axiomatic that the child's interests come first. But this is not valid for the sake of the child only: since children are the citizens of the future, who will soon have to run their society, whatever is best for their development is best for society too. (This is, of course, not to say that the present procedures of educating 'normal' children are optimal – far from it. What we mean is that personal self-centred preferences of parents may not be indulged in at the expense of the real – not necessarily fashionable – interests of the education of their children; and that by 'education' we understand not merely the teaching of skills, but the guidance of their development towards happiness and responsible citizenship, with all its social and moral requisites, will by now have become clear.)

We wish we could give concrete advice to the parent of a one-parent family, beyond saying that if at all possible a father should, even with very young babies, either attempt to play the mother's part as fully as possible or arrange for a stable substitute-mother (and also, if the parent is a woman, to try to see to it that her child receives loving attention from at least one substitute father). For contact with other children, playgroups are of course especially important (and not only for a child in a one-parent family, but also for an only child).

Early detection is of course easiest for experienced mothers, who know more or less how normal babies 'ought to' behave, for they have handled babies before and have, with the keen interest of the directly involved, watched how other mothers deal with their children. With one's first baby one cannot be expected to know fully how to proceed, one has to rely to quite an extent on the advice and example of experienced grandmothers, friends, health visitors etc. Yet one need not of course follow slavishly what they say; one has to exert a certain amount of discrimination and listen most to those whose judgements one has reason to consider to be wise and knowledgeable. This is, of course, difficult for those young mothers who have missed out on the early, informal programming for motherhood that we have described as natural for our species, but they can learn a great deal from watching and listening to experienced mothers who, even though they may do some things wrong, are also likely to impart knowledge and wisdom that are not to be found in manuals written by experts, or passed on by doctors or nurses in clinics. (Those mothers who rely exclusively on manuals run a risk of becoming *opinionated* rather than *good* parents.) The need for *willingness* to go on learning cannot be over-emphasised. Mothers of only children who 'know it all' may in effect deny their child aspects of parental care of which he is in real need.

It is partly because of the difficulties of early detection that so many autistic children are not recognised as such until long after they have begun to show signs that the experienced eye would have recognised early as incipient disturbed behaviour. Also, as we have said, too few doctors have the ability or the willingness to be of much use to parents. This is not to say that even if autism is not discovered until the child is three or four years old (when he behaves too abnormally to ignore his condition any longer), it is too late to start treatment; but we agree with the experts who say that recovery becomes less likely the further parents and child have travelled on the downward spiral. Yet we are convinced that attempts at rehabilitation are worth undertaking *at any stage*, for we have seen late attempts succeed. When one remembers that autists are sometimes given the label 'schizophrenic' when they grow up and when one then knows that nowadays new methods have been developed that can help at least some adult schizophrenics towards complete recovery, one will feel less reason for despair even if one becomes aware that one's child is in an advanced stage of autism.[3]

Emotional adjustment of parents

Having tried to alert parents to early warning signs, our next advice to parents who have spotted such early signs of withdrawal in their baby is not to panic; not to believe unquestioningly what so many authoritative books on autism say: 'that autism is hardly ever curable; that the prognosis is necessarily poor'. Whatever your doctor and your friends may say, do remember that this view is based on the poor rate of success in the past, and that new and more promising ways of curing autistic children are not merely theoretically possible but have actually been found, even though the official literature has so far hardly taken notice. Remember also how many 'do-it-yourself' mothers have been successful. You may find such a mother in your home town or among your acquaintances who is willing to have her brain picked or, better, to be observed in action. It can also help to look back and try to find out whether the early conditions in your baby's life contained some of the factors we have called 'autismogenic', perhaps even before he was born. This might not only protect you from unwarranted feelings of guilt, but also help you to believe that some of these early influences might be counteracted and the harm undone. If you cannot find much in the child's early history, perhaps he is one of those highly susceptible babies, perhaps one who has some otherwise highly valuable traits in his personality? It certainly is more helpful to try to discover what he *is* interested in and whether he has special gifts than to dwell too much on what he is *not* interested in, for any positive quality can be used as a 'bridge' towards socialisation.[4]

If you do suspect either that your child has been exposed to autismogenic conditions (if, for instance, you have moved to a new life or place, perhaps while you were under considerable strain – see our list on pp. 121–37) or that he may be a supersensitive child, or both, you may (even though your *reason* tells you that you cannot be blamed) nevertheless *feel* guilty, and this may make it needlessly difficult for you to make a constructive effort. Of course, the best way to cope with this would be to convince yourself that you *are not* to blame. Or, if that does not work, you might try to think: 'So what? We have done our best. Anyway ideal parents, who never make any mistakes, do not exist. No use crying over spilled milk; what matters *now* is: how can we cure him?' We also know mothers (parents) who, sometimes wrongly, *did* blame themselves, and have, with astonishing strength of character, said to themselves: 'I (we) produced that damaged child; it's up to me (us) to undo whatever harm I (we) have done'. But such people are extremely rare, and no one need feel inferior who cannot emulate their example. What we think *is* unhelpful and, in fact, an evasion of the issue is to accept without questioning the view that such a child is, in the terminology of the insurance policy, 'an act of God', a cross you have to bear and which you cannot, and therefore need not, even must not, try to do anything about. It may help you reject this meek way out to realise that to declare a child ineducable amounts to passing a terrible life sentence on him, to condemning him literally to lifelong misery. In our view the only defensible attitude is: 'As long as it is not proved beyond any doubt that attempts at rehabilitation are futile, we must at least try'.

Of course it can be extremely difficult to build up such a positive, constructive response to the disaster of seeing your child 'derail'. However, do remember that we have seen how soon a negative, despairing attitude can change into its opposite if and when one's first attempts at establishing contact are rewarded by a change for the good, however small. We ourselves are always happy to recall the story of a little girl of 20 months ('Fae', whose history we describe in Ch. 10) who recovered completely in a few months. This case may well be representative of quite a number of similar, seemingly trivial but in our opinion very important and by no means rare reversals of incipient autism, which therefore deserves close attention. The point we are making now is that early detection and speedy recovery are no distant ideal but could very well be achieved with exactly the same happy result, and this alone can give any parent in the same position great encouragement. With luck, a normal degree of sensitivity and, admittedly, a degree of perseverance that may at times be hard to maintain, many more parents will be able to save such children than is now professionally believed. Certainly, the personal experience of, for instance, seeing a smile appear, seeing a stereotypy become rarer – *any* sign of progress, however small and however still behind the normal stage of development, even however much slower than normal the *rate* of progress may still be – the awareness that all this means that recovery is on the way can do wonders for the parents' confidence.

They need this confidence, because even when overall progress is good, there will inevitably be numerous setbacks.[5] It is essential for parents not to be discouraged by such setbacks – and if possible to find their causes and profit from the insight so acquired – but to keep reminding themselves that one step forward is more important than the many steps back, for they are only temporary interruptions of the overall progress. *Do* try to believe that it is the improvements, however rare and slight they may be at the start, that show the child's real potential!

This is in fact the attitude that all successful mothers and teachers of withdrawn children have or develop: the confidence, the unshakeable belief, the *certainty* that the child will come out of his shell. It is this belief, that bouts of normal or even exceptionally promising behaviour are the true indicators of the child's potential, which enables them to accept the setbacks and disappointments without becoming too discouraged. (Please note that we do *not* advocate a light-hearted, passive belief that 'all *will* come right in the end', but an attitude of optimistic determination to *make* it come right.) Conversely, we must also warn against an attitude that we have met more than once, one of forgetting about the progress made and of immediately worrying about the many things the child can*not* yet do. It does help a great deal to remain aware of signs of progress, however little – to be grateful for small mercies. This is also where the father's attitude is of great importance. Even though the resocialising of a derailed child is at first mainly the mother's task, she will be greatly helped in getting over moments and periods of despair if her husband gives full support and, as is soon necessary, begins to play an active part. There is no doubt that an autistic child can become an almost intolerable stress on the marriage bond. We have seen cases in which the father, immersed in his work as the breadwinner, washes his hands of the whole affair, with a virtual break-up of the marriage as the result; but we also know fathers who take a full part in the rehabilitation efforts, and in our experience it is when both parents take their share (though their roles differ and, we believe, have to differ) that the chances of recovery are best.

Of course all this is more difficult for some to achieve than for others; in our experience there are, on the one hand, parents such as those just mentioned, for whom (so to speak) one little sign of their child's potential is enough; at the other extreme, there are parents who find it next to impossible to develop this all-important belief in their child. Unfortunately, the prevalent 'official' attitude tends to weaken the morale of this latter category even more.

The way in which *outsiders* can best help the 'non-believers' varies of course from case to case and involves all kinds of imponderables. Some parents will be quite prepared to take other, happier families as their examples; others may be put off or may bristle at the slightest suggestion that their attitude is not helpful to their child and that other parents might perform better; much depends of course on who gives advice and how it is given. At any rate, any outsider has to be aware of the fact that many parents are, understandably, very sensitive on the subject. He has to realise all the time that, as we have said, it is not just the child who has derailed but that it is the child–mother dyad, or the child–parents triad, often even an entire family that has become 'ill', has been 'driven round the bend'. This means not only that no two cases can be approached in the same way, but also that empathy and tact are always required in whoever does the counselling. Which combination of diagnostic statement and criticism on the one hand and of encouragement on the other is best has to be considered in each individual case, and this makes it impossible to give more than general advice. We certainly do not want to add to the burdens of parents – we try to be helpful, and certainly *encouragement* is often of crucial importance.

Attitude to doctors and other professionals

We would be evading an important issue if we did not alert parents to the fact that doctors, even the most specialised consultants, are fallible and, as advisors about autism and similar disorders, all too often of little or no use. As we have argued, this is often due to ignorance, often to their adherence to the thesis of the 'ineducability' advocated by most books on autism, often to a laudable but in effect not always helpful habit of reassuring parents by saying that the child will 'grow out of it'. What are parents to do in the face of this unhappy state of affairs? We are afraid that the best advice we can give is to try to apply self-help.

To begin with, although one has to turn first to one's own family doctor, then perhaps to a specialist: treat their opinions with a grain of salt. In some cases of clearly bodily illness, at least when the doctors concerned admit or show that they are at a loss to understand what is wrong, one can, often with their active help, ask for second, third and even more opinions. Most doctors will not take this amiss unless it is done in a discourteous or irritated manner. But with mysterious mental disorders, and especially with emotional childhood disturbances, there are at least two reasons for avoiding such a course. First, it will not do an autistic child any good – on the contrary – if he is taken to doctor after doctor or clinic after clinic.

Secondly, doctors might well (understandably, because they have to cope with too many hypochondriacs and other bothersome surgery *habitués*) come to consider an over-insistent parent a nuisance.

We believe that the best advice we can give as to how to react to the doctor's first reaction is: study the way he goes about his business. Does he show real interest and concern? Does he observe the child? Does he ask you for relevant factual information and does he listen to it? Does he show awareness of the vulnerability of an emotionally disturbed child or does he straightaway prescribe a drug or recommend a host of clinical tests? Does he seem aware of the alternative views on autism, other than those to be found in most of the standard books? With all due respect for the practising medical profession – and this is considerable, though qualified – we feel we have to advise parents to treat medical opinion with reserve, and critically. If your doctor, in reaching a diagnosis, ignores information you give him, if he recommends without proper examination such things as an observation period in hospital, the taking of electro-encephalograms, blood tests, or even merely a set of standard psychological tests (in the clinic rather than at home), you would, in our opinion, be wise to hesitate and to discuss with him your misgivings about too rough a diagnostic procedure. The least you can insist on is that you will be allowed to be present when such tests are done. If you cannot have confidence in what he intends to do, there may be nothing for it but to refuse to have your child submitted to what, after studying the relevant literature, you think might harm him further. However, we can do no more than advise caution; to refuse sensible medical help can be as irresponsible as to accept help that one distrusts. It is the parents who have to decide, and we can only alert them to what we consider to be the biased attitude of most of the experts and of those among their friends who believe experts too readily.[6]

If it is difficult to obtain a responsible *diagnosis*, the dilemma may become even more acute for parents when it comes to deciding on what *treatment* to give their child. As will by now have become clear, we feel we have to convince parents of two things: (a) that for many, if not most, autistic children the notion of ineducability, of their inability to understand and to 'make sense' of their surroundings and their perceptions and all that goes with this view, is rash and in most cases downright wrong; and (b) that, as we have explained in Chapter 6, a number of promising new lines of treatment are being tried out, as yet perhaps still on an experimental, tentative basis, but together clearly evolving into what may well become an effective therapeutic procedure. To what extent any particular parents can work along the new lines depends on a variety of circumstances in which they find themselves: first of all on their own determination and their parental or rather superparental abilities, then also on what help is available to them. We can do no better than suggest once more that all parents do their own reconnaissance in this respect and try to find the best possible solutions by discussing their problems with other parents in the same situation, by exchanging experiences and information about the possibility of founding a special playgroup or infant school, and by trying to find an experienced therapist who shows understanding of what autistic and other emotionally disturbed children need.[7] The teachers to avoid are those who do not believe in the educability of autistic children and those who try to educate them by 'drilling' them in the various ways we have criticised in this book. How to get the education authorities to agree with unconventional ways of educating one's child is again a problem that parents must try to solve for themselves; fortunately, however strict the law may seem to be, many officials concerned often show a considerable degree of flexibility.

Assuming that permission for home tuition and other unconventional regimes can be obtained, we can only repeat that willingness to learn from the example of clearly good parents, therapists and teachers is an attitude to be cultivated in oneself. All this, including contacts with fellow parents, can help one not only in building up one's own method of helping one's child, but also in maintaining one's, at times sorely tried, morale.

We realise full well that this advice, in its generality, puts an enormous load on the shoulders of the parents concerned, but under the present unsatisfactory circumstances we find it impossible to recommend full, uncritical acceptance of what doctors or other experts say or prescribe. But we must hope that these circumstances will not prevail for too long. It is our own belief that the most urgent task for the professions concerned will be to acquaint themselves with, and seek training in, the application of methods based on Dr Welch's procedure in the first place, ideally supplemented and enriched by the various approaches we have discussed in Chapter 6. Small 'mothering centres', such as Dr Welch and her mother Mrs Jane Welch have pioneered, could form the nucleus from which a more effectual treatment of autistic children and their parents could grow.

Our readers might think that the various Societies for Autistic Children, which have so creditably alerted public awareness of autism (according to some, at the cost of otherwise handicapped children), would be the obvious organisations to which to turn for advice and help. Unfortunately, most of these societies are at least for the present, certainly in the English-speaking world, prejudiced, almost possessed by the idea of ineducability or at any rate limited educability. Among the many utterances and publications of their leaders, one has to distinguish clearly between the moral message ('autistic children and their parents deserve help') and their practical advice ('this is the way to help them'). We agree with the moral message but think that their practical directives and educational methods have to be judged critically.

Finally, we have to remind parents of autistic children of the fact that, as we mentioned briefly in note 22 to Chapter 5, very few people, doctors included, have any idea of the extent of the deterioration in the quality of our food that has taken place over the last decades, and that is resulting in a frightening deterioration in general fitness. Although, as we have seen, the links between food and autism are only just beginning to be investigated, parents of autistic children (and of all children) would be well advised to read up on reliable nutritional literature, and certainly to give their children well balanced vitamin supplementation.

After this general preamble, we shall now try to make some specific proposals.

Restoring the emotional bond

Whether or not professional assistance of the right kind is available, all parents of autistic children will have to bear the brunt of their child's actual treatment themselves. As we have stressed before, it is in the nature of our species that the very first stages of bonding, the affiliation proper, are very much a matter between child and mother. We believe that by far the best a mother of an autistic child can do is to take a leaf out of Dr Martha Welch's book and to build the treatment on her method of establishing, or re-establishing, a bond between herself and her child by 'holding' (see Ch. 6 & Plates 5–11). This will be the more effective the younger the child is, but experience so far shows that it is beneficial for children of any age.

Holding sessions should take place if possible every day, preferably when mother and child both feel like it, but also, if at all possible, when either or both may feel: 'not just today'. Certainly at the start of the treatment, few days should be without at least one holding session. It is best to select a comfortable couch, or a suitable site (e.g. a mattress) on the floor in a room where one will not be too easily interrupted.[8] The first sessions may last uncomfortably long, *for it is essential that one does not stop as long as the child is still struggling and resisting; he must be held until he really snuggles up to his mother!* Dr Welch also finds it desirable that, whenever possible, the father gives his wife moral support (e.g. by putting his arm round her shoulders) while she is holding the child. If the father is not available, the mother's mother can help in this way (see Plates 7–10).

It is important to realise that it is not just the mechanical act of holding (not just the giving and receiving of *any* 'touch stimuli') that counts; it is the 'psychological' (especially the *emotional*) content one gives to it, and this depends very much on the way one behaves during holding. Doing it mechanically, dutifully, in a bored, or worse, in a reluctant or hostile manner will help neither child nor mother.

We repeat once more: whatever the child's age, think of him and treat him as if he were very much younger, in fact at the start as if he were a babe in arms. Be kind and loving, make little jokes, cuddle the child, kiss him, pat his behind or his head, stroke his back, pull his arms around your chest, put your own arms firmly around his body, and talk to him intimately, encourage him to talk and respond. If he struggles, hold him with your legs as well if need be, but do try to achieve as much chest-to-chest contact as possible. (Teenagers must preferably not be held on one's lap but in a sitting position next to the mother, although it seems as if even with relatively old autistic children one need not expect that sexual responses are easily aroused.) Remember all the time that, however fiercely the child struggles and tries to keep his distance, he *is* ambivalent and does at the same time *want* to be held; remember also that he *wants* to be treated as a baby. Even if one puts a teenager at one's side, he too does need to be touched, patted, stroked and kissed etc. His resisting expresses only part of his being: it belongs to and is at the root of the illness you want to treat. Teenagers can even become so upset that they may lash out and fight back but, according to Dr Welch, their fighting is always inhibited and not as dangerous to the mother as their physical size and strength might make one fear.

Remember all the time that holding sessions may at times last long, be physically and emotionally exhausting, and even psychologically hurtful: it takes a great deal of devotion to remain kind and warm when you are violently rejected, and especially when (as happens occasionally with more advanced children) the child begins to hurl verbal reproaches at you about events that have hurt him in the past and which you may have totally forgotten. (but however unjustified the reproaches might be, remember that what counts is that the child has *experienced* them as hurtful or as rejecting).

The mother should not give up too easily when the child begins to give signs of being bored. One mother wrote to us that her child fell asleep during a holding session, which made her feel silly and at a loss as to what to do next. At the same time, however, she felt elated at the trust the child showed in her (but it *might* have been one of the child's ways of 'opting out' – the instantaneous interpretation of such incidents is often impossible).

If you become bored yourself and your child is quiet, yet without actively snuggling up to you (as he will usually end up by doing), the session may be helped along by the telling of stories that are interesting to the child and that may also provide new opportunities for increasing the physical contact, and by singing nursery rhymes etc. Some autistic children respond best if the story is not told directly to them but in a way that simulates a conversation with oneself. Do not be misled by the child's seeming indifference; remember all the time that the idea that an autistic child 'does not understand speech' is for almost all of them simply nonsense, based on poor observation. But the talk must as a rule be adjusted to the 'mental age' of a very young child. A little commonplace trick that is often forgotten is to bring one's own head down to the level of the child's head. All this will have to be done in a flexible way – like normal children, autists respond in more mature ways at one time than at another, and it would seem to be a mistake to use *nothing but* simplified talk. As always, monitor your child's reactions and try to recognise the moments or times when he seems receptive for speech more appropriate to his age. As we have said before, the father will also have to play his role, but one that differs from that of the mother. He can help for instance by playing with the child; often, in a specifically father's (or elder brother's) way, by romping with him in 'rough-and-tumble' play, by crawling along with him on the floor, by playing peek-a-boo, by moving him about on a swing, by playing ball games etc. Soon he can take his child for walks (with, if necessary, many pauses in which he has simply to stand around and watch, or explore the world together with his child). The nature of his role too has to be adjusted to the child's 'mental' and emotional age. It is also of great importance to the child (whether normal or autistic) that he be allowed and gently encouraged to observe his father in all the little practical jobs around the house that he does anyway: washing dishes, mending things, digging the garden or gathering garden produce etc. But be careful not to *force* an autistic child into such roles; rather, allow him to begin with to observe you from afar and 'out of the corner of his eye'. Autistic children do have 'eyes at the backs of their heads' and, never mind what so many experts say, most of them take in much and make very good use of what they observe in such situations. Some prodding, or at times telling him firmly not to be too passive may be necessary, but caution is advisable. To find the best balance on each occasion is no doubt impossible, but it is worth trying to approximate it. It should be added here that the kind of interactions we recommend are not based on the fashionable, but actually ill advised and biologically simply unsound idea that a child requires a great deal of 'stimulation'. That general term 'stimulation' is one of the extremely misleading and in our opinion really harmful red herrings pulled across the path of parents and teachers. A little reflection will show that what children need is stimulation *of special kinds*, namely those that elicit and guide healthy behaviour patterns such as social and exploratory and at times eating and sleeping behaviour etc. (Also, when they are not apprehensive, or are in need of stimulation, they will often seek and find it themselves.) What is definitely *not* wanted and to be avoided is *over*-stimulation, and *one must certainly not provide fear-or-panic-inducing* stimulation. We cannot warn enough against uncritical acceptance of this notion that children have to be given 'more stimulation' in general – just as it is wrong to stress the need for touching and being touched in general. As we said before, these terms, so fashionable just now, reveal and lead to careless, sloppy thinking. If anything, conditions in our modern society tend to be harmful by providing 'information input *over*load'; and too much stimulation, even of an intellectually positive kind, must therefore in our opinion be *avoided*, certainly in those middle-class families that tend to over-emphasise 'cerebral' development. Children must have time to indulge in their own activities and not be interrupted all the time. Just to mention a few examples: an autistic child can be over-stimulated by increasing his fear and tendency to withdraw; one can also only too easily bore a child by irrelevant or too intrusive interference, and it can have adverse effects if one interrupts him when he is actively (though perhaps surreptitiously) socialising or exploring (untimely interruptions to which some well intentioned or self-indulgent parents and grandparents are often prone). Less easily recognised are those occasions in which too much stimulation causes a *conflict of interests* in the child. We have seen a striking example of this when a one-year-old boy was interrupted while he was engaged in a delightful bout of rough-and-tumble with his father. While this game was going on, someone turned on the radio and, since the boy was exceptionally musical, the music at once caught his attention. He stopped romping, yet could not quite tear himself loose from his father and give his full attention to the music. The expression of intense conflict on his face and in fact in his whole body was downright painful to observe. Fortunately, the radio was soon turned off and the two could resume their play. We have observed similar unfortunate occasions of conflicts caused by simultaneous kinds of clashing stimulation in schools for autistic children; in many cases they were caused by teachers who, believing in the false thesis of autism as a 'cognitive' defect, exposed the children to a near-bombardment of too many and too different kinds of input. So do realise that much of this talk about the need for 'stimulation' is a passing fashion and has applicability only in very special cases, of which autism is definitely not one.[9]

One also has to guard against impatience and taking over from a child when he is working at a task in a fumbling way. It is only too easy to say 'let me do it' and so deny him many opportunities for developing skills at his own pace and in doing so build up his self-confidence.

Other aspects of rehabilitation

Having argued that in our opinion the restoration of the 'emotional balance' must be the primary aim of any treatment of autistic and similar children, we add straightaway that the holding method is not necessarily the all-sufficient way of achieving this. We suggest that it should form the core of the therapy, but it can probably be supplemented and enriched by a great variety of other procedures, some of which we discussed in Chapter 6.

To begin with, although we always stress the need for treating an autistic child at least in many respects as if he were much younger than he actually is, often even as a baby, it must of course not be forgotten that in other respects he may be precocious, nor that even a normal baby is not continuously being held by his mother. Every baby is at times quite happy, and may even be busy socialising and exploring and practising when he is merely aware that his mother or other members of the family are around. This awareness comes to him through various sensory channels, among which familiar sounds, a familiar physical environment, familiar smells and toys such as pram beads (and of course his own fingers and feet) are undoubtedly very important. As an *autistic* child improves, the 'security umbrella' can likewise be progressively provided 'by proxy' and less and less often. What counts is that he *feels* secure, and that in this respect he needs the treatment normally needed by younger children. As his progress continues, it becomes if anything even more valuable for him to have available his own private, secure yet secluded corner or, later, room, perhaps only a corner merely screened by a half-partitition. In between bouts of contact-socialising – not all the time – he may have to be put there or to be allowed to retreat. It might well be useful to have, in such a 'den', a mattress or merely a blanket or a piece of furry material. We also believe that this could be the place where he can have some of his own personal toys, and perhaps also (for the purposes of socialising and exploration of a peer) a full-length mirror, for a mirror image is often less frightening than a real person – not only because it is the child's own size but also because it will of course never intrude when the child himself withdraws! Raun, the boy described in such detail by his father, B. N. Kaufman (see Ch. 10), seems in one stage of his recovery to have been fascinated by his interactions with his mirror image. (Kaufman's interpretation of Raun's 'mirror play' seems to us a little fanciful but, as we shall argue in the next chapter, one has to read the published case histories with discrimination, distinguishing between often valuable factual information and at times less valuable theorising.)

If not used as a *permanent* retreat, such a private den is useful to any child in many ways. Autists particularly will, when they believe themselves to be unobserved and when relaxed, practice on their own a number of skills of which even their parents may not have the slightest suspicion; for instance, they may sing surprisingly well, and sometimes speak, even if they never do so in company. (Parents may be convinced that their child does not do these advanced things even in his den, but they may forget that an autist especially is excessively sensitive to even the slightest signs of possible intrusion; he may, for instance, withdraw into his shell at the faintest sound of a creaking staircase. To 'stalk' such a child effectively one may have to develop very sophisticated 'field craft' indeed, comparable to that of the (good) hunter or the (good) naturalist – of whom there are surprisingly few in our modern society.)

We are still far from knowing what autistic children actually do when in their dens, but we know of three girls who from an early age had books, including some Shakespeare plays, hidden under their mattresses and revealed often that they read them; another girl who would, when in company, type only when she held her tutor's index finger, with which she then pressed the keys, was found to type on her own (though only a series of separate characters, not words) while she was alone in her room. The boy Dibs (described by Axline, Ch. 3, note 8) read, painted, listened to music and did all kinds of technical things when he was in his own room; he also looked a great deal out of the window and became, for instance, attached to one particular branch of a tree next to the house (we also suspect that he may well have talked a lot with the gardener who, apart from Dib's grandmother, was for such a long time the only person who somehow must have given him loving attention). Sandy played with his toys and built villages and railways when alone.[10] We are afraid that autists also use their dens frequently for just being bored (but at least out of touch with the frightening outside world) and for less desirable self-exploration such as masturbating; but even so we believe that the advantages of a den outweigh by far the disadvantages, at least if withdrawal is allowed in moderation.

One of the important things to remember is the child's continuous and often very 'tense' ambivalence: even when he withdraws, he may nevertheless at the same time *want* to receive reassuring, distant signs of the presence and interest of others. It is important to make sure that one senses if and when he wants such contact and that one does not reject him then (and even ignoring is a form of rejecting). We have known many normal children who, at ages between two and four years, had a special contact call (different for each child, often originating in actual imitations) to which, especially in a strange environment or when they had strayed just a little too far from their mothers, they expected a reply (often the same call), which then fully reassured them. The function, parallel with the contact calls of many social animals, is striking. One of our own children used the curious sound 'koye-kaye-koye' for this (of which we never discovered the origin); another one used 'gogglygoggly gooo' (which we happen to know was mimicked originally from our chickens, and then formalised). In our experience, it is very important to such children, whether normal or merely a little insecure or autistic, that their contact calls be answered *every time they utter them*. (As we indicated earlier, they are really announcements and questions in one: as Selma Lagerlöf[11] has put it, they convey 'I am here, where are you?'.)

It seems also to work as reassurance and bonding devices when the mother, while doing something for or with the child (e.g. helping him climb the stairs or even, long before that stage, when changing his nappy), sings or semi-sings some tune; speaks, softly, a kind of running commentary on what she does, preferably mixed with endearments, smiles etc.; or, later, counts (perhaps in a ritualistic way, in the manner of 'one, two, three-four-five – once I caught a fish alive . . .'). Since normal, 'natural' mothers do these things unconsciously and as a matter of course, in fact out of deeply felt need, we have in the course of our lives learned, with growing astonishment, that there are many mothers who have to be taught these simple, seemingly trivial but in reality so very important elements of mothercraft. We have known a gifted mother of eight children who literally always had a little rhyme or song ready for every occasion. Her stock in trade was a vast number of nursery and children's songs, helped by a great ease of rhyming and singing. She had a rather broken voice, but her instant reactions endeared her to very many children. No child, when feeling hurt, strayed away from her lap until it felt consoled. It is surprising how soon one overcomes inhibitions if one 'has no voice', 'is not able to sing' etc. once one has experienced how children take to the sound of a singing voice. We recently read a newspaper account of a school for autistic children in Ontario, Canada, where the staff routinely had to sing instead of talk to the children. It was claimed that the children of that school made remarkable progress, undoubtedly not just because of the singing – rather, it seems to us, the 'singing rule' was an indicator of the general attitude of the staff.

The means used by a good parent for encouraging socialisation are not only numerous but they also change as a child grows up. The more secure a child becomes, the less direct the 'we love you' signals need to be. For instance, many children want to receive some kind of welcome when they return home from school, or from whatever little venture they have been out on. One of our own children would invariably, up to the age of nine years, call out 'Mother!' when she came home from school and when answered (and reassured that Mother *was* at home) would say straightaway 'I am going out to play'. But if the answer did not come immediately, the 'Mother!' call was repeated on a crescendo of anxiety until the reassuring answer came.

Some children can be reassured indirectly, for instance by finding a little snack in an agreed place; others may be happy with any other sign that they have not been forgotten – with *any* 'welcome by proxy'. Again those who find it difficult to 'think up' a sufficient variety of such interactions can, if willing, learn a great deal from parents who are more gifted in this respect. It may seem to be merely a skill, or even a trick, but through developing this skill and experiencing the happy reactions from children, parents will often find their motivation growing as well, and with that their competence.

This is the place to remind parents that a chaotically run household may be a contributing factor towards autism; a certain amount of predictability, even of rules, is reassuring to any child, certainly to an autistic child.

Lest we should be understood to advocate that autistic children must at all times be mothered or interacted with, we should like to point out that, since socialising and exploring by autists clash with their anxious reluctance to do so, too strenuous invitations to socialise can carry in their wake the over-arousal that, we have argued, must be considered the inevitable consequence of living in this kind of conflict. This is why we think that autistic children so often have sleeping difficulties. There is, therefore, certainly a need for them to be able to withdraw frequently from social contact, and to have regular periods of rest. We know two schools for autistic children where a period of (communal) rest after lunch is an obligatory part of the daily routine, and this seems to have a beneficial effect.

Encouraging independence and initiative

A real difficulty with any mothering programme with autistic (as with normal) children is how to strike the balance between mothering and sheltering them, and allowing or even encouraging them to engage in some independent exploratory or practising activity. Some children are over-cautious, while others may over-compensate at times by being too reckless; the parental influence must therefore be adjusted to the personality of each child. But autists and many over-carefully sheltered children easily develop the attitude (only too prevalent nowadays even in many 'normal' middle-class families with few children) of expecting *all* initiative to come from their parents or teachers; waiting, for instance, for their coats, mittens, shoes etc. to be taken off or put on for them. The utter dependence and lack of initiative of autistic children makes special 'teaching to take the initiative' of great importance, the more so the longer a child has been involved in the downward spiral and the more reluctant he has become to take initiative of any kind. Also, of course, the age of the child concerned is a factor *per se*, irrespective of when he has become autistic. What is important to keep in mind all the time is that all autistic children are pathologically timid and unenterprising and that even the smallest step towards initiative is, for them, an act of great courage. This deserves some special attention.

Much of what we have said so far has focused on how to restore a child's socialising behaviour and so make him feel more secure. But just as by doing this we hope to revive and encourage him to accept social instruction and to join in a variety of activities that are normally done in a social context, we must remember that exploratory behaviour in the widest sense (going out into the world beyond his family or his inner circle of friends) is likewise dependent on being socially happy – in this case having a secure home base. Just as we believe that restoring the child–mother bond alone is not enough for autists of long standing but that they must be helped with accepting instruction and learning from joining in, so it seems to us clear that all exploratory behaviour must also be encouraged along with the emotional treatment. A very common parental task, with normal and with autistic children, is to help them venture into the water. Most children, normal or autistic, young or old, indeed many adults, loosen up emotionally, often in a most striking way, once they are in the water. But to make them try to swim, and literally to take the plunge into deep water, can meet with frantic resistance. Here a few children respond well to 'being thrown in at the deep end', but we would never advise this with an autistic child. What we know to be often helpful, once a child is judged ready for the next step, is to make him take this step *together with the parent*, either father or mother – whoever has the child's confidence for this kind of support. The difficulty is to find the right moment. Probably it is best to go by the child's own slight intention movements. These can be observed all the time, for many autistic children have exceptional courage and want to force themselves to be brave. Even quite mildly autistic or simply very timid children will walk up and down at the edge of the water, will now and then come to a halt, face the water and take up a preparatory stance, but withdraw after a shorter or longer time of hesitation. The moment one senses that the child is almost 'about to jump in' may be the best moment to take his hand and say 'shall we jump together?' As always, perception and quick responses are required.

This progressive loss of initiative in autists, and the need for reversing this by a little prodding, may apply to autism at many levels and with respect to many activities. The girl Carla who, while mute, expresses herself very well on the typewriter, explained that the effort of plucking up the courage to speak was simply too great for her; she claimed that she wanted to speak very much but 'could not bring herself' to do it.

This loss of initiative, the ever-increasing helplessness, has been studied both in animals and in people by the American psychologist Martin Seligmann, who has devoted an entire book to what he calls 'learned helplessness'.[12] In his view, it is typical of many deeply depressed, anxious and also of some schizophrenic people, especially of those who have been hospitalised for a long time. He describes how patients can be coaxed back towards taking more initiative by being subjected to some moral pressure to do tasks that had been done for them for years, such as making their own beds (the 'graded task' procedure). If this is done step by step, every time, perhaps against the will of the patient who has at times to be coerced, many of these patients are reported to recover their initiative to quite an astonishing extent, and to feel much the better for it. As we have said in Chapter 6, it is especially in this respect that we believe Dr G. Waldon's procedures to be so valuable. Apart from his reassuring fatherly behaviour, he undoubtedly helps his pupils to experience the satisfaction and joy of achievement and so to foster their courage in tackling tasks from which they had for so long shrunk back. There is a striking parallel between these views and those expressed by the Dutch psychiatrist Jan Foudraine, who has treated a variety of patients (among them an 'adult autist', Sylvia) in very much the same way. Quite a number of them had been institutionalised for years, several of them under the label 'schizophrenic' and other diagnostic tags.

Carla who, when 16 years of age, was hospitalised in a psychiatric 'lock-up ward' and kept under a variety of drugs, 'told' her tutor on the typewriter that she deliberately adopted an attitude of being a 'complete fool' or an 'imbecile' in order to be left alone and to raise no expectations in the staff at all. Such an attitude may well be more common in the early stages of institutionalisation, and very few doctors and even staff seem to see through it, or to suspect that a little prodding might be a good thing.

Dr Welch has argued to us that initiative, in the social sphere as well as in the exploratory sphere, comes back of its own accord without the child having to be prodded at all. As we have said before, we feel that, at least with autists of long standing, we cannot rely fully on this, and that with such advanced autists the extra, specific help, not only with the acquisition of skills of all kinds but also with wanting to take initiative, can be useful, provided it is done in such a way that the rebonding remains basic and the child does not feel too harassed and so becomes *more* apprehensive.

We recently heard of one autistic boy who, when unable to jump into the water himself where his sisters were already enjoying themselves, was pushed in by his mother. She jumped in immediately after him, and he was then, before he could indulge in panic, self-pity or anger, playfully tossed round by mother and sisters. from one to the other. It would seem a risky thing to do, but it worked; the boy at once began to enjoy himself.

There are more indications in the literature of the healing function of occasional, and at times quite vigorous prodding or even forcing, of some kinds of 'being thrown in at the deep end'. Examples of this will be found in the fascinating story of Ann Hodges (which, like so many 'popularly' described case histories, is largely and quite wrongly ignored by professional students of autism).[13] After her father had noticed sudden improvements in Ann's behaviour following some accidents which at the moment of occurrence seemed to be the last one would wish for an autist to experience, he began to think that 'violence' of some kind was the effectual element in these occurrences, and he developed a system of creating some kinds of 'violent' situations when he thought they were called for, including simple slapping. This seemingly risky procedure (for which 'violence' is of course not really the right term) did seem to work and, although we believe that it would be dangerous to advise all parents to proceed along these lines, it would seem that some specially gifted parents can apply it with success, at least with some children.

In view of the tendency, which seems to have developed in some clinics, of systematically using slapping or other physical penalties for behaviour modification in general, we need perhaps not repeat that such near-indiscriminate use of violence is something quite different from Mr Hodges' procedure. Unless done by a gifted and perceptive parent, such routine slapping could easily degenerate into ineffectual (and, worse, cruel) symptom treatment of the kind that we criticised in Chapter 6.

'Naughtiness', destructiveness, hostility and the need for discipline

A special difficulty, which puts a heavy strain on the parents of many autistic children, is the children's frequent 'naughtiness', in which they sometimes indulge in curiously stubborn ways and by which they can drive parents (or teachers) to distraction. Before we discuss this, it is good to remember that the word 'naughty' does more than describe the *child's* behaviour; often it has just as much or even more to do with the adults' inability to tolerate ways of behaviour that are very inconvenient or irritating to *them*, yet may, upon cool reflection, not really be objectionable at all and could even be quite natural – in cases may even be said to be the child's right! Toddlers have a *right* to explore (yet have to be taught which things are out of bounds); all children have a *right* to move about a lot (yet must sit still during meals or lessons, at least for limited periods); they have a *right* to talk (yet have to learn that sometimes they have to listen or wait rather than interrupt others). Just as parents of normal children have to ask themselves frequently 'Do I really have to forbid this?', so parents of autistic children will have to try to see the child's point of view. Even so, some 'naughty' behaviour simply cannot always be tolerated; the difficult question is how to keep it within bounds and how to help the child drop such habits. Very much the same applies to truly hostile and at times destructive and even aggressive behaviour. We cannot claim to know the solution for all eventualities, but a few helpful hints can be given.

Often, 'naughty' behaviour is an autistic child's way of indulging in exploratory or experimenting activities that one would accept in very much younger children and for which one would create 'toddlerproof' conditions, in which one would be able to allow and even to encourage the child to do more or less as he likes. For instance, we know autistic children who sneak off time and again to the lavatory and play with the water in the lavatory bowl, even drink it, pull the chain time after time and study attentively the movements of the water. Such children may well have missed out on this (for young children one of the most generally fascinating) phases of exploratory behaviour and feel an irresistible urge to catch up, yet are prevented from doing it because 'they are too big to mess about in such a childish' and (it must be admitted) often very disruptive and unhygienic way. In such cases we believe that a combination of two procedures is to be recommended. (a) One can lure the child away from undesirable behaviour by giving him plenty of opportunity to engage in acceptable and harmless water play; giving him plenty of long sessions with a few inches of water in the bath; giving him the run of the garden or a waterproof corner or room indoors with facilities for a variety of water games; and where possible (in a swimming pool or on the shore or in other natural, shallow waters, of course with the usual safety measures such as water wings) letting him go and joining him. Quite apart from the 'intellectual', educational value of such games, being half immersed in water clearly has itself a remarkably soothing, almost mentally uplifting effect (and not only on autistic children). Some schools have a swimming pool for this very reason, and we have seen autists 'thaw out' in the water. We know of some mute autists who spoke their first words while in the swimming pool.

Very much the same problem as that of 'loo play' is raised by, for instance, playing with mud, or even urine and faeces.[14] Here, one has to overcome to a certain extent one's own distaste and recognise that a (very brief) period of getting to know the unpleasant properties of, for example, faeces is a quite normal, possibly universal little lesson for every child (or at least *was* before the age of plastic pants); autistic children may just need longer because they often do not seem to learn (or not to act on what they have learned) from the feedback to which a normal child reponds almost at once. Older children may go through a period, sometimes lasting months or years, of switching electric light switches on and off; this too might be a phase they have to go through if they are to make further progress. Experienced parents have of course witnessed such juvenile exploration and experimentation periods in many different forms and at many different stages. But while each phase lasts a relatively short time with normal children, autistic children may have to repeat the same thing time and again for very long periods.

Yet with all these things, simply luring the child away is only half the answer; it is often essential (b) that the child learns at the same time that there are places and times in which this catching-up behaviour simply cannot be tolerated. This curbing of behaviour that threatens to get out of hand can often be done by quiet yet firm and (it should never be forgotten) *consistent* prohibiting, or by reasoning with the child, or even by an occasional angry utterance; in whatever way discipline is imposed, the main thing seems to us that the child must not feel the prohibition to be arbitrary and unjust. We know a mother who allowed her autistic child (Olga – see Ch. 10) to go out and play, suitably dressed, in the garden during any weather and make herself as dirty as she wished; but there was an inflexible rule that during meals she had to be clean and, for instance, must not throw her food about.

Another example of managing these difficult situations comes from the tutor of an adolescent, severely autistic girl who, like so many others, has a strong tendency to masturbate. She has been told, and has gradually accepted as an iron rule: 'If you *have* to masturbate, go to your own room if you wish, but I don't want you to do it in my presence'. With all these and similar cases one has to keep in mind that after all the urge to repeat childish behaviour and ingrained 'bad habits' is part of the child's illness, that it may have to be endured, but only up to a certain level, and that it is essential to pay close attention to the problem of how best to cure him. The number of childish things that will have to be treated along these lines is almost endless (because individual children differ so much), but water, mud and faeces play, and messing round with food are some of the more common ones. We begin to see more and more indications that, if a child is treated the right way and improves emotionally, these infantilisms often disappear 'of their own accord'.

The reasoning involved may have to differ from child to child and from one occasion to the other. Sometimes a blunt statement that 'I don't accept this' may be the right thing (remember that autistic children often understand just as well as normal children *why* their behaviour is unacceptable); often an autistic child will respond well if one points out that 'naughty' behaviour hinders or hurts other children. Also, of course, it is important to spot incipient bad habits as they begin to form and nip them in the bud; and as always one has to be as consistent as at all possible. It must always be remembered that a set of good rules creates security and predictability – children hate unpredictable chaos.

There are undoubtedly occasions when 'being naughty' is due to quite different motivations, e.g. when it is a method of desperately trying to attract attention. It may be very important to recognise such attempts at socialisation for what they are and to try to meet them with positive social behaviour, e.g. holding.

Another reason again for 'naughty' behaviour can be extreme fatigue, or the beginning of an illness. In such cases rest may well be the best answer, even though the child may (with half his being) resist, and it is then probably best to ignore his resistance and give him the care he needs. Some people have an intuitive almost uncanny feeling for what the child really wants or what drives him, and respond in an effective way. It is difficult to write a set of directives for coping with *all* these forms of 'naughtiness'; perhaps the best advice we can give is again: realise that other mothers may have special gifts in this direction and pay attention to how they cope. As we grow older ourselves, we have developed a growing interest in observing such parents and we take delight in (and also learn a great deal from) seeing real 'champion parents' in action.

Often autistic children who have been allowed to 'get away' with, for instance, temper tantrums have formed deeply ingrained bad habits, which can drive their parents to distraction. Yet, if this has happened, it is never too late to undo the harm, but it may be necessary to be very strict for a time. This, as with normal children, will not cause an emotional breach, *provided* it is done in a way that does not make the child imagine that he is no longer loved. We know of a mother who solved scenes that arose in such a way by saying after the event 'I can understand you are feeling angry now, but never mind, I love you enough for both of us'. Perhaps unexpectedly, the child understood and the ploy worked.

Quite wild outbursts of destructive behaviour can occur when a child is severely frustrated because he wants to socialise and, for instance, enter into discussions but cannot do so either because he is afraid or because he is mute. The girl Carla, mentioned before, smashed up crockery for this very reason and did a great deal of damage in the school that had taken her in (we know her reasons because, as will be remembered, she is one of those who communicates very well by writing). This particular girl also throws severe tantrums when people treat her as if she is a 'halfwit' at moments when she wants to speak but cannot. Such outbursts can be coped with by realising that, while the child concerned may be mute and in many respects very childish, he is in other respects quite mature, intelligent, experienced and often remarkably perceptive and sensitive, and the underlying rebelliousness can be reduced and even turned to advantage by talking to the child at an advanced level. The difficulty of course is to know when the child wants to be left alone and when he wants to socialise.

Very much the same seems to us to apply to those occasions when a child is 'naughty' because he is simply extremely bored. Again, some people are much better at detecting what lies behind this kind of 'naughtiness' than others, but we repeat that perceptiveness and ability to cope can be fostered by being willing to learn from others.

Finally, 'naughtiness' often takes the form of really hostile and aggressive acts. It is true that the child, even when attacking, is to a certain extent inhibited and will not readily harm another person seriously, but even so there may be unpleasant and quite upsetting clashes. We saw one father deal with such an occasion in what we consider to be a near-perfect way. His (very mildly autistic) son of eight years resented being told to go and have 'a wee and a wash' before the family, who had been visiting us, would leave on a three hours' car drive. Irritated by the 'command' the boy pinched his father's skin as hard as he could and, with a furious expression on his face, said as he did so 'That hurts!' The father simply said in a very neutral tone 'Yes, John, that did hurt; now go and do as you are told'. This totally defused the whole situation.

The problems raised by naughtiness are part of the wider one of discipline. Must one and can one discipline autistic children? In some strata of our modern society it is quite common for parents of normal children not to bother to discipline them and to expect the school teachers to do this for them (a teacher of our acquaintance expressed this aptly by saying that 'many modern children are not being *brought up*, they are merely *allowed to grow up*').

Here too, the extent to which prohibitions have to be instituted and enforced, as well as the extent to which children must be merely allowed to do things or have to be encouraged or even coerced, depends of course in part on the nature of each child concerned; just as there are over-timid and over-reckless children, so there are over-complying and over-rebellious children – among normal as well as among autistic children. But another difficulty is that modern urban society has not yet really adapted itself to the changing circumstances and tried to work out norms for finding the right balance between a 'permissive' and a controlled, disciplining approach to child-rearing. Yet modern conditions have created new demands. For instance, it has now become quite urgent that parents teach their children curb drill of some kind; the need for adhering to some rules within the family circle remains as real as ever, as is the need for instilling in one's children honesty, responsibility and a sense of good citizenship; but many parents seem to do little about either the old or the new needs for discipline of any kind. Again, this applies to the parents of autistic as well as of normal children. We do not pretend to know the answers for this range of problems. Once more, it would seem to be best for parents of autistic children (as for many others) to let themselves be guided by the examples of parents in their own environment whose success they admire.

Here again, it is clear that some parents can go much further than our interpretation of autism would make us expect, at least with some children. As we shall describe in one of the case histories of a 'do-it-yourself' mother and her child, this mother did know when to apply, at times some very severe, forms of disciplining; she even describes how she once said, with flashing eyes and angry emphasis 'Don't you *dare*!' But again, we believe that the pros and cons of 'losing one's temper' when dealing with an autistic child have to be considered very carefully by every parent or teacher concerned.

Help from co-therapists

ANIMALS

Although the mother has to be, if at all possible, the main therapist, it stands to reason that, if insufficient socialisation is at the bottom of autism, other people and/or (if the child rejects them) even animals can form the bridge towards a more social attitude.[15] In fact, it is known that some autistic children form attachments to, for instance, dogs more easily than to persons. Provided such a bond does not lead to an obsession to the exclusion of people, pets can therefore be expected to have potential as co-therapists. (We must anyway beware of taking the danger of such 'obsessions' too seriously; think of how, for instance, 'horse-mad' girls and eccentric dog-lovers usually remain socially well within normality.) A more serious danger with pets is that the parents, in particular the mother, may show more affection to the animals than to their autistic child. We know from personal observations that this does occur and that it can make the child envious and hostile – to pet and mother alike. As we have already reported, it is not only dogs or cats or other small animals that can be useful in this way, but even horses; Mr Royds, whose pony rides therapy we discussed earlier (p. 190), reports that of the mute children who have had pony rides under his direction, no fewer than 27 spoke their first words ever when they were on horseback! He thinks that a mentally handicapped child 'being up on a horse, elevated physically, senses a completely unprecedented psychological advantage'. (To which we would add, in addition to a genuine affection for the horse.) In March 1979 alone, more than 130 special schools all over Britain made use of this facility, offered by the National Society for Mentally Handicapped Children's Riding Fund.

(Of course the possibility of roping in animals as co-therapists must not deflect us from the need to help autistic children to socialise with their parents and with other children. With regard to parents, more and more centres where, admittedly, 'holding' is not taught are trying to engage their active help in school or clinic. This seems to be sound because direct observation of a successful therapist at work can teach parents very much more than even lengthy texts. But parents must realise that relegating themselves (so to speak) to acting as assistants to the professionals also carries risks, because with all successful bonding with persons other than the parents and even with animals there is a danger that the 'therapist' in effect usurps the parents' roles and that, when the therapist and child must separate, the child experiences true and unnecessary bereavement.)

HELP FROM OTHER CHILDREN

As we have seen, children can also do their share in helping autists. This is not just because in normal society children do come together and play together a great deal but also because, as observant mothers know perhaps best, the ties between young sibs can in some ways be even more intimate than those a child has with his mother. For instance, young children have a special smile, which we have seen often enough but cannot yet describe, which they reserve for each other. As one mother of our acquaintance put it: 'When Jane smiles at Tom in this way, it makes me quite envious'. Children can no doubt play important parts as co-therapists; the subject certainly deserves further exploration. We believe for instance that both Down's children and autistic children may profit from being schooled and taught together. The friendliness and quiet insistence on making social contact which is typical of Down's children makes them often acceptable, indeed irresistible, to autistic children. Because Down's children do not object to being taught, teachers tend to spend more time on instructing them. This reduces, for the autists, the intrusiveness to which they object, but it does give them the opportunity to learn a great deal from simply watching and taking in much of what is being taught to the Down's children. Thus this kind of arrangement can reduce the load per teacher and yet benefit both types of children. Similar arrangements may well include other emotionally damaged children, although of course aggressive and otherwise interfering children do not qualify as co-therapists.

More use could also undoubtedly be made of normal children to play their parts as co-therapists. This is in fact now being done in more than one country. As Dr Sasaki's film *All are friends* (already mentioned in Ch. 6) shows so convincingly (and as we ourselves have seen in a very promising pilot scheme in England, that however has not so far been reported on in full), it is quite possible in well-run normal schools, expecially primary schools, to attach a limited number of even fairly severely autistic children to such normal schools in a loose way and with the part-time support (carefully adjusted to the special needs of each child concerned), of 'home tutors'. Certainly too many children are, in our opinion, put too easily into the special schools for 'educationally subnormal', 'severely subnormal' and other children who are difficult to educate, and are so denied access to potentially more suitable educational opportunities. Admittedly, the integration of autistic children in normal schools is not easy, but simply to dump autistic children in schools that are intended for children with totally different handicaps smacks too much of an easy way out. Such unsuitable placing could well be avoided once the reasons for under-performance of autistic and other emotionally disturbed children are better understood. Much depends, of course, on the degree of understanding of the individual teachers concerned, but we believe that the reservoir of potentially helpful teachers, and of available home tutors, is so far not being tapped nearly as much as would be possible with better 'teacher training'. Of course, the modern trend of reducing the number of teachers and of overloading the remaining ones by giving them larger classes would seem to make this idea impracticable. But to society as a whole, extra money spent on schemes such as we suggest could well lead to a long-term reduction of expenditure which would otherwise be needed for accommodating non-cured autists in institutions for the duration of their lives.

Nor should the potential of sibs within each family be underrated. What we have so far seen and heard ourselves has convinced us that, dependent on the insight and the attitude of the parents, sibs can be either a destructive or a constructive element in a child's rehabilitation. We know of families in which, following the example of the parents, an autistic child's brothers and sisters have developed an apologetic (but to their autistic sib very hurtful) way of making clear in a variety of explicit and implied ways that 'he is an autist; he can't do this or that', or 'you must ignore his odd mannerisms'. It often surprises us to see how insensitive and thoughtless otherwise kind and far from cruel members of the family can be simply because they assume, explicitly or tacitly, that autistic children, especially the mute ones, cannot understand speech. It should not be glossed over that even very good-willing parents and sibs can now and then reveal the damaging side of the ambivalent attitude they cannot help having towards the autistic member of their family, and can occasionally, in exasperation, or even truly maliciously, say things that hurt and that can on occasion undo a lot of the helpful support they give as a general rule. Examples can be found in Park and Beck.[16]

It has only recently and gradually become clear to us that an autistic child can sometimes, perhaps at critical moments in his life, respond with alacrity to a request, best made by his parent(s), to 'help other children even more unhappy than himself' or sick people or animals; and that giving such active help can have a strikingly beneficial effect on the child himself. (For two revealing examples, see the case histories of Judy and George in Ch. 10, first section.)

'Retardation'

Parents of all children have experience of the curious combination of traits a child can display that seem to be contradictory and never cease to surprise them: on the one hand, the child's unexpected brightness and, one would almost say, maturity when he is at ease delight them; while on the other hand, the signs of immaturity which that same child can show at other moments present an odd contrast with those impressive and hope-giving signs of growing up, and cause worry and anxiety to his parents. The same is true of autistic children, only 'even more so'.

On the whole, most of them are, as almost all experts emphasise, more or less severely retarded. On the other hand, many and perhaps all of them do present us with those 'islets' of good or even excellent performance that can baffle us so much. This extreme form of the dual nature of children presents parents and teachers with one of the most difficult problems: how is one to deal with these awkward 'mosaics' of backwardness and, in some cases, precociousness that so many autistic children display? We shall first discuss the retardation aspects and then try to say something sensible about the islets.

As we have argued, the retardation of most autistic children is in the first place of an emotional nature, and this is why we believe that the Welch therapy of forced holding works so well. But it is one thing to be aware of this general fact, and quite another to recognise what specific kind of emotional need a child has at any particular moment, since these needs express themselves in such a great variety of forms. The task of judging at what age level an autistic child wants to be treated at any particular moment keeps caregivers continuously on their toes, guessing at 'what is upsetting their charge *now*' and, if possible, trying to find the right answer. Yet this must be done if at all possible, for failure to do so may lead to explosive tantrums or destructive behaviour, or to sudden withdrawals. The child himself will only relatively rarely take the initiative and reveal in what respects and when he wants extra emotional support; most often the adult will have to read these needs from very subtle signs, or will even have to guess.[17]

Most parents of normal, timid children will have experienced occasions when their child's development has a sudden setback. For instance a bereavement, or even a move from one place to another, certainly to a foreign country, can put children of ages between 8 months and 4 years or so back half a year or more; children who had begun to socialise well with other children and played well on their own become suddenly withdrawn,[18] suck their thumbs a great deal, and revert to following their mothers around like puppies; they may also become incontinent again, may begin to wet their beds etc. In our own experience, such setbacks are best dealt with by giving some extra attention and by adjusting the form of this attention to their emotional age – by treating them as temporarily younger than they had been before. This applies in general also to autistic children, only more so. Admittedly this suggestion 'to adjust' is a tall order; for instance, when a child of 8 or 10 years, or even older, suddenly wants to be taken on mum's lap and be cuddled like a baby, it is the *contradiction* between his physical size and these infantile demands that can make mothers understandably reluctant to do this 'with such big lumps' (and one should not be surprised when at such moments the cat is a more inviting 'baby'). Yet, in view of the beneficial results of Dr Welch's 'forced holding' procedure, which she has on occasion applied even with non-autistic, disturbed teenagers and older patients, we would advise every mother who is willing to try this therapy, if only occasionally, to do so. Many people also find it difficult to have patience with a 14-year-old who follows them around the house like a puppy; yet we believe that it is best to bear with this (and to interact with him), provided of course that one does not totally give up attempts at prodding him into some degree of independence; only the level at which one aims must be adjusted to this (often temporary) lapse into a younger emotional stage. In such phases, an autistic child will also fall back to a variety of infantile forms of exploration, including self-exploration, and this too has simply to be accepted, and tolerated, in the hope that, as so often in the past, giving the child more security will be the most efficient way of helping him over his lapse, his flight into childhood (which is often only temporary). *Patience* (though not *resignation*) is the watchword, and not succumbing to despair; and as we said, this becomes easier as one learns to notice and take delight in even the smallest signs of real progress one sees in the child's better periods.

One of us (E.A.T.) has repeatedly demonstrated her way of assessing and adjusting to the 'emotional age' of even severely autistic children in playrooms in clinics, while the other (N.T.) watched, together with the staff concerned, from behind a one-way screen and gave a running commentary. The reaction of such staff has invariably been: 'I had no idea how cautious and patient your contact-making was, and how rapidly that child could be made to behave more maturely until I saw you do it'. Yet they assured us more than once that in one session of less than an hour the child had come out of his shell further than they had ever seen him do before. In trying to assess a child's emotional level as it fluctuates from day to day, it can be helpful to pay special attention to his behaviour when one meets him first thing in the morning. The way in which he moves, the general level of his clumsiness (or the reverse), can be a more sensitive indicator of the level of achievement on the day to come than other signs. Experienced teachers and mothers know by this sort of 'indicator' whether, in the day just started, they can aim high or have to refrain from making too heavy demands (see for an example of this, the case history of George in Ch. 10).

There is little point in going into more details about the kind of infantile behaviour one has to expect and adjust to, as long as the general principle is understood and the adult concerned has a minimum of experience with the behaviour of young children; in most cases the obstacle is not so much lack of knowledge (although there are parents who are much more ignorant and helpless than they may realise themselves) as the *will* to adjust, and patience; and these come only when one believes in our view of the causes of the retardation of autistic children.

The opposite of the overall retardation of autistic children – their special gifts or 'islets' of good performance – can best be discussed in the context of skill teaching, to which we turn now.

The teaching of 'skills'

Because autists are overall so strikingly behind in their emotional and 'executive' development (by which latter term we mean perceptual and motor shortcomings or under-achievements as well as intellectual under-performance, including poor speech), many parents and teachers have the understandable desire to help them catch up not only, or even not so much, on their emotional maturation as, especially, in the development of all these achievements that we group here under the convenient, if perhaps not precise, overall term of 'skills'.

The older the child becomes and the longer he has been engaged in the 'downward spiral', the more his parents tend to feel the urgency of this. This in turn is largely due to the pressures of our modern society, in which the passing of exams and the obtaining of diplomas at the 'right' age have more and more become a *sine qua non* for effective incorporation into adult society; fewer and fewer people without 'qualifications' have a chance of earning a living, standing on their own feet and so earning self-respect. We know a number of children whose parents, still more or less confident of recovery when their children are still young, approach a state of panic as the years fly by and the 'academic' hurdles to be taken are looming up. The way they choose for helping their children tends to increase the pressure for acquiring such skills as are demanded by the educational and examination systems.

But as a rule this does not work and we should emphasise that it often has the opposite effect. Unless the skill teaching is, so to speak, made into part and parcel, is embedded in and is almost a by-product of the treatment at the emotional level, autists respond to attempts at 'drilling' them by becoming obstructive, by offering passive resistance (fed in part by intense boredom), by becoming destructive or even aggressive, and on occasion by throwing tantrums and even having 'fits' or 'seizures'.

It is just in this context that the new insights which begin to emerge have important, we believe crucial, implications, for they suggest a very different approach.

As we have argued in Chapter 6, we get promising results if we base our educational efforts on our view and that of Dr Welch that autistic children are primarily damaged emotionally and are in particular over-anxious, withdrawn and unenterprising and that, if only we can reduce this anxiety and provide security, their achievements in a variety of skills will improve rapidly, sometimes indeed by leaps and bounds. This is partly due to the fact that they begin to want to learn, partly to the pleasure they derive from the overt performance of skills they have already learned 'latently' while they were still severely autistic and gave their caregivers the (wrong) impression that they suffered primarily from a 'cognitive-cum-language handicap'. We have seen the most astonishing examples of both this latent learning and of the rapid, explosive catching-up in learning. Concealed in published case histories, examples can be found of both; here we shall confine ourselves to mentioning a few.[19] Dibs (who is admittedly a very special case – see next chapter) developed and also began to show already acquired skills and intellectual abilities in his first play sessions with Axline; d'Ambrosio's Laura (mentioned in our 1972 paper) showed even more spectacular leaps forward. A less dramatic but equally significant example came to our notice not so long ago. A boy of our acquaintance, who was fairly severely autistic and had with great caution and much help by a home tutor been gradually taken into a normal primary school, had at the age of 14 years still not managed to tie his own shoe laces. When he was about to go to a secondary school, his mother took him shopping to buy, among other things, a new pair of shoes. She chose elastic-sided boots, but he insisted that she buy him shoes with laces. When his mother reminded him of his inability to tie laces he said: 'But if you show me once more, I promise you I can do it'. This she did, and he did in fact learn at once to tie his laces properly. Examples of latent learning, often done when no one is watching, are in our experience by no means rare. The most striking example we have come across is that of a mute eight-year-old girl who showed, when she began to be able to write (in her native English), that she had acquired an excellent knowledge (of 'O'-level ability!) of French, and also a quite reasonable understanding of printed German. This same child had also taught herself so much mathematics that her home tutor had to call in the help of a mathematics undergraduate to teach her further. Her father was a teacher of German and French and had as such quite a library in these languages at home. He had never even tried to teach her to read, nor had anyone else. The child must in some way have taught herself without parents noticing. (This has been confirmed by what she has later written down in response to questioning.) Of course this kind of thing happens in all those children whose 'islets of good performance' have been noticed. Our experience suggests that there is a high proportion of autistic children who develop such islets, but with the prevalent dearth of good field work most of them go unnoticed, although many parents often do know about such special abilities. Part of the trouble is that so many 'experts' do not believe what tutors or parents tell them (and to be fair, it is often near-impossible for them to know what to believe and what not – for this they would have to do more 'fieldwork').

It is in this context worth saying that, as we have learned only recently, many very young normal children learn to read well before school age by watching and hearing television commercials; this might well apply to some autistic children too.

Needless to say, it is of the greatest importance that parents and teachers try to discover these hidden developments; it may stop them wasting a lot of time in unnecessary attempts at skill teaching and save them – and the children – a great deal of frustration. We remember a television programme which showed a well-intentioned but unimaginative psychologist busy subjecting a girl of about 8 years old to simple shape and colour discrimination tests of the conventional type; in the filmed samples the child invariably chose correctly at once, but displayed the most striking signs of the utmost boredom; nevertheless, the tests were endlessly repeated. We were irresistibly reminded of the famous story, already mentioned in Chapter 6, of the prominent psychologist Donald Hebb, who as a young man was shaken out of his preoccupation with such discrimination tests with chimpanzees when his (equally bored) test animal began to hand to *him* the slices of bananas that he had been giving her as rewards for correct choices. Finding a child's true but hidden abilities rather than routinely applying the standard tests has the additional, considerable advantage of raising both the adult's and the child's morale.

We are convinced, however (as we have said before), that *exclusive* reliance on treatment at the emotional level and *total* trust in the child having done a lot of latent learning and in his ability to catch up on what he has really missed are not maximally effective. They may work, as far as our experience goes, with children whose autistic deviation has been spotted at a very early age (such as was the case in Fae and, at a slightly less early age, in Sonia – both described in more detail in the next chapter). Prompt incorporation into the family circle in the case of Fae, and extremely patient and understanding emotional support from the parents in Sonia's case have indeed worked wonders, in fact both children are completely cured (and have since proved to be quite bright). Dr Welch reports on two similar cases (Appendix I).

However, autists of longer standing have inevitably missed out on much that normal children learn as a matter of course, not just at school but during normal socialising and exploring. With such children we suggest that the adults concerned try to find ways of supplementing the emotional treatment with ways of teaching skills, while continuing to encourage the emotional recovery. We believe that we can learn a great deal from the cases described or referred to in the next chapter and, in particular, from a careful study of the books we list there that report on more or less striking successes. An important aspect of this is that the adult tries to respond quickly to any signs of willingness to be taught that a child shows, sometimes only momentarily. A child may perform something quite clever in the course of his own play or during socialising sessions. Even if this interrupts what the adult planned to do, he may then probably do well to take up the child's initiative, certainly to acknowledge his achievement (without offending him by over-praising) and allow or even encourage him in a subtle way to develop his activity. These occasions may not come often, or one may miss the chance. But we believe that it is a good rule to watch out for signs of awakening interest and to try to provide opportunities for indulging even in what may border upon obsessional play. Certainly, acknowledging a positive achievement would seem to be a good course to follow; we feel that the way in which this can best be done is described most impressively in Axline's story of her sessions with Dibs. Provided it is done with caution, it also may be helpful to arouse a child's interest actively – if teaching by arousing interest is good for normal children, it is even more desirable for autists.

It is often said that autistic children have a short 'attention span', but in our experience this is true mainly when they are asked or coerced to do things in which they are not interested, or of which they are afraid; when engaged in their obsessional activities their 'attention span' could be said to be exceptionally *long*; and of course their attention span for potentially frightening things or events is near-infinite! ('Attention span', like 'stimulation', 'touch' and numerous other terms, is often used in a generalised way even when the facts show that they have no general applicability – yet another 'red herring' thoughtlessly thrown across our path!)

We repeat that it seems to us that it is especially here that the methods applied so successfully by Dr Geoffrey Waldon are relevant. As we said before, we believe that his kind of teaching helps a child not only to develop a great variety of perceptual, motor and intellectual skills (and so contributes greatly to the restoration of his confidence and sense of enterprise), but also to restore his emotional balance – in Dr Waldon's case, we think, in part because he plays many of the roles normally played by a child's father.

In this area of rehabilitation, there is no doubt a great need for variety and for educational inventiveness, and some parents are undoubtedly much better at this than others.[20] It is to be hoped that Dr Waldon will in the not too distant future publish his many valuable views and experiences in print (but see Ch. 6, note 17); in the meantime the best advice we can give is again to study what successful parents do and see whether one can take leaves out of their books. Observant parents will also undoubtedly notice that a child often shows signs of wanting to be helped. He may not be fully willing to accept straightforward instruction, but very often what he wants is to be given the opportunity to watch someone perform certain tasks, to a certain extent join, and perhaps imitate, him without, however, being taken too much notice of. What in our experience does often work wonders is when an adult acts, as naturally as possible, as if she is for her own sake absorbed in a task which in reality she wants the child to master, and to comment, again as if to herself, on every step in the process of doing so, including making remarks about her tentative ideas and her mistakes. Most people can easily acquire the kind of seemingly uncommunicative 'thinking aloud' that for instance some (BBC) television programmes on chess matches ('The Master Game') do so very well. In our experience it is not too difficult to 'deceive' an autistic child in this way and make him think that one is really struggling with tasks for one's own sake, and it is surprising how often such a child will begin to participate – usually at first by (almost reluctantly, certainly guardedly) observing the adult, then by giving some sign of joining (even though this may at first take the form of obstructing) and then, if one has patience, by joining in fully and, later, taking over the task himself, sometimes in a brief flash of daring. We have seen a boy at an infant school for disturbed children who did nothing but run around, flicking on and off the electric switches until he drove the teachers almost to despair. At the same time one of the teachers was helping a girl doing a jigsaw puzzle. At one stage this child got stuck with a piece that seemed to her not to fit in anywhere. Suddenly the boy, running past, picked up the bit and put it quickly in its correct place, literally 'in passing'! Observant adults can see such proofs of in fact very good 'cognitive' abilities on many occasions; many examples are described in Clara Park's *The Siege* (see also Furneaux & Roberts).[21]

It is our experience that, just as autistic children can at times display exceptional courage in overcoming their fears, so they may show great perseverance in mastering a skill. This seems to us most likely to occur when such mastering boosts a child's self-respect or gives him status among his fellow children. What easily kills this enterprising mood is impatience and contempt or even derision from either other children or adults; we know mildly autistic children who actually say quite openly 'I know I won't ever be able to do that'. Much can also be taught, as we have already indicated elsewhere, by 'latching on' to a child's more or less stereotyped behaviour and, in a playful way, forcing him to invent and venture out into variations. Professor N. L. J. Kamp of Utrecht University has shown us a film that demonstrates beautifully how he helped a girl, who at the sound of music began to rock (rather in the monotonous, mechanical way of a dancing bear), to develop her 'stereotypy' into steadily more variable and soon more imaginative dancing by (walking behind her and holding her by the hands) initiating at first slight then steadily more pronounced and irregular variations. This dancing became a play, which the child obviously came to enjoy greatly. We shall discuss some more examples of this kind of 'invitation to play' elsewhere in this chapter.

The case history of Paula mentions the good influence of her joining music sessions. In general, we recommend that a great deal of attention be given to music and dancing; these two activities (and many other types of 'movement') naturally belong together. Music teachers are often in effect music therapists if they have an understanding and a love of children. In several countries a great variety of interesting procedures is being tried out in this field. The range of activities that can be developed with the aid of music and dancing is very wide indeed and can, for instance, be linked with play acting.

Another way in which a special interest and ability can be utilised for teaching other skills is to use the obsession that quite a few autistic children have with counting, with numbers and with arithmetic. Good examples of this are described by Marion Beck, and also by Clara Park; and, in a later report, on the use of a 'counter' by Elly Park's father.[22]

It is in this context that we can well discuss the extreme cases of 'islets' of good or even exceptionally advanced performance found in so many autists. From the few examples mentioned in some detail in the literature, one might easily form the impression that such islets are rare. Admittedly, cases such as that of Nadia,[23] whose extraordinary talent for drawing has been publicised by the book by Lorna Selfe, of Joe Carter who, while still autistic at the age of 24, had become an outstanding pianist, and of other 'autistic savants' have attracted attention, but rather as oddities, as exceptional cases. Here again, however, a closer study of 'everyday autists' reveals that many, if not indeed all of them, possess islets or pockets of normal or above-normal either autistic or intellectual abilities.

As we have said, we know two autistic girls well, who though mute or near-mute can express themselves very well indeed in writing or on the typewriter; one of these girls writes stories and reports about her own experiences that reveal a command of English (and an insight into human nature) that is well beyond that found in normal children of her age. The other girl is not only a quite gifted artist (with a very distinctive style of her own) but, as we have mentioned, has also managed to teach herself a remarkably good level of both understanding and use in writing of more than one foreign language. The case histories of these two girls are not included in our book because their tutors intend themselves to publish accounts of them in due course.

Certainly, it is very common to find an extraordinary sensitivity for *music* in autists. Already in 1972 we described a few facts about a boy of our acquaintance who showed (very mild) autistic traits from approx. 20 months on and who combined this with an extraordinary interest in and understanding of music. At the age of almost 3½ years he once said, pointing at the television screen 'it says Mozart' when the name Mozart appeared on the screen without being spoken at all (he knew the configuration of the printed name from one of his gramophone records). Yet no one had (at that time) any inkling of his ability to read. Even more striking was the ability of this same boy, at five years of age, to recognise the style of Haydn in one of this composer's lesser-known symphonies when he heard it for the first time, and which his (musically quite sophisticated) parents had said to be Mozart. The boy was adamant and he was proved to be right.

Everyone who is familiar with autistic children knows of similar, often quite astonishing 'islets'. One can even find examples of this, well described, in books by authors who are so preoccupied with their children's backwardness that they do not seem to notice the contradictions in their own reports. Thus Kaufman, in his book on his son Raun, has been so captivated by the claim, made (wrongly) by Delacato and others, about the low level of cognitive ability of autistic children that he fails to point out the discrepancy between this overall view and the fact that Raun, at the age of 17 months, could, on being given a rectangular shoe box for the first time and after examining it closely by touch and sight, balance it on one of its points and even make it spin like a top! Everyone who has even *tried* to do this will know that it requires considerable insight and skill.

On the surface, the question of how to deal with the islets would seem to offer no special problems. Commonsense might seem to dictate that their further development could be left to the child, and educational efforts could be concentrated on the central issue of socialisation. But it could equally well be argued that such exceptional talents should be given special opportunities for their development. We believe that the 'islets of good performance' are activities which the child can learn either by distant observation or by solitary practice or both, but there is obviously more to the story. Certainly, if (as we suspect) there is a degree of correlation between having such gifts and being exceptionally susceptible to autismogenic influences, the problem of how to help those children becomes especially acute. Part of the problem is that some of these activities may possibly enable a child to bear his loneliness more easily, and that encouraging him *too much* in indulging in them might, by enabling him to evade more normal social behaviour, aggravate his autistic deviation. We have ourselves seen how a child who was at a very early age obsessed with classical music, and was given exceptional opportunities to listen to gramophone records, began to use listening to these records as a sort of soother, as a means of having company; and it seems to us not impossible that his socialisation and his general venturesomeness, his readiness to take initiatives, has lagged behind for a time as a consequence of this. We know a knowledgeable and sensitive psychologist who is convinced that special talents in autistic children must *not* be fostered and developed. However, we cannot believe that this is right, at least as a general principle.

A study of a case such as that of Nadia[24] presents us with a dilemma, for there is no doubt that Nadia's quite exceptional brilliance as an artist has withered during the education she has received. (Of course this kind of thing – the shrivelling-up of quite promising creative talents soon after schooling has started – is not at all rare in normal children. We ourselves happen to believe that in many cases the more or less regimented character of institutionalised teaching has to do with this.) Seeing that Nadia's treatment has been in the hands of psychologists who take a view of autism totally different from that developed by us, and who have therefore applied educational principles which in our opinion do not tackle the emotional core of the disorder, we consider it quite possible that the drying-up of Nadia's drawing talent is the consequence not only of the loss of her mother but also, perhaps largely, of having been given an education that was aiming at the development of skills such as speech. Whatever the explanation, Nadia is unfortunate in that she has lost her talent without having got much in return. Nigel Dennis, who wrote a thoughtful review of the book in *The New York Review of Books,*[24] considers that Nadia is a victim of insensitive treatment, and we are inclined to agree with him. It seems to us significant that, when Nadia's mother returned from three months in hospital, Nadia (then aged three) was not only 'overjoyed to see her', but that it was also 'at this time that Nadia began her drawings' (Selfe, p. 4). This casts doubt on the view that allowing such a child to indulge in these exceptionally talented activities somehow makes his recovery more difficult; it certainly looks (and this would conform to many experiences and to our overall view of autism) as if Nadia's association with her recuperating mother stimulated rather than suppressed her drawing.

Yet in view of the uncertainty in this respect, it seems to us that education of autistic children with special gifts is best run along the lines we recommend for all autists, i.e. by concentrating on treatment 'at the emotional level', yet without neglecting the further developement of these talents. We believe (rather in what we take to be the spirit both of Dr Waldon's procedures and of those that apply the 'graded task' method) that the 'islets of good performance' should be used (though without neglecting play and work on under-developed skills) as the starting points for overall cures, as opportunities for building social bridges and for giving the child the confidence, so badly needed, that he is 'good at something' and certainly not overall incapable. In other words, we incline to the view that special gifts must certainly be given scope, but not at the expense of socialisation. Since drawing and painting have so often a communicative motivation and function, there would not need to be any incompatibility between nursing *this* type of 'islet' and socialisation.

At any rate the education Nadia has had seems not to have made her either happier or socially more acceptable than if she had become an active, creative, be it perhaps rather odd and withdrawn artist. We must leave the question open, but we do feel it to be a shortcoming in Nadia's education that the psychologists involved (Dr L. Selfe and Dr E. Newson) seem not even to have considered the *possibility* of 'treatment at the emotional level' as an alternative to, or at the least part of the treatment.

The importance of being playful[25]

One more aspect of the way to treat autistic children deserves consideration: the need to avoid an over-serious, tense atmosphere at home and at school. It is on the whole, alas, inevitable that there are in modern societies ('Western' as well as communist) strong pressures towards an increasing amount of institutionalised teaching, in which specialist instructors are engaged to help children develop the many skills they will need if they are to take their places in adult society. We have already discussed how this emphasis on being instructed, on exams and diplomas, is in our view a lopsided development and that other settings for learning, which are at least of the same importance for a healthy development, are unfortunately becoming rarer. Our entire society has moved into efficiency-consciousness and competitiveness, and its prevailing mood is one of seriousness and of preoccupation with getting ever more things done ever more efficiently. The result is a loss of relaxed playfulness, in children and adults alike, and *yet play*, not just with peers but also with adults, *is an invaluable educator* as well as a relaxant for all. We must add here that during play of all kinds children not only learn a variety of skills, but they also develop healthy *social attitudes* of an emotional nature, such as social perceptiveness, co-operativeness and responsibility.

In the arrogant, still very widespread belief that our modern society is somehow superior to 'primitive' societies, it is appreciated by hardly anyone that the lack of cheerfulness, the overall seriousness and trend towards efficiency are, if compared across cultures, exceptional and, to those who have lived with 'primitive', not yet westernised people (Eskimos, Bushmen, Amerindians and many others), this over-seriousness and lack of true playfulness of modern 'civilised' peoples are clearly pathological. We are firmly convinced that this over-seriousness of our achievement-bent, competitive society acts as a severely damaging stressor on children.

There seems to us little doubt that autistic children are even more in need of a playful atmosphere than normal children. It is one of the very important things they have missed. But their social avoidance and their parents' unhappiness about the near-impossibility of getting through to them make it extremely difficult to start any playful interaction. We believe that this unhappy situation can be changed best if one begins by applying the various methods of reducing the children's apprehension, which we described in Chapter 6. Although it is difficult to change an adult's overall attitude to her child, a number of quite useful 'tricks' of the recommended procedure can be learned and taught; and, as we have said before, once a child begins to respond to an overture by approaching, however tentatively, this 'feedback' from him acts as an extremely powerful reward on the initiator. To be approached by a child who hitherto was so hopelessly withdrawn and rejecting can create a happy switch in any adult, which then makes it easier for her to forget her misery and to enjoy, and then to seek playful contact with, the child. This is not just a theoretical claim; for instance, five out of six mothers of withdrawn and otherwise disturbed children whom we saw at Mrs Jane Welch's Mothering Center in Greenwich, Connecticut, testified spontaneously that the positive social approaches by their children made them much happier and also more inclined to be playful themselves; and we believe that their response is typical.

With normal children initiative can often be left to the child, who invents so many games that one need only 'enter into the spirit' and respond properly. Most mothers will discover that they soon become playfully inventive too, and before they know it they are engaged in a mutually satisfying game. With autistic children more is required of the adult's initiative, and the responses to the child's overtures have to be subdued, so as to avoid at all costs 'answering' in a way that, exhilarating though it may be to normal children, often frightens off the autistic child. Since parents of autistic children are inclined to be sad, serious and preoccupied, perhaps by nature, partly perhaps as a consequence of their upbringing, but certainly as a consequence of having such a damaged child, they need extra support, even instruction in how to start this entire process. We are convinced that many over-serious parents are not by nature unplayful but have underdeveloped or suppressed their cheerfulness. Although it sounds paradoxical that one should be, so to speak, trained or 'drilled' in the skill of how to become playful, we believe that these particular parents may need at least some specific instructions for taking the first steps, just to release their inhibited potential for playful parenting. Once these work, and the child's responses touch the parent emotionally, further play may come more naturally.[26] The following are some directives for taking those very first steps.

With autistic children, the initiative to play, normally taken now by the child, now by the parent, will, as we have said, have to come more often from the parent, who can at least try to 'latch on' to a playful overture of the child and enter into the playful spirit. This can be done every time contact of some kind has been established. Not surprisingly, we have found that many autistic children respond well to games that are suitable to normal children of a much younger age: for example, games that involve the sense of touch – a gentle pinch, rhythmic patting, occasional tickling (which, however, must not be overdone). Such games can be started best in a way that the child considers safe.

The following is a typical example of how E.A.T. applies this very often.

'I was observing a severely withdrawn autistic boy of 6 in a small school, who was playing intently with building blocks, which he used first for building a tower, then for constructing a staircase, then for putting them back in their fitting slots in a box. When he made a (consistent) error (in itself interesting but not relevant here) and the teacher wanted to interfere, I asked her by a quick gesture to leave him alone. After each self-imposed task he stood quietly and, with obvious satisfaction, looked at what he had done. The last time he did this he began to clap his hands together, softly and rhythmically. When he stopped this I reciprocated by repeating his clapping pattern in the same rhythm. He turned his head towards me and gave me one fleeting glance, then, looking in front of him again, he answered by repeating his clapping. This "dialogue" went on for a while; then I changed the pattern and to my delight he followed exactly. This too went on for a while, and then *the boy* changed the rhythm to a new one; in which I then followed his "directive". Now, still engaged in our "conversation", he began to amble round the room, and after some seemingly aimless wanderings ended, in the inconsequent way autistic children have, "by accident", near me, where he lay down on his tummy in the passage next to me. Significantly, his feet were nearest me and just within reach of my hands. I now started to clap the rhythm on his feet, which seemed to please him, for he shuffled a little nearer to me while "replying" by clapping his own hands. By reaching out while he moved nearer and nearer to me as well, I could gradually reach his legs, then his behind, and could finally tickle a bare patch on his back between his jeans and his shirt. He gave a delighted giggle and wriggled even nearer to me. Unfortunately at this moment another adult entered the room and our game stopped. The boy's teacher, who throughout had sat perfectly still, told me that she was amazed to see him take initiative and to hear him vocalise – things he had not done for several weeks.'

As we mentioned before, such touch games are always good ways to make contact with young children and with autists – even with those who initially shy away from actual touching or being touched. Closely related to touch games are those that use the child's natural rhythms and his kinaesthetic sense. We have already mentioned Kamp's film of how he used the curiously clumsy and monotonous rocking movements of an autistic girl as a starting point for what became real dancing. Many parents have, of course, used a very similar procedure for a kind of fun and games: whenever one supports, from behind, a toddler who insists on walking up the stairs, it is natural and satisfying to both sides to make a game of this, by counting, perhaps in a singsong; by introducing unexpected variations and, by laughing, letting the child feel that this is fun; by seeking further inspiration from what the child does in response (a child – and, though less openly, an autistic child – often enters very happily into the spirit of playing such jokes). Of course such games are at the same time extremely 'useful' in that they teach the child such skills as, for instance, counting – with, as a further step, becoming *numerate*.

Psychologists now begin to put on scientific record what normal parents have of course 'known' (acted) for aeons: that joking begins long before a child begins to speak.[27] Our colleague Jerome Bruner once told us an amusing and highly instructive example of very early joking interaction between a young mother and her baby, who did not yet speak and had just entered the stage of being spoon-fed. The naturally gifted mother initiated the joke by once, instead of moving the loaded spoon into the baby's already wide-open mouth, withholding it in 'mid-flight', suddenly smiling with her 'joking face' at the baby as she played this trick on him. The baby responded by laughing and was then, before he could become impatient, fed as normal. The next time the mother brought the spoon to the child's mouth, he surprised her by suddenly closing his mouth, with an amused, 'defying' smile on his face, before she could feed him. Good mothers (and fathers and sibs) play a great variety of such jokes with young children; our point here is that even very young babies take delight in this and show inventiveness. Also, we stress that it does not matter whether one has to learn a repertoire of jokes by heart or invents them on the spur of the moment (though the latter is of course the higher achievement) and that 'laughing together' (in young as in adults, and even if it has to be done at one's own expense) is one of the most effective and satisfying bonding mechanisms of our species. It is even important for children to know that their parents and other companions have a repertory of jokes, some of which they want to play time after time. It would seem that a certain balance between inventiveness and conservatism is best; and that even to have, within the family, a set of standard 'in-jokes' that cannot be shared by outsiders seems to us an important factor in bonding by means of joking.[28]

As a child develops, his playful behaviour and playful interactions with his parents, sibs and friends of all kinds grow with him. In a happy family, joking involves all members, each in his own role. Fathers joke in a way different from mothers; children have their own play and joke culture. We believe that many skills of a high order are developed in such contexts, for instance the skill of quick repartee (verbal and non-verbal), that of social adjustability; that of inventiveness etc. And – we must always remember – much of what has 'educational' value with normal children has 'therapeutic' value with disturbed children.

We repeat once more that we ought all to realise that in our society, which is in danger of forgetting about ways of learning other than by mass instruction, yet another educational context is greatly underdeveloped: that of observational learning and learning by practice. Everyone who has seen, and enjoyed, how a boy can sit and watch intently an older boy or a man at work on some manual task, and who has seen young girls asking Grandma 'could they help' her with laying the table, or with dusting or polishing furniture, washing up etc, will have realised both the socialising and the educational skill- (and stamina-) developing functions of this. Unfortunately, much in our modern world fails to create the opportunity for this – fathers do incomprehensible work far from home; washing up is done by the dishwasher, dusting is done with the hoover – and our modern mechanised ways such as the use of electrical appliances, motorised garden tools etc. make it even dangerous for a child to join in. And, most significantly here, the modern parent is so often in a hurry! Thus we lose the institution of 'apprenticeship' in the family context, which used to promote observational learning, practising under supervision and, so to speak in passing, effecting social bonding and co-operation as well. It is therefore of great formative value to create opportunities for such 'apprenticeship' conditions in the family. Fortunately, the need for taking one's part in domestic chores does exist to a certain extent, or can be created, or extended even in the modern urban family without paid domestic help.

To many, it may sound 'unnatural' that such parental behaviour may have to be taught, that 'parentcraft instructions' may be necessary at all. Many will find it difficult to believe that one can, so to speak, 'learn parenting by heart'. We agree that those who have learned a great deal of parental behaviour when, as children, they saw and did a great deal of parenting in a playful context, will undoubtedly on the whole develop into more effective parents than those many members of modern urban societies who have missed out on this early 'apprenticeship'. But in practice, it is our experience that at least some parental behaviour, such as the first few steps in establishing contact with a shy or even an autistic child that we have described, *can* be learned by heart, by following instructions if one's own intuition fails one. Even ungifted or untutored parents soon *do* supplement their sub-optimal parental behaviour by responding to their children's responses in the give and take of playful interactions. Even slight overtures by the parents can elicit responses in the children that give them new ideas or at least a new stimulus or impetus, and can so develop the interaction further, stimulate parents' inventiveness and (most importantly) lead to greater self-confidence in the process – in *both* 'partners'.

Again, the key principles in playful interaction, as in all social intercourse, are: *observe, monitor* the child's behaviour continuously though, if possible, not tensely; *retreat* as soon as the child shows a wish to withdraw (e.g. reduce the fear-inducing 'boo' part of a 'peek-a-boo' game); *avoid* in general all too intrusive approach behaviours (including, at the start, even looking straight at the child) and (except when beginning a 'holding' session) *proceed only* when the child shows that he is ready to take up contact again. Admittedly, this requires a kind of tightrope walking, but practice does help one find the right balance.

More even than normal children, be prepared for having to repeat particularly successful games time and again. The parent may be sick and tired of the game but the child often is not, and likes the security of the ritual. Adding a new game (or adding a variation to the old game) may in the end make it possible to drop the 'stale' game. (This, incidentally, may suddenly be *demanded* by the child, who sometimes may have continued the game because he thought that the *parent* really liked it!)

How much of parentcraft is innate and how much is due to learning we do not really know, but we probably are not far wrong when we say that the general *readiness or wish* to respond parentally to the friendly and happy behaviour of a child is largely innate and irrepressible (although it can atrophy), while the *ways in which we do it* are largely learned, first during one's own childhood but then, with new impetus, when one becomes a parent oneself. Even if a number of insecure, sad or inexperienced mothers and fathers need to be taught how to be playful, the feedback from successful first attempts and 'replies' from their children will 'strike a chord'. Thus, both the skill and the motivation grow with experience of happy interactions.

Finally, we stress once more that in treating autistic children one has to have *stamina* – parents of an autistic child may have to adjust their entire life to his needs, and can hardly ever relax. Only when the condition is recognised at a very early stage can one, with luck, expect quick results. In Chapter 10 we describe some examples of the 'superparenting' that some people manage to do. The point is worth making time and again because many parents, even those who mean well, do not realise that they give in fact less attention to their child than they believe. We have heard of a doctor who asked parents to record on audiotape how they interacted with their child at the start of their treatment; when these tapes were, at a later, more advanced stage, played back to them, these parents were astonished to notice how little they had in fact occupied themselves with their child. 'Having stamina' means that once a 'course' of treatment has been started, *it must not arbitrarily be stopped. To do so may do serious harm.*

Conclusion

We could elaborate these educational guidelines almost *ad infinitum* without catering for all needs; how much advice and how many detailed instruction parents require varies from case to case. We have tried to meet the needs of what we believe to be 'the average parent' of an autistic child; but we have to keep this chapter within reasonable bounds within the framework of the book as a whole. We should like to emphasise that much of what we have said is tentative, based as it is on the exploratory, still searching attempts at designing new ways of treating autistic children which are now being pioneered by so many colleagues. It is natural for parents to ask, as one correspondent in a Dutch journal of *Orthopedagogics* did: 'When will all these experts on autism give us concrete guidelines for coping with our children?' Honesty compels us to reply that, as long as autism is so little understood and methods of treatment are being tried out in such a searching, inevitably almost haphazard way, it is simply not yet possible to give perfect advice that will meet all cases and that will invariably lead to success. But there is a certain justification in this cry for help, for it cannot be denied that 'the experts' have, by writing so much, in such an authoritative style, about autism, created the impression among lay people that they had much more knowledge and understanding than is actually the case.

The reason why we have nevertheless tried to suggest that some ideas and procedures be tried out is that we want to encourage participation by parents, caregivers and teachers in the search for understanding and for better therapies, and to make known – either through the medium of one of the many existing journals on child care and related subjects or in case histories in book form – how they have proceeded and what measures of success they have had. The problems of autism and related disorders are so varied and so complex that it will only be by such a co-operative effort that new, and (we are convinced) better, treatments can be worked out. Certainly, this must not be left entirely to the experts; as we have stressed throughout this book, we believe that both our understanding of autism and the search for effectual treatments would profit immeasurably from collaboration between all persons involved.

Notes and references

1   Park, C. C. 1972. *The siege*. London: Penguin.
       A friend of the Parks began to wonder about Elly when she was 8 months old: 'seeing Elly lying in her baby-tender, content without even a rattle in her hand.' (p. 25). When Elly was 22 months old, the doctor said to her mother 'if you are not worried, I am.' (p. 41); but, as so often, hospital tests did not reveal any abnormality (see Ch. 3 of *The siege* for further details).

Useful tips are given to mothers, doctors, nurses and health visitors by Dr J. A. B. Allan of the Department of Counselling Psychology of the University of British Columbia in Vancouver, Canada. In his 1976 paper 'The identification and treatment of "difficult" babies. Early signs of disruption in parent–infant attachment bonds.' *Canadian Nurse* **72**, 11–16 (which is an abridged version of a lecture given in 1974) he distinguishes three types of such attachment-disturbed babies, which he calls the hyper-kinetic or excessively irritable type; the excessively limp and passive baby; and the excessively rigid baby. In his experience these three types require each their own, slightly different ways of holding. It is even possible that the way to restore the mother–infant bond has to be slightly different depending on whether the baby has been 'odd from birth' or has become socially withdrawn at a later stage. We agree with Dr Allan that there is a great need for home-visiting healthcare personnel to be properly informed and experienced about these early warning signs, so that, on their postnatal checking visits, they could spot trouble and alert mothers at an early stage as well as instruct them how to act. Such properly trained, alert 'manwatching' barefoot counsellors could render quite a number of services, acting as the home-visiting arm of maternity clinics, many of which are too sedentary and often too test-oriented to engage in this kind of fieldwork. In Britain at least the basic personnel structure is there, and the workers involved are undoubtedly keen to extend their considerable expertise to incorporate this kind of 'psychological trouble shooting.'

2 Hutt, C. 1975. *Males and females.* London: Penguin.

3 See, for example, Foudraine, J. 1974 (Ch. 2, note 8) and Rimland, B. 1978 (Ch. 5, note 40).

4 See, for instance, the case history of Paula (Ch. 10) whose mother joined her in pushing chairs around the room; and see the description in Kaufman, B. N. 1976 (see Ch. 6. note 19) who describes how Raun's family joined him in making plates spin.

5 Elly Park had a severe setback when her family went to Britain for her father's sabbatical leave. Another autistic child we know had severe regressions whenever her parents (who were about to separate) had a quarrel; this same girl severely damaged her finger by biting it at school when her home tutor, who had told her that she would collect her at 11 o'clock, was ten minutes late. A 10-year-old girl whom we know quite well (Carla, whose case history will, we hope, be written up by her tutor) regressed very badly for an entire month after she had watched a television documentary about autistic children in which one mother was seen and heard to say about her autistic son that, rather than send him to an institution, she would 'put him to sleep' (we never heard why this girl was allowed by her parents to watch the programme). The last two girls mentioned were mute and the first was practically so – so much for the 'cognitive defects' of autists! Judy too (Ch. 10) regressed badly for some time when she fell ill shortly before Easter 1980, but she soon recovered and once more became her (perfectly normal) self.

6 For instances of unhelpful medical reactions, see, for example, Kaufman (1976, pp. 16, 17, 18) – see note 4 above; Park (1972, Ch. 9 about *The professionals*) – see note 1 above; Copeland and Hodges (1973, p. 23) – see Ch. 5, note 28; Beck, M. 1978. *The exorcism of an albatross* (obtainable from the author 'send $7.50, which includes postage within Canada, to Marion Leslie, 95 Hudson Drive, Regina, Canada S4S 2W1').

On the other hand, Axline (see Ch. 3, note 8) relates on pp. 76–7, how Dib's parents, who had asked the advice of a psychiatrist, had been told frankly that Dibs 'was the most rejected and emotionally deprived child he had ever seen'. In the words of Dibs' mother (speaking to Axline) 'He said that my husband and I were the ones who needed his help, and suggested treatment for both of us.' According to Axline, the parents ignored this advice.

7 While the Parks were in Britain, Mrs Park saw an analyst who visited Elly at home and managed to place her in a nursery school for normal children. The description of this

school and the teacher's way with Elly reminds us of the schools to which two of the girls whom we know went (viz. E., whose case history is being written down by one of our colleagues, and Judy, whose story we relate in Ch. 10). In all these instances, the school had a strikingly good influence on the children concerned. See also our section 'Children as co-therapists', p. 189 (Ch. 6).

8   The bad effect of interrupting a child at the wrong moment is well illustrated in the case history of George (see Ch. 10); see also note 9 below.

9   Montessori gives clear descriptions of the adverse influence of 'stimulation' at the wrong time, e.g. during the 'false fatigue', when the children at her school after the morning's early work on familiar, well-mastered tasks has been done, prepare themselves for the next tasks. Montessori, M. 1965 (first published in 1917). *Spontaneous activity in education*. Cambridge, Mass: Bentley. (See p. 100 and beyond.)

10   Wexler, S. S. 1970 *The Story of Sandy*. Winnipeg, The North American Library of Canada: Signet.

11   Lagerlöf, S. 1958. *The wonderful adventures of Nils*. London: Dent. (Original Swedish edition published in 1906–7.)

12   Seligman, M. E. P. 1975. *Helplessness – on depression, development and death*. San Francisco: W. H. Freeman.

13   Copeland, J. and J. Hodges 1973 (see Ch. 5, note 28).

14   We believe that it is not generally known that many, if not all, normal children, unless denied the opportunity, learn to avoid handling their own faeces 'because of the foul smell and taste'. They learn this as babies when hard faeces fall out of their nappies or get within reach in some other way and, when still naïve and in the phase of oral exploration, they manipulate them, as they do any new objects, and put them into their mouths. It is when they taste them that they will cry bitterly until cleaned up, and it seems that one such experience is enough for them to learn not to 'play with their faeces'. The survival value of this instant conditioning against faeces is, of course, clear: the danger of re-infection with intestinal parasites is a severe selection pressure and must have been so for many millions of years. This is perhaps also why our sense of smell is particularly sensitive to 'skatol' and 'indol'.

15   See Chapter 6, note 25.

16   Park, C. C. (see note 1 above) and Beck, M. (see note 6 above).

17   A striking example of a mother realising that (and why) she had missed one of the rare chances of making contact with her autistic child was given in an interview on (we believe) B B C radio, when she was asked 'Have you ever felt "If only I had done this or that I might have established contact"?' She replied: 'yes, once my son and I were together in the kitchen while I was cooking the dinner. On an impulse I put the lid of a saucepan on my head instead of on the saucepan and balanced it there for a while till it fell off. My son actually laughed at this and I feel that, had I gone on with the game, we might have entered into a relationship, for however short a time. But I was too tired, in fact exhausted by having to cope with all his odd behaviour and problems, and let the chance slip by.'

A good example of realising a child's need and prompt reaction to it is to be found in Judy's case history, when the family decided to leave their friends' home (where they were staying and where Judy objected hysterically to the new baby) and, in snow and sleet, went on a camping trip instead.

Carla's parents decided at one time, when she was 13 years old, to go camping with the whole family, and for weeks beforehand kept telling her that 'she would like it so much'. This led to outbursts of destructive behaviour and, when asked why (by her tutor, for whom she wrote willingly) Carla wrote: 'I see their point and I accept that they like camping, and also that I will have to come along, but I resent being told over and over again that I will like it. It will be even worse than staying at home, more chaotic and unorganised.' During the camping week Carla was 'naughty' and rude to other campers when they tried to jolly her into communal play. Other examples of how to (or not to) meet a child's needs can be found in, for example, Beck, M. (see note 6 above) and in many other books.

18　From what we understood of Zappella's accounts in *L'enfant poisson* (see Ch. 5, note 34) and his later book *Il bambino nella Luna* (1979, Milan: G. Feltrinelli), we thought that he believed that the elective mutism that he describes of rural children who are suddenly sent to more urban schools could be an incipient and temporary form of autism, but during recent discussions with him at Oxford, he expressed doubt about the relationship between the two conditions. We feel that we must keep an open mind about this.

19　The fullest discussion of 'autistic savants' has been given by B. Rimland (see Ch. 5, note 40), but most books on individual children give some examples. We ourselves believe that the available evidence points strongly to the conclusion that special gifts of some kind and predisposition to autism (and other emotional disturbances) are closely correlated, even more closely than is at the moment evident, because such special gifts are often not detected, or are considered 'odd'.

20　C. Park in *The siege* (see note 1 above) gives numerous examples of this kind of inventiveness and we have seen fine examples in some of the families we visited.

21　Park, C. (see note 1 above) and Furneaux, B. and B. Roberts (see Ch. 1, note 4).

22　For Beck, M. (1978) see note 6 above; for Park's *The siege*, see note 1 above; for the story of Elly's counter, see Chapter 6, note 21.

23　See Chapter 5, note 37.

24　Dennis, N. 1978. Portrait of an artist. *The New York Review of Books*, **25**, 8–15.

This is an exceptionally thorough and penetrating review of Selfe and Newson's book. Dennis draws attention to two paragraphs in particular, and we repeat his comments here because we feel that they hit the nail squarely on the head. Selfe's lengthy text leads up to the (none too surprising) conclusion that 'In all respects human behaviour presents the most difficult challenge in the history of science – it is far more complex than the dark side of the moon or the D N A molecule. Nadia remains an enigma.' (p. 128). E. Newson concludes her 'Postscript' with the following astonishing paragraph: 'Is this a tragedy? For us, who love to be astonished, maybe. For Nadia, perhaps it is enough to *have been* a marvellous child.' (emphasis is Dr Newson's) 'If the partial loss of her gift is the price that must be paid for language – even just enough language to bring her into some kind of community of discourse with her small protected world – we must, I think, be prepared to pay that price on Nadia's behalf' (p. 130). We feel that this remark indicates a lack of sensitivity; we also wonder whether the authors have realised that art is often a powerful form of communication. Dennis is even more outspoken; he writes 'Every line of Dr Newson's cozy summary is thoughtless and bad. How can a psychologist believe that when you are fat, fifty and feeble minded it will buck you up to think that you were a world-beater at five? . . . As for us, "who love to be astonished", it is surely our business to take a more intelligent' (and we would add, loving) 'view of what genius has to give us, and to see tragedy in its thoughtless destruction' (p. 14).

If readers think that we have exaggerated when we wrote that we found 'this corner of psychiatry in disarray' (Tinbergen, N. 1974, p. 209; see Ch. 1, note 8), these few quotations may convince them that we have shown considerable restraint.

25　Tinbergen, N. 1975. *The importance of being playful* (see Ch. 4, note 14).

26　We have only gradually discovered how extremely difficult, indeed near-impossible, it is for quite a number of mothers to play with their children. We observed repeatedly one mother of a mute, severely autistic girl of (then) five years old, start a simple game with her child, facing her and on her lap, holding her by the hands and gently letting her bend back and then pulling her up again. The child was at the start anxious and rigid, but gradually let herself go. But as soon as, in this more relaxed phase, she touched her mother's legs, the latter pulled her up sharply and stopped the game.

Another mother, who tried out a form of 'holding' with her 10-year-old son, told E. A. that at times both she and her son became 'so terribly bored'. E. A. suggested to her that she tell her child some stories, whereupon the mother said 'But I don't know any stories!' It turned out that she herself had, as a child, never been told stories, nor learned nursery rhymes!

These mothers are examples of an entire class of mothers of autistic children who have in common that they have themselves been poorly mothered when they were children. (Of course, this must not be reversed: it hardly needs repeating that the best of parents can have the misfortune of having an autistic child!) The 'three generations phenomenon' (of a near-normal grandmother, a poorly mothered but still fairly normal mother, and an autistic or otherwise disturbed child) is undoubtedly not uncommon.

27 Very young children are, of course, great natural jokers. One little girl of our acquaintance who, for a time when she did not feel quite secure, was allowed an old-fashioned soother, was used to taking it out of her mouth when offered a cup to drink from. Suddenly, with a twinkle in her eye, she put the soother back just when her mother was about to bring the cup to her (the child's) lips. No doubt every normal mother knows this kind of preverbal joking of her own children; they play jokes endlessly and often with great inventiveness.

28 Joking, of course, often of the most 'silly' and repetitive kind, can not only bridge long periods of enforced boredom or tiredness, but, for example, during a long car drive or a train journey or when coming home from a long walk, can actually play an important part in strengthening the family bond. One father we know could keep his children laughing for half an hour at a stretch during long car journeys by such games as (Father asking) 'What do we like? Peanut butter!' 'Yeees!' 'What do we like? Strawberry jam!' 'Yeees!' 'What do we like? Our little brother!' 'Yeees!' (laughter because of the switch in the meaning of the word 'like'). 'What do we like? A red traffic light!' 'Yes – noooo!' (laughter) etc.

Our two youngest children, when approximately two and six years old, would always have their bath together, E. A. would have to wash four hands and there was for months a standard joke of taking first a hand of the younger child and then one of the larger child, with the comment greatly enjoyed 'What a funny child; she has one large and one small hand.' This had to go on day after day, so that E. A. became thoroughly sick of it. Then, as happens so often, the eldest suddenly said one day 'Must we play that silly game every day?' Again, every family knows innumerable examples of the bonding function, but we know families with an autistic child where this is simply never done. Few clinicians ever hear of these and similar, highly significant aspects.

10

Some case histories

Introduction

This final chapter consists of two batches of case histories. Two additional
sets are presented in Appendices I and II, especially written for this book
by two psychiatrists who have been applying the 'forced holding'
technique. Almost all of these histories have a more or less happy ending;
some of them early in life and after prompt acting on early warning signs;
others before or around adolescence, and most of these after very long,
sustained uphill struggles, always with many a setback. All of them have
been brought as much up to date as possible; those collected by ourselves
up till May 1981; others by using the latest available evidence we could
find.

None of the evidence presented here is the result of real, 'controlled', let
alone 'double blind' experiments (which we maintain are not only
impossible to do but would, if possible at this time, needlessly prolong the
agony of thousands and thousands of families) nor is it even the result of
comparisons between 'matched samples' (which are at the moment simply
not available). But we claim that these four groups of cases do, by sheer
numbers and by the detailedness, relevance and critical recording of
relevant information, compare favourably with most case material to be
found in the literature on autism.

This is not to say that we shall not *ever* need the accumulation of
'matched samples' evidence, nor (perhaps) in the long run, of large-scale,
long-term experiments. But before such further work could make sense at
all, the stage has to be set for it and this is what our book, including this
final chapter, is intended to do. This 'setting of the stage', the decisions on
what has to be done and how it can best be done, can be done sensibly
only if we spend a considerable time 'watching and wondering'; and this
last chapter is intended to show in detail how this can be done, something
which the earlier parts of our book describe in a more abstract way.
Beyond this we present what, at the present stage of knowledge, are fair
descriptions of what kind of circumstances can make children autistic (and
how these vary from case to case), and also how the damage can be undone.

We present this material in four parts. First, we give condensed
descriptions of the six most conscientiously recorded cases (part of a larger
number) of 'do-it-yourself' treatments that have not been published until

now. Next, we present brief abstracts of six books, several of which have been available for a long time, and all but one or two of which have never been taken seriously by professional students of autism.

The two appendices to this chapter are up-to-date reports by two professional psychiatrists, who have been working for years in isolation, disbelieved and largely ignored by those who have, by prolific writing and by organising the various societies for autistic children (which, as we have argued, contain a non-representative sample of parents of autistic children, namely those whose children have not recovered), dominated the scene for so long, but whose 'adherence to sameness' is now beginning to be noticed by an increasing number of their colleagues (see the quotations in note 6 to Ch. 1).

The first of the two appendices has been written by Dr M. Welch of New York, whose method we have described in the main text of Chapter 6. The original paper was prepared several years ago but, concise though it was, has been rejected by more than one professional journal, or accepted only on the condition that it would be condensed to a fraction of its length, in which the crucial points could not even be listed, let alone argued. Because we consider publication to be of paramount importance, we are glad to have found both Dr Welch and our publishers prepared to add her story to this chapter.

The second appendix, like Dr Welch's, was written by a psychiatrist who had until recently worked in complete isolation and developed his theory independently, but whose two short books had so far been published only in Italian and French respectively, and had received little attention. The author, Dr Michele Zappella of Siena, and Dr Welch met in the autumn of 1980 at our home for a 'minisymposium' of a couple of days, during which we looked at their videotapes and listened to their reports and views, and so could judge for ourselves what degree of successes they were gradually achieving. Dr Zapella's story is of special interest because of the clear elucidation of the steady growth of his ideas under the impact of what he experienced. Also, of course, both Dr Welch and Dr Zappella stand out because, unlike the largely clinic-based armchair experts whose views we have criticised, they do field work; they know the children and their families intimately and in this respect they too could be called true 'ethopathologists'. We are deeply grateful to them for having allowed us to incorporate their reports in our book.

This chapter seems to us important for yet another reason. In Chapter 6 we argued that a therapy can be derived either theoretically, viz. from an analysis of the nature and of the origin of a disorder, or empirically, rather more by trial and error, by seeing what treatment happens to lead to recovery. We argued that it was encouraging that these two lines of approach had led to virtually the same conclusion. It is in this chapter that the conclusion about the (so far) best therapy is supported by much more evidence than could be expected as little as 10 years ago. Its procedure by 'the proof of the pudding' enables us to come (so to speak) full circle and return to our introductory remarks, in which we challenged the validity of the myth of 'ineducability'. The prognosis may still *be* poor for many autistic children, but it *need* no longer be poor; the outlook is becoming better.

Nor are these two psychiatrists the only representatives of the new school. We are in touch with several others, but they are either preparing their own stories or are not yet far enough to be able to report in full. Our chapter, we *know*, is only the advance guard of a growing supply of new evidence that is 'in the pipeline', and this new evidence on the curability of autism will be of vital importance for parents of autistic children, already born or still to be born in our increasingly stressful society.

Lest we raise false hopes, we do have to add that it is as yet impossible to justify the claim that *all* autistic children can be cured. As we have said, there are cases who seem to defy any attempts made so far at curing them. This, we think, is largely because their persistently severely autistic behaviour has literally driven their parents to distraction. But we do claim that even among these cases there is a number who could recover, if only because their parents could nurse new hope and receive practical guidance from the success stories we publish here. Some of them show that the task that *seemed* impossible, turned out in the end not really to have been so. The more we learn about autistic children, the more confidence we get in, and admiration we feel for, the incredible resilience and urge to survive that so many of them show in the face of such awesome adversity.

Six 'do-it-yourself' cases

PAULA – REPORT BASED ON INFORMATION SUPPLIED BY HER PARENTS

Paula was born on 6 August 1961, the youngest of five children. Her father and mother, who very kindly received us at their home when Paula was 17, are obviously competent, warm, concerned, devoted parents. The father is a busy practising physician. During our visit Paula came in and joined us normally.

The following is largely taken from notes kept by the mother from 1964 onwards, supplemented by the father's comments.

After a normal pregnancy, the baby was delivered without complications but two weeks premature. She was definitely not unwanted. She was not really 'odd from birth', but the parents report that 'from the start Paula was a "lazy drinker"; she was also exceptionally quiet and good.' Because Paula 'took no trouble' when put to the breast, the mother (who had breast-fed most of her previous children but none for longer than a few weeks) switched to bottle feeding. The baby seemed contented but she drank too little, developed persistent diarrhoea and lost weight; an infection was therefore suspected and she was, when six weeks old, hospitalised (on her own) for three weeks' observation and a penicillin cure. 'The paediatrician considered Paula to be a "neuropath" '. When her mother visited her, Paula did not smile at her, not at other people, though she did smile 'at herself' or some situations, e.g. a moving object, or a ball thrown past her ('later she became especially interested in balls and could soon play with them surprisingly well'). The first indication that Paula did not live up to normal expectations was when, at the appropriate age, she was offered a biscuit and 'clearly did not know what to do with it', although she ate it when it was put into her mouth. It was then that her mother saw 'a blank, empty expression on her face' and that both she and her husband began to be worried.

Upon her return from hospital, no striking change was observed in her already withdrawn behaviour; she seemed 'contented' and did begin to babble at the normal time when she was put in her playpen, 'but this stopped when she was 15 months'. When Paula was 18 months old, the parents began to think that her hearing must be faulty or impaired, even though she did react to some (non-social) sounds 'such as the falling of a metal ashtray, a sound she seemed to like . . . She never showed affection for us or for other persons.'

As soon as she could sit and crawl, the playpen was put away so as to give her freedom of movement. She showed interest in, for example, a black spot on her white chair, in the electric light when it was switched on ('she understood the connection between the switch and the light'). When approximately 20 months old, she would play with a ball for hours, and at other times she would shove a chair around, often balancing it on one of its legs. *In these games the mother often joined her for hours in an attempt to establish contact.* Paula was now also fascinated by the sound of passing cars.

When, at 20 months, 'we had become resigned to the idea that Paula was at least "hard of hearing", we were delighted when one day she crawled towards us from an adjoining room after we had called her name' (obviously it was her ignoring socially significant sounds that had worried the parents). At that time, Paula did walk if she was not in a hurry, when she would crawl, as so many normal children do.

Even now 'she acted as if she did not know her mother, and when she was taken out on shopping trips she cried pitifully, even in shops she knew. When she was almost two years old, we decided to take her on a camping holiday at the seaside. We took her daily to a sandy beach, but for ten days she did not leave her pushchair in this environment. On the camp site she would walk only when going to her own cot. We drew her out by endless invitations to ball-playing, by which we finally overcame her excessive clinging to her pushchair.' In this period she began to show attachment to her mother. She still showed 'odd' behaviour (stereotypies) such as *shaking her head, incessant tapping with knives, spoons, plates. She often took her mother's hand and pushed it towards 'everything'.*

At 2½ years, Paula was taken by her parents to an ear, nose and throat specialist, because they still had doubts about her hearing. Here she showed no reaction to an alarm clock (!) set ringing behind her (but she could hear all right, indeed exceptionally well – see later).

Paula now began to push chairs around, day after day, in an obsessive manner; to hammer on the heating radiators; to bang with cutlery; or alternately to lie on the floor for long periods. 'But she made no social contacts at all.'

In January 1964 she fell ill with respiratory trouble and fairly severe German measles, but she stayed at home. On 13 January her mother played to her on a recorder. Paula was at once 'in ecstasy' and the mother immediately showed her sympathy. The reward came when, during daily playing, a stronger bond developed between Paula and her mother – 'real contact'. Yet she remained frightened and apprehensive when, after her recovery, she was taken for walks in park or wood.

At Easter 1964, she got severe 'blue' measles and pneumonia of the right lung. 'She now became a very anxious, extremely thin little girl; she did not want to leave her bed, did not dare look, enter the room, stand or walk alone.' When she recovered, her parents resumed taking her for regular walks, keeping her between them. In view of Paula's obvious interest in music, they now bought her a toy piano, on which she played at once a familiar tune. She could now be lured from room to room by moving this piano about. The parents began to notice an overall improvement. Paula showed that she had a special liking for classical music (e.g. Bach). She loved hearing and playing a xylophone and soon also a recorder; got them out of their drawer and carried one of them with her when she was taken to other homes. She also began to show an understanding of speech and, for instance, tried to make her mother take her to the ducks in the park by taking her by the hand, looking intently at her and saying something like 'haak-haak'. When she was three years old, she was often given jigsaw puzzles with pictures of animals, with which she played a lot in the summer of 1964. That same summer, when again on the (sandy) seashore, she ventured away from her mother and paddled cautiously (*not* recklessly) in beach pools.

Upon their return home she was sent for regular sessions with a logopedist (continental term for speech therapist) but this was unsuccessful; she never responded but played endlessly one special lullaby on her little piano! Even so, there was gradual improvement: she began to play on a swing in the garden, and became more or less toilet trained. From about this time on, the mother often played music to her and she was given a triangle when the little piano broke down.

At Christmas 1964 Paula once more fell very ill, now with pneumonia of the left lung; her behaviour regressed: she refused all social contact, and had to be fed in a prone position. 'We are desperate; the whole family suffers; we consider taking psychiatric advice.' She was given a new small piano. But she recovered and became less withdrawn, 'and we decided to forget about the psychiatrist'. Next she was taken to a group for rhythmic movement, dance and play at the sound of *Dalcroze* music (a continental type of music play and therapy). Here she was at once fascinated by the piano, 'forgot her mother, did not want to leave, had to be dragged home, where she cried incessantly, which stopped only when her parents put a Mozart record on the gramophone. Paula set out all her musical instruments in a semicircle round her and was completely happy. From then on Paula improved strikingly, began to eat in a well mannered, even deft way, became fully toilet trained, but was at first still mute. The Dalcroze sessions were continued; and soon Paula began to speak. ('Piano' was her first word, but she soon began to say – and understand – more, although she seemed to find abstract and general terms difficult. Thus, asked to 'take the mail' from the letter box she looked blank but acted appropriately when 'the letters, papers and cards' were asked for.)

Spring and summer 1965 brought spectacular progress, which we will describe in some detail. Paula became more or less obsessed with gramophone records, both of classical music and of popular tunes. 'We bought a real piano', on which she played a number of tunes. By March 1965, she played real melodies, with her mother accompanying her. On hearing Bach she once said 'a swing' and ran outside to play on the swing. This association remained for a long time. Now her speaking improved by leaps and bounds; she began to play outside, became much more social, but was afraid of dogs. On 23 March she showed that she did not like babies. Hearing Bach music made her draw a swing and make swinging movements with her hands. On 6 May she asked for a violin concerto on the gramophone; during the music she told her mother to make the bowing movements that belong to the violin music. On 8 May she attended a semi-public performance of her Dalcroze group. When the children appeared holding a balloon each, she (verbally) asked 'could she have one too'. When the children of the group were lined up on the stage she called out 'train' (having just a few days before been on a much enjoyed train journey). One girl acted as the conductor of the group; Paula said 'man who beats (time)'. When triangles were beaten she said 'xylophone'.

On 17 May 1965, Paula gave a clearly meaningful answer for the first time: when she motioned to an aunt and uncle, urging them to join her in drawing swings, and her parents said 'why don't you draw them yourself?' she replied 'no, can't draw'. When she did not want to play the piano she cunningly said 'the piano wants to sleep'. With a violinist friend of the family, she made contact through her music by playing a simple tune until he began to accompany her. When she was visited by other children she allowed them to listen to a gramophone record the way other children will lend a friend a doll (we know this offering of playing a record as 'one's most precious gift' of other autistic children as well; it is of course completely logical, though of course rarely effective!).

Paula still disliked crossing into a new room and often lay down on the doorstep between rooms, crying complainingly. Her mother took her every day to the park and the ducks, and had to tell the same little story every day ('There are the ducks, "quack, quack, quack" says the little duck' etc.). Once, when her mother was depressed and failed to sing, Paula sang the tune and also 'Now we are almost home again'.

In September 1965 Paula, now four years old, entered a nursery school, which her next elder sister, Diana, was already attending. She still seemed to have difficulty in understanding complicated phrases; for instance, she did not react when the teacher asked her to 'put this on top of the chest of drawers' but did it at once when another child did it first. In the story of Little Red Riding Hood, she did not seem to understand the phrase 'walking along the path in the forest' until she was taken to a wood and had walked along the path there.

In this nursery school she made friends with a boy, and she often played next to him though not *with* him. She commented 'John's nice, his mother is kind person' (John's mother played on the piano for her).

After a few 'dry runs' to the dentist (who lived opposite) to prepare her for later treatments, Paula soon went across alone for her periodic checks. Once a tooth had to be drawn; Paula went alone after having been told what would happen. She returned home with the tooth in a matchbox, and when asked what had happened drew a head with one big tooth in it. She was asked to a party; when her mother expressed her delight, the other mother said 'Paula elicits all that's best in my girl'. In the course of this year she gave numerous signs of good understanding and thinking, though her speech was still in brief 'skeleton' sentences. In the summer of 1965, when the family once more went to the seashore, the mother had to draw piano keys in the sand and play on them endlessly.

When Diana left the nursery school to pass on to primary school Paula was very upset.

When Paula herself reached six years of age, her 'intelligence' was tested and judged to be 'that of a two-year-old' (!) but both the nursery school teacher and the primary school teacher realised that she had something special, and it was decided not to put her in the equivalent of an ESN school but in the normal primary school – one teacher saying 'it's all or nothing', another saying 'let's start normally; we can always change tack'. She soon read well but had difficulties with arithmetic. She now began to attend weekly ballet lessons and acted little parts. Next she began to speak to neighbours and visitors and asked them 'where do you live?' She began to use dolls to re-enact scenes that had happened and fascinated or upset her at school; she made these daily sessions into extremely lively performances. Her contact with her parents improved steadily but she was still often lonely and missed, for instance, a friend who went home for weekends. ('I love Monica; she smiles so nicely.') She made some contact with two of her elder sibs.

After the usual six years at primary school, the parents and the teacher considered her too young to go to secondary school and in order to give her time to mature she was permitted to stay down for one more year. Being still the odd one out at school, she was still often teased. When she left primary school the teacher predicted a good future 'for this plucky child. She has been teased so much; she has gone through hell'.

At the secondary school ('Gymnasium', a type of grammar school with emphasis on the classics and the humanities) she made steady progress. Her main handicap was in the beginning a poor idiom; then, as she acquired the art of expressing herself, a certain bookishness of language which her parents thought to be due to her having, in her younger years, taken in too little of what was said in her environment.

When we visited her and her family in 1979 (Paula was then 17 and was preparing herself for her final examination, at the same time making plans for her further education) she was a perfectly normal person, with an excellent use of language, charming and with quiet social poise. Her parents spoke of a fairly recent 'breakthrough' and gave us as examples her increased independence (as instanced by her expert shopping and cooking during her parents' absence abroad, her growing circle of friends, with whom she had frequent contacts) and the disappearance of her former feeling of being a relative outsider compared with her sibs, who still had a richer social life.

E. A. visited Paula once more in her home (while her parents were abroad on holiday) in September 1980. Paula had in the meantime gained entrance to university where she had started reading history; she had given up her original plan to train as a child-care worker or a similar profession because 'she wanted to get away from anything that would remind her of the unhappy past'. She was a completely self-possessed, courteous and friendly hostess, and did not hesitate to inform E. A. about what she remembered of the past, but said that she would prefer to be forward-looking. She was about to take a room of her own in her university town, and had joined a students' society and a dramatic society. While E. A. was with her she received a telephone call from her grandmother and, although E. A. did not want to listen in, she could not help noticing that Paula chatted away cheerfully and with great animation. At the start of the hour with E. A. her speech was 'a little young for her age and achievements' but as they became re-used to each other (this was only the second time Paula had met E. A.), her conversation became normal. Her repeatedly expressed wish was now to 'live among normal people'. 'A mature, normal and interesting personality.'

Now (mid-May 1981) her parents report that socially and academically Paula has adjusted very well to the new circumstances. She has had a boyfriend for some time but broke it off because 'she did not agree with having sex before marriage'. She is to all intents and purposes a normal, happy and independent university student, has been invited to go on a sailing trip with a friend and her family, and plans to go abroad, with another friend, for a fortnight this coming summer, paid for with self-earned money.

Authors' comments

This is another case of a child who was clearly 'quiet from birth' though not clearly autistic. Paula has undoubtedly had bad luck very early in life; the lonely hospital stay with the (doubtless painful) penicillin injections must have made her more withdrawn than she already was (compare with Olga's history). According to the father, who had throughout a very busy practice, the 'do-it-yourself' treatment was very largely the work of his wife, who never gave up trying to make contact with Paula and even joined her in some of her odder behaviours; who made perceptive use of Paula's love of music; who played a great deal with her but prodded her occasionally into taking initiative. The parents always 'accepted her as she was' and had endless patience. They kept searching for ways of fostering her mental and emotional growth. It is in our experience typical of D I Y ('super') mothers that Paula's mother does not feel that she has done anything special. As she said simply: 'the child clearly needed my help'.

OLGA – REPORT BASED ON INFORMATION SUPPLIED BY HER PARENTS AND HERSELF FROM 1977 ON

Olga's parents were married in July 1939, a few months before the outbreak of World War II. Their first child, Helen, was born in June 1940. The father, a schoolmaster, later headmaster, was called up in 1942 and served in Europe and the Middle East until December 1946, with occasional home leave.

Olga was born in May 1946, after a normal pregnancy but in uncertain, in many respects anxious and generally stressful times. The mother, a nurse and later an infant teacher, had stopped working 18 weeks before Olga's birth. Labour started a day early, but on arrival in the nursing home it stopped, and was then induced at the mother's request. The baby was born after only four hours' labour; the birth, though painful, was not abnormal; Olga's weight was approximately 3½ kg. She was not given to her mother to be fed until the day after her birth. She was breast-fed for approximately six months. Both parents had wanted the child and felt very happy with her.

During the next ten years the family had to cope with an exceptional series of misfortunes. Three days after her birth Olga contracted pemphigus, and mother and child were, together with some other mothers and babies, transferred to an isolation ward, where they stayed for approximately a week. For a number of days Olga had, every three hours, a penicillin injection (which was then still very painful); her mother could hear her scream but was not allowed to comfort her, although at other times of the day she could continue to breast-feed her. (Whenever Olga's cot was lowered before the injection it made 'a screeching noise'. Three years later the mother's treadle sewing machine, when moved, produced a similar sound, and then 'the child screamed in terror and covered her ears'.) After completion of the cure, mother and child were allowed to return home, i.e. to the house of a bachelor-farmer for whom the mother kept house *in lieu* of paying rent.

Six weeks later, when another blister appeared on Olga's skin, mother and child were once more taken to hospital, where the mother was allowed to take care of Olga. While the father was still in the Middle East, the mother had first lived with her eldest child in a remote cottage on the Norfolk coast, without electricity or warm water; then in the house of the farmer already mentioned. But 'his pub crawling, after which he often returned in a very provocative, aggressive mood, forced her, when Olga was 11 months old, to 'put our furniture into storage and to dump myself and the children on my father, who lived in a tiny bungalow with few facilities'. (Olga's father, by now demobilised, had obtained a teaching post in another part of the country far from his family. It was not until September 1947 that he could join his family in their newly acquired home in South Yorkshire, where he had found a position as lecturer in a Mining and Technical College.)

Before this, when Olga was six months old, her mother had to go away for a day, and the baby was 'parked' for 12 hours with good friends, 'whom Olga did not know well'. Here she cried incessantly and refused to be fed. But the first real signs that all was not well did not come until Olga was 11 months old, the time when her mother, still on her own with the two girls, moved into her father's bungalow. Here 'she began rocking her pram, once so violently that she overturned it'. She also rocked her cot. (We have no information about possible earlier warning signs, although we suspect that signs of withdrawal and tension must already have been present.)

Throughout Olga's early youth her father, a hard worker, had not only his normal work but was also studying for higher degrees in his spare time; he became headmaster of a secondary school in 1952. His nerves were often on edge, and at all times there was quite a lot of friction between the parents. Yet he did what he could to help his wife, financially, actively and morally, to cope with the stressful situation, of which Olga's slow development formed only a part. The mother's unmarried brother, who after a period of unemployment had found a job, lived with them for quite a time; he was not difficult but his presence did complicate the mother's task. From the parents' notes we see that Olga 'reached the usual milestones (standing, walking, cutting her first teeth) at a normal age'. She was, however, 'lazy about eating solids'. She was a 'good and undemanding baby' (a familiar aspect of many case histories). When 16 months old, she did not reach out to things even quite close to her, nor did she hold on to them when they were placed in her hands. She did not respond to her name and appeared deaf; she would not look at her mother nor at other people. When she was two years old, she had only one word: 'bluebell' (enunciated clearly, used in the general sense of 'flower').

At three years, she showed an exceptional interest in music and when on one occasion the mother, walking Olga up the stairs, sang 'doh-ray-me' etc. up the scale, Olga sang the words too and perfectly in tune, then 'copied me when I sang the words down the scale'.

The mother remembers many tantrums, mainly when Olga was between three and six years old. 'Olga often touched and stroked people's clothing – particularly velvet, fur or hair.' She had her stereotypies: 'turning her head to one side and peering at the sky through her fingers, whirring her hands round, making peculiar grimaces and sometimes spinning round without appearing to become dizzy'. She also showed attachments to 'unusual objects, insisting on taking a huge red engine and a large tablespoon to bed, which left little room in the cot for herself.' At times 'she walked long distances on tiptoe'.

At five, before she went to school. Olga and her mother had a meeting at a clinic 'with the full array of specialists in child health'. The mother was told that Olga 'was probably brain damaged; that she would most likely prove to be ineducable, and that she would never earn her own living'. However, the report to the headmistress (as the parents heard years later) mentioned that Olga was 'severely autistic'.

When Olga was 5¾ years and still in the echolalia stage, she was admitted to a normal state infant school. The mother 'warned the headmistress that Olga might often be disruptive but asked for her to be treated as much as possible as a normal child'. During the three years at that school Olga's improvement began. 'Just how they managed I shall never know, but at age eight she was reading, her speech had leapt forward, and when she was relaxed she was perfectly normal.' After these happy and probably decisive years at this first school Olga had to move on, in September 1954 (8½ years old) to a junior school (likewise in Yorkshire) but after the first term there the family moved to Suffolk. 'In the first school in Suffolk – separated from the first friend she had just made in Yorkshire – Olga stayed less than a year because she was most unhappy. Other children danced round her and kicked her and generally made her life hell. She never fought and did not know how to answer back.' (In this respect – see some of the other case histories – autistic children often behave like very young normal children in the first days after being introduced to their first play school.)

Yet between January 1955 and October 1964 (when Olga gained admission to the Royal College of Music, see below) she attended six different schools. In spite of unhappy experiences at some schools and overall stresses hitting the entire family, but mainly through attending good and sympathetic schools, and throughout receiving exceptional parental, in particular maternal, care (for her mother was both very devoted and determined) she continued to develop and gradually recovered completely. When Olga was six years old her mother had concluded that 'possibly we, the parents, had unwittingly caused the trouble' and that she 'had to start again at baby level'. The father, though busy, with his nerves always on edge, did support his wife, although he said afterwards that 'the main credit was due to her'. ('It would be more honest to say that my support was material rather than unreservedly moral . . . I do not think I was fully aware of the magnitude of the problem . . . Sure she was a problem and a headache but she was ours . . . but from the beginning my wife did the fighting and the initiating in the battles for our children; I supported her though sometimes almost grudgingly . . . But until recently I did not share my wife's confidence that Olga would grow up to be the able, rounded personality that she is . . . As regards autism, I grew to hate the subject . . . after my wife's return from the Autistic Society's conference in York in 1976 I was very upset by what they had done to my wife . . . who had been met with disbelief and even hostility.') (This in spite of the fact that Olga had (on her own initiative) gone to York with her mother – so to speak as 'Exhibit A'.)

In April 1951 a third daughter, Mary, was born. For this delivery too the mother went to hospital. Helen and Olga were cared for 'in the home of a very kind couple who loved all children'. 'Olga seemed to blossom here, especially since she was allowed to play the piano. Afterwards our friends said to us: "Do you realise that she never plays a discord?".' Olga also had a talent for acting; when, some months before Mary's birth, the mother had taken her along to a child guidance clinic where she was advised to let Olga attend a playgroup for one hour each Monday (reduced to half an hour because she was too difficult to manage), 'Olga did a brilliant impersonation of the doctor greeting me when I arrived'.

In September 1951, when Olga was 5½ years old, her elder sister Helen contracted polio and was admitted to hospital. She spent seven weeks in an iron lung and years in hospital; later she was at home in a wheelchair, attending a local grammar school, and spending much time with Olga, with whom 'she had a close sisterly relationship (including arguments and much fun-making!)'. Helen's mind was not affected, but she died in 1965. This was the greatest grief the family had to cope with, but by that time Olga had recovered (see below).

The following incident gives us a glimpse of the difficult situation as well as of Olga's condition at that time. While Helen was in hospital in the iron lung and the youngest a baby of half a year (late September 1951, when Olga was 5½), Olga contracted whooping cough and the matron suggested that she be nursed in the same hospital. After one night, the doctor told the parents that he was sorry but Olga could not stay any longer because 'she has been scaring us to death by jumping from bed to bed and wandering from ward to ward; not to mention perching herself somewhere near the ceiling'. (When Olga was 33 she told us that she remembered the incident very well and that she was trying to find her sister. This tallies with her information that later, when she once ran 'away from home' she was actually running *to* a place well known to her. We have evidence from other sources suggesting that such 'running away' is not merely avoiding home but at the same time going to an already familiar and well-liked place. Thus such observations need not – as they might well seem to do at first sight – contradict the claim, which in our view is correct, that autistic children are reluctant to enter unfamiliar terrain or tolerate situations new to them.)

When Olga was six, her mother, determined (as we have said) to 'go right back to baby level with her', decided to ignore the verdict about 'brain damage' because 'I thought that her problems were rather of an emotional nature' (this was long before the parents had ever heard of autism, and when anyway professionals had not yet hardened into their 'ineducability' stance, and had also less experience with autistic children than they have now). 'To me, Olga was just a very puzzling child who I hoped and trusted would improve over the years.'

While Helen remained dangerously ill for two years, Olga had to (and did) accept her mother's daily visits to Helen's hospital. Olga was then fetched from school by a senior girl. Later, when her mother could be at home more often, Olga was still left very free, often in the garden, with the mother exerting a degree of discipline ('mainly to reduce disruption in the family, but also to protect Olga from being ridiculed by other children; further treating her as much as possible as a normal child'). Already before this time, discipline was often enforced. For instance, when Olga was four, her mother said to her in a stern voice 'don't you *dare*!' when Olga was about to spit out her food during a meal. When Olga once threw a kitten into the air, she was told something like: 'Poor pussy! That is *cruel*! I won't let you have her when you do that!' 'I tried in general to inculcate kindness to others.' In dealing with Olga's tantrums the mother had in fact already practised the art of going back to babyhood. 'Olga used to roar at the top of her voice, rather frightening at times. But I felt these tantrums were due to the frustration she felt when I could not understand what she needed or she could not understand what I wanted her to do. My instinctive response was to hug her tightly and try to reason with her or explain simply.' (In fact, of course, she was 'doing a Welch'.)

When we asked the mother to explain exactly how she had reared Olga during her autistic phase, she wrote: 'I had no definite plan at all, not knowing anything about autism, but I had been an infant teacher from the age of 18 and knew quite a bit about normal children. I was simply a housewife trying to supply the needs of the family . . . Much of my time went on cooking and laundering, or sewing and knitting to clothe my children. Olga would either potter about outside or stay in the kitchen with me, perhaps playing with the contents of a drawer. We occasionally went for a walk as a family or went for a picnic. We always had birthday tea parties and a children's party at Christmas.' (which the father could not bear to attend). 'My husband and I went rarely out together since we could not afford a babysitter . . . Once when we went to a horse show I let go of Olga's hand and in a twinkling she was hugging the hind leg of a horse! (age 3½). At age four, when we were strolling along the sea front we noticed that Olga was carrying a bucket she had pinched from one of the stalls! Usually we ignored incidents like these and did not scold her because she did not know better at the time. I treated her rather as a normal very young child, but as one merely different from the others . . . I think Helen's illness made Olga do things for the family because she seemed to sense that the family were in desperate straits . . . I also think that the birth of her younger sister Mary was a godsend to her because through her she learned to play.'

Olga's speech developed gradually, first with the use of single words, or two- or three-word sentences; then on to uttering real sentences. Even very simple utterances could, when some trouble was taken to try to understand her (e.g. by paying attention to the accompanying non-verbal behaviour), be seen to be communicative. For instance when, at 4½ years, she was asked by her mother's brother to 'help Mummy dust' she looked straight at him (for once) and said distinctly 'too work', refusing to do what was too much like work, or something to that effect . . . 'I never had to teach her to speak. Nor was her speech or lack of it ever discussed in front of her. I just treated her as a toddler and the speech came naturally.' When, during the whooping cough episode, an aunt came to care for her at home, Olga once, by design or accident, locked her out while she was out in the rain taking the washing off the line; then asked through the door 'Are you getting wet, Auntie Molly?' At about the same time she once came to the landing and called down 'If you don't come quick Auntie Margaret I shall be sick down the banister!'

During the years when Helen was in hospital, both Olga and Mary 'had to spend endless time in cars visiting Helen in numerous hospitals . . . Our finances desperately low, I started work as soon as I could when both children were settled in the same school. First I worked as a nurse, then, because the nursing hours were inconvenient, as an infant teacher . . . Helen was 14 when she went to a residential school for handicapped children in London. After three months there she developed pneumonia. We fetched her home as soon as she was well enough to travel and I nursed her myself (this was why I gave up the nursing job).' Another impression of the stress on both parents is revealed by a remark of the father about 1952: 'I remember well my dilemma in Newark when I was motoring south and Olga suddenly demanded a toilet. I could not take her into the gentlemen's and dare not risk allowing a strange woman to take her into the ladies'. My wife was at the hospital helping Helen through one of her life-and-death battles; she slept with our daughter in the hospital for seven nights.'

In spite of all these upsets, Olga made steady progress.

In Suffolk, in 1956, 10 years old, Olga formed her first stable friendship, with Harriet (about whom Olga herself told us later that 'she liked her because she was not bossy or a bully'!) 'Like Olga, Harriet was also a "loner". Olga was made welcome in her home, in a family where children were given freedom and the mother was warm and kindly to all children. I could now allow Olga to spend a day there now and then and mix with the four other children'. Yet: 'When Olga was 10 she still made grimaces, whirred her hands round at eye level, had a peculiar gait and caused the other children to say that she was a "nut case". She was still occasionally tormented by other children.'

'On her first try Olga did not pass her eleven-plus examination, which disappointed and humiliated her' (both her sisters, she wrote to us later, seemed to be cleverer than she). 'But she learned to ride a bicycle and played a great deal out of doors on the playground of the school where her father was headmaster.'

Olga now had to leave primary school and was sent as a day pupil to a local private school 'where children were expected to work but where there was a happy, fairly relaxed atmosphere. Olga thrived and made excellent progress – even won prizes'. She was considered for grammar school but arrived there for her interview before she was expected. When asked why she was so early she replied (with typically autistic honesty) "because I wanted to get out of geometry". Needless to say, she lost her chance of a grammar school education.'

'In the next year Olga made little progress (according to Olga: "because she was in the 'secondary school stream' not in the 'grammar school stream' she had become demotivated") and she was rather a nuisance at school, playing up the teachers' (often a sign of progress in an autist). 'But she was still very absent-minded. She also found another good friend in Audrey, who sometimes spent the weekend with us; Olga would also go and stay at her home.'

From now on, Olga progressively lost all her autistic peculiarities. At 13 she became a member of the local choral society 'I think she was 15 when we realised that she no longer appeared different from other children.' Parents of a four-year-old autistic boy could not believe that 'Olga had been exactly like him' and outsiders considered her normal. Her interest in music and especially singing grew, and she had ambitions of becoming an opera singer (as mentioned before, she had a talent for acting).

Since her school did not have a sixth form, she went for two years to 'the best school in the area. This school did nothing special for her except enable her to continue her music, and they taught her to swim. But she had no friends there (mainly because she was a day pupil who had arrived at an already well established boarders' community) . . . After she had an audition at the Royal Academy of Music we were told that she would get in "standing on her head". But her acceptance also depended on an interview and at this she gave a poor account of herself, sadly lacking in confidence when speech was required . . . Later that year, still 18, she was accepted at the Royal College of Music after an audition and an entrance examination.' (Olga said later: 'this came about after one of the RCM's professors had heard me sing and win a class at a local music festival'). When Olga was going to live in London, her mother felt it necessary to go with her for the first time 'to be sure she was competent to travel on the Underground and to warn her of the dangers of city life. But she was only too glad to leave home, where tempers were still often frayed.' She was, as she said later, 'excited at starting a new life and having an identity of my own'. After three fairly happy years ('marred by the loss of my sister at the end of my first year. But I established a few good friendships and had many acquaintances'), she passed her ARCM singing (performing) at the first attempt. She was quite active in church activities connected with the hostel where she was staying, and was 'soaking in as much music as I could'. 'I went out with a boyfriend now and then'. But 'behind the surface happiness I was deeply apprehensive about how I was going to cope with the world on leaving College . . . I dreaded the thought of leaving, having had only occasional and incidental experience of employment such as singing before an audience and invigilating at an entrance exam, by which I earned myself a little cash . . . My only other work experience at this time was a couple of monthly spells working at a local firm, "Haverhill Meat Products"; this was assembly line work . . . I gained my ARCM singing (teaching) in December 1968' (on the advice of her professor she had stayed at college a fourth year and, part time, a fifth year). 'But I had reservations about my vocal technique – I was always trying too hard I guess.' In the fifth year she started part-time work as a sales assistant in an Oxford Street shop. Before long she became an assistant librarian in London and 'was satisfying her growing thirst for knowledge'. In 1978 she was promoted to a post as Senior Library Assistant in the London borough where she had been employed since September 1970. As a sideline, Olga is a fairly prolific oil painter and has exhibited in Suffolk, London and Mildenhall. 'My confidence in my voice returned after a few years' silence from 1974 onwards, and I have had varied solo experience in high standard London amateur opera groups, e.g. as Amneris in Aida and Elisabeth in Don Carlos.' Olga is now well established in London, where she lives in fairly poor accommodation, but this she considers 'part of living in London'. While content with her life in London, she keeps up contact and has good relations with her parents, appreciating what they have done for her in the years of her illness.

Now (May 1981) she is 'moderately happy in her work although she does not find it sufficiently challenging. Realising that she may never achieve her ambition of becoming a full-time singer she is trying to improve her status in libraries. For this she is, with her usual persistence, taking the various exams that are required. With a full-time job, a flat to run and rehearsals with the Carlos Opera Group she drives herself pretty hard . . . Her recent performance as Lady Macbeth in Verdi's *Macbeth* was described by a normally fairly severe critic as "fabulous" . . . She still manages to find time for the odd party, has several girl friends but as yet has not met Mr Right. This would have to be a caring man who treats her as an equal . . . and does not insist on sex before marriage. She would also love to have children.'

Authors' comments
Both from the 'official' diagnosis (at the time given to Olga's headmistress but not passed on to the parents and confirmed later by Dr L. Wing on the basis of the full information given by Olga's parents) as well as from the many details of Olga's development, of which we have given a sample, it is clear beyond any doubt that she has been severely autistic. Nor can there be any doubt that she has made a full recovery. But she was not one of those 'odd-from-birth' cases; by all accounts she was at the start a healthy, normal baby and there were no nursing difficulties at all, nor was there lack of *rapport* between her mother and her. But as her history shows, she has been subjected, starting with the pemphigus experience, to a veritable bombardment of circumstances and events of the kinds that we have listed as autismogenic. (The delay between her birth and the first breast-feed, though not ideal, has been accepted by so many mother–infant dyads that we feel we can ignore it here.) In fact, she must be a mentally and emotionally very resilient person. She also has very clearly at least one 'islet of good performance' in spite of years of retarded development.

The main credit for her recovery must undoubtedly go to her mother, who rightly or wrongly decided that 'the parents had unwittingly caused Olga's troubles and that they *had* to help her recover'. Here too it is interesting to notice (both in her written notes and in personal discussions) that she herself does not take the slightest credit for having been what we call a 'supermother'; in fact she considers that she has behaved normally. Equally interesting is the fact that, although neither she nor her husband, nor anyone among their acquaintances knew anything about autism, she considered (as we do) that Olga had *emotional* problems. She did intuitively what we believe is required for a successful cure, including early (in fact pre-Welch!) application of the Welch method of 'holding', and treating her child as a normal, but very young child: starting from the baby stage, giving the child playful encouragement yet disciplining her where necessary, no talking about her disabilities in her presence etc. It is sad indeed that when, in 1976, the mother tried to be helpful to other mothers at the York conference of the

Society for Autistic Children, her offer was rejected in so hostile and misguided a manner. But, as the readers of this book will by now know only too well, this is unfortunately typical of the present unhappy state of affairs. Too many parents seem to have become afraid of nursing any hope.

SUSAN – REPORT BASED ON INFORMATION SUPPLIED BY HER MOTHER WHEN THE GIRL WAS 19 YEARS OLD

Susan was a second child, and clearly developed autistic traits very early. From the start she 'responded in no way to people', 'disliked being handled', 'cried most of the time', 'did not sleep', and 'looked very unhappy'. She 'never liked being touched, certainly not to be cuddled or kissed'. Because she refused to be fed from the breast and fed only reluctantly from the bottle, she 'did not thrive from birth on'. Various causes were suspected but the doctor came to believe that she was allergic to cow's milk, and prescribed watered-down 'Cow and Gate' milk powder. The milk content was so low that Susan lost weight and, drinking so little, became dehydrated. A second opinion was obtained from a retired paediatrician who had his doubts about the milk allergy and suggested, since the girl was starving anyway, that her mother risk giving her a full diet of fresh cow's milk. This doctor did not make a definite diagnosis, said something about 'not knowing whether she was perhaps subnormal', but predicted further feeding difficulties. On his second (and last) visit he was satisfied with Susan's improved physical condition. When this doctor died the mother 'decided to disregard unhelpful medical or other advice and bring up the child on her own'.

Throughout the first year of her life Susan continued to reject social contacts of any kind, but she gradually formed some kind of bond with her four years older sister. For instance, she wanted to have a bath only if her sister joined her; even at five years old, she would eat only if her sister was present and, preferably, ate the same food, but she would avoid eye contact with her, and both children faced the wall consistently even during such meals.

The typically autistic 'insistence on sameness' expressed itself in a variety of ways. She rarely ventured out of her bedroom on her own and preferred to stay in bed, rocking, banging her head etc.; even, until late adolescence, she slept deep down under the blankets 'so that she is now worried over the fact that she must be breathing in her own carbon dioxide'. She has always had pronounced 'food fads' and was late in switching over to solids. For a couple of years she would not take solid food at all other than 'Heinz chocolate pudding, mashed banana, and scrambled eggs; at four she began to eat a little fish, after five she now and then had some chicken, and she ate great quantities of chocolate'. She was greatly attached to a furry animal doll which she held against her nose; she has had several of these. She disliked new clothes: 'they had to be familiar'. She kept preferably to fixed routines; for instance she 'had to' feed the cat every day at 5.50 p.m. exactly; 'we have many examples like this'. But, 'since we incorporated many of these routines into our daily family schedule we tend to forget that they originated as adjustments to her addiction to routine'.

Susan has always been extremely perceptive. Although she could not bear being looked at and did not look openly and directly at other people, she 'never missed a trick' and you 'could see her observing everything through lowered eyelids'. 'She was obviously acutely perceptive and all her senses seemed to be hyper-aware: smell, touch, hearing etc.'

As to stereotypies, Susan spent a great deal of time banging her head against various hard surfaces (cot, bed, wardrobes, her chair), and she did a great deal of rocking, as a baby in her high chair, and in bed: 'She often did not much else all night and all day if she could'.

During family holidays on the water she somehow developed a liking for boats, and she 'became a skilled boat hand'. 'But she had no initiative in undertaking anything new of her own accord.' She learned to swim and to paddle a canoe and became a good (single) canoeist; from age nine years on 'she goes in all weathers on trips, preferably to lonely, remote places'. She became a good cyclist at age six years. A chance observation gave some idea of how Susan sometimes 'broke out' of her adherence to sameness; during a trip to Sweden 'where the family stayed in a hotel miles from anywhere on a wild beach, . . . she ventured into breakfast, having no intention of eating anything except a bar of chocolate in her hand. She was surprised at the huge cold table and watched as I helped myself to cheese and pickled herring. It was all beautifully set out. Someone told her that all Swedish children had goat cheese for breakfast and they had a special one for children, of which she was offered a thin sliver. She tasted this and liked it, with the result that all she ate at every meal for ten days was goat cheese. We went to that hotel for the next two years at her request and she still eats goat cheese.'

A trait of Susan that is not common to otherwise so severely withdrawn children is that she 'developed speech at the normal time'. Yet she often spoke in a negativistic, rejecting sense ('I don't want to . . .' with reference to a number of different things whilst rocking and banging her head) – her way of 'throwing a tantrum'? – and she often talked in repetitive and seemingly non-relevant sentences; for instances, during the first sea crossing she banged her head all night shouting all the time one special, totally irrelevant phrase from a nursery story (which reminds us of 'verbal stereotypy' as mentioned in Ch. 4, note 5). However, she developed 'a special interest in words and language, wrote as a child good poetry and won a national prize for essays'. (Her speech, or rather verbal communication, was therefore a curious mixture of autistic and non-autistic traits, and but for the fact that she did speak she resembles in her gift for and interest in language the girl Carla whom we have mentioned in our main text. It seems to us possible that this kind of seemingly contradictory behaviour can develop in autistic children whose 'islet of good performance' is in the literary area.)

In other subjects Susan did not perform very well – 'was not interested in maths, physics, chemistry, French, art, music, dancing or any team games. But she was interested in certain aspects of science, especially natural history; on her canoe trips she liked to observe water life, and she read on science subjects . . . She surprised everyone with her "general studies" paper for "A"-level in which she wrote knowledgeably about Darwin, Madame Curie etc.'

Susan always had sleeping difficulties and only slept when she was really tired. She often goes to bed well after the rest of the family and, from age six on, read and still reads a great deal (often in secret) before falling asleep; 'we have found complete Shakespeare and Roget works well hidden under her bed'.

As to what made Susan autistic, she seems to have been one of those babies who have been described in the literature as 'odd from birth'; of the possible autism-inducing factors that we have listed, the only ones that might apply are prolonged labour and a fairly drastic and possibly traumatising forceps delivery. The parents were *not* inexperienced and the child *was* welcome, even though the father would have preferred a son. She grew up in a cheerful family, although later the atmosphere occasionally became subdued as a consequence of the difficulties caused by her abnormal behaviour. The mother, who was a housewife, though originally trained in fine arts (especially sculpture) stayed at home with Susan for five years, until the girl went to school and so freed her mother, who then took an MSc in psychology and became a professional psychologist.

Perhaps the most interesting part of Susan's history is the fact that her mother coaxed her back to normality (the father has and had a busy doctor's practice), and how she did it. When we discussed this, 19 years after Susan's birth, the mother impressed us as an intelligent and imaginative, energetic, no-nonsense and honest person with a strong enough motherly motivation to have devoted much of her energies to the rehabilitation of her child. But she told us that she did not at all consider herself to have been a 'supermother' or to have done anything out of the ordinary (we have often found that these D I Y mothers believe that they have done 'only what any mother would do under the circumstances'). But she certainly had a strong motherly motivation, which expressed itself not only in what she did and to what extent she concentrated on the child's well-being, but also in the fact that she remembered so much about her child's history (in our experience a good indication of maternal commitment). She had not done any holding in the Welch way (probably because the child resisted being touched so much; Susan also said herself that until she was approximately seven she could never approach other people closely 'because they smelled funny'). But the mother had made it her job 'to be with the child as much as possible, for instance by taking the child with us into the living room and bolting the door, and also sitting in Susan's room at night while she banged her head'. She certainly put up with a great deal of discomfort by tolerating the endless and noisy head-banging. 'My approach to the child was to realise intuitively that she was under stress and to try and find ways of alleviating this to enable her to fit into the family . . . I suspect that she finally realised that whatever she did in no way altered my approach to her, *which was basic approval of her as a human being*' (emphasis ours). 'I have only once smacked the elder child and never the younger one . . . Food seemed to be one of her main problems, so I merely gave her whatever she wanted to eat. I would never cook anything special for her, except chips. I always offered her what we were eating, but accepted her refusal without any emotion. Since my own favourite foods are good bread and butter and potatoes with lots of butter, of which I haven't yet tired, I didn't see why she shouldn't eat what she enjoyed . . . As we never went anywhere for about five years I managed to avoid outside criticism.'

Now (May 1981) Susan is 19 years of age. Even though her achievements at secondary school were not outstanding, she has been accepted on interview by a good drama school where she is reading for an honours degree in drama. After having had to find her feet in the first term away from home, she has had a good and happy second term. She is in general doing well and fits well into society. She has good relations with boys and girls – even had a 'steady' for two years – but does not use the pill and certainly rejects casual sex even while having to live in a sexually loose-living, promiscuous student community. She has not so far formed a serious tie with a prospective partner. She is now quite a gourmet, although she is fussy with regard to her food and, for instance, makes sure that salads etc. are properly washed. Her life is still full of rituals. She still takes nightly, rapid baths, keeping the bathroom door open 'in case there are spiders'.

Authors' comments

Susan's syndrome has clearly not been entirely typical of early childhood autism. She did display all the usual 'nine points' in one way or another, but was unusual in her ambivalent attitude towards speech and language. On the one hand she has shown rejecting and non-communicative aspects in her speech; on the other she has a great sensitivity for words and language, and has written poetry and essays of merit. But she has used clear 'verbal stereotypies' and as a child has been reluctant to communicate directly with others. Language may have her interest as one of those puzzling 'islets of good performance'. But she certainly belongs to the category of children about whom we have been writing in this book.

Apart from the prolonged labour and the possibly traumatising forceps delivery, we have not been able to find any of the factors in her early history that we have listed as 'autismogenic', and we can suggest no explanation of the origin of her autism.

Her rehabilitation has certainly succeeded either completely or to such a remarkable extent that she now fits well into the normal range. Although her mother does not consider that she has done anything out of the ordinary, it seems to us clear, and significant, that she has not allowed Susan to withdraw totally from the family, and that she has even spent much extra time and effort with her, e.g. has throughout accepted her as a 'human being' and has done the equivalent of the later phases of 'holding': keeping company and interacting. It is impossible to say, but seems likely in view of the mother's overall attitude, that she would have held her child bodily in a quite normal way and perhaps even more persistently than she would have done had the child been normal, for Susan's incessant crying and other signs of discomfort would have made her do this; but the child's determined resistance made this practically impossible.

FAE – REPORT BASED ON INFORMATION SUPPLIED BY HER PARENTS

Both Fae's parents are university graduates; her mother has a PhD. In November 1974, when they had been married for five years, they took in a foster child, a four-year-old, very affectionate and active boy, Adrian, who thrived with them from the beginning. On 11 November 1975 Fae was born. The pregnancy was terminated early by inducing labour because the mother was losing weight. Delivery was by forceps; birth weight approximately 3 kg. The mother's inverted nipples made it impossible for Fae to suck effectively, but during the first days no-one realised that she received no nourishment. After four days she was taken into intensive care because she screamed incessantly and ran a high temperature. She was first sedated and then, when she had calmed down, was fed through a tube. She had contact with her mother every four hours. During the next four days she was bottle-fed by her mother with the latter's own milk after attempts to breast-feed her with the aid of a nipple shield had failed.

On 21 November mother and child returned home. Two days later the mother contracted a severe gastro-enteritis, lost about 6 kg in two days, and her milk dried up, so that she had to bottle-feed Fae with 'formula'. It took four weeks of bottle-and-breast-feeding before the mother's milk production was fully restored.

On 4 January 1976, i.e. when Fae was less than two months old, the father had to leave to take up a new position 300 miles away from his family. Just before his departure a severe gale cut off the electricity supply, which left the mother without electricity for four days.

During the next six months the family was visited only occasionally by the father for brief stays. He came back at Easter for two weeks, and after that on most weekends. The mother and the two children did not join him until 22 July 1976, to live at first in temporary accommodation. The sale of their old house, the move, and finding a new house took a great deal of the parents' attention and caused them considerable anxiety.

After one week in their new quarters the children were 'parked' with the mother's parents while she herself went off to take care of the transport of her two horses. This took six instead of the anticipated two days.

After two weeks in the new living conditions, Adrian began to feel increasingly unhappy, mainly because he had no friends. Partly because of this, the whole family went to stay for a week with friends in their former home base, where Adrian was happier.

Two months after this on 1 October 1976, the family moved into their present home in the countryside. By this time Adrian, though still missing his friends, had become more settled.

On 20 December 1976, when Fae was 13 months old, a boy, John, was born. That winter was exceptionally cold with much snow and severe frost; apart from John's room and the kitchen, the house was unheated. In addition the parents had financial worries. Four months later they decided to sell part of the house; this sale caused problems which were not solved until eight months later.

In August 1977, when Fae was 21½ months old, we visited the family for the first time after the parents' marriage. We knew nothing of their circumstances but resumed personal contact because we happened to be spending our holiday not far from them. On our arrival we found John asleep in his pram in a sheltered place in the courtyard, and Fae sitting up in her pram in the garden, out of sight of John. The mother, with Adrian nearby, was working in the garden some 70 yards away. Fae, whose toys were lying scattered on the ground around her pram, did not look at us, did not invite contact but neither did she cry; she stared just past us, and repeatedly shook her head in a stereotyped way. When, later, her mother took her from the pram the girl faced away from us or looked past or 'through' us, frequently head-shaking. The mother told us later that she did this head-shaking a great deal when meeting strangers, when upset, 'and frequently when she hears other people speak disparagingly about her'. She did *not* head-shake when they said nice things about her (revealing, of course, quite good understanding of speech, at least of tone and mime). The parents told us that she was a 'very good' baby and was left much on her own, 'because we had come to the conclusion that this was the way Fae wanted it'. Fae did not walk or stand unsupported and used only two words: 'bottle' (to denote the bottle by which John was fed and from which she herself was fed orange juice, but also to indicate John himself); and 'Adrian' for the eldest boy (with whom she was on good terms and had regular eye contact).

The parents told us that the mother's mother and the health visitor had both expressed concern about Fae's slow progress, but the parents themselves (having experience only with the much older Adrian) were not unduly worried and had decided 'to wait for things to happen'.

A few days after our visit, we wrote to the parents to tell them that we too felt that Fae gave cause for concern. Without mentioning the word autism, we suggested that her development might pick up if, instead of being left so much on her own, she were taken into the family and so exposed to normal family life and, we hoped, be stimulated to interact with parents, sibs, perhaps with pets and with friends. Just after our letter arrived, Fae and John (according to a pre-arranged plan) went to stay for a week with the mother's sister whom Fae knew and liked, who is a professional caregiver of mentally handicapped young children and who herself had a six-week-old baby and another child three months older than Fae, very bright, extrovert, and kind to Fae. The parents themselves took Adrian with them for a visit to the mother's brother in France. Adrian was taken along because he had shown signs of being jealous of the father's affection for Fae. Upon the reunion, the parents, who had been prepared for initial rejection by the younger children, were delighted to be at once warmly welcomed by both.

From now on the parents began to act on our advice. Seven weeks after their return from France the mother wrote to us that 'Fae is now quite a different child; everyone has been remarking on it . . . When we returned from France she was walking and talking more too . . . We put Adrian and Fae in the same bedroom. They chatter together in the morning for about an hour . . . Her vocabulary grows daily, and she strings two and three words together, e.g. "Adrian smart shirt"; "off we go". She is far more entertaining and outgoing; and she is becoming very helpful, taking off her coat and putting it away and then putting John's away too. She also takes things to people when requested.' John's pram and her own were now put close together in the afternoon. She began to make jokes: 'I was most amused to hear her say "grr" behind me and be dug in the back one day. When I turned round I saw that she had my red washing-up glove on her hand in front of her face; after saying "grr" once more she collapsed into giggles, saying "Fae hord monter" (Fae horrid monster), no doubt derived from games played with Adrian.'

Four months after our visit the mother began to take Fae to a 'mothers' and toddlers' group' where she could meet strangers and play with other children. This group met twice a week for two hours at a time. Activities were not organised by the adults; the mothers chatted to each other and played with the children. There were toys, books, paints and jigsaws. The children played alongside rather than with the others. At Fae's request,

Adrian took her to Sunday school one morning (she usually went to church with her parents). Both children came back 'full of it'. Her friendship with Adrian became even closer, and she soon began to take part in his many 'pretend games'.

We visited the family again for the day in December 1977. Fae now walked very well, was initially a little shy of us but no more so than a normal child, and she soon began to interact with us, making normal eye-to-eye contact and speaking well. Her head-shaking had subsided, having appeared only briefly and barely noticeable at our arrival, and once, more vigorously and repeatedly when, walking with us on a country road, she was badly frightened (naturally) by a car that suddenly and inconsiderately hooted loudly less than 50 yards behind her. Throughout this visit she took a normal, cheerful part in the (clearly warm and happy) family life. Again, her mother said that 'she was now so much more fun'.

Next August (1978) we paid another one-day visit. When we arrived, Fae again showed slight and quickly passing gaze aversion, again no more than most normal children of our acquaintance. Within 15 minutes she had climbed onto E. A.'s lap to show her a decorated box and her multicoloured plasticine. Pointing at the pictures on the box, she said 'what's this?' and echolalied E. A.'s replied ('That's a dolly's head'; 'here are her arms' etc.), which again we consider fairly normal. Soon afterwards she approached N. and joined him cheerfully in simple hand-to-hand games. During lunch (with, apart from the family, an adult guest, two visiting children and us two) she interacted with all in an alert, lively way. Her speaking was now well above normal for children of her age; for instance, later that day she told E. A. a long, fairly complicated story about herself and two other people, expressing herself clearly and using good phrasing.

The mother comments: 'I think Fae reacted mostly to lack of maternal care. I felt I had failed her in hospital, and that she disliked me. For instance, she would cry when I picked her up, but was soothed when I handed her to my husband. This negative response to me passed after approximately one month.'

Mid-May 1981, the mother added in a letter to us: 'Both Fae and Adrian always remember you despite the infrequency of your visits (approximately once a year) . . . Fae is a quiet and fairly slow worker but progresses evenly on all fronts . . . This was confirmed by her teacher . . . She does not fiddle with things she doesn't understand . . . She is intensely feminine and motherly, adores babies and mothers us all ("Poor Mummy, *I* think you are beautiful" . . . "Poor Daddy, *I* think you've made the greenhouse base level") . . . She is demanding in wanting help, getting paint mixed, pastry out, hair band fixed, etc . . . They say at school that she is showing signs of taking the lead in play . . .'.

Authors' comments

In our experience, this case is representative of numerous others which do not come to the attention of doctors because the child's derailment is detected early, and is speedily corrected by good and properly adjusted 'extra parenting' and by life in a good family. We have no doubt that, by all criteria applicable at such an early age, Fae's early behaviour deviations were incipient autism.

The following circumstances seem to us to have been autism-inducing: possibly the forceps delivery; in hospital the mother–child interaction was seriously disrupted in the first few days; the baby had sucking difficulties which were not detected at first; she was switched from (ineffectual) breast-feeding to bottle-feeding and back to breast-feeding; the family had to make a drastic move and had to adjust to new conditions while the parents were under stress of various kinds; the next sib was born only 13 months after her own birth. Her consequent withdrawal elicited a well intentioned but almost certainly harmful withdrawal by the parents (which was intended as an adjustment to the child's needs). Both the retardation and the stereotyped formalisation of the conflict-head-shaking had occurred as secondary, long-term results. The father and mother, themselves without experience of this type of child, showed their parenting gifts by responding immediately and fully to constructive advice. It seems as if the one week's stay with her experienced caregiver–aunt and her family had come at a crucial stage. Fae's re-introduction into her obviously good family circle and her joining a toddler group made her return quickly to normal; in some respects she is now well above normal, mentally and socially.

We called unannounced at Fae's family's home in early April 1981. The parents were abroad and the paternal grandparents were staying with the children. Adrian was away during the two hours we spent with the grandmother and the two other children, who were both playing indoors because Fae was recovering from a throat infection for which she had been given antibiotics. Fae and John hardly recognised us but had within minutes dropped their initial slight shyness and began to show us their colouring books, dolls, and soon their little plastic farm animals and the toy farm in their playroom. Both children were outgoing, lively, very alert and listening to and telling stories, Fae obviously taking delight in her first steps in learning to read. The grandmother had clearly forgotten about Fae's initial difficulties but remembered once we recalled them. Fae and John played well together; all in all a delightful pair of bright and cheerful children with a great sense of humour.

GEORGE – REPORT BASED ON INFORMATION SUPPLIED FROM 1979 ON BY HIS FATHER AND MOTHER

We have corresponded with them for some years, and E. A. stayed with the family for one day and one night in the late summer of 1980, when George was 12 years old.

George is the youngest of four children of two teachers: the father has a demanding outside job; the mother, likewise a hardworking person, lives at home.

The parents report that George's birth was normal and that at first 'nothing out of the ordinary had been noticeable'. But 'he was such an easy child that he almost escaped his father's notice.' It was not until he was approximately two years old ('when he should begin to show some initiative') that his parents began to realise that he tended rather to withdraw into himself and avoid contact with others. When they tried to hug or caress him he pushed them away, sometimes even slapped their faces. When taken to bed in the evenings he hid quickly under the blankets. In the mornings he preferred to stay in bed, and when his mother lifted him up gently he would turn his face away and try to avoid any contact. He would always begin by refusing to drink or eat, but would accept food after his mother had held him on her lap for some time. As soon as someone said something to him, or even about him, he would slide down, lie flat on the floor and would often even crawl under the table (where he tended to spend a great deal of his time). 'It was always quite a job to take and hold him on your lap because he resisted, kicked and lashed out.' On such occasions the mother found that the best way to cope with him was to go or stay alone with him in a room and to press him firmly against her body, not speaking but merely rocking him for a long time. This made him gradually give up his struggling. But as soon as one of his sibs would enter the room, perhaps calling 'hello!', he would renew his struggles and might even throw objects such as plates from the table. But once he stopped resisting, allowed himself to be stroked and was willing to drink and eat 'the worst part of the day was over', and he would let his mother clean, wash, dress and feed him.

George had and still has various styereotypies: head shaking ('no'), nail biting, sucking at several of his fingers (which the mother suppressed by painting them with a distasteful substance), and violent back-and-forth rocking of his head when someone approached him when he was in bed. His speech developed 'a little late' but was of good quality and content, but when upset he began to speak softly and to slur his words. His walking started late but was normal. However, when he was about two years old, it began to strike his parents that 'many simple activities which normal children of his age master easily, caused him difficulties, and when he engaged in them he did so listlessly.' 'He was approximately seven when he first started dressing himself' and 'he did not tie his shoelaces until he was ten'. Relatives and friends began to say that he was being spoiled and ought to be handled more firmly. 'But on occasion he could astonish everyone by his exceptional technical abilities.' Any moving objects or contraptions fascinated him and once, returning home with his mother from a visit to one of her friends, he rushed round the house and collected all sorts of materials. In no time at all he constructed a cardboard model of a cuckoo clock that he had observed at the friend's home. He made a hole in the centre through which he fixed a piece of wire to form a pendulum, which he moved by hand. 'Whenever George worked on such projects one could hardly imagine that this was the same child who was being criticised for being clumsy, listless, uninterested and unenterprising.'

A problem arose when, at three-plus years of age, he had to be taken to an eye specialist because of a 'lazy eye'. His 'good' eye (which was not all that good either) was covered to force him to use his 'underemployed' eye. His mother, 'as always firm and consistent', ensured that the treatment was applied without interruptions. It was successful, but 'George did react to this episode by withdrawing even more and taking an increasing part of his mother's time'. 'To make him do anything one had to do it together with him' for he did very little of his own accord. Much of his time was spent 'playing with a radio', under a table in the corner of the room, where he would stay for hours, until his mother would take him out into the open.

The parents now decided that the father had better give up part of his job so as to have more time for his family, and to lighten the work load of his wife.

Whenever George was unwell, he reverted to wanting to stay in bed, hiding under the blankets, lying motionless with his face to the wall, refusing social contact and also rejecting food and drink – 'I won't get better anyway'. The parents felt that he needed them in order to want to live, yet rejected them. This spurred them on to giving their utmost in devotion, love and patience.

When four years old, George went to a nursery school. This was 'a terrible experience' for him. In the mornings he once more began to refuse to get up; when taken out of bed he resisted being washed or dressed. He again refused food and drink. But by starting early and having endless patience and perseverance, his mother managed every day to get him to school on time.

In this school George kept himself completely isolated, from the children as well as from the teacher. The children found him 'odd' and soon began to kick, scratch and bite him, but George did not retaliate. Sometimes he returned home with his hands covered with blood. The teacher said that 'she could not prevent this'. George once more suffered an overall setback and became unmanageable even at home. His parents decided to take him away from this school and to teach him at home until he would be old enough for primary school. This had a good effect, though much of his autistic behaviour persisted. However, when the time came, he had recovered sufficiently to be accepted in a normal primary school.

Here matters did not go well either. George made no contact with the teacher, and probably none with the children, for he did not learn the names of any of them. At home he once more began to refuse to get up in the mornings, would withdraw socially, and lie for long times on the floor, 'playing with his radio'. Attempts by his parents to encourage him to play with other children failed. The family began to be regarded by the local community as 'being incapable of bringing up children; they are rather peculiar people'. 'No wonder their children behave so oddly.' (The family came from another part of the country; the children read a great deal of rather unusual books: novels, books on astronomy; the daughters were sometimes given tools as birthday presents.) When the parents invited other children to their home, the invitations were accepted by the parents concerned, but on the day not a single child turned up.

A new teacher at school now tried to make George work by keeping him in after hours each day, but this had no effect. When the parents suggested that their child might well work only if the teacher were to befriend him first, this opinion was ignored. Once more George began to regress at home to his earlier behaviour, including bedwetting, refusing to get up in the morning, refusing food, hiding under the table etc.

The parents, who are both qualified teachers, then decided to exercise their legal right and take George out of school and teach him at home themselves. At once he began to improve and began to show interest in life and the outside world, and to make progress in his work. The father, a music therapist who works in a school for children 'with learning difficulties', had among his pupils a girl who behaved autistically. By teaching her together with a one-year younger boy, and encouraging the girl to help this boy, he had made her 'emerge' from her self-isolation and form a friendship with the boy: she cheered up whenever she saw him, made him join in simple games, pointed out pictures to him, pronounced words for him and spoke short sentences for him. This experience made the parents decide to try out a similar procedure with George. This worked: when he was asked to help others he proved keen to do so. When members of the family fell ill, he began to take care of them and in the process became more capable. His overall progress was such that at the start of the new school year the parents considered him ready to go to school once more. A new teacher treated him more suitably than his predecessor: he encouraged George rather than coerced him, and helped him when he floundered. If such help was not forthcoming, George regressed once more to infantile behaviour. Every change in his environment frightened him. Whenever this happened his speech, which had always been so well up to standard, would become soft and slurred, as in the past, so that people could not make out what he was saying. When he was eight he was reported to be 'still unable to learn the multiplication tables, but to know difficult and sophisticated electronics terminology'. He gladly took his turn to give a talk to his form, but the teacher had to remind him: 'Don't talk about too difficult things, George, or the others won't be able to follow you'. Once started, he was self-assured, made appropriate jokes, and aroused and held the interest of all the children. 'But when the classroom was visited by a group of parents he hid like a frightened little bird, losing all his confidence.'

When George was 10 years old, the family moved from the small town where they had been living to a more rural community, where they acquired a house with a large garden. This meant, of course, another change of school and of teacher. In his new environment George thrived. He became friends with a delicate and vulnerable boy, both becoming mutually considerate and helpful to each other. In contacts both with children and adults, George began to be 'gentle and careful not to hurt them in any way'. The family acquired a few geese and sheep; these became George's special friends. 'He is particularly gentle with them and they trust him; in fact, he is the only one in the family who can reassure the geese when they shy away from anyone else; they even let him take them in his arms. He also spends much time with the sheep, stroking them and talking to them. He treats them the way his parents always treated him, and calms them when they are apprehensive; he explains that this reassures them.' But although George now developed well, he remained vulnerable. Yet, while he had 'for years' failed to learn to swim, a new teacher taught him, and in a short while George passed two grades.

When E. A. visited him and his family in the autumn of 1980, George was 12 years old. Together with his mother he met E. A. at the railway station. He was for a while just a little shy, but from the start behaved in an open, friendly manner: he shook hands with a smile on his face and made perfectly normal eye contact. His manner, like that of the other three children of the family, was trusting and endearing, and a twinkle in his eye often enlivened his talk. He 'coped well in a normal secondary school but still needed occasional help'. Although the change from primary to secondary school had caused a fairly severe regression, no one could now have suspected that he had ever been so deeply disturbed. His speech was fluent and he showed a very good command of his native language. He was still keenly interested in animals (not only in the sheep and geese but also in his stick insects). He was well integrated in the family. He wrote stories in which his animals were often the main characters. His interest in all things electric had persisted. Like so many other children, George was vulnerable because he had and has a trusting attitude towards the world. There was a warm and harmonious family atmosphere, with the father taking full part in family life in spite of having a demanding job. All in all, the boy had clearly recovered at least as far as Judy (see the next case history).

Authors' comments

Although the parents had not heard of autism until years after George was born, and although no official diagnosis of autism was made, their descriptions of George's behaviour show him to have been a fairly typical autist: at two years of age he had developed pronounced social withdrawal, apprehensiveness of the unusual ('adherence to sameness'), a tendency to stay in bed, and several stereotypies. While it is true that his speech developed merely 'a little late' and developed well, it deteriorated whenever he was under social stress, in an unfamiliar environment or when unwell; he then spoke softly and in such a slurred manner that he became incomprehensible and to all intents and purposes non-communicative, perhaps even stereotyped. Although his autistic behaviour did not attract the special attention of his parents until he was two years old, the symptoms as described were then well advanced. Since he had been one of those over-quiet babies, and because his parents were hard-working people who had already three older children, it seems more likely that there may have been what we would now recognise as early warning signs (see, for example, Fae's report and Allan, Ch. 9, note 1) but that they had not been recognised as such.

We have not been able to trace much in George's early history that could account for the onset of his withdrawn behaviour. Being already 'over quiet' from birth, he may have elicited less attention than a more demanding baby would have done (his father, after all, did not notice him much at first), and the parents told us that when George was six months old the family moved out of their house (for a thorough reconstruction) and returned there five months later when the house looked quite different. These moves, and the many changes of school, teachers and other circumstances that caused temporary regression may have exacerbated an initially mild condition.

In May 1981, the parents wrote that George was now coping well, at school and socially, but that he still needed occasional help and support; he had, since September 1980, had one mild regression when both parents were exceptionally busy, but he had recovered as soon as the mother gave him more attention. He acquires excellent knowledge and understanding of things that arouse his interest.

There are two aspects of the way in which his parents have treated him that in our view deserve special emphasis: (a) the mother's intuitive and very successful application of what amounts to 'forcible holding' in the Welch manner when George was very young; and (b) the father's 'brain-wave' in cashing in on what he had, with admirable insight, initiated at school: encouraging George to extend help to others – sick people, another vulnerable boy, animals. Finally, the father writes that he has since been in contact, as a teacher of children 'with learning difficulties', with quite a number of autistic children. He made the following general comments on his experiences, which we find worth passing on.

(a) Few of his colleagues recognise early autistic traits in pupils, nor do they find it necessary to give such children more than normal attention (very serious, advanced cases do not as a rule reach their school).

(b) Those adults who are themselves by nature diffident and vulnerable achieve the best results with this type of children.

(c) Autistic children need *above anything else love. The more they reject loving approaches the more they need them* (emphasis ours).

(d) Even when such children develop well, they remain sensitive and vulnerable persons (yet the determined way in which they overcome their fears often reveals remarkable courage).

JUDY – REPORT BASED ON INFORMATION SUPPLIED BY HER PARENTS

Judy was a planned, wanted first child of relatively young parents. The mother is an English graduate, the father was at first a student (without a grant), then a music teacher; the mother had to be the breadwinner until just before Judy was born. The baby was due in mid-February 1970 but, because of severe hypertension and toxaemia, the mother was admitted to hospital shortly before Christmas 1969. She was allowed a brief stay at home over Christmas, but was back in hospital on 4 January, where she was put in a dark room, with a sign 'silence' on the door and with instructions 'not to move' etc. On 8 January, the birth was induced, four or five weeks early. The 'doctor did not have much hope for the baby, and felt that there was risk for the mother – about even chances'. When in the evening there was not enough progress, the mother was sedated, and a night nurse sat with her throughout the night. Next day the mother was 'hurried on'; an incision was made and then, with 'just a lift with the forceps', Judy was born. The mother heard the surprised comment from the senior registrar: 'The baby is in quite good condition!' Her weight was about 2 kg. The mother was shown the baby but, without her glasses, she could not see much; then Judy was taken to the incubator and the mother went back into the darkened room. She felt 'inflated by a ridiculous pride'.

Judy showed distressed breathing for which she was given oxygen; she was fed through the navel yet lost some weight. On the fifth day the mother was wheeled to the baby, who was then being fed through a nasal tube. When, on the eleventh day, the mother was discharged, Judy stayed behind in hospital. There could be no breast-feeding because the mother was on steroids. The mother visited Judy twice daily for the bottle-feeds the baby had energy for; tube-feeding took care of the rest of Judy's ration. She was in hospital for one month and 'had much attention from one particular nurse, who spent approximately three hours each day caring for her'.

Like many babies in the ward, Judy had a chronic sore bottom (she was fed on 'Regal', for which the hospital had a contract). She made a 'dopey and dull impression'. When once given 'expressed breast milk' she was at once more alert. Then she was given 'SMA' (another formula milk) and began to do better.

When Judy came home 'everyone had a streaming cold' and she was given 'Vick' between vest and nightie. The mother now put her on demand-feeding; because she was weak she was given many small feeds. She soon began to 'yell for a feed' as soon as she woke up. She smiled clearly at five weeks. At six weeks she lifted her head well. While cooking, doing some of the housework etc. the mother carried her round a great deal, holding her on her hip. At five months, Judy stood without help if she had a chair to hold on to. She babbled very early and was heard to say 'Dada', but her manual skills developed slowly (yet later she became very good on the violin, for which, however, the physical skills had to be acquired by a great effort). She talked early, with good communication and phrasing.

The first summer 'was idyllic for us all'. Judy spent the mornings in the garden; in the afternoons her mother wheeled her to the park, where she could crawl in the grass. When wheeled under the trees Judy 'would sing with joy'. The mother made daisy chains and chatted non-stop with her. At the end of the afternoon they would collect the father from his work. 'At this time we were rather an inward-looking family.' When Judy was approximately one year old, the parents bought their small new home. Judy took the move quite well. At the same time the mother became pregnant again.

Now Judy could walk well over several hundred yards but she made sure always to hold on to at least one finger of one of her parents; she was 16 months before she walked alone. She loved food, and was 'just getting around to spooning for herself' when the mother, with her pregnancy halfway, had the first of four admissions to hospital because of her high blood pressure. This first time it was just for a weekend's observation. The father took leave so as to be with Judy. The parents had always explained to her that her mother might have to go, but could not predict when. For the last three weeks of the pregnancy the father's mother came to stay and help out. 'It soon became clear that Judy was unhappy. When her father came back from work she dashed to him, climbed on his knee and refused to be dislodged until bedtime.' The father's mother greatly disapproved of this, 'we were making a rod for our own backs, spoiling her etc.' She also reported that 'during the day she did not talk to Judy so as not to over-excite her'. Although the father gave Judy full attention during the evenings, 'she became quieter, less jolly apart from slightly crazy laughing spells or crying'. The grandmother rarely changed her nappies; the father did this before he went off to work, at lunch time, and in the evening. His mother told him: 'Judy never fusses, she is quiet and no trouble.'

When the mother's second pregnancy was in its 38th week she was 'listed for induction' but as it happened she started labour spontaneously after a short rest in hospital 'and a brisk walk'. In spite of her urgent requests, she had been refused permission to rest at home, which she wanted because she was worried about Judy. After an easy delivery the second child, Anne, was born (during the birth the father was not allowed to be present because at the last moment a film crew, whose original subject 'did not perform as hoped', was 'given' the mother as a substitute). After four days, Judy's mother was allowed to return home (with the new baby); Judy was now 20 months old. When the mother 'took Judy to see the baby, Judy responded by saying unhappily: "oh dear, dear, DEAR!" and by turning away'. 'From now on Judy screamed frantically whenever Anne appeared, or even when I went to the fridge to get the milk . . . She regressed in many ways, e.g. in the way she managed her food; by a great deal of thumb sucking and chewing her "fringey", she talked less well although what she said was intelligible; she also developed a "nervous tummy" (her nappies were plastered about half a dozen times a day in a way that had never happened before) . . . We remarked (out of earshot) that it needed only a return to crawling to make the picture complete.' At this time she also began to have feverish ear infections with deafness, loss of appetite and even refusal to eat. The visiting midwife commented that 'in her 20 years of work and raising her own family she had never seen a child so disturbed by the arrival of the next baby'. She suggested that the parents give Judy sedatives, which they did not do. (The severity of the upset might, of course, have been due to the previous periods of separation and the unsuitable behaviour of the father's mother.) The father's mother, who had stayed as long as the mother was in hospital, now went home and the maternal grandmother came to help instead.

The mother, who knew something about 'next baby rejection' was 'puzzled by the *way* Judy showed that she was upset'. 'She clung to me desperately but in absolute terror of Anne.' As a consequence, Anne received very sketchy treatment from her mother, who was always rushing to Judy to soothe her and sing to her. She told Judy time and again, particularly when Judy was about to fall asleep, 'I'm not going away again. I did not want to leave you before but was told to go to hospital because I was ill. Anne will love you and will later be very proud of her big sister' etc. The father helped a great deal too but he had to be away from 8.15 a.m. till 7 p.m. The only time when Anne received full attention was after Judy had gone to bed, when she was potted or fed etc.

'Judy became terrified of going into any room except her own bedroom. When she was given chocolate to stop her screaming she was too tense to swallow and the chocolate simply streamed down her chin.' Soon *any* baby, *any* stranger, *any*thing to do with hospitals, especially doctors, *any* sound of crying, *any* loud noise (e.g. the rumbling of the fridge, the sound of passing lorries, the vacuum cleaner, the sound of someone knocking next door) and also the sight of a cat or dog would set her screaming. She even began to hate the parents' best friends (with whose child, of her own age, she had been friendly); if she saw them she would call 'goodbye, goodbye!' and run inside and close the door.

Walks together became impossible; Judy would go rigid and yell as soon as she was put on the pram seat, even if Anne was asleep in the pram. A little bag of 'Jelly Tots', her cuddly blanket, were no good. If anyone came to visit the house, she would whine 'put her to bed' and would go to her cot (the use of 'her' for 'me' was of course a typical regression). She was sometimes found cringing in a corner sobbing silently, and with fresh (self-inflicted) scratches on her face and elsewhere on her body. Trying, at the sensible advice of the family doctor, to help Judy 'associate Anne with happy things' did not succeed; Judy would not relax until Anne was carried off.

Walks became more or less possible when Judy was allowed, though held by the hand, to lag far behind the pram.

Her screaming now developed into 'spectacular tantrums', and the parents decided that they had to try to discipline her (see below). Both parents became seriously overwrought and the father completely withdrew for a time, but recovered from his depression after treatment. 'Curiously enough, Judy became reconciled first of all with Anne, the cause of all the trouble. All other children still terrified her but she could play alongside Anne.'

Then, when Anne was approximately one year old, the family went to stay with an old college friend of the mother. But the friend had a baby and Judy went back to 'stage one': 'on hunger strike, hiding under her bed, withdrawing by cringing on top of the washing machine, excessive thumb sucking, holding and rubbing her "fringey" against her nose etc'.

'After three days' screaming and starvation we left to go camping. With teeth chattering as we drove off in driving rain and sleet Judy said: "That's a lot better, isn't it, Daddy, a *lot* better".'

The breakthrough came when her three-year-old cousin Peter came to stay. At first Judy avoided him consistently, but when her mother said: 'Judy, Peter is very sad because he hasn't got his mummy with him. Could you try to comfort him a little?' Judy *ran* downstairs, took him by the hand and said: 'Come on Peter, let's go and see the squirrel!' From then on the two were inseparable and went everywhere hand in hand.

'Still, a year after Anne's birth, Judy was safe only at home.' Then the parents considered sending her to Smallbridge Nursery School – 'a kill or cure idea'. She still had tantrums – a doctor staying with the family gave her a sedative, 'which produced a rare four hours' sleep'. At about this time disciplining started in earnest. This was done as follows. Rule I: food could be left but not slung around. Penalties: (1) warning; (2) severe warning; (3) slap and end of meal. 'This was a total success. She needed something to come up against.' Rule II: no tantrums at mealtimes. 'If you cry you'll have to leave the room', and if she cried she *was* sent out. Rule III: no tantrums while Mother is telephoning (it was explained to Judy that it was vital that Mother got the many messages for Father all right). She was slapped if she transgressed.

Soon afterwards the mother asked Judy after a long tantrum: 'Why do you do it, Judy? It does not help at all'. Judy replied: 'I don't know', then pointed into her open mouth and said: 'It's inside Judy'. Tantrums now became rarer, and always when Judy was frustrated. Once, when a plane flew over, the mother talked about aeroplanes and how people travelled in them. Judy asked her to bring it down and when her mother explained that this could not be done, Judy threw a tantrum, and was smacked. About this time she also threw a tantrum (cause unknown) while the family had a picnic in the garden. She was warned, then banned to an upstairs room. 'Terrific tantrum – might she not break the pane she was hammering at so furiously?' She also kicked the door (which was not locked). Then she called: 'Mummy, are you deaf?' Then: 'Mummy, are you *dead*?' 'We sat it out and gritted our teeth.' Finally, after long screaming, banging and kicking, she calmed down and then said: 'Mummy, I am sorry'. Mother went upstairs at once and 'we had a splendid reconciliation'.

Going to bed had to be regularised slowly. Judy began to come down time and again, was sent up, even smacked, and finally a compromise was agreed on: her mother would come up every half hour and 'have a peep'. Judy accepted this gradually, but once came down to complain that she 'had not been peeped'.

The parents did indulge Judy in many of her rituals. Thus, at bed time her 'fringey' was always draped round her body 'just so': Judy had to put her finger through holes in it in a specific order: while she had one thumb in her mouth she would wave the fringey back and forth with her other hand. When she got a new bed she wanted to hear its precise history, including that of all the people who had slept in it before. The mother would have to sing one of a small repertoire of songs while she held Judy's hand.

When Judy was three years old, she was moved into the same room as Anne. She bedwetted that same night. Asked why, she explained that she could not leave her bed while Anne was in the same room. She was given a room of her own and the bedwetting stopped.

Judy went to Smallbridge School ('a very fine school' – mother) a few days after her third birthday. Before the great day, the parents 'did a lot of sales talk' and the mother had taken her along more than once to let her look over the wall at the children who played during the break. They also had an accidental meeting outside the school with one of the teachers.

When the mother started taking her, she weaned her by easy stages: 'First she got off my knee, then ventured across the room, then allowed me to wander into other parts of the school. I always told her if I was leaving the room . . . After a week or so she could be left. There was always a last-minute ritual at the door: "Goodbye Judy, have a good time! I'll see you at 11.30". Reply (lips trembling) "Goodbye, see you at 11.30".' Final wave, the teacher would lift her to see her mother go, waving until she was out of sight. When the mother came back, Judy always flung herself at her, but she had always enjoyed herself. Sometimes she cried when leaving school 'because she had not been able to do everything she had wanted to do'. In the first six weeks, whatever else she did, she always 'washed up' at least once a day and ended up with wet sleeves. Once she wet her pants and the teacher told her off briskly, without any baby talk: 'Don't let it happen again, will you, Judy?' – 'Judy wanted to explore and to make friends, but dared not accept contact at first; when a child approached her to give her something she would press herself against the wall, tense and rigid.'

When Judy was 3½, her teacher expressed concern about her shyness; she was still reluctant to play with (as distinct from alongside) other children. When told that Judy was not, as the teacher thought, 4½ but a year younger, and her history was described, the teacher said: 'It's the way she talks of course that misled me'. In this period Judy often made quick switches back and forth between babyish behaviour and that of 'an advanced four-year-old'; she could, for example, show 'good verbal expression and understanding'.

'At school she got over her fear of doctors. She had a tantrum when she had to undergo the first routine check by the school doctor. Afterwards she asked whether she could apologise, was taken to the room where the doctor was, and said in a rush "sorry I made a fuss" and bolted.' She got another chance the week after when the doctor came for the children she had not seen on her first visit. The mother prepared her for this occasion and pre-enacted what would happen, reassuring her etc. Judy said: 'I am going to smile all the time' – and she did, though tensely. Then, 'characteristically' she began to play doctor all the time, examining and bandaging the whole family. She was still scared of animals and was taken aback when she was given a rocking horse; she was keenly interested in it but did not want to sit on it 'because the horse had a bad back and I would hurt it'. The mother suggested that she bandage the horse and wait a week. This worked.

'Now things began to improve quickly.' Judy began to listen more to music and recognised, for instance, Bartok's string quartet. She listened to the mother's singing and the father began to teach her the violin. Although he was a demanding teacher, she thrived and loved it.

When Judy was 4½, the teacher suggested that she stay on for one or two more terms at Smallbridge.

While she was there, the doctor decided that she would have to have her tonsils out. The mother explained to Judy carefully and well beforehand what was going to happen. She went to hospital with Judy and all was well – 'Judy was now very much pro-doctor'. The adventure seemed to build up her self-esteem. She behaved very pluckily, also later when she was rushed to hospital because of an asthma attack and also on two subsequent visits, for the treatment of ear infections.

At about this stage the mother taught her to read, and soon she began to read aloud to Anne, which strengthened the bond between the two girls.

When, at five years old, Judy went to primary school, there was no fuss. At a music festival that winter she stood up and played a violin piece in front of an audience without fear. She went alone for a stay with her grandmother and 'behaved beautifully'. When the father, mother and Anne came to collect her, Judy exclaimed: 'Anne!' and embraced her, then said: 'Oh, Mummy and Daddy too!'. Her weight, which had been down to 25 lb at 3½ years, was now back to normal. From now on the two sisters were inseparable and played many lovely pretend games. Once the mother overheard them handling pretend babies while sitting at the top of the stairs. Judy said 'This is Judy's baby; this is Anne's baby. *This is Mummy's baby, let's throw it downstairs!*'

There were setbacks. For some reason Judy became terrified of the possibility of fire and screamed when she saw smoke coming out of the top of a chimney, and also when a visiting friend lit his pipe. She was also terrified of death.

The family then made a difficult move into a large house, which had to be rebuilt by the father. This made Judy regress a little. She often ran out from school into the street where she was found crying on the pavement by other parents. At the new school she often hid in the lavatory, found a hideyhole to protect herself from the lunch playtime; at home she begged to be taken back to her old school etc. Often she wept long into the night. One night she even dressed, and packed, intending to leave home so as not to have to go to school, but decided halfway that she could not take this desperate step. At the same time she developed remarkably well. She helped her father rebuild the roof, and climbed up to him where he was sitting astride the roof beam, and handed him slate after slate, on top of a four-storey house! She hiked 20 miles with the family, climbing Sca Fell on the way. 'She was enraptured by tiny living things'. But once, returning to a camp site after a year in town, she threw a tantrum 'because a much-loved caterpillar was no longer sitting on the same plant'. She made good progress on the violin. At school, some staff members thought her 'almost backward', others 'wise beyond her years'. 'This was entirely dependent on whether she withdrew or opened up.'

She did not make new friends at first. When she complained that 'nobody liked her' her mother suggested that she show friendliness to other friendless loners. She did this with alacrity and 'soon collected a motley crowd of infant drop-outs' round her (all of these came to tea, but one at a time, because they did not befriend each other).

At age six years, Judy was so fond of Anne that, when she had a nightmare, she would join Anne in her bed, where the mother found them the next morning with Anne's arms round her elder sister.

Now (May 1981) Judy is to all intents and purposes fully normal; she even shows clear signs of being well above normal in literary and musical ability and even talent. When she is ill, she still becomes very clinging, but she is doing very well at school, is a delightful companion and guest and is very gentle and altruistic in her relations with other people, especially small children.

In April 1981 we had a good opportunity to see an example of the courage such children display in their struggle to overcome their fears: when N. T., showing them round a nature reserve which harboured many adders, asked: 'Who is coming with me to see an adder?' (some of which he had been shown by the reserve's warden), Anne said 'Not me!' but Judy, confessing that she was afraid of poisonous snakes, said, clearly overcoming her apprehension 'I'll come'. And they did find one of the adders at home; Judy was keenly interested, and admired the delicate beauty of the slightly fearsome animal, and was afterwards glad (and not a little proud) that she had decided to go.

Authors' comments

Here again is a case in which a child was not 'odd from birth' but became traumatised by a series of unfortunate events in her early environment. We happen to know this family well, and so have not only followed their struggle but also obtained a more detailed description from them than is usual. Since the father in this case had to work exceptionally hard to make sure that he could offer his family what they needed, much of the story seems to centre on the mother, but we know that both contributed to the utmost of their capacity to the rehabilitation of their eldest daughter (the younger was never in any danger). It will be clear from the report that these parents too proceeded at the 'emotional level', trying to provide (with success) for their child the security she so badly needed, and yet at the same time being very strict and at times even seemingly hard when vital matters of discipline were at stake. A nice parallel to, for instance, George's story, is the striking and good effect which an appeal for help for a 'still more unhappy child' had on Judy. We refrain from giving fuller comment; the story speaks for itself.

Six published monographs

KAUFMAN, B. N. 1976. *To Love is to be happy with.* London: Souvenir Press. (American edition: 1976. *Son rise*. New York: Harper & Row.)

This is an extraordinarily interesting, important account of a successful D I Y treatment. The boy Raun was the first son, born when his older sisters were aged seven and three years. His birth 'was normal' yet he was at first 'steel grey' (which soon turned into a rosy pink). According to standard tests he seemed normal, but his mother was uneasy; he cried almost constantly and was unresponsive when approached.

Soon there was no doubt that he was becoming autistic; at 17 months of age practically all the signs were present (e.g. spinning objects, staring, rocking, solitary play with the same toy in the same place, no pointing, no gesturing, loss of vocalisation, certain obsessions etc., but no self-destructive behaviour). Doctors tried to reassure the parents that Raun would 'grow out of it', but the parents, who had by now read up on almost everything written about autism, came to the conclusion that there was no doubt, and Raun certainly was a near-classical example of a child who is a little odd at birth, and develops the syndrome steadily in the first 1½ years.

Little bits of information about his history are given, such as 'steel grey at birth' (surely anoxia?); a nasty middle ear infection when he was in his fourth week, for which he was sent to an intensive care unit in hospital; he received antibiotics; both eardrums became perforated. During the next four months he was withdrawn; he seemed normal at the end of the first year, yet he did not put out his arms when his parents approached him to pick him up. There are many details about the visits to doctors, some of whom suspected autism, but advised the parents to come back later (the usual confusion); the atmosphere at home became (understandably) restless, tense and worried as the parents, at their wits' end, tried almost feverishly to find out what was wrong and what to do. Altogether there was quite clearly an 'autismogenic' atmosphere in the Kaufman home. When Raun was 17 months old he was still very withdrawn and had a vacant stare, was spinning objects and rocked a great deal.

The parents, aware of the chaotic and contradictory state of expert opinion, now decided to treat Raun themselves. They mention an anonymous, helpful expert on the 'option method' but decided finally not to proceed exactly according to his views, and it seems clear to us that they rejected Bettelheim's view of parental guilt and opted for Delacato's view that 'nerve paths' were undeveloped and that what was necessary was 'stimulation . . . even overstimulation' (p. 48). This rationale runs through the whole book, with the confusions we have pointed out in our main text between 'stimulation' in general and *special forms* of stimulation. What comes out more clearly than in the accounts that Doman gives of his methods (so very similar to Delacato's) is the loving commitment of the parents, an attitude which, though (as in other accounts by D I Y parents) not pointed out explicitly as important, can be deduced from numerous little remarks; thus Raun's mother often joined Raun in his spinning sessions for up to two hours (!) at a time; she sat with him up to eight to nine hours (!) a day, fed him, talked, hummed and sang to him, sometimes gave a running commentary on what was happening and, on occasion, very sensitively and inventively, called his attention by gently blowing on his cheek. Interestingly, she made Raun look at her by making the spoon with food approach from the direction of her eyes (compare with Clancy's method), and soon Raun did begin to look more often at his mother's eyes. But – most importantly! – the parents began with a fortnight's close observation of Raun's behaviour before they decided on a plan for his treatment. Raun soon began to react more socially in general, but only fleetingly and only now and then.

On pp. 68–9 a helpful summary is given of Raun's condition after the first eight weeks of treatment, when he must have been about 19 months old. On pp. 74–5 a 'work' schedule is given as followed at that stage. Four weeks after this, Raun had a sudden setback and rejected the work he used to do. There were more ups and downs. After a down he might suddenly make progress, e.g. speak better. Since the stimulation programme seems to us a little too demanding, we think that Raun may well have rebelled now and then; or he may have been involved in an internal struggle, bracing himself for the next leap forward. As we have said in our main text, we feel that some of the information given in the book is self-contradictory; Raun has some fine, admittedly obsessive skills; the parents do stress that he could not observe, analyse, reason logically; yet there is the incident when, given a cardboard shoe box, he studied it carefully and then managed to make it spin standing on one of its corners, an example of quickly grasping the possibilities of a new situation, and of very dexterously handling this awkwardly shaped object.

Yet, even if the account given contains such seeming contradictions, and although Raun is often confused and retarded, he is at the same time bright, and we feel that the parents may well have underrated Raun's capacity for cut-off in defence against their, in a way, relentless efforts at overstimulation.

Yet there is not the slightest doubt that this is a success story; at four years of age Raun had completely recovered. In spite of this, the parents did go on with their demanding regime, partly because Raun had turned out to be so very bright, partly because he remained still vulnerable.

Although we ourselves would have preferred to read a more soberly written book, we do recommend it warmly; it deserves very close study and Raun's parents are in many respects superparents. We feel, but cannot really substantiate it, that the Kaufman's are or have been in danger of falling into the 'Doman trap' of trying to make a 'superkid' of their son. One of the most important aspects of the Kaufman procedure is their ethologically sensible decision (found so rarely among psychiatrists, and even among biologists of many kinds) to spend the first fortnight deliberately refraining from intervention, but merely observing intently what exactly Raun did do.

Kaufman has since written at least one other book which, however, we have not read so far. But we did read his article 'A miracle to believe in', in *Family Circle* of 24 February, 1981, in which he describes how a Mexican couple comes to see him and his wife with their young son, who had been diagnosed as 'autistic and retarded'. The Kaufmans agreed to spend three months on trying to find out whether they could help this family. Again, they began by doing 'marathon observations' of how the boy actually behaved. The Kaufmans' story is once more a mixture of fact and (not necessarily valid) interpretations (about 'memory dysfunction', the 'monitoring functions of the reticular formation' and the 'self-stimulating' function of his mannerisms etc.). What concerns us here is that they applied to this boy roughly the same procedure as they had followed with Raun, and that the boy made spectacular progress in the one and a half years he and his mother (the father had to return home earlier) stayed with them.

The stories of Raun and of this Mexican boy, unfinished though the latter one is, join the ranks of the accounts that invalidate the 'ineducability' myth.

WEXLER, S. S. 1971   (original edition 1955). *The story of Sandy.* Winnipeg: Signet.

This story of the recovery of an autistic boy is a very worthwhile book. It seems that Sandy had not been officially diagnosed as autistic, but the behaviour descriptions show all the familiar symptoms: at 14 months he did not yet walk, although he began to walk clumsily before he was two; when he was two years plus, a younger sister was born, and he then stopped what little walking he had in the meantime mastered; he regressed in several other respects: lost the few words and sounds he had used before, went limp in company, became completely withdrawn, spent much time rocking, made no eye contact any more, etc. A fairly exceptional detail is that when he was especially anxious he used to put his finger into his throat and vomit. (Vomiting as a result of anxious tension is, of course, not unusual in normal people.)

Sandy was not 'odd from birth'. His mother was a very unstable person, now depressed, now elated. Her twin brother committed suicide the day Sandy was born, which made the mother deeply depressed. Sandy spent two weeks in a residential nursing home while his mother's depression lasted, and his nursery at home was not fixed until he came back. He was put on the top floor, out of earshot of the parents! Feeding and care were irregular and not dependable. Sandy cried for long spells without his mother taking notice. When he was eight months old his mother again went into a deep depression and had to have psychiatric help. She was very ambivalent towards Sandy. When he was one year old she wanted him to be more independent, yet she also wanted to board him out, presumably to ensure that he would be properly cared for. When Sandy was 22 months old the mother realised she was once more pregnant; she tried to have an abortion because she did not want another child; she developed various stress symptoms and Sandy was to all intents and purposes forgotten. When the new baby was three months old and Sandy about 30 months, the mother decided that Sandy was a 'congenital imbecile' and ought to be put in an institution.

Sandy's father, who had himself been raised by a childless couple from his tenth year on, went to these step-parents (the 'grandparents') and asked them to take Sandy. They adopted him and treated him with great love and understanding. When Sandy arrived he was still very withdrawn, but when held up he urinated in a glass jar, which he had not done for six months. A paediatrician examined him next, said he was in excellent physical health and advised them 'to let him settle down; love and patience are the only medicine . . . Consult an expert in childhood mental disorders later'.

The move to this loving couple, his 'grandparents', started Sandy on his long way back to normality. After six weeks with them he began to invite company by patting on the ground, he began to make eye contact, to imitate the behaviour of others, began to walk again, and to make some sounds. When Sandy was almost three years old, the 'grandmother' risked a four days' separation, and upon her return Sandy patted the floor and said 'down' to her. At this stage the 'grandparents' also started a teaching programme adjusted to a toddler. They gave him a gramophone, which he learned to handle with great dexterity; his eating manners had also become well controlled. When Sandy was 3¼ years old he was seen (at home) by an expert, who did not make a diagnosis but did not give him a clean bill of mental health either; she said that he was still too young for psychotherapy. She advised the 'grandparents' strongly to keep the child: 'I think you are the only chance he has' and 'one thing I am absolutely sure of: if you hurry this child he will go backward' (p. 61). She also warned against overstimulation.

Because of their relatively advanced age, the grandparents (who had legally adopted Sandy) arranged for continuous help; although a succession of persons was involved, they were clearly very carefully instructed. Sandy then began to make slow but steady progress. At three-plus years the results of psychological tests put him in the 'imbecile' class; about nine months later he was considered a 'borderline case' and was accepted for one hour daily in a nursery school where he stayed for two and a half years. This started an overall improvement, with good speech development (e.g. use of 'I' for the first time), but he still walked a lot on tiptoe and showed other autistic signs. When he reached 4¾ years, a series of psychotherapy sessions was started. Here he had a sudden regression, for which the cause was discovered: the therapist had a large rubber giraffe in the office, and Sandy's mother had often called his father her 'pet giraffe' or 'Petty'! Sandy had a second regression when a babysitter called him 'Petty'.

At 7½ years, Sandy was accepted in an ordinary school, but he could not yet stand the strain and was put in a much smaller school for deviant children; this worked. Tests then showed that he had 'average intelligence'. At 9½ years, Sandy was sent, after thorough preparation and acting his role, to a summer camp for 'children with problems' (some physical, some mental), which led to his spending the next two and a half years in the boarding school that had organised this camp, returning for the holidays to his 'grandparents'. In these years he showed steady emotional improvement but, due to poor teaching, not much academic progress. At about this time contact with Sandy's father (who had had a divorce and had remarried) was re-established; the relationship was quite good, especially with Sandy's new stepmother. Then Sandy was accepted by a state school, in a class for children two years his junior. Here he managed emotionally, but was bottom academically. He rose in status when he turned out to be good at soccer, football and swimming; he learned to dance and began to show 'conventional' interest in girls (real interest did not come until his college days). Slowly becoming normal, Sandy went to normal high school, and from there got a place in a state university. He still had a slight speech impediment, but this disappeared when he was debating and when he gave an address in public (which was well phrased and well delivered, read from a script but with a number of little impromptu asides).

Sandy's story is a clear one of rejection, primarily by his mother but also – in desperation – by his father, and then acceptance by loving substitute parents, and later by his father's second wife. The substitute mother sums it up at the end of the book, when Sandy has finished college: 'I have never felt that special credit was due to us. Sandy had within himself the resilience to recover . . . Between Pa-Joe (her husband) and Sandy lies the deepest tie I have ever seen . . . We took Sandy into our home . . . because we had a home and he had none . . . We came to love Sandy as a shared blessing (shared between the elderly couple, Sandy's father, and his second wife) . . . Pa-Joe cared more for kindness then for success; admired humility . . . more than fame . . . With small imperfections and a little handicap in his coordination . . . Sandy has made the grade – handsome, lovable, wise beyond his years.' Surely we recognise this attitude: it is that of the good 'do-it-yourself' mother!

BECK, M. 1978. *The exorcism of an albatross – the story of a very special relationship*. Regina, Canada: Zephyr Printers.

This is the story of a boy, described and diagnosed as autistic, written by his mother when he was approximately 16 years old, although the major part of the book deals with his first 14 years.

The boy, Stephen, was born when his elder brother was four years old. He seems to have been normal to begin with, but to have become more and more autistic in the next 30 months. Before he reached that age, the following events happened (among others) which might have pushed him into autism.

He had five separations from his mother (among them a week spent alone in hospital and, on another occasion, 'days' when his mother was away in hospital); since Stephen was a quiet baby and his mother was exhausted after a severe haemorrhage at his birth, she spent little time with him and much with his elder brother. When Stephen was 1½ years old, the family went on holiday, changing motels practically every night. Before then, when Stephen was approximately nine months old, the mother had begun to be very uneasy, for he began to be 'very withdrawn and remote'. At 20 months he began to show an obsession with water, e.g. he played with, and drank, water from lavatory bowls. He developed speech very late and at first very poorly, and did not often respond to what his parents and others said. He started rooting in dustbins at 2½ years and to wander off, seemingly unaware of traffic etc., but he always returned home safely. At 25 months he bit and scratched his newly born baby brother. At three years he discovered 'Lego' and built all the time the same aeroplanes and bungalows, throwing tantrums when he made a mistake. He was examined by doctors – but in their surgeries, not at his home. An ear, nose and throat specialist concluded that he was not deaf; a speech therapist diagnosed 'autism'.

Stephen's father was away from home for his work a great deal and the mother noticed that Stephen missed him. When Stephen was 3¾ years, the family flew to England for a two years' stay; the departure greatly upset Stephen. In England he became attached to his maternal grandfather, whom he then missed very much when back in Canada.

In spite of these and a number of other damaging experiences, Stephen did gradually improve, although even at 16 he was not normal. Yet he talked, had a friend, mastered a variety of skills (e.g. cooking) etc. The mother's narrative abounds with details about his development and about the way she has dealt with him. Although she had been told that if a child is 'once an autist he'll always be an autist', she and her husband did not abandon him, but what they actually did do with him is in our view a mixture of 'good' and 'not so good' things (such as the visit to

England – compare Elly Park in *The siege*). In the mother's own words (p. 79):

> 'I didn't do any of those things I've read about in the other stories. I didn't imitate Stephen when he was in his own world so that he would let me in to help him. Nor did I try to shake him out of it persistently and consistently so that he would learn to behave in an acceptable way. Or learn new skills. Nor did I sit, hour after hour, slowly trying to help him say sounds. Or purse his lips and blow. Or all the other routine things these other dedicated parents did so tirelessly and patiently.' (She has read Kaufman's story *Son rise*.)
>
> 'In fact, I sometimes wonder if Stephen succeeded not because of me but in spite of me.
>
> 'Or did he?
>
> 'When I go back through the years, a pattern emerges and the strongest thread in this is cooperation. Even in the hardest moments Scott (her husband) and I never pulled in opposite directions. And if we disagreed with the other's approach, we discussed it later in private. And we always worked with and not against his teachers. From the very beginning we used Stephen's own interests to help him, teaching him to go to the store in Leeds years ago, for example, and to cook that dreadful Christmas when he was taken off his tranquillisers. And we learnt that we must be consistent. I found this the hardest lesson of all, for it was such a luxury sometimes not to bother. But I always paid for these lapses . . . Apart from that one brief (*sic*) spell in England, we always took him with us on walks and to libraries and shops . . . In time, I even learnt to be selfish too. Or perhaps learnt to establish my priorities . . . What else have the years taught me? To be firm above all . . . and to expect some setbacks. To expect things of Stephen too. I have learnt that I must not be over-protective and to accept that he can cope with most situations if given a chance. I have learnt to present him with new challenges, for . . . he still needs some direction in how to use his spare time . . .'

The story, written up more or less chronologically, is full of interesting details. It is interesting to notice (and, we think, revealing) that, when Stephen's mother found that, after having wandered off on his own, 'he always came back' (p. 17), she 'let him go without following him'. But on the first occasion his parents had been very worried about these disappearances and when his father, who had found him 'wandering around in a wood nearby, brought him back', his mother 'held him (Stephen) close in relief'. But such 'holding' was not always done at appropriate moments, thus (p. 37) when 'the most wonderful moment came when he came running into the house from the cab one afternoon and said "Mummy!" for the first time . . .' there is no mention of a similar hugging response on her part. Yet, even though the book sounds as if the mother is a little self-centred and (as she says herself) at times bored with her son, Stephen does recover to a large extent. The degree and speed of this recovery may be judged from such facts as that Stephen did attend school from approximately age six years onwards; that he became quite articulate, kept a diary, 'started to pun' (in our experience a phase in the acquisition of language that also fascinates many normal people when they begin to learn a foreign language). He learned rhyming slang and used it jokingly.

Although Stephen's story does not end in complete recovery (at least up till his 16th year), it is – considering how confused the guidance (and lack of it) has been that his parents have received, and given in their turn – a story that rather lends support to our thesis that autistic children can be helped to recover, provided the parents and especially the mother are sufficiently motivated. (Our mentioning of the fact that Stephen's mother was at times rather bored with him and seemed not always to act 'supermaternally' must not be taken to imply criticism; the story told so honestly, without glossing over any mistakes that may have been made; reveals a greatly caring and devoted parental attitude and behaviour.)

COPELAND, J. AND J. HODGES 1973 *For the love of Ann – the true story of an autistic child,* London: Arrow.

This is a straightforward, typical success story written by a journalist on the basis of the information supplied by Mr and Mrs Hodges – Ann's parents.

Ann was the second child, born 16 months after her elder brother. The birth was normal, but she became accidentally chilled just after birth so that she had become 'blue with cold'. (But later, the medical opinion was that she had a bout of near-asphyxia – see below.)

From the beginning she was an exceptionally quiet baby, it was 'easy to forget she was there' (p. 19). Gradually it became clear that her development was not normal, and she developed all the well-known symptoms of autism: she did not gurgle or coo at the age when a baby is expected to, she slept very little, her parents had difficulty in making her take solids; she began to have long screaming bouts, which intensified when her parents tried to put a paper shade on the light in her room; although at 10 months she began to walk, at 14 months she clearly resented being picked up, stared vacantly, threw tantrums when taken by the hand, banged her head against the wall and the floor, became attached to a chair (in which she rocked ceaselessly) and to a doll – 'her world was a chair . . . and "dolly". Always "dolly",' (p. 35); she pulled out her hair and stuffed it in her mouth; when at two-plus she was knocked over by a large dog, she screamed 16 hours non-stop and from then on was quiet only when in her pram; at three the screaming was so bad that a policeman called at the home because he thought that a child was being molested. When Ann was six years eight months, after visits to many doctors and clinics, a doctor diagnosed her as autistic, adding that she was 'unlikely ever to be educated . . . or for that matter even to recognise you as her parents'. Apart from the 'chilling' (or, more likely, anoxia) incident (which might very well have been the main cause of her autistic derailment), the parents cannot think of any other possible autismogenic factors; superficially this looks like an 'odd-from-birth' case, but to us it looks very much one of sudden traumatisation just after birth. Exacerbating factors that came later were quite possibly: the birth of a third child when Ann was 20 months; the death of her maternal grandmother at about that time; and the dog incident mentioned already.

There are interesting details about the way Ann was treated. First of all, her parents loved and cared for her from the start, and even after the shattering message given by the doctor they decided firmly that 'Ann was not a mental defective' and that 'they would never put her in a mental home' (p 16).

For the rest this is just a typical 'do-it-yourself' story. Throughout, Ann is a member of a loving family. This, and the resultant discovery of what made her panic after the Hodges moved into their new home, illustrates beautifully the great importance of patient observation and of wondering about what causes each setback. For instance, pp. 36–9 describe how the parents found out that the sight of a large privet bush swaying in the wind threw Ann into paroxysms of screaming. Cutting the bush down had an immediate effect.

But an equally important part of the loving behaviour of the parents was the considerable effort they put into forcing Ann to do things she 'refused to do' (shrank back from doing), such as making her feed herself with a spoon, toilet-training her, taking her all round the house and, ignoring her screaming protests, making her touch things etc. The way this forcing (a kind of putting-through, but more than just that) was developed, reveals both the constant attention given to her problem by her parents and, time and again, a flash of inventiveness: once when, at the seaside, at age 5½ years, Ann had refused to leave her 'trolley' (push chair) to play in the sand, her trolley fell over so that she was literally catapulted into a new situation. She did protest, and even panic, but after a while she began to play with the sand, something so unexpected that the parents 'had a feeling of elation' (p. 32). Days later, the father, who had kept wondering about this and other incidents, woke up in the night shouting 'violence!', meaning that it must have been the very shock of falling down that had made Ann take a 'leap forward'. Together with his wife, he then decided to try out a step-by-step programme of forcing Anne now and then, if necessary even slapping her.

Another interesting aspect of the story is the way in which a teacher of educationally subnormal children, George Glover, became involved with Ann's rehabilitation. First of all he supported Ann's parents in their habit, already well established, of observing and recording as much as they could about Ann's behaviour, and about how certain incidents seemed to affect it; secondly, he engaged the help of other children in his school. (The children did this so enthusiastically that they had at times to be restrained.) The authors also mention George Glover's story about a boy of two years old who fell into a river in spate, managed to hang on to some tree roots, 'screaming for two hours' before he was rescued, and who after that had become suddenly withdrawn, mute and 'autistic'.

When Ann was 21 years old, she was practically normal, happy and capable, had learned typing and had shown increasing initiative, agreed to co-operate in a film of her story, had greatly improved her speech and had made other obvious improvements.

The 1976 edition of the book adds that Ann, then 24, had appeared on many television programmes in Britain and in Ireland; had a boyfriend, was a good driver, and insisted on attending the funeral of George Glover. The medical information about her having turned 'blue with cold' was then interpreted as near-asphyxia. Up till this point it would seem that she had done as well as any normal young person; in fact, according to the author, she was determined to have 'just the same opportunities as others; it is likely that she will just try that bit harder'. And there, as far as we know, the matter stood in 1976.

AXLINE, V. 1972. *Dibs – in search of self.* London: Penguin.

This book, a veritable little gem written by the clinical psychologist who is one of the pioneers, if not *the* pioneer, of play therapy, is unlike any of the other books listed here. Written in a deceptively sober style, it combines the selectivity, almost sketchiness of a novel with the incisiveness and, in places, precision of a scientifically responsible case history. It is an important and also extremely moving book.

Axline herself, recognising the unusual nature of her story (although, in the light of what we know now, it turns out not to be all *that* unusual) refrains from labelling Dibs' disorder, although she does mention, tentatively and rather in passing, the term autism. From the descriptions of his behaviour, however – which are undoubtedly not meant to be complete – it is perfectly clear that he belongs to, is even fairly typical of, the class of children with which we are concerned in this book: in the classroom and, at the start of treatment, in the playroom (Axline did not study Dibs at his home), he showed most of the time extreme withdrawal, lay for hours crouched under the table, scratched with a stick in the mud when in the garden, hugged the wall, behaved passively, spoke at best in single words or toddler talk – 'No go home! No go home!', 'Dibs go out' – had frequent tantrums, buried his head in his arms, crawled rather than walked when not at ease, was retarded in many respects, rocked, chewed his hand, sucked his thumb, struck out at children who approached him etc. Yet he could at other times behave very intelligently, for instance he explored (though often by touch and even smell, although it is clear that he has also looked, listened and read a great deal), sometimes he took books from the shelves and studied them, and he had obviously formed some kind of warm relationship with his grandmother and, clearly, with the gardener whom he could see and, it seems, hear from the window of his room at home.

Not much is said about his history, but Axline is told that a child psychiatrist had called him 'the most rejected child he has ever seen'. He was the first child (he has a younger sister) of two scientists, the father (according to the mother) 'brilliant', the mother certainly totally committed to her scientific work. Both seem to have been fairly taken aback, and unpleasantly surprised, when they realised that they were going to have a child, and they seem to have been rather cross with Fate when Dibs turned out to be almost the opposite of brilliant. It seems that the father responded mainly by withdrawing and being *in effect* cold and cruel to his son (on the rare occasions that he bothered about him); the mother was deeply hurt and when the story starts had withdrawn into an attitude of hopeless acceptance of her fate of having an idiot son. In their curiously cerebral way they had given the child 'everything' in the way of toys etc. that a child should have for his maximum *intellectual* development; but they 'kept' Dibs, rather like an inconvenient animal, in his own room, often locked up (something that Dibs later reveals to have resented bitterly). He was sent to an infant school, more or less to be rid of him and to let the staff cope. Typically, there were some among the staff who loved Dibs and firmly believed in his considerable intellectual and generally human potential.

The bulk of the book consists of detailed descriptions of a limited number of sessions that Axline has had with Dibs in a special playroom. Calmly observing him; accepting him as a fellow human being with possibly great potential and certainly with his dignity to be respected; speaking with him by acknowledging what he says and does, yet being very firm at times (e.g. expecting him to take off and put on his coat himself instead of doing that for him as he expected); adhering strictly to certain rules, such as when each session has to end; now and then very perceptively introducing a little re-enacting of what she suspected might have hurt him in the past; not usurping the role of Dibs' mother; patiently waiting for 'this astonishing child' to come out of his shell and also for the mother to approach her (Axline), in case she wanted to step in and take her part; Axline observed with mounting near-incredulity the emergence of the 'real' Dibs, who turned out to be an exceptionally gifted, perceptive, extremely sensitive and vulnerable child who had been deeply hurt by social rejection.

Critics have often said (a) that 'Dibs was not an autist' (why, we can only guess, but in some cases we know it is 'because he recovered so quickly'), and (b) that his case is highly exceptional and of little value for understanding autism. On both counts the critics could not be more wrong, and although the combination of Dibs, an infant school with exceptional teachers, the arrival on the scene of an Axline at exactly the right moment (although her arrival earlier or later might also have had spectacular results) and a mother who (whether or not under Axline's exceptional influence we must leave open) has the moral courage, and the love (however atrophied or suppressed by her disappointments) to reject all her wrong ideas about Dibs and to change her behaviour towards her son so completely – although this *combination* of circumstances may be rare, the story carries an important message to all who have to do with autistic (or otherwise emotionally damaged) children. Outstanding is Axline's self-restraint, in dealing with Dibs, with his mother, and in the great care she takes not to usurp the mother's role. Much remains unsaid in this story – for instance about Dibs' early experiences, and about the degree of maternal commitment of Dibs' own mother once she stopped rejecting him – but these gaps are undoubtedly the consequence of Axline's determination to keep her involvement and her interference at a minimum. Parents of autistic children who read the story without realising what has been left out and what exactly it is that makes the story exceptional may be misled by the seeming simplicity of the book and by the seemingly 'magic bullet' effect of the treatment. But with children whose emotional imbalance is discovered very early or, as in Dib's case, has been healing under the surface, and who are then treated warmly, in and by their own family, such magic recoveries are certainly *not* rare; the case of Fae described earlier in this chapter is representative, though the Dibs' story is not.

PARK, C. C. 1972 (original edition 1967). *The siege – the battle for communication with an autistic child.* London: Penguin – a Pelican Book.

This is perhaps the most detailed, though not the most encouraging, story we have found in the literature of a family's struggle to help an autistic child. Its very richness of detail (buried in a fairly verbose, in places chatty text) makes it impossible to write a short précis of its contents, but the book's importance is beyond doubt, both because of the parents' obvious commitment and good moves and for their, frankly reported, mistakes.

Elly was born in July 1958, the last of four children – two sisters and a brother preceded her. At birth she seemed to be healthy; she developed colic fairly soon but not for an excessively long time; she smiled at seven weeks; reached for objects at the usual time (two months); when her father took a snap of her in her bath at age five months, she laughed, looking at the camera. A photograph taken at eight months shows her looking at the camera very seriously. Already at eight months a neighbour had begun to wonder whether all was well; and her mother remembered that after the colic period Elly had become very quiet and contented. When she was 12 months old Elly did not play 'peek-a-boo', and at 19 months her mother realised that she had never seen Elly point at something or someone. She was slow in sitting, crawling and walking, but then so had her sibs been. At 22 months she occasionally spoke a few words. From 18 months on she had begun to puzzle her parents more and more (little eye contact, little smiling at persons, happy on her own with very few toys, distress at trivial changes in routine, no normal speech development, seeming lack of a sense of touch, of visual and auditory perception; she often went limp when picked up or touched, she used other people's hands as tools, did not explore etc. – the book is full of such details which, together with the results of repeated examinations and testings, leave no doubt that Elly had become a typically autistic child). At the end of the book, when Elly was eight years old, her parents agreed that Elly's father had characterised the causes of her aberrant behaviour very aptly when he said 'It's the sense of purpose that is missing!'. He deduced this, obviously correctly, from the seemingly contradictory facts of, on the one hand, serious though gradually diminishing shortcomings in her overall achievements and, on the other hand, on many occasions clear signs of surprisingly good, even very good, intellectual functioning in many spheres (throughout the book the emphasis is rather on skills and intellectual development, less on social and emotional aspects; and this may well account for the incompleteness of Elly's recovery).

What could have made Elly autistic? One can only guess on the basis of the mother's very candid and honest, though perhaps not in all respects complete, descriptions. The child was unplanned, and not really wanted; the mother could not take up the work she had hoped to do; and although she adjusted remarkably well, she was disappointed that Elly was not a boy. When she had been pregnant for six months, the mother had measles. Elly developed colic shortly after being born (which can be a genuine obstacle to warm mother–infant relations), but the mother breast-fed her for nine months, and enjoyed it. But, as the fourth child, Elly received at first less attention than the others had had in their time. When she was six months old, Elly had mild chicken-pox (even so, the doctor remarked 'What a lovely baby!'). When she was just four years old, her parents took the whole family to England and Austria during the father's sabbatical year. Not surprisingly, the child reacted by a pronounced withdrawal, including even initial refusal of food and drink. During this year she was seen at a clinic in Hampstead, London; mother and child received psychotherapy, yet the parents also went for a visit to Paris, leaving Elly for 11 days in the care of 'a trusted help'. But England had its compensations: a very good analyst visited the family twice (p. 164) and helped get Elly admitted to a nursery school for normal children. This 'benefited Elly more than any other single thing that has been done for her' (p. 165).

The parents were clearly concerned about their youngest and did what they could, or thought best, but they were obviously (as are most parents) confused by the literature and, faced with contradictory opinions and advice, they made their own choice and became more and more 'do-it-yourself' parents. There is no doubt that they had appreciable success, but there is no denying either that it was only a partial success. We ourselves are convinced that their not-quite-successful treatment of Elly may well have been the consequence of their difficulty in taking their pick from the self-contradictory literature. Thus they found the books of L. Wing, contributions by Lovaas, Bettelheim's book and Delacato's ideas helpful but, as we have said, it looks as if their decisions about what to try with Elly were based on a rather cerebral view of child development. Even so, they did often do more or less what the best D I Y parents have done, though they mixed it with a clearly harmful behaviour, such as taking Elly to England, and even leaving her for 11 days for their Paris visit. However, both parents are clearly loving and caring, and they have persistently tried to help their child. They did take and keep her in the family, and showed both considerable sensitivity and inventiveness; witness, for instance, the number of things they observed and recorded, the variety of things they tried in their treatment (such as the experiment with the counter mentioned in our main text – Ch. 6, p. 188). Also, the father had 'a flair for jokes . . . excitement . . . games' (p. 115). Yet the mother did take a part-time outside job when Elly was two years old and admits that in the hour(s) spent in Elly's company she was sometimes 'bored' (p. 245); this reveals, in our opinion, a certain degree of lack of conviction that her child might recover fully (not astonishing in view of the defeatist tone of much of the literature); perhaps she was often plain tired; perhaps she was also not fully aware of the need of an autistic child for being 'simply mothered', not just intellectually stimulated. We think that the decision to take this part-time job was a mistake, which seems not to have been corrected later. Instead the parents engaged a series of girls as helpers (p. 114) – as we know now, with hindsight, this is not the ideal thing to do.

A few pages can never do full justice to the exceptionally informative, rich content of *The siege*, nor can we justify the inclusion in our book of the very long abstract the book certain deserves. For reasons quite different from those applying to, for instance, *Dibs* or *For the love of Ann*, *The siege* is eminently worth having, and reading time and again, though critically. The book is better known and accepted as worthwhile by the profession than the others we have mentioned – whether this is because of the successes it reports or because it can also be taken to support the idea of at least 'limited educability' is anybody's guess.

Elly's further development has been studied carefully by her parents; and her father, together with one of his colleagues from M I T, has reported on one aspect of this development until she was 16 years old (Park, D. and P. Youderian 1974. Light and number: ordering principles in the world of an autistic child. *J. Aut. Childhd Schizophrenia* **4**, 313–23).

Not surprising in the light of (a) Elly's early preoccupation with numbers and arithmetic, and (b) her still (though only slowly) growing verbal communication, Elly had, especially in her twelfth year but also, less obsessively, later, in fact until the time of reporting, developed a highly sophisticated language of her own, in which numbers (and integers and a very great variety of complicated calculations which, once done, she knew by heart) played a major role, together with some other symbols (such as the level of juice in her glass – the happier she felt, the higher the level; also the Sun, representing happiness; clouds, representing sadness; and doors, representing the barriers needed to make sources of extreme, not quite bearable happiness acceptable – we understand, as a kind of graded series of obscuring filters). She had a consistent code in which these non-numerical symbols were connected with the numbers. The authors write that, in part aided by Elly's (limited) speech, in part by their own mathematical insight, they were able to understand the rules, the 'grammar' of Elly's private language fairly well. They stress that this language had been created by Elly, who was 'always ahead of us', and it also seems that the fact that someone understood her was a source of great joy to her.

We do not claim to understand this development, but we would like to offer a suggestion. The authors report that she was still 'gravely affected' at the age of 16 years, and that her speaking and writing were a mixture of verbal expressions and these other symbols. Making an inspired guess, it would seem to us that, with her verbal language and, consequently, her interpersonal communication so impaired (which we keep seeing as a secondary consequence of her basic emotional imbalance), Elly had, based on one of her 'islets of good performance' (her other one was love, though a purely passive one, of music), created a language of another kind which, in itself, made perfect sense. The sad thing about this was that, until her father and his colleague succeeded at least partially in 'breaking' her code, she could not be understood by anyone but herself; she was in fact (so it seems to us) satisfying her urge for communication by at least talking to herself (that she had this urge seems clear from the fact that she did speak to a certain extent, did write letters, and now and then wrote with great speed a message in numbers when people seemed not to understand her). She also drew the Sun and clouds, and wrote the number of doors under them. Three examples are printed in the paper.

This fascinating though sad story focuses our attention once more on the issue that we discussed in the main text of this book (Ch. 9): 'To what extent should one encourage, to what extent discourage an autistic child's islet(s) of good performance?'. It seems to us not impossible that Elly developed this one-person code as a second-best to her poorly developing speech. At least she managed to create *something*, and so seems a little happier than Nadia, whose artistic talent shrivelled up but who got nothing in its place. Personally we consider that it would have made for a happier Elly if she had been treated consistently in the way we recommend and document – at the 'emotional level' – but once she had recovered only partly and had developed this scientifically interesting ability, this documenting and interpreting of her private language made her into a potentially useful object of study of the effects which the autistic derailment can have on a child's thinking. One need not give up all hope for Elly's recovery – Foudraine's 'adult autist' who recovered when she was 46 years of age comes to mind – but then, we venture to suggest, her treatment should change tack. She is, after all, still maturing, and can 'view this earlier experience with detachment and humour' (p. 314).

Appendix I: retrieval from autism through mother–child holding therapy

Martha G. Welch MD
952 Fifth Avenue, New York, New York 10021, USA

Introduction

Autism is caused by faulty bonding between mother and child. The fact that the children cured of autism through mother–child holding therapy show no residual organic pathology suggests that environmental factors, namely aspects of the mother–child interaction, play the largest role in the etiology of autism.

Children are born with different sensitivities and vulnerabilities. However, some mothers will not give up on a withdrawn child. Others will conclude that he prefers to be left alone. Still others will neglect a child's needs, albeit unwittingly, until he gives up from frustration and hopelessness.

The benefit of holding therapy accrues equally to the mother and to the child. The mothers seem to lack normal instincts toward their autistic children prior to treatment. They are unable to understand their needs or to respond in any normal fashion.

It is understandable that a mother should have difficulty in the face of months or years of rejection she has experienced from her autistic child. However, once a mother starts holding her autistic child, she invariably gets enough positive reinforcement from the child to overcome her own resistance and aversion. Once she makes enough contact to see the possibility of a normal relationship, she is more able to behave toward that child in a normal way, i.e. setting limits, demanding appropriate behavior, and expecting mutuality.

The cases presented in this paper fit the classical criteria for autism.[1, 2] However, regardless of whether a given case fits completely the classic definition by Kanner,[1] or the further refined definition by Rimland;[2] regardless of whether there is originally some biologically determined predisposition; or whether the cause is purely postnatal environment, holding treatment predicated on mother–child bonding can effect radical improvement, if not essential cure.

Despite the fact that this paper presents only a few cases, the results are clear-cut and unambiguous. All the cases unequivocally suggest a severe disruption of the mother–child relationship and a dramatic response to rebonding through holding therapy.

Review of the literature

Kanner set forth the main criteria for the diagnosis of early childhood autism: disability to relate to people and situations, lack of speech or non-communicative speech, obsessive insistence on maintenance of sameness, and early onset.[1] Additional criteria which are recognized to be part of early childhood autism are developmental retardation with areas of higher functioning, mannerisms and abnormalities of motility,[2] and abnormal perceptual responses such as apparent deafness.[3]

The literature on the treatment of autism is extensive. The papers cited here include some classic works, some review articles, and some of the most recent thinking on the subject. Attempts at treatment of autism range from the use of shock[3, 4] which has been largely abandoned; to the use of pharmacologic agents[4-8] which remains a symptomatic treatment used as an aid in improving the child's receptivity to social and educational modalities; to educational measures[9-19] which have had some positive though limited results difficult to maintain outside the treatment situation; to using parents in the treatment[20-25] which is regarded as more promising both in terms of manpower efficiency and effectiveness; to play and analytically oriented psychotherapy[17, 26-32] which have not yielded generally better results[17, 33-9] than any other modality; to institutionalization[3, 32, 40, 41] as a last resort.

A few sporadic cases of cure of autism through psychotherapy have been reported in the literature. One case of retrieval of a young autistic boy by his parents without the help of therapy is recounted in a book by the father.[42]

O'Gorman in *The nature of childhood autism*[3] postulates that the child's withdrawal from the rest of the environment is an extension of his initial withdrawal from, or failure ever to make, a normal relationship with his mother.

Zaslow and Breger[43] say that the autistic child and his mother are trapped in a 'locked system' of negative emotional responses.

Animal studies of the past few decades involving mother–infant bonding are enlightening. One study[44] disrupted the bonding process by separating mother goats and their infants at birth for a few hours. The mothers then did not recognize their own infants. However, normal bonding could be effected by confining mother and infant in an enclosure and restraining the mother so she could not butt away the infant. Successful permanent bonding was effected in an average of ten days.

The absence of an effective treatment for autism stems from the failure to recognize that it is a problem of two people, a mother and a child. Bowlby states that the most significant recent development in child psychiatry has been the recognition that problems are not confined to individuals but usually develop between two or more members of a family.[45] Bowlby suggests that secure attachment results when a mother is sensitive to the child's signals and the child discovers that his initiatives succeed in establishing a reciprocal interchange with his mother. In the extreme absence of these conditions, attachment failure and even some forms of autism result.[46]

Winnicott says that 'the development of a capacity to use an object is another example of the maturational process as something that depends on a facilitating environment'.[47] Therefore, the greater the failure of the mother–child relationship, the less able the child is to derive benefit from another's help or therapy. Until the primary bond is established, no one, including fathers and therapists, has an easy access to the child as does the mother.

Method of treatment

Since normal development proceeds when there is a strong mother–child bond, the task of treatment is to establish such a bond between the autistic child and his mother.

The treatment with the best chance of success is one in which the therapist does not interpose himself between the mother and child. Nor should the therapist attempt to substitute for the family. Rather he must draw into the treatment the father, grandmother and extended family when possible.

Any action that reunites the mother and child will help retrieve the child from autism. However, since autism is a withdrawal and a refusal to make or to allow contact, bringing mother and child together is very difficult. The therapist must resolve the conflicts of both mother and child. The therapist must overcome both the child's resistance or unresponsiveness, and the mother's own reservations or inhibitions. The mother requires an enormous amount of support to persist in face of the child's rejection of her. The father and the maternal grandmother are key figures in providing the necessary support. For the holding therapy to proceed well, the therapist must help the mother to resolve the conflicts with her husband as well as with her own mother.

Physical contact is the best way for the mother to reach through the child's autistic barrier. Autistic children resist intense physical contact. The mother must hold on to the child until the child accepts the contact.

When the mother begins to feel she is successfully making contact with her child, she can then be instructed in setting limits for and making demands on him. This is an area in which parents of autistic children are particularly inept. The mothers, especially, feel that they cannot, or have no right to, set limits. Once they begin to provide positive interaction with their children, mothers then feel they can be appropriately demanding. One grandfather succinctly stated his conflict about disciplining his autistic granddaughter: 'I have no right to reprimand her when I don't spend any nice time with her'.

Initiating holding therapy is a complex task for which the therapist must utilize all his psychotherapeutic skills. He must remain a keen observer at the same time as he is bringing mother and child together.

It is best to begin the holding at the very first interview, as soon as the family is introduced. The holding is both a diagnostic tool and a treatment. The difficulties both mother and child experience when brought so close together illustrate for the family where the core of the problem lies. At the same time it gives the mother a concrete way of relating to her autistic child. This effective method of relating in turn gives the mother hope of retrieving her child who has been estranged from her for so long. Even in the first holding encounter, the child will make some sort of response which will signal the mother that she can be successful in reaching through the autistic barrier. More often than not the mother is able to pinpoint the circumstances which led to the autistic withdrawal once she starts holding her child.

A soft couch is the best place to carry out holding therapy. There will usually be a violent physical resistance by the child. A soft couch or mat protects the pair from physical injury.

The mother is asked to hold the child on her lap, face to face. The father is asked to sit beside and put his arm around the mother. The child sits astraddle the mother with knees bent, one on each side of the mother. The mother places the child's arms around her and secures them under her arms. She then is free to hold the child's head with her hands in order to make eye contact. This position is not necessarily comfortable for either person.

The therapist must remain near enough to closely observe and interpret the mother's and child's actions and reactions. The mother is usually easily discouraged and rejected by the child. The therapist must confront her with the child's misery and need for rescue. Although the child is in fact rejecting the attempts at interaction, he invariably demonstrates his ambivalence. The therapist must then show the mother how the child is expressing mixed feelings, both the wish to get close and the wish to withdraw. For example, even the larger and stronger children do not exceed the strength of the mother when they fight 'to get away'.

At first, the mothers do not hold very well. Like their autistic children, they fail to grasp with the open palms of their hands. The holding is often awkward and weak. The therapist must urge the mother to hold tightly and securely.

At first, the mothers do not want to hold their children. Even if they seem willing to do it under the therapist's instruction, they do not feel comfortable pursuing their child in this way. They must be made to understand that the actual holding will help them to feel like doing it. The mothers are apt to let go before a good resolution is reached. They must be exhorted to hold on until there is a good interaction.

Eventually, in the course of many sessions, the mother's feelings and attitudes toward the child and toward herself change. Her frozen or seemingly absent feelings for her child begin to emerge. After three months of therapy, one mother wept with relief at finally feeling love for her child. Also, the mother's self-esteem is greatly enhanced by her ability to reach her otherwise unreachable child. Her sense of failure caused by the failed relationship begins to be replaced by her triumph at retrieving her child.

Holding treatment benefits the mother as much as the child. The mother's conflicts as well as the child's are mobilized through holding. Maintaining contact physically ensures that the conflicts do not precipitate a break. The conflicts are then available for analysis and interpretation.

Ideally, the father should participate in this therapeutic process. In addition the maternal grandmother should be brought in as well. She becomes even more important in cases where there is no father available.

The essence of the mother–child holding sessions is as follows.

The mother is asked to physically hold the child.

Autistic children resist being held.

The mother must not be allowed to give up. She must hold the child closely and try to establish eye contact.

Eventually a battle ensues. The child may scream with rage and terror, bite, spit and hit.

The mother must hold on until the child relaxes, molds to her body, clings, gazes into her eyes, explores her face lovingly and gently, and eventually talks.

The mother must do this holding at home as well. She must hold the autistic child at least once a day plus whenever the child signals distress. Each holding lasts at least an hour.

In the sessions with the therapist, such a holding sequence must take place each time. These sessions are more complex because the holding is used to evoke the mother's feelings, to help her to examine them, and to help her resolve conflicts. When the father participates there is the further task of resolving conflicts between the two marriage partners as well as working on the father–child relationship. One problem which emerges frequently is the competition between the parents for reaching the child. The father must be helped to support the mother, not to replace her. The father's direct holding of the child must be a supplement to the mother's holding, not a substitute.

The therapist's role is complex.

First: to encourage, exhort or impel the mother to hold the child despite her child's resistance or her own reservations or inhibitions.

Second: to observe and translate the signals the mother and child give, but which each fails to understand.

Third: to analyze and interpret the conflicts, first between mother and child and then between mother and the other important family members. In a large family the task seems overwhelming at times.

Fourth: to tolerate the rage and depression the mother and child experience without withdrawing, thus providing an important role model.

Fifth: to engage the father's help. The mother and father must hold each other. The father at times holds the mother while she holds the child. He must learn to hold the child himself. He must hold the other children while the mother holds the autistic child.

Sixth: to work through the mother's problems in relating, particularly with her own mother and with her husband.

The therapist must not do the holding. It is important to let the family do the holding.

The same holding therapy process. must be done simultaneously between mother and father, otherwise the mother will be unable to sustain the intense effort necessary to retrieve the child. The therapist must teach the parents to physically hold on to each other, especially when they are angry. Anger is a potent cause of distance between marriage partners. When they learn to hold on through the anger, a new level of rapport is achieved. This rapport is communicated to the child through the mother's increased ability to give of herself.

Mother–child holding therapy thus involves the intensive treatment of the entire family complex. It is an exhausting undertaking, only worthwhile because of the positive results.

Case material

CASE 1

H.M. was referred at age 3½ years because he was mute, unable to relate to people, hyperactive, developmentally retarded, bizarre looking, and obsessed with flushing toilets and aligning blocks in an exact line. He had a tantrum whenever his obsessive activity was interrupted. H. M.'s mother was cold, distant, and intellectual.

Autism is a disruption of the mother–child bond was explained to the mother, and holding as the means of reaching the child was suggested. She declared that she had not held H. M. since the age of eight months except as necessary for clothing or feeding him. Just then H. M. had a tantrum because someone interrupted his obsessive toilet-flushing. His mother picked him up and started to hold him. H. M. protested at this intrusion into his defensive withdrawal. He screamed with rage and terror and tried to escape his mother's embrace. His mother held on until H. M. calmed down. After six weeks of daily sessions, H. M. spoke for the first time. After one fierce holding battle he said, 'Thank you for holding you'. He progressed from no speech directly to full sentences in one leap. From then on, his speech developed rapidly. Concomitantly his eye contact improved. Within six months he was playing happily with other children. By age 4½ years he was showing reading readiness. Now, at age eight years, he is in the third grade and functioning above grade level. He has excellent reasoning ability, a vivid imagination, tremendous curiosity and drive to learn. He has no behavior problems. Through holding he has achieved a mutually gratifying relationship with his mother who is now a warm, loving, gently persevering mother in contrast to the cold, distant, intellectual person who presented initially. H. M. strongly identifies with his father, with whom he is now very close.

CASE 2

P. R. presented at age seven years because he was unable to relate to people, hyperactive and destructive, developmentally retarded but showing signs of good potential, bizarre looking (including such gestures as hand flapping), speaking but only in non-communicative gibberish, and obsessed with aligning objects. He had tantrums whenever he was prevented from his obsessive behavior.

P. R. developed normally until around 13 months of age, when his brother was born. He had begun to speak but ceased all sound production until age four when, after speaking one meaningful sentence, he spoke only gibberish in English. His parents spoke only Spanish. P. R.'s mother was punitive and cold toward him. After one year of mother–child therapy, P. R. was no longer hyperactive. He was able to speak both English and Spanish. He read several grades above level. He was able to adjust to change and deal with his feelings verbally. When treatment was terminated after one year, he said, 'Can nothing stop you from leaving?'. When he was told no, he said, 'Then I won't talk anymore'. His first impulse was to withdraw. However, his mother, who had become lovingly persistent with him, continued to hold him and he continued to develop.

CASE 3

H. I. presented at age 2½ years, referred because he was developmentally retarded, unrelated to people, mute, bizarre looking, and fixated on spinning objects. He was an adopted child who seemed unresponsive to the adoptive mother right from the start and was left to himself because he seemed more content if undisturbed.

H. I. had been in mother–child pair treatment for two years prior to holding therapy. At the start of mother–child holding treatment, at age 4½ years, he was still unwilling to establish eye contact, unrelated to people, retarded, bizarre, still fixated on spinning objects, and had tantrums if he was not allowed to obsessively maintain sameness.

H. I. initially allowed himself to be held as long as he could avert his face from his mother and suck his thumb. When she insisted that he turn his face toward her, H. I. closed his eyes. When she persisted, a flood of emotion was released. After a holding session, H. I., like the other children being held, would explore his mother's face with his hands and with his eyes. He began to mold to his mother's body and to cling. H. I.'s mother held him daily as well as anytime he had a tantrum or showed another signal of distress. Holding the child during a tantrum was important because the underlying reason for the distress was his inability to relate in a more functional way. Holding re-established contact and helped the child to take consolation from his mother instead of from withdrawal.

After a year of treatment, H. I. had become warmly related to his mother as well as to other people. Now, at age nine years, three years after formal holding therapy was terminated, he is in the fourth grade, functioning above grade level. He is considered to be a gifted student. He plays normally and adjusts to change. He deals with his feelings verbally. He asks for daily holding with his mother who willingly gives it.

CASE 4

H. K. presented at 22 months, having been misdiagnosed as retarded. She was placed on phenobarbitol for one year, which led to further autistic withdrawal. When first seen by this observer, she was immobile and unresponsive. She was born with a severe eye muscle problem which prevented her from establishing eye contact with her mother. The mother was very depressed around the time of birth and felt that H. K. did not like her. Around the first year of life, the child began to be slightly more responsive, but two subsequent hospitalizations resulted in her complete withdrawal. At age 22 months she was developmentally retarded, unrelated, mute and hypokinetic.

H. K. responded immediately to enforced holding. She tried to avoid gaze, closed her eyes, cried, screamed and battled for at least an hour and a half. This reaction was altogether more emotion than she had shown in her life. Then she calmed down and allowed herself to be held. Afterward she said 'Grandpa' to her grandfather, called another person by his name, and began to play with a doll for the first time. Now she uses words and sentences and babbles and vocalizes the way a normal younger child does.

Her legs had been under-developed from disuse atrophy. She now walks well and likes to explore the world. Her curiosity is expanding weekly. She loves music and is now taking piano lessons. After three years of holding therapy, H. K. is not yet normal. She is reluctant to talk and recently said to her mother, 'Blah, blah, blah, I talk too much'. However, the therapy is still in progress and the changes continue. H. K. is just beginning to use speech to express her conflicts. Last week she told her mother that she hates her. Often she has verbalized her love for her parents but this was the first use of speech for negative feelings.

With H. K., as with the other children, each holding session repeats the same sequence: holding leads to crying, screaming, and fighting. H. K. clenches her hands to prevent open-palmed contact with her mother. When her palms are prized open, she clenches her toes. After 30–60 minutes she relaxes, molds, clings, makes eye contact, explores her mother's face, and often speaks.

CASE 5

L. G. presented at age 10 years, having been a resident of an institution for autistic children since the age of six. He was mute, unrelated to people, hyperactive and destructive, developmentally retarded, and bizarre in his movements and postures. He rocked and toe-walked, flapped his hands and drooled.

The initial history given by the mother indicated that L. G. had been a quiet and undemanding baby although he was normally responsive until age two months, after which time he seemed unresponsive. Subsequent to that time the mother remained preoccupied with supervising the building of their new house through L. G.'s first year and a half. She reported having left him alone in the car for hours at a time and day after day.

L. G. spoke after the first holding session. The damage from the lack of relating occurred in this case, as in the others, over a period of years. Surprisingly, the added injury of having been institutionalised did not appear to have made L. G. less reachable. However, it may have had irreparable effects on the mother's ability to rebond with L. G. She said that she would not send L. G. back to the institution if he would only speak. When he said a few words for the first time in his life, she immediately declared 'That's not enough. I will send him back'. Whereas he had begun to establish eye contact during the session, on hearing this he again avoided gaze and began banging the door. The withdrawal was marked and immediate.

Over the course of a few sessions of holding treatment, he did stop his destructive behavior. Because he no longer needed constant supervision, the family continued to keep him at home. When his mother held him and forced him to look at her, he began to cry for the first time and to show emotion like a normal child. The mother seemed at this moment to be profoundly moved by the appearance of his feelings.

These progressions occurred despite minimal contact between them. The mother slept late each morning while her younger daughter, age eight years, helped L. G. get off to a special school for autistic children. Generally she returned from work between 6.30 and 7.00 p.m. Often, but not regularly, she held L. G. for 30 to 45 minutes before he went to bed. If they came for their therapy appointments at all, they came one or more hours late. The father, who also attended the holding therapy sessions, was unable to be helpful. Therapy was interrupted in the summer when the parents elected to put their three children in eight-week camps so that they could go away together. They have not returned to treatment.

CASE 6

C. C. presented at age six months with a 5½-month history of disturbed behavior. From two weeks of age he was fussy, unco-operative and antisocial. He actively resisted contact by arching his back, averting his face, and often screaming and squirming to get away. He did not seem to differentiate his mother from other people. Responsive smiling only occurred from a distance of several feet. There was no anticipatory response to being picked up. He did not seem responsive to toys. He did not coo or babble. He refused solids or even baby food. Even when he nursed from the breast, he pushed his mother away with one arm as he sucked. He would allow himself to be held only if he could suck a pacifier and avert his gaze. Attempts at further contact elicited uncontrollable screaming and struggling.

C. C.'s mother had planned to have him and had wanted a boy. C. C. was her fourth child. However, she had had misgivings during the pregnancy about being tied down and about C. C.'s well-being. She had many worries about abnormalities. When C. C. was born with a precipitous delivery, the mother was upset because the doctor was not there. C. C. had an inturned foot and a bulging navel, two defects that confirmed his mother's premonitions about his being 'abnormal'. Then, when he developed jaundice, she felt even more convinced that C. C. was 'not as good as her other children'. These negative feelings interfered with her attachment to C. C. In fact, she reported that she had no feeling for him. She did not know that her lack of attachment to C. C. could be communicated to him because she nursed him as she had her others and had cared for him herself.

After two weeks of holding therapy, she began to feel protective of C. C. She held him daily. He cried, squirmed, tried to avert his gaze but eventually calmed down. He smiled at her, molded to her body for the first time, and began to cling to her. His development began to proceed normally. After three months of holding therapy, C. C.'s mother began to feel love for him. Now, at 13 months, he appears to be a normal, socially responsive, appealing little toddler. He shows the signs of good attachment to his mother as well as to his father. He is appropriately shy with strangers and is intensely interested in other youngsters. The mother's attitudes and demeanor toward C. C. are now those of a normal mother.

Discussion

The successful retrieval of several autistic children through mother–child holding therapy demonstrates that the prevalent view that autistic children will never achieve normal development is less secure than it once was.

Normal development proceeds in the context of a strong social tie between mother and child. In autism, this social tie is absent or, at best, very weak. It follows that creating or restoring a strong social tie between an autistic child and his mother will lead to normal development. In fact, this is the case.

Autism is the end result of faulty attachment between mother and child. The attachment or bonding process begins during pregnancy and is on-going throughout life. Although birth is a crucial time in the bonding process, and therefore subject to serious disruption, such as in the case of premature birth or other neonatal complication, the on-going attachment can be disrupted at any time in development. In general, the earlier the disruption, the more severe the attachment failure.

Any situation or event which interferes with the on-going attachment can lead to autism. For example, a sudden or prolonged mother–child separation can cause a child to withdraw. If a reconciliation is not effected, the withdrawal can become fixed, i.e. autism. However, just as the attachment can be disrupted at any time, so too can it be repaired at any time.

Autism is a problem of both child and mother. The conclusion that the problem arises from the interaction does not imply that the mother is to blame. The mother is just as much a victim as is the child. In each case I have examined, a situation or life-event interfered with the on-going bonding process. The result of the interaction was that the child withdrew, whether out of hopelessness, fear, frustration or anger. When the mother failed to retrieve the child, the withdrawal became fixed. All the cases I have seen were in a fixed state of failed relationship: the mothers depressed and hopeless about their children, or even worse, accepting of their children's autistic condition, and the children in autistic states of varying degrees of severity.

No life-event in and of itself will necessarily cause autism. Only in so far as the event catastrophically disrupts the mother–child relationship does it lead to autism. Consequently, any event or situation that severely disturbs the mother can cause some children to withdraw. At the moment of the disruption the mother is as deeply affected as is the child. The child's response, even if it starts with protest, eventually becomes one of withdrawal. The mother's response is failure to act in a way that retrieves the child from the withdrawal. There is a failure of reconciliation. The mother and child both adjust to this changed and deteriorated relationship, the child by an intensification of the autistic withdrawal, the mother by whatever mechanisms she has available to her. By the time she has adjusted, the child appears to be unreachable. By the time the pair are seen for diagnosis, both have settled into their adjusted states. The mother seems rational and able to cope, in contrast to the child who is obviously abnormal. However, a close look at the mother–child interaction will reveal that the mother in her own right is distanced from the child. In one severe case of autism, it was noted that the child made 20 physical approaches to the mother's one.

The mothers are generally more distanced from their autistic children than are the fathers. Before treatment, the fathers are strikingly more connected with the children and make more attempts to connect with the children than do the mothers. Another important observation is that the fathers are more motivated to establish contact with their children than with their wives. In some families, the parents display open rivalry over the child. In other families, the mother backs off further in face of the father's greater ability to deal with and relate to the child. In such cases, the mother is angry and rejecting toward the father. In all cases, there is faulty communication of feelings between the parents. The therapy must refocus the father on the mother. When the father can be helped to support and take care of the mother, the mother gains the resources to pursue the autistic child.

In the cases where the retrieval from autism to normal development was rapid, the difficulties between the parents were resolved quickly. In the slow cases, the mother and father resisted working on their problems of relating to each other.

In all cases, there were serious problems in the relationship between the mother and maternal grandmother. Also there was little or no physical contact between the two. In some cases there were outwardly good relations but on further examination there were fundamental gaps between mother and grandmother.

In the cases where there were siblings, the parents reported that the autistic child behaved better toward the sibling than toward the parents. A hallmark of the sibling interaction was that the sibling demanded more from the child – and got it. Parents of autistic children have difficulty raising their expectations of them.

Mother–child holding therapy provides the child with an avenue of escape from autism. The mother, in forcibly breaking through the autistic barrier, offers herself as the guide. In doing so, her capacity for love of her child is enlarged. The positive consequences of the effort begin an upward spiral that results in retrieval from autism. In giving so much of herself to save her child, the autist's mother feels she can permit herself to set limits, make demands, and create structure for her child instead of allowing him to live in a world of his own.

The most important aspect of the therapy is to motivate the mother and father to participate in it. All the children subjected to holding have responded positively. Not all mothers have been willing to do it, in spite of their children's readiness to be engaged.

Conclusion

The cases of autism studied and treated by this author demonstrate that it is possible to restore an autistic child to normal development by establishing a secure mother–child bond. The fact that these children responded to the repair of the mother–child relationship with normal development suggests that the sufficient cause of early childhood autism is the failure of the mother and child to establish or maintain a normal bond which is so vital for healthy development.

A treatment with the greatest probability of success consists of treating the mother–child pair by techniques that do not interpose the therapist between mother and child, but instead help the mother to break through the autistic barrier.

The therapeutic process described in this paper is not an easy solution but rather a hard, painful process for the treating psychiatrist as well as for the mother and child and their family. It is only because the results have been so impressive that this worker has been able to persist in using this technique.

The fact that normal learning and normal development followed the restoration of a close mother–child attachment suggests that this technique may have implications for treatment of other psychiatric disorders.

References

1   Kanner, L. 1972. *Child psychiatry,* 4th edn. Springfield, Ill.: C. C. Thomas.
2   Rimland, B. 1964. *Infantile autism. The syndrome and its implications for a neural theory of behavior,* 7–15. Englewood Cliffs, N J: Prentice-Hall.
3   O'Gorman, G. 1970. *The nature of childhood autism,* 2nd edn. New York: Appleton-Century-Crofts.
4   Fish, B. 1976. Pharmacotherapy for autistic and schizophrenic children. In *Autism: diagnosis, current research and management,* E. R. Ritvo, B. J. Freeman, E. M. Ornitz and P. E. Tanguay (eds), 107–19. New York: Spectrum.

5   Bender, L. 1955. Twenty years of clinical research on schizophrenic children, with special reference to those under six years of age. In *Emotional problems of early childhood,* G. Caplan (ed.) 503–13. New York: Basic Books.

6   Campbell, M. 1975. Pharmacotherapy in early infantile autism. *Biol. Psychiat.* **10,** 399–423.

7   Hawkins, D. R. and L. Pauling (eds) 1975. *Orthomolecular psychiatry.* San Francisco: W. H. Freeman.

8   Weiner, J. M. 1977. *Psychopharmacology in childhood and adolescence.* New York: Basic Books.

9   Fenichel, C. 1974. Special education as the basic therapeutic tool in the treatment of severely disturbed children. *J. Aut. Childhd Schizophrenia* **4,** 177–86.

10   Fisher, I. 1970. Programmed teaching of autistic children. *Arch. Gen. Psychiat.* **23,** 90–94.

11   Frankel, F. 1976. Experimental studies of autistic children in the classroom. In *Autism: diagnosis, current research and management,* E. R. Ritvo, B. J. Freeman, E. M. Ornitz and P. E. Tanguay (eds), 185–97. New York: Spectrum.

12   Graziano, A. M. 1970. A group treatment approach to multiple problem behaviour of autistic children. *Exceptional Children* **36,** 765–70.

13   Koegel, R. L. and A. Rincover 1974. Treatment of psychotic children in the classroom environment I. Learning in a large group. *J. Appl. Behav. Anal.* **7,** 45–59.

14   Lansing, M. D. and E. Schopler 1978. Individualized education: a public school model. In *Autism: a reappraisal of concepts and treatment,* M. Rutter and E. Schopler (eds), 435–52. New York: Plenum Press.

15   Lovaas, O. I., L. Schreibman and R. L. Koegel 1974. A behavior modification approach to the treatment of autistic children. *J. Aut. Childhd Schizophrenia* **4,** 111–29.

16   Lovaas, O. I. 1977. *The autistic child: language development through behavior modification.* New York: Irvington.

17   Ornitz, E. M. and E. R. Ritvo 1976. The syndrome of autism: a critical review. *Am. J. Psychiat.* **133,** 609–21.

18   Rutter, M. and F. A. Sussenwein 1971. A developmental and behavioral approach to the treatment of preschool autistic children. *J. Aut. Childhd Schizophrenia* **1,** 376–97.

19   Wing, L. 1976. *Early childhood autism: clinical, educational and social aspects,* 2nd edn. Oxford: Pergamon.

20   Freeman, B. J. and E. R. Ritvo 1976. Parents as paraprofessionals. In *Autism: diagnosis, current research and management,* E. R. Ritvo, B. J. Freeman, E. M. Ornitz and P. E. Tanguay (eds), 277–85. New York: Spectrum.

21   Hemsley, R., P. Howlin, M. Berger, L. Hersov, D. Holbrook, M. Rutter and W. Yule 1978. Treating autistic children in a family context. In *Autism: a reappraisal of concepts and treatment,* M. Rutter and E. Schopler (eds), 379–412. New York: Plenum Press.

22   Kugelmass, N. 1970. *The autistic child.* Springfield, Ill.: C. C. Thomas.

23   Lovaas, O. I. 1978. Parents as therapists. In *Autism: a reappraisal of concepts and treatment,* M. Rutter and E. Schopler (eds), 369–78. New York: Plenum Press.

24   Schopler, E. and R. Reichler 1971. Parents as cotherapists of psychotic children. *J. Aut. Childhd Schizophrenia* **1,** 87–102.

25   Schopler, E. 1978. Changing parental involvement in behavioral treatment. In *Autism: a reappraisal of concepts and treatment,* M. Rutter and E. Schopler (eds), 413–22. New York: Plenum Press.

26   Axline, V. 1964. *Dibs – in search of self.* New York: Penguin.

27   D'Ambrosio, R. 1971. *No language but a cry.* London: Cassell.

28   Des Lauriers, A. M. 1978. Play, symbols and the development of language. In

Autism: a reappraisal of concepts and treatment, M. Rutter and E. Schopler (eds), 327–36. New York: Plenum Press.

29 Rank, B. 1955. Adaptation of the psychoanalytic technique for the treatment of young children with atypical development. In *Emotional problems of early childhood,* G. Caplan (ed.), 491–502. New York: Basic Books.

30 Szurek, S. A. and I. N. Berlin 1956. Elements of psychotherapeutics with the schizophrenic child and his parents. *Psychiatry* **19**, 1–9.

31 Waal, N. C. 1955. A special technique of psychotherapy with an autistic child. In *Emotional problems of early childhood,* G. Caplan (ed.), 431–49. New York: Basic Books.

32 Ward, A. J. 1970. Early infantile autism: diagnosis, etiology and treatment. *Psychol Bull.* **73**, 350–62.

33 DeMyer, M. R., S. Barton, W. E. DeMyer, J. A. Norton, J. Allen and R. Steel 1973. Prognosis in autism: a follow-up study. *J. Aut. Childhd Schizophrenia* **3**, 199–245.

34 Kanner, L. 1971. Follow-up study of eleven autistic children originally reported in 1943. *J. Aut. Childhd Schizophrenia* **1**, 119–45.

35 Kanner, L. 1971. Approaches: retrospect and prospect. *J. Aut. Childhd Schizophrenia* **1**, 453–9.

36 Kanner, L., A. Rodriguez and B. Ashenden 1972. How far can autistic children go in matters of social adaptation? *J. Aut. Childhd Schizophrenia* **2**, 9–33.

37 Wenar, C. and B. Ruttenberg 1976. The use of B R I A C for evaluating therapeutic effectiveness. *J. Aut. Childhd Schizophrenia* **6**, 175–91.

38 Tinbergen, N. 1974. Ethology and stress diseases. *Science* **185**, 20–27.

39 Tinbergen, E. A. and N. Tinbergen 1972. *Early childhood autism: an ethological approach.* Berlin: Paul Parey.

40 Bettelheim, B. 1967. *The empty fortress: infantile autism and the birth of self.* New York: Free Press.

41 Goldfarb, W. A. 1970. A follow-up investigation of schizophrenic children treated in residence. *Psychosocial Process* **11**, 9–64.

42 Kaufman, B. N. 1977. *Son rise.* New York: Warner.

43 Zaslow, R. and L. Breger 1969. A theory and treatment of autism. In *Clinical cognitive psychology,* L. Breger (ed.), 246–89. Englewood Cliffs, N J: Prentice-Hall.

44 Hersher, L., J. B. Richmond and A. U. Moore 1963. Modifiability of the critical period for the development of maternal behavior in sheep and goats. *Behavior* **20**, 311–20.

45 Bowlby, J. 1969. Attachment and loss. Vol. 1: *Attachment,* 349. New York: Basic Books.

46 Bowlby, J. 1969. Attachment and loss. Vol. 1: *Attachment,* 346. New York: Basic Books.

47 Winnicott, D. W. 1971. *Playing and reality,* 89. New York: Basic Books.

Appendix II: treating autistic children in a community setting

Michele Zappella MD
Head of the Department of Child Neurology and Psychiatry,
Ospedale Regionale, Via Mattioli 10, Siena, Italy

This report summarises eight years' experience in treating autistic children through fostering reciprocal interaction between such children and the people amongst whom they lead their everyday lives. At first, the treatment involved mainly therapists, but later the children's families were increasingly involved, with the parents playing the key roles. Our therapeutic 'strategy' evolved as a result of growing experience and of work done by colleagues abroad.

The work was initiated when special classes and institutions for 'difficult' children were being closed, so that the children concerned had to return to living with their parents and attending day schools only. This in turn prompted the therapists and psychiatrists concerned to visit and observe these children in their homes, schools and villages and to find ways in which they could be encouraged to make more contact with people and objects around them. This switch away from institutions and towards the community, and from clinic or institution to 'fieldwork', soon proved particularly fruitful for the treatment of autistic children.

From the first, I was impressed by the natural ability of some non-professionals found in these communities; for instance, some students, teachers and even normal children were able to establish and develop a kind of 'dialogue' with autistic children and in the process elicit in them many more responses and make them show much more general interest than I had previously seen in the hospital setting. In this early stage it was the paper by Tinbergen and Tinbergen (1972) that helped me to interpret and understand much of what was happening, and make sense of the positive (as well as of the negative) results.

In the schools we found that some children even showed a preference for making contact with an autistic child, took him by the hand, talked to him and, partly by guiding his hands, made him take part in a variety of activities. They were throughout kind to him, made a great deal of bodily contact, oriented themselves often sideways rather than face-to-face with him and were obviously strongly motivated. The same was true of the successful adults who concentrated on autistic children. In this setting it was also obvious that autistic children could learn a great deal by observing others from a distance; during gymnastic games, for instance, an autist could often be seen to place himself behind other children, observing and then successfully imitating them. Or he could be seen to observe other children playing during the morning and then, after school was over, trying on his own to repeat some of the play sequences he had observed. Through this observational learning and also by being guided ('put through') in a number of movements, the autistic children could be induced to undertake a variety of activities, including, for instance, building with blocks, finger painting and drawing. Our general policy or 'strategy' was to treat the children with a combination of kind, sympathetic and non-intrusive behaviour and, on occasion, more vigorous and even intrusive, instructing interference. These two approaches were mixed and applied in alternation in a variety of ways, dependent on what close observation and intuition made us feel was best at any given moment. Throughout, we tried to discern the children's deeper needs and to foster their trust in people and to promote their mental growth. As a result, the autistic children in our charge almost invariably began to relate emotionally to people and to the outside world.

Guided by these experiences, I began to search – among therapists, teachers, children and other members of the communities involved – for individuals with the right emotional attitude and motivation for establishing this kind of 'dialogue' with autistic children. I also found that, apart from selecting individuals who showed natural gifts in this direction, I could to a certain extent educate them for their roles. For example, when the child described in Case 1 (p. 340) began to emerge from his lonely autistic state and began to hit smaller boys in his classroom, then run to another class, tell the teacher what he had done and proceed to beat up other children, thus creating chaos on an entire floor, the teachers did not interfere, partly because they were afraid of intensifying the boy's aggressiveness, partly because they were afraid of being criticised for constraining the boy, yet at the same time aware of the danger of children being really injured, or made into misfits in their turn, with possibly police interference as a result. When I was called in, I spoke to all the teachers on the floor and impressed on them the need not only for sympathy with autistic children but also for disciplining them when necessary. When I visited the school again a month later, the teachers had acted on this seemingly paradoxical advice, order had been restored, and the boy's progress had continued.

This combination and alternation of attempts at understanding and supporting autistic children and at disciplining them was applied by me in many different ways, adjusting the 'strategy' to the needs as I saw them. What emerged in this phase of my work was that under this type of treatment autistic children can profit from being members of a community and can show striking improvements in their condition, provided they can live in a stable and emotionally rich environment.

As part of this procedure, I visited the children often, together with an occupational therapist or nurse, in their villages, their homes and their schools, and I also invited the children with their families to regular visits to our out-patients' department, all the while trying to find new ways to enrich the children's ability to communicate and to master their environments. However, I was still far from thinking that the family could be the focal point of treatment; most of the time the children were dealt with outside their homes. This stage of my thinking is reflected in my book *Il pesce bambino* (1976), Milano; Feltrinelli (French translation, *L'enfant poisson* (1979) Paris; Payot).

Follow-up studies on these children showed me that only those of them whose families had developed an intense, rich and varied 'circulation of emotion' made further progress, whereas other children deteriorated after our treatment ended. It turned out that the latter children lived in families with a certain degree of internal disharmony, friction or disunity.

Among the successful cases, I mention a child whose mother had rubella during her pregnancy, who was born deaf and, when seen by me at 3½ years, was severely autistic, mute, incontinent, showing many stereotypies and no functionally useful behaviour. When treated along the lines described above, he almost recovered and this recovery became even more striking when his mother began to take part in his 'orthophonic' rehabilitation and developed an intense bond with him. He is now 11 years old, attends with good results the fourth form at school and shows an adequate emotional and social adjustment.

Another child came to my notice when he was 3½ years old; he was very withdrawn and showed consistent gaze aversion, was able to repeat only a few words in an echolalic manner and came from a family full of intense conflicts. The family situation became much more harmonic when the mother was sent away from home and the child remained with his father, his sister and his paternal grandparents. A warm relationship developed between the boy and this 'pruned' family. He was sent to a nursery school where he was dealt with carefully under my periodic supervision. By the age of six years, he had become quite normal in language and in his cognitive, emotional and social behaviour. He is now 9½ years old, attends with good results the fourth form and has remained entirely normal.

In other cases, however, conflicts and difficulties in communication within a family could prevent or reverse progress. I was in particular impressed by the catastrophic deterioration of a child who during two years of treatment had, in spite of disharmony in the family, become near-normal, when the parents decided to break off the treatment; when they returned with him after a year and a half all the progress had become undone and the child was again in a most desperate autistic isolation.

At about the same time I began to receive requests for treatment from families living in distant towns. The combination of family disharmony as a cause of failure in an initially successful treatment, of successes with children in a harmonious community and family, and requests from families who could not find local help yet lived too far away for me to see them regularly, made me decide to aim at a more direct involvement of the family in the treatment of autistic children.

The following is a summary of one of a number of cases reported in my book, *Il Bambino nell Luna* (1979), Milano: Feltrinelli.

CASE 1

Antonio, the only child of two young parents, was first seen by me when he was 6½ years old. He lived withdrawn from people, spoke mostly in the third person or in an echolalic, often unintelligible way, and showed occasional gaze aversion. He had bouts of extreme anxiety, especially during thunderstorms or when he was hurt. He was able to draw complex, tube-like figures but did not draw human beings. He had initially developed normally, but had begun to show autistic traits at two years of age, after which he progressively deteriorated. There had been friction and disharmony between the parents at the start of their marriage, when the child was born, and afterwards.

To start with, Antonio and his parents came to see me or were visited by me at their home every ten days; we also had meetings with his teacher and with other teachers at his school.

Following my advice to become more involved with their child, the father responded first by engaging in playing with his son, building with blocks with him and supporting him in learning to read and write. A strong bond developed between father and son. The mother, partly encumbered by conflicts with her husband, partly by domestic demands and partly by feeling guilty and a less adequate parent than her husband, succeeded far less well in establishing a bond with her son.

During repeated discussions with both parents (in which I told them of very similar feelings of inadequacy I had had myself after my first child had been born) the parents' difficulties were discussed, which helped to dissolve the guilt feelings of the mother and the less strong feelings of guilt of the father, and soon the mother began to take a more active part in building a bond with her son. The family became better organized, and the child's imaginative and quite artistic achievements, evident, for instance, in his ability to transform numerals into amusing animal forms, were encouraged. For some months the father, who was on friendly terms with the boy's teacher, attended Antonio's school for approximately two hours every day, giving him moral support until he could be left at school entirely on his own.

One year after the beginning of this treatment, Antonio was speaking normally, was able to read and write, had an adequate contact with his parents and with other adults and, apart from a residual shyness in his relations with his peers, was normal in every respect. He has subsequently been seen by me at six-month intervals and now, three years after the end of the treatment and 10 years old, he has a greatly improved social ability, behaves on the whole like a normal boy of his age and attends with good results the fifth form of his primary school.

This and many similar cases strengthened me in my conviction that autistic children could often be helped by involving their parents and other non-professionals in the therapy, and that this succeeded best when there was harmony within the family and the community, whereas disunity and friction within the family held back improvement or caused deterioration. I helped establish or restore harmony in a variety of ways: sometimes it was helpful to separate the parents during part of the day so that now one, then the other, could be occupied with the child, thus freeing the partner for other tasks; in other cases, both parents could become involved in a common project with their child, such as making puppets and then organising little theatrical performances with him; and other activities in which the parents together joined their child's activities of an intellectual, imaginative, creative or artistic nature, and in general helped him in extending, elaborating and enriching his development. As with normal people, such sharing of the experience of the 'marvellousness' of even every-day life is mutually stimulating and growth promoting. In my experience it is especially in this direction that autistic children both want and need special nurturing.

My conviction that autistic children can be helped by engaging the help of their parents, family and the community was strengthened and made more explicit when, in 1979, I heard of the work of Dr Martha Welch of New York, to which Professor and Mrs Tinbergen drew my attention. Dr Welch allowed me to read a paper she had prepared (the precursor of the contribution printed here as Appendix I) and we met in Oxford for discussions and a first study of each other's videotape records, and later when Dr Welch visited me in Siena, where I had the chance to work at her side for a day. This contact led to the third stage of the evolution of our strategy: it induced me to add progressively three additional therapeutic procedures: (a) making more use of face-to-face interaction (whereas up till then I had considered side-by-side orientation preferable); (b) encouraging the mother to engage in maternal behaviour that instinctively and culturally form part of any normal mother's role, including but going beyond simple 'holding'; and finally (c) having the mother provoke her child in various ways to foster his growth, followed always by warm, affectionate bodily contact with him. I found that this new, close, frontal 'scenario' for the mother–child relationship was indeed important for the recovery of an autistic child and of his mother alike, but that it also entailed certain risks, such as that of sliding off into the mere mechanics of holding, with resulting monotony and passive, non-stimulating behaviour of the mother. As Dr Welch emphasises, it is reciprocal, warm, affectionate behaviour which we have to help both mother and child achieve. (Note by T. and T.: as is clear from our main text, we believe that the return to earlier phases of affiliation is an equally important aspect of the Welch method).

The following cases, all treated in this third phase, i.e. in the year ending April 1981, illustrate the importance of adding elements of the Welch procedure to my earlier therapy.

CASE 2

George was six years old when I first met him; he was affected by Leber's disease, a rare congetical condition which involves loss of foveal vision, though peripheral vision is functional. His older brother was also affected by this disease, while the firstborn, a girl, was normal. George's birth had been normal and he had begun to walk alone and say his first words at 11 months. In his second year, however, speaking and spontaneous walking had stopped. When I first met him he spent most of his time alone, sitting or lying down, making continuous, repetitive hand-flicking movements, not uttering any words or responding to speech; he showed gaze aversion and could take no more than a few steps unaided. He lived with his parents, sibs and paternal grandparents.

Treatment began with 'maternal holding' and, although the mother did this consistently and in long sessions, no progress was made in the first three months. At first the family visited our out-patients' clinic once every fortnight, but I soon began to visit them in their home. I noticed then that the mother's schedule consisted of mornings of domestic work in their large living quarters and, in the afternoons, driving her children to and from various outside destinations. After a visit of a few hours, I could suggest a number of alterations in their life-style, such as the provision of more and new toys and a number of changes in personal and social attitudes about which I had not known before.

Shortly after, a change occurred when the mother had taken George to the hairdresser and, when he started his usual vigorous resistance, had taken his head firmly in her hands, held him close face to face, and had angrily told him to be quiet and behave properly. He suddenly complied. At home she continued to give him a number of very firm orders and obtained from him a number of achievements she had never before seen of him.

I asked the mother to re-enact what she had done and to put into it all her energies and spontaneity. She took him in her arms, held him face to face, spoke loudly to him, asking him to call her 'Mummy' because she had had enough of his silence; then she held him down under her, repeating her request for several minutes although the child was screaming; then suddenly he said, weeping, 'Mummy, Mummy!'. She then took him again in her arms, talked to him now very sweetly, now jokingly and even teasingly, whereupon he began to laugh and repeated several of the words she was saying.

On this occasion the mother told me of her pride in having achieved this of her own accord; so far she had never felt confident as a mother and also felt inhibited by her parents-in-law. Now she decided to devote entire afternoons to occupying herself with him (during the mornings he attended school).

In the following four months she continued her sessions of face-to-face contact with George but varied the procedure; for instance, she soon stopped holding him but maintained a great deal of bodily contact. She began to demand that he dress and undress himself, and began also to guide his hands in building towers etc. of blocks, and other activities. While showing great educational ability, she did need occasional moral support for keeping her motivation at the required level. During this period a degree of disharmony between the parents became noticeable which, while probably harmless in a normal family, may well have added to the strain caused by two sensorily deprived children (the elder son had also at times related poorly to his parents and others).

Now, four months after his mother's discovery of her own parental ability, George can articulate at least 50 words, can say short, appropriate sentences, eats without help, is able to dress and undress himself, walks and runs about, plays with a ball and other objects and has a close, warm contact with his parents, the rest of his family and his teachers. Many of his stereotypies have stopped.

Throughout the treatment, George's father and the grandparents had understood the need for the mother's central role and had given her full support.

CASE 3

I met Simon first when he was 5½ years of age. He showed consistent gaze aversion and was seriously hyperactive. He was able to open doors, but could not catch objects in his hands. His speech was largely an unintelligible 'salad' of words with some echolalic features. He was an only child in a disturbed family. His father had been diagnosed as 'psychotic'; he was aggressive and critical towards his wife, had ideas of grandeur (which were probably due to basic feelings of insecurity) and often left home for needlessly long days. In his work as a shop assistant, he was fairly efficient. The mother was a passive, resigned woman, openly called 'mentally retarded' by other members of the extended family living with them – the paternal grandparents and a sister of the father. Since Simon's parents were considered inadequate, he stayed usually with his maternal grandmother, the domineering figure of this group, and with his paternal aunt.

An initial period of 1½ years' treatment, with periodic sessions involving the entire extended family and also the nursery school, failed, and at seven years Simon was only marginally better than at 5½ when this treatment began. I then initiated weekly sessions of occupational therapy in which his mother's presence was requested. She took part in some of these sessions and co-operated with the therapist in attempting playful interaction with Simon. A few weeks later, the entire extended family moved to another town, but at my insistence Simon and his mother stayed behind, for I considered her a potentially perfect capable mother.

While the occupational therapy sessions and school attendance continued, I recommended to the mother that she hold Simon in her arms every day for long periods of time. When I first saw her after the departure of the rest of the family she was very happy and told me that she felt for the first time that she was in sole, full and satisfying charge of her child. She held him regularly in her arms and took a number of initiatives to foster his development in such things as catching objects, eating without help, and even drawing. Her husband, until then so remote from her and from his only child, now began to return often for short visits and became actively involved in the treatment. When, after six months' separation, the rest of the family returned, the situation had completely changed. Both parents were transformed and played their parental parts in full; the mother was now full of energy and decisiveness in matters concerning her son; her husband was close to her and to his son, acting as a modest, simple father without a trace of his former psychotic behaviour. Now, one year later, Simon is capable of speaking fluently in full sentences without any echolalia, looks directly at people, makes bodily contact, is no longer hyperactive, makes drawings of the human figure, can name colours and shows rapid and continuing progress.

CASE 4

Joseph was four years old when he first came to our out-patients' clinic. He showed mildly autistic features, such as keeping his distance from others, speaking often in the third person and at times showing echolalia, but he did not avert his gaze and he asked an occasional direct question. He was able to build a simple tower with a few cubes, but never took a pencil in his hand. He had two older sisters aged seven and eight, very intelligent and active, but they did not relate much with him. When I met them, there were no signs of friction between the parents but they had in the past had some difficulties.

I asked the mother to take Joseph in her arms in a face-to-face position, look him in the eyes, soothe him for at least one or two hours every day, and I asked the father to engage with his son in a variety of rough-and-tumble games. Both parents were co-operative and, when I saw their child a month later, his autistic features were rapidly disappearing: he was speaking directly most of the time, was less withdrawn and played a great deal with others. In subsequent months, these improvements continued and our treatment began to concentrate more on helping him overcome his cognitive retardation. Now, a year after the first visit, he relates normally to adults and children, shows no autistic features at all, draws (for instance) houses in considerable detail and climbs steadily towards the level of ability normal for his age.

CASE 5

Olivia, when first seen at three years of age, was severely autistic. She showed extreme social avoidance, had a sad facial expression, banged her fists, held one over the other almost continuously on the substrate, showed gaze aversion and did not respond to speech, and her vocalisations were unintelligible sequences of sounds.

Her development had apparently been normal during the first two years, but autistic traits developed when her mother became overworked: Olivia was put in a nursery from 8 a.m. to 6 p.m., the family moved house and lost contact with relatives to whom she seemed to have been attached, and there was a sudden change of all the teachers who had been involved with her in the nursery.

Treatment began by giving the parents a number of practical directives, such as advising the mother to take her daughter in the bath with her, to caress her and speak kindly to her while sitting side by side and encouraging similar friendly but not too direct interactions with other members of the family. I urged them to play simple games with Olivia, such as pat-a-cake and hide-and-seek, and to adopt a warm smiling attitude. After the first session, the parents decided by themselves to leave town and to return to live with the mother's parents, both peasants living in the country. I then encouraged them to let Olivia play with animals, which she obviously loved to do. It was soon seen that she handled objects frequently when she thought herself unobserved; she was therefore put slightly behind her parents during meals and allowed to take food with her hands without others watching her. I also encouraged the mother to take Olivia to bed with her and to talk to her and caress her.

In a month, Olivia had become an apparently happy, frequently smiling little girl; she could eat without help, though with her hands only; she now went up and down the stairs; and some intelligible words could be heard in her otherwise still chaotic babbling. But she still continued her fist-banging. At that time the main therapeutically effective person in her environment was probably her grandfather, who had an extraordinary ability to glance and smile at her without moving the rest of his body, or to do a sort of dance with the upper part of his body while remaining seated; this made the child laugh and scream for joy, dance around him and even jokingly call him, and beat him in the face. At that time I heard of the Welch treatment and I began to add this to what was already being done. During the first two months, however, there was little further improvement. Then her mother, paternal grandmother and aunt took her to the seaside for a month's holiday while her grandfather stayed behind. Olivia became very nervous, and often cried and screamed, calling desperately for her grandfather. It took six months after their return to the grandparents' home for Olivia to regain her previous level. The parents were deeply depressed about this setback and felt that Olivia would never recover. I then asked the mother to stop working for at least three months, to stay continuously with Olivia, to hold her, look her in the eyes, urge her to repeat words she said to her, caress her and joke with her. I advised both parents to guide her hands to touch and grasp objects, to keep her hands in theirs and close to their bodies. Now Olivia improved rapidly, and the parents began to initiate a number of imaginative new activities and situations; her father, for instance, gave her a pony ride every day, which she enjoyed very much. In this time she also showed signs of artistic sensitivity: in the out-patients' clinic she kept going to some attractive paintings made on a glass door, touching them and exclaiming 'how beautiful!'.

Three months have now passed since Olivia's mother stopped working away from the home; Olivia has entirely stopped banging her fists, she uses at least 30 words appropriately, speaks short sentences, eats without help, and displays a rich variety of facial expressions, sometimes slightly melancholic, but more often happy and smiling. She no longer averts her gaze, she responds to speech and relates to her parents, to her relatives and to us in a rich and varied way and shows hardly any autistic behaviour any more.

Conclusions

My experiences to date (15 April 1981) have strengthened me in my view that autism is essentially the expression of a child's inability to enter into reciprocal relationships with people, and that it can be cured by helping him to establish such relationships. The relationship may be made with any person in the child's environment, but I agree with Dr Welch that, in general, the child's mother seems naturally and culturally best suited to initiate the required socialisation.

I have now followed three children for three years after the end of my treatment, viz. the maternal rubella child described above, the child mentioned after him and the child of Case 1; and all three have remained normal throughout this follow-up period and their emotional relations with their families and others are good, and have developed in the normal way. The children treated in the last 12 months (cases 2, 3, 4 and 5) have lost most of their autistic traits, and in every case this has come about when they began to develop emotional attachments with one or more members of the family. Interruption of contact with such an attachment figure can cause disastrous setbacks, as was clear in Olivia's case.

In the last 12 months I have been treating four more autistic children. Two of them are identical twins; their condition has improved considerably but they are still fairly withdrawn and show occasional mannerisms; their treatment has to be continued, but already shows great promise. A third child was withdrawn from the 'holding' treatment (which the mother had initiated very ably) when, during the first six months, serious frictions began within the family which I was unable to prevent; this, the lack of progress of the child and the fact that the family lived 500 miles from Siena and could not be properly instructed and supervised by me, probably discouraged the parents and made them give up the treatment. The fourth new child has likewise made little progress, but he too lives far from Siena (250 miles) and certain disruptive features of his family too may well explain the slight progress made so far. Therefore, 9 out of 11 cases have profited greatly from our type of treatment, to which the incorporation of the Welch technique has been a valuable addition, even though the earlier forms of treatment-by-the-family had already proved effective. The two twins have not been under treatment long enough for a definite assessment, and the two failures are in all likelihood due to insufficient contact between the parents and us, combined with disruptive elements within the families.

Our experience so far has led to the following guidelines:

(a) Families with an autistic child are in need of the advice and supervision of a therapist or group of therapists who live not too far away, so that frequent contacts in clinic or at the family's house can help the parents and school teachers develop appropriate strategies – which involve alternating between minimal and maximal intrusiveness. Thus kindness, cuddling, low-tone speaking, avoidance of direct eye contact etc. must alternate with at times enforced 'putting through' or other ways of firm guiding, face-to-face confrontation, firm holding etc. At times the parents might also well express their sorrow at their child's unco-operativeness and urge him to grow up and 'be his age'. Non-verbal interaction, including rough-and-tumble play and non-verbal joking, can help the child develop verbal interaction. Animals can be introduced to take their part in starting social bonding.

(b) The child's natural delight in the beautiful and the 'marvellous' can be enhanced by introducing him to beautiful things and inducing him to join others in admiring and enjoying them; this, such shared happy experiences and joking together with others, may help in developing emotional bonds with them.

(c) Parents as well as teachers need occasional, repeated moral support and encouragement, especially to help them overcome disappointment about temporary setbacks or lack of progress.

(d) A harmonious atmosphere within the family is of the utmost importance, and the therapists have a vital part to play in trying to discover and then to smooth out disruptive conditions and attitudes. Sometimes it is necessary to allocate separate roles to the two parents, sometimes they have to be confronted, at times almost brutally, with their shortcomings; yet at the same time they must be helped to maintain hope. If the therapist succeeds in restoring harmony within the family, he enables the parents to support each other in their difficult task of 'superparenting'. It has on occasion proved helpful when the therapist could tell parents that he himself had experienced difficulties with his own spouse or children. This again is easiest if the members of a team of therapists can exchange such experiences amongst themselves.

Finally, it will be clear that our therapeutic procedures are still in the process of further development; even so, the cases described here demonstrate that, and how, autistic children and their parents can be guided back to normality and happiness.

Postscript*

After we had completed the text of this book, we received new information about the effectiveness of Dr Welch's method of 'forced holding' from Dr Jirina Prekop, Senior Clinical Psychologist at the Paediatric Centre of the Olga Hospital in Stuttgart, Germany. She told us that her decision to give this therapy a try was made when, having read newspaper reports about a lecture given by N. T. in June 1981 in Lindau, and having heard about our visit to a family with an autistic child in Southern Germany in that same summer, she had obtained more detailed information from us. Another consideration was that she had so far, in her long practice, not succeeded in really curing autistic children. Beginning in July 1981, Dr Prekop tried to initiate 37 couples living in her area (Baden-Württemberg) who each had an autistic child, into Dr Welch's method. The results in the first half year were so striking that she decided to publish them in a preliminary report, which has been accepted for publication in the summer 1982 issue of *Autismus*, the journal of the German Society for Autistic Children (Hilfe für das Autistische Kind). We are grateful to Dr Prekop for permission to add the gist of her report here, and to Messrs George Allen and Unwin for their willingness to incorporate this new evidence in our book.

In eight of the 37 cases, the child concerned proved either too strong physically for the mother, or the mother was not well enough to undertake the holding, or she felt she did not have the time, or the parents did not believe in the method ('too simplistic in view of the fact that even the best experts have failed'). The 29 remaining cases were divided by Dr Prekop into:

(a) 19 cases in which the child showed 'the typical autistic syndrome as described by Kanner';

(b) six cases of 'clear autistic psychopathology with high intelligence (Asperger children)';

(c) four cases in which structural brain-damage had been demonstrated and where autism had developed as a secondary effect of this ('consequential autism' – T. and T.).

The ages of the children ranged from 2½ to 17½ years; their average age was 7½ years. Of the 25 children in categories (a) and (b), 21 had been strikingly quiet, 'good' babies from birth, who did not elicit much motherly attention. Six of these 21 positively disliked bodily contact; the mothers of 12 of them reported that, when they had been crying, they

* The material on pages 351 and 352 has been added in the second impression.

calmed down most quickly if they were left alone. Four of the 25 had been 'criers'; of these one had always been cuddled a great deal until he stopped crying, while in the three others such extra motherly care had been irregular. All the mothers of the quiet babies 'had always responded normally to their other children when they cried', and these normal sibs had all developed into contact-loving, initiative-taking, charming children; this suggests that these parents were capable of rearing children normally, and that the autism in their other child was primarily due to the personality of the child.

Interestingly, Dr Prekop discovered that not one of the official case histories of these children (not even those she had written down herself) had mentioned whether or not any of them had wanted, and received, maternal approach and consolation. To discover this she had in every case to conduct a special interview. She remarks that she then realised that case reports 'contain as a rule objective, measurable, tangible information about such things as body weight, size of head, amounts drunk, age when the child had begun to walk, to talk, etc., as if affective behaviour were not important or not recordable'. (This is of course where the ethological approach can be so helpful – T. and T.).

Twenty-four of the autistic children had previously been treated under Dr Prekop's supervision for a considerable time: some for four years, others for only a few months; the average length of previous supervision had been two years. The procedure in this 'pre-Welch' phase had been an integrative one (as described in J. Prekop, Förderung der Wahrnehmung bei entwicklungsgestörten Kindern. *Geistige Behinderung*, issues 2, 3, and 4, 1980 and issue 1, 1981) but the results had been disappointing with the autistic ones.

With the 29 autistic children mentioned in the present report, forced holding was introduced between August and December 1981. As a rule, holding was done with each child once or twice each day, for periods of about one hour.

Results

Without a single exception all these children – whatever their age; irrespective of whether they had first received different treatment or not; and whether 'typically autistic', 'psychotic' or structurally brain-damaged – became more relaxed, more quiet, more receptive, more alert and more cheerful, and they quickly began to make more contact with their mothers, including more and more attentive eye contact. Holding therefore caused a profound change, more striking than had ever been achieved with the previous treatments. The extremely strong initial resistance against being held soon gave way to obvious delight in the contact with the mother. The relation with the mother became altogether more intimate and 'more conscious'. In none of the children was the disturbed behaviour strengthened; on the contrary, the ill-temper, the restiveness and the destructive tendencies waned.

All the mothers, however reluctant they had been at the start, however hard they had to work, however much they had disliked intimate contact, were soon overjoyed to see the change in their children. Some of them thanked the therapist for having coerced them; all of them acknowledged that the holding had started a real emotional improvement in their children. They also began to gain confidence, and none of them wanted to abolish the holding in the future.

Dr Prekop ended her original report by emphasising that it covered only the first six months, so that, however real the progress had been in every single case, none of the children had yet completely recovered. She writes that *in themselves* these results justify neither euphoria nor *a priori* rejection of the Welch procedure.

Latest information

In an updated progress report for this impression, and now after 28 months of experience involving 104 cases, Dr Prekop states:

'Whereas behaviour therapy, perception exercises, therapies to promote activity, etc., had led at best to partial improvements, the Welch therapy made it possible for the first time to achieve astonishingly high success rates.

Of the 104 autists treated:

- 13, aged between 1½ and 7½ years, lost all autistic symptoms and developed into contact-loving children of normal and above-normal intelligence;
- 19 improved greatly – with some of these complete recovery may be within sight;
- 72 improved only slightly because of excessive physical strength, parental inability (see above), shortness of treatment so far, and brain damage (29 confirmed cases). Though autism became milder, a mental handicap persisted (children with pre- or perinatal brain damage are apparently particularly susceptible to autismogenic influences).

It can be confirmed that *all* "held" children became more sociable, more cheerful and easier to manage. *In no case was holding harmful*. Parents became more assured in their educational behaviour and their self-confidence improved.

General findings

- The more intensively a child acts out his resistance, the more successful the holding. Confronting him with his fears is the only possible way of desensitising him. Without previous tension and fear, the relaxation that follows cannot be experienced as joyful.

- Vestibular-kinaesthetic tactile stimulation, such as dynamic rocking, stroking, kissing, tickling, etc., has proved the best mode of comforting a child.
- In order to awaken the enjoyment of variety, the manner of holding, comforting and the stimulation of communication should be varied and pleasurable.
- Guidance to parents should include an explanation of the rationale of holding and a relief from feelings of guilt. Not the mother, but an autismogenic, "technocratic" lifestyle is responsible for autism.
- Holding is not a total therapy. It merely opens an emotional pathway for future learning. In the first place, there is a need for persistent attempts to prevent stereotyped behaviour, by guiding the child to other, preferably productive, activities, using holding to overcome resistance.
- Parents should watch out for developing omnipotent forms of behaviour; for once children discover their capacity for social contact through holding they may try to dominate them.
- All children who had been "cured" suffered setbacks if their emotional security was threatened through sibling problems, moving house, etc., but all recovered when holding was resumed.
- Moreover, holding is indicated in disturbed relations resulting from other deprivations – such as the omnipotence–symbiotic syndrome, hospitalisation, psychogenous fits, phobias, fear of rejection, etc.
- Holding is not a purely "rational" treatment and must never degenerate into a technical, mechanical routine. It needs to be performed with intuition and affection. Indeed, this profound experience of love should in the first place be regarded more as a way of life than as a therapy.'

88 Lonsdale Road,   E. A. Tinbergen
Oxford OX2 7ER   N. Tinbergen

References

Further factual information about the progressive improvement over weeks and even months after the start of 'holding' is given in the following papers:

Müller Trimbush, G. and J. Prekop 1983. Das Festhalten als Therapie bei Kindern mit Autismus-Syndrom, Teil 2. *Frühforderung Interdisziplinaer* **2**, 129–39.
Prekop, J. 1983. Das Festhalten als Therapie bei Kindern mit Autismus-Syndrom, Teil 1. *Frühforderung Interdisziplinaer* **2**, 54–64.
Prekop, J. 1983. Anleitung der Therapie durch das Festhalten nach Welch und Tinbergen. *Autismus* **15**, 32–9.
Prekop, J. 1984. Zur Festhalte-Therapie bei autistischen Kindern. *Der Kinderarzt* **15**, 798–802, 952–3, 1043–52, 1170–5.
Prekop, J. 1984. Festhalten. *Behinderte* **7**, 6–22.

Author index

Subject index

Italic page numbers refer to text figures; plates are referred to as, e.g., 'Pl.4'.